Immigrant Adaptation in Multi-Ethnic Societies

Routledge Advances in Sociology

For a full list of titles in this series, please visit www.routledge.com.

45 **Changing Relationships**
   Edited by Malcolm Brynin and John Ermisch

46 **Formal and Informal Work**
   The Hidden Work Regime in Europe
   Edited by Birgit Pfau-Effinger, Lluis Flaquer, and Per H. Jensen

47 **Interpreting Human Rights**
   Social Science Perspectives
   Edited by Rhiannon Morgan and Bryan S. Turner

48 **Club Cultures**
   Boundaries, Identities and Otherness
   Silvia Rief

49 **Eastern European Immigrant Families**
   Mihaela Robila

50 **People and Societies**
   Rom Harré and Designing the Social Sciences
   Luk van Langenhove

51 **Legislating Creativity**
   The Intersections of Art and Politics
   Dustin Kidd

52 **Youth in Contemporary Europe**
   Edited by Jeremy Leaman and Martha Wörsching

53 **Globalization and Transformations of Social Inequality**
   Edited by Ulrike Schuerkens

54 **Twentieth Century Music and the Question of Modernity**
   Eduardo De La Fuente

55 **The American Surfer**
   Radical Culture and Capitalism
   Kristin Lawler

56 **Religion and Social Problems**
   Edited by Titus Hjelm

57 **Play, Creativity, and Social Movements**
   If I Can't Dance, It's Not My Revolution
   Benjamin Shepard

58 **Undocumented Workers' Transitions**
   Legal Status, Migration, and Work in Europe
   Sonia McKay, Eugenia Markova and Anna Paraskevopoulou

59 **The Marketing of War in the Age of Neo-Militarism**
   Edited by Kostas Gouliamos and Christos Kassimeris

60 **Neoliberalism and the Global Restructuring of Knowledge and Education**
   Steven C. Ward

61 **Social Theory in Contemporary Asia**
   Ann Brooks

62 **Foundations of Critical Media and Information Studies**
   Christian Fuchs

63 **A Companion to Life Course Studies**
The Social and Historical Context of the British Birth Cohort Studies
Michael Wadsworth and John Bynner

64 **Understanding Russianness**
Risto Alapuro, Arto Mustajoki and Pekka Pesonen

65 **Understanding Religious Ritual**
Theoretical Approaches and Innovations
John Hoffmann

66 **Online Gaming in Context**
The Social and Cultural Significance of Online Games
Garry Crawford, Victoria K. Gosling and Ben Light

67 **Contested Citizenship in East Asia**
Developmental Politics, National Unity, and Globalization
Kyung-Sup Chang and Bryan S. Turner

68 **Agency without Actors?**
New Approaches to Collective Action
Edited by Jan-Hendrik Passoth, Birgit Peuker and Michael Schillmeier

69 **The Neighborhood in the Internet**
Design Research Projects in Community Informatics
John M. Carroll

70 **Managing Overflow in Affluent Societies**
Edited by Barbara Czarniawska and Orvar Löfgren

71 **Refugee Women**
Beyond Gender versus Culture
Leah Bassel

72 **Socioeconomic Outcomes of the Global Financial Crisis**
Theoretical Discussion and Empirical Case Studies
Edited by Ulrike Schuerkens

73 **Migration in the 21st Century**
Political Economy and Ethnography
Edited by Pauline Gardiner Barber and Winnie Lem

74 **Ulrich Beck**
An Introduction to the Theory of Second Modernity and the Risk Society
Mads P. Sørensen and Allan Christiansen

75 **The International Recording Industries**
Edited by Lee Marshall

76 **Ethnographic Research in the Construction Industry**
Edited by Sarah Pink, Dylan Tutt and Andrew Dainty

77 **Routledge Companion to Contemporary Japanese Social Theory**
From Individualization to Globalization in Japan Today
Edited by Anthony Elliott, Masataka Katagiri and Atsushi Sawai

78 **Immigrant Adaptation in Multi-Ethnic Societies**
Canada, Taiwan, and the United States
Edited by Eric Fong, Lan-Hung Nora Chiang and Nancy Denton

Immigrant Adaptation in Multi-Ethnic Societies
Canada, Taiwan, and the United States

Edited by Eric Fong,
Lan-Hung Nora Chiang and
Nancy Denton

LONDON AND NEW YORK

First published 2013
by Routledge

Published 2016 by Routledge

711 Third Avenue, New York, NY 10017

Simultaneously published in the UK
by Routledge
2 Park Square, Milton Park, Abingdon, Oxon OX14 4RN

*Routledge is an imprint of the Taylor & Francis Group,
an informa business*

First issued in paperback 2016

© 2013 Taylor & Francis

The right of Eric Fong, Lan-Hung Nora Chiang and Nancy Denton to be identified as the authors of the editorial material, and of the authors for their individual chapters, has been asserted in accordance with sections 77 and 78 of the Copyright, Designs and Patents Act 1988.

All rights reserved. No part of this book may be reprinted or reproduced or utilised in any form or by any electronic, mechanical, or other means, now known or hereafter invented, including photocopying and recording, or in any information storage or retrieval system, without permission in writing from the publishers.

Trademark Notice: Product or corporate names may be trademarks or registered trademarks, and are used only for identification and explanation without intent to infringe.

Library of Congress Cataloging-in-Publication Data
Immigrant adaptation in multi-ethnic societies : Canada, Taiwan, and the
   United States / edited by Eric Fong, Lan-Hung Nora Chiang and
   Nancy Denton.
      p. cm. — (Routledge advances in sociology ; 78)
   Includes bibliographical references and index.
   1. Immigrants—Social conditions. 2. Immigrants—Cultural
assimilation—Canada. 3. Canada—Ethnic relations. 4. Cultural
pluralism—Canada. 5. Immigrants—Cultural assimilation—Taiwan.
6. Taiwan—Ethnic relations. 7. Cultural pluralism—Taiwan.
8. Immigrants—Cultural assimilation—United States. 9. United States—
Ethnic relations. 10. Cultural pluralism—United States. I. Fong, Eric,
1960– II. Chiang, Lan-hung Nora. III. Denton, Nancy A.
   JV6342.I44 2012
   305.9'06912—dc23
   2012012969

ISBN13: 978-1-138-95235-5 (pbk)
ISBN13: 978-0-415-62854-9 (hbk)

Typeset in Sabon
by IBT Global.

Contents

List of Figures ix
List of Tables xi

INTRODUCTION

1 Introduction 3
ERIC FONG, LAN-HUNG NORA CHIANG, AND NANCY DENTON

IMMIGRANT/RACIAL/ETHNIC RESIDENTIAL PATTERNS IN MULTI-ETHNIC CITIES

2 The Dynamics of Immigrant Residential Incorporation in the United States: Theoretical Issues and Empirical Challenges 15
JOHN ICELAND

3 Partial Residential Integration: Suburban Residential Patterns of New Immigrant Groups in a Multi-ethnic Context 31
ERIC FONG

4 Asian Immigrants in Vancouver: From Caste to Class in Socio-Spatial Segregation? 54
DAVID LEY

5 Are Native "Flights" from Immigration "Port of Entry" Pushed by Immigrants? Evidence from Taiwan 64
JI-PING LIN

GROUP RELATIONS IN MULTI-ETHNIC CITIES

6 Diversity in People and Places: Multiracial People in U.S. Society 109
NANCY DENTON

7 Openness to Inter-ethnic Relationships for Chinese and South Asian Canadians: The Role of Canadian Identity 138
RICHARD N. LALONDE AND AYSE K. USKUL

8 The Contradictory Nature of Multiculturalism: Mainland Chinese Immigrants' Perspectives and Their Onward Emigration from Canada 159
ELAINE LYNN-EE HO

9 The Perception of Social Distance in a Multi-ethnic Society: The Case of Taiwan 170
YU-HUA CHEN AND CHIN-CHUN YI

IMMIGRANT ADAPTATION IN MULTI-ETHNIC CITIES

10 Diversity of Asian Immigrants and Their Roles in the Making of Multicultural Cities in Canada 199
SHUGUANG WANG AND PAUL DU

11 Family Forms Among First- and Second-Generation Immigrants in Metropolitan America, 1960–2009 223
TIM F. LIAO AND BERKAY ÖZCAN

12 Different Voices: Identity Formation of Early Taiwanese Migrants in Canada 255
LAN-HUNG NORA CHIANG

CONCLUSION

13 Conclusion 285
ERIC FONG, LAN-HUNG NORA CHIANG, AND NANCY DENTON

Contributors 289
Index 291

Figures

2.1	Dissimilarity scores by race, Hispanic origin, and year: 1980–2000.	18
2.2	Information theory index (H) values: 1980–2000.	22
2.3a	Dissimilarity of Hispanics, by race and nativity, from Anglos: 2000.	23
2.3b	Dissimilarity of Hispanics, by race and nativity, from African Americans: 2000.	24
5.1	Low-skilled foreign labor volume and share as Taiwan native-born labor.	69
5.2	Regions and prefectures/cities.	76
5.3	Distribution of low-skilled foreign labor relative quantity and classified regions of FLI.	82
5.4	Metropolitan areas.	86
5.5.1	Immigration impact on the out-migration rate of native-born labor.	97
5.5.2	Immigration impact on the in-migration rate of native-born labor.	98
5.5.3	Immigration impact on the net migration rate of native-born labor.	99
6.1	Population of two or more races, 2010.	125
9.1	Acceptance of immigrants from six countries or regions.	177
10.1	Distribution of the Chinese and South Asians in Vancouver CMA.	209
10.2	Distribution of ethnic Chinese supermarkets and shopping centers in the Toronto CMA.	212
10.3	South Asian temples in the Toronto CMA.	214
10.4	Chinese associations in the Toronto CMA.	214
10.5	Changing interactions between the receiving society and ethnic groups.	217

11.1	Percentages of vertically extended households by year and region of origin.	235
11.2	Percentages of horizontally extended households by year and region of origin.	236
11.3	Predicted probabilities for the five origin groups.	251

Tables

2.1	Dissimilarity from Native-Born Non-Hispanic Whites by Race, Hispanic Origin and Nativity, and Year of Entry: 1990 and 2000	19
2.2	Generalized Linear Regressions with Levels of Dissimilarity of Black Hispanics, by Reference Group: 2000	26
3.1	City and Suburban Distribution of Blacks, South Asians, East and Southeast Asians, and Eastern Europeans, 1996	39
3.2	Distribution of Blacks, South Asians, East and Southeast Asians, and Eastern Europeans in Neighborhoods with Different Levels of Concentration by Location, 1996	40
3.3	OLS Regression of Group Composition and Immigrant Composition on Proportion of Blacks, South Asians, East and Southeast Asians, and Eastern Europeans in Neighborhoods by Location, 1996	44
3.4	OLS Regression of Group Composition and Immigrant Composition on Immigrant Proportion of Blacks, South Asians, East and Southeast Asians, and Eastern Europeans in Neighborhoods by Location, 1996	46
5.1	Size of Samples Selected from the 1996–2000 MUSs for Study	78
5.2	Sample Statistics by Some Selected Variables Derived from the 1996–2000 MUSs	78
5.3	Relative Quantity of Low-skilled Foreign Labor to Native-born Labor and Internal Migration of Native-born Labor by Region, Metropolitan Area, and Regional Level of FLI: Average in 1996–2000	85
5.4	Internal Migration of Native-born Labor by Level of FLI: Average in 1996–2000	87
5.5	Estimation Results of the Most Preferred Departure Model	90
5.6	Estimation Results of the Most Preferred Destination-choice Model	93

xii *Tables*

5.7	Migratory Responses of Native-born Labor to Changing Levels of Low-skilled Foreign Labor	96
6.1	Growth of the U.S. Population by Race and Hispanic Origin, 2000–2010	113
6.2	Growth in Specific Combinations of Races, 2000–2010	116
6.3	Age Variation in Specific Combinations of Races, 2000–2010	122
6.4	Percentage of Total Multiple Race Population in Each of Six Specific Combinations, by State, 2010	126
6.5	Dissimilarity of People of Two or More Races vs. Non-Hispanic Single Race Groups, 2000–2010	128
6.6	Dissimilarity of Children and Adults in Specific Multiple Race Combinations from Non-Hispanic Single Race People, 2010	131
7.1	Correlations between Cultural Identity Variables and Attitude Measures	146
7.2	Correlations between Cultural Identity Variables and Study Measures	151
9.1	Attitudes toward Acceptance of Migrants from Six Countries and Regions: Differences among Three Ethnic Groups	178
9.2	Distribution of Typological Attitudes toward Acceptance of Migrants from Six Countries or Regions	179
9.3	Descriptive Statistics of Independent Variables (N = 1867)	180
9.4	Results of Multinomial Logistic Regression Predicting Taiwanese's Acceptance of Migrants from Japan	183
9.5	Results of Multinomial Logistic Regression Predicting Taiwanese's Acceptance of Migrants from South Korea	185
9.6	Results of Multinomial Logistic Regression Predicting Taiwanese Acceptance of Migrants from China	186
9.7	Results of Multinomial Logistic Regression Predicting Taiwanese Acceptance of Migrants from South East Asia	188
9.8	Results of Multinomial Logistic Regression Predicting Taiwanese Acceptance of Migrants from Europe	189
9.9	Results of Multinomial Logistic Regression Predicting Taiwanese Acceptance of Migrants from North America	190
9.10	Summary of Predicted Effects of Independent Variables on Attitude toward Acceptance of Migrants from Six Countries or Regions	192
10.1	Asian Immigrants in Canada by Country of Birth, 1996 and 2006	201

10.2	Asian Immigrants in Canada by Age Group, Canadian Official Language Ability, and Period of Landing	203
10.3	Education Qualifications of Asian Immigrants in Canada by Country/Region of Last Permanent Residence, 1980–2005 (in percentage)	205
10.4	Distribution of Asian Immigrants in the Top Ten CMAs in Canada, 2006	207
10.5	Distribution of South Asian and Chinese Immigrants in the Toronto CMA, 1996 and 2006	208
11.1	Summary Statistics by Subsamples of Immigrants' Regions of Origin	233
11.2	Estimates from Mixed-Effects Logit Models, First- and Second-Generation Hispanic Immigrants	238
11.3	Estimates from Mixed-Effects Logit Models, First- and Second-Generation Asian Immigrants	240
11.4	Estimates from Mixed-Effects Logit Models, First- and Second-Generation European Immigrants	242
11.5	Estimates from Mixed-Effects Logit Models, First- and Second-Generation Canadian and U.S. Territory Immigrants	244
11.6	Estimates from Mixed-Effects Logit Models, Non-Immigrants	246
12.1	Trend of Population Increase of Taiwan-born in Canada, 1961–2001	258
12.2	Profile of Respondents	264

Introduction

1 Introduction

Eric Fong, Lan-hung Nora Chiang, and Nancy Denton

INTRODUCTION

We have entered the "globalization of international migration" era (Castles and Miller 1998). This wave of immigration, beginning in the 1970s, has two major flows. The first is the large-scale immigration from non-European countries to developed countries as a result of the abolishment of discriminatory policies in major immigrant-receiving countries, such as Canada and the United States. In the United States, more than 31 million individuals obtained legal permanent residence in the country between 1970 and 2010 after the 1965 change in immigration policies (United States Department of Homeland Security 2011). Its northern neighbor, Canada, accepted close to 18 million individuals between 1970 and 2010 after a similar policy change (Citizenship and Immigration Canada 2011; Employment and Immigration Canada 1989). These immigrants arrived in their new countries with diverse socioeconomic backgrounds, ranging from unskilled workers to highly educated professionals (Alba and Nee 2003). They emigrated for various reasons, from independent migrants seeking economic opportunities, to individuals joining family members in the new country. The second major flow of the wave of immigration beginning in the 1970s is the growing stream of international migration within the Asia-Pacific region (Castles and Miller 1998). With the dramatic economic growth in the region, compounded by the decline in the fertility rate in some places in Asia, such as Taiwan and Japan, there was considerable labor migration from less developed to more developed places within Asia. After their contracts were completed, many of the laborers stayed at their new destinations, legally or illegally.

The most distinctive consequence of the large number of immigrants from non-European countries is the growing racial and ethnic diversity in cities in most major immigrant-receiving countries. In the United States, the representation of Asians and Hispanics continues to grow in major cities. In Chicago, the proportion of Asians increased from 3.5% to 4.6% from 1990 to 2000, while Hispanics rose from 12.1% to 17.1%. Similarly, the proportion of Asians in San Francisco increased from 19.9% to 22.5% in the same period, and Hispanics from 14.5% to 16.8%. This growth reflects the continuation of a large volume of immigration as well as births to earlier immigrants (Hao and Fong 2011). Studies based on the last U.S. census documented a growing diversity in smaller cities as well (Lichter and Johnson 2009). In Canada, the situation is similar. The non-white population (i.e., visible minorities) of Toronto increased from 40% in 1996 to 43% in 2006, while in Vancouver it rose from 27% to 42%. The non-white population also increased in smaller cities, e.g., from 14% to 16% in Ottawa and from 14% to 22% in Calgary (Statistics Canada 1996, 2008).

A similar growth in ethnic diversity has been observed in many countries in Asia. The increase is the result of the recruitment of labor from other nearby countries due to labor shortages as the economies of the host countries grow. According to Castles and Miller (1998), the foreign population in Japan jumped from 817,000 in 1983 to 1.4 million in 1995. Many of them were Koreans who stayed in Japan. The increase came largely from China, Brazil, and the Philippines. In Singapore, foreign workers represent 19% of the labor force, drawn from Malaysia, Thailand, Indonesia, Philippines, and Sri Lanka. In Malaysia, while many citizens have emigrated to other countries, the number of immigrants has increased, coming mainly from Bangladesh, Philippines, and Thailand. Hong Kong has recruited high-skilled workers in financial and management sectors from different parts of the world, including the United States, Canada, and Singapore. In Taiwan, the foreign labor policy in 1992 laid the foundation for future recruitment of foreign workers. According to the Taiwan National Immigration Agency, about 325,572 legal workers and 17,193 ferreted illegal workers sought job opportunities in Taiwan in 2010. At the same time, marriage migrants, mainly from Mainland China and S.E. Asia contributed close to half a million (461,121) to the total population of Taiwan in 2012, forming the fifth largest social group.[1]

This racial and ethnic diversity in cities due to immigration suggests that the study of immigrant adaptation and intergroup relations are closely intertwined. The discussion of immigrant adaptation has to be situated in a multi-ethnic context. Considerable debate has been generated in recent years (Alba and Nee 2003; Schiller, Basch and Szaton-Blanc 1992; Zhou 1997) by the limitations of using a minority-majority model to understand immigrant adaptation when urban areas are developing more racial and ethnic diversity. These studies have concluded that it is necessary to go beyond a minority-majority focus to understand intergroup relations.

In addition, the emerging migration within the Asia-Pacific region poses new challenges in studying international migration. Most theoretical understanding of international migration is based on the North American experience (Portes and DeWind 2004). Given the different cultural, social, and economic dynamics in Asian countries, and their growing racial and ethnic diversity, it is pressing to learn how much the existing theoretical frameworks are useful in understanding international migration patterns in

Asia. Unfortunately, there are not many studies that provide a comparison of international migration in Asia and North America.

This edited volume will situate the study of immigrant adaptation in a multi-ethnic context. Included in the discussion are Canada, Taiwan, and the United States. The volume makes three major contributions to the literature. First, we analyze immigrant adaptation in a multi-ethnic context. Second, we explore the intergroup relations of immigrant groups in a multi-ethnic context. Third, we bring a comparative perspective to the understanding of immigrant adaptation in a multi-ethnic setting. The comparison of experiences among countries is important to advance our theoretical understanding of the topic of current immigration, and it also allows us to appreciate some common issues related to the adaptation process of immigrants in various multi-ethnic contexts.

We chose Taiwan as the place in Asia for comparison because of its rich history of immigration in Asia. Based on the National Immigration Agency, Ministry of Interior of Taiwan, about 2%, or 464,930 persons, were foreign residents in 2011, a percentage larger than most Asian places. More important, the 1992 policy of active recruitment of migrant workers to occupations with a high demand has triggered a drastic increase in migrant workers in Taiwan (Castles and Miller 1998). Because of lax controls, many migrant workers have stayed beyond the permitted period, usually two years, either legally or illegally. This situation, compounded with the rapid industrialization of the 1970s, makes Taiwan an ideal location to study immigration in Asia (Castles and Miller 1998).

Since the area of immigrant adaptation is a vast topic, this book focuses on three areas: immigrant and racial/ethnic residential patterns, intergroup relations, and intragroup diversity. These three perspectives address the topic at the city ecological level, between groups, and within groups. Together, the chapters will facilitate in-depth discussion at multiple levels from comparative perspectives.

IMMIGRANT/RACIAL/ETHNIC RESIDENTIAL PATTERNS IN MULTI-ETHNIC CITIES

The study of residential patterns of racial/ethnic and immigrant groups has been a major focus in social science for decades (Alba and Nee 2003; Fong and Shibuya 2005; Iceland and Scopilliti 2008; Lieberson 1980; Massey and Denton 1993). From the early Chicago School ecological perspective, when Park observed that physical distance reflects the social distance of groups (Park, Burgess and McKenzie 1967), residential patterns among groups have been viewed as a reflection of intergroup relations. Although governments can prevent discrimination in housing markets through legislation, they cannot do as much to ensure representation of different groups in neighborhoods as they can in workplaces and schools (White and Glick 2009).

The residential patterns of groups shape their opportunities for intergroup contact (Massey and Fong 1990). It has been well documented that living in neighborhoods with lower co-ethnic concentration fosters intergroup relations, reduces group misunderstanding, and cultivates shared values (Massey and Fong 1990). Thus, the residential patterns of groups are excellent indicators of group relations. In addition, residential patterns can reveal the life chances of groups living in particular locations (Alba and Logan 1991). Neighborhoods are associated with sets of physical and social amenities that can influence the social and economic opportunities of their residents. Clustering in neighborhoods with less desirable amenities suggests that the life chances of group members will be restricted (Logan and Alba 1993).

Iceland (Chapter 2) provides an excellent review of residential segregation among groups, with specific attention to the theme of the book. He succinctly summarizes the three major theoretical perspectives that have been guiding our study of residential patterns of immigrants: the spatial assimilation perspective, the segmented assimilation perspective, and the ethnic stratification perspective. Drawing from American studies, he suggests that the three perspectives have different outcome expectations, ranging from complete convergence of groups, to different outcomes across immigrant groups, to persistent patterns among groups across generations. Iceland identifies four issues that can affect the evaluation of the integration of immigrants from different racial and ethnic groups. First, studies based on cross-sectional data that refer to integration patterns that occur over a period of time and across generations may come to different conclusions and implications from those based on longitudinal data. Second, the choice of reference group can affect the conclusion. This issue is especially important in the study of a multi-ethnic society and the disproportional distribution of immigrants from several racial and ethnic groups. Third, the level of analysis, whether individual or group, will affect the conclusions. Individual levels of integration may be different from the group level of integration. The factors affecting individual integration may be different from those affecting group integration. Finally, the judgment of whether findings support a particular perspective can be challenging, given that findings may provide mixed evidence to support certain perspectives. In short, this chapter clearly identifies some of the issues in studying the residential patterns of immigrants and racial/ethnic groups in a society with growing racial and ethnic diversity.

Fong (Chapter 3) explores the residential patterns of groups with high concentration of immigrants, using census data from Toronto (the largest city in Canada). The study reflects the issue of choice of reference group discussed by Iceland. Instead of comparing residential patterns with those of the majority group as most previous studies have done, Fong compares the likelihood of these groups sharing neighborhoods with the immigrant and Canadian-born members of other groups. Though groups with large proportions of immigrants seem to share neighborhoods with other groups as they stay longer in the new country, Fong's findings show that immigrant groups are more likely to share neighborhoods with immigrants of other groups, but they are less likely to share with the Canadian-born population of the same groups. Fong suggests that this pattern of seeming integration may mask a clear understanding of the integration of immigrants.

Ley (Chapter 4) traces how immigrant neighborhoods have been viewed in different periods of time in Vancouver, a major immigrant gateway city in North America. This approach addresses one of the issues highlighted by Iceland (residential patterns across time), and it discusses the meaning of segregation in society over time instead of simply documenting the level of segregation as a reflection of integration. His study explores "the contexts of Asian immigration to Canada through three periods of hegemonic belief and practice at the level of the state and civil society." He traces how the colonial pluralistic society before the 1940, the multicultural policies of the 1960s, and the neoliberal government in recent decades of the Canadian government shaped society's view of Chinese neighborhoods in these three periods. Ley makes an important point that there have been changes in the meaning of segregation of immigrants, apart from trends in the measure of segregation. Therefore, we should be aware of how policies shape the meaning of segregation.

Focusing on an Asian context, Lin (Chapter 5) uses his study of Taiwan's Manpower Utilization Surveys from 1996 to 2000 to explore how immigration flow affects the residential movement of native labor away from the immigration port of entry. Though the topic has been discussed in North America, there has been little exploration of the situation in Asia. The experience of immigrants may be different in North America, because most recent immigrants to the continent are physically distinctive from the majority of residents in the host country. However, most immigrants in Taiwan are from other Asian countries. Still, Lin has shown that in Taiwan, as in North American cities, the ecological factor, i.e., the size of the immigrant group, affects the movement of native workers, especially those with lower levels of education, away from the immigration port of entry.

GROUP RELATIONS IN MULTI-ETHNIC CITIES

As a set, the four chapters in the next section testify to intergroup relations in a multi-group setting. The boundaries of groups are less distinctive and less consequential when groups share resources and power. However, the boundaries of a group can be rigid when the group or its members experience prejudice or discrimination (Alba 2005; Telles and Ortiz 2008). Group relations in a multi-ethnic society can be complicated, because the focus is no longer the relationship between a minority and a majority, but the way in which each individual group relates to a number of other groups (Fong and Shibuya 2005).

The obvious consequence of growing racial and ethnic diversity in the society is an increase in the multiracial population. The growth of this population reflects growing intermarriage or more precision in ancestry identification. Denton (Chapter 6) provides a careful and detailed understanding of the group. She shows that the group is varied in immigrant gateway states and less segregated from whites than other racial groups. As the multiracial population continues to grow in the United States, they comprise a larger segment of the population and have significant implications for the color boundaries of the country.

One of the long-standing approaches to studying intergroup relations is to explore intermarriage patterns. Since the work of Gordon (1964), "marital assimilation" (his term) is one of the important dimensions by which to explore group relations. A higher rate of intermarriage is one of the major indicators of integration. It signifies the final breakdown of group boundaries, as a higher rate of intermarriage suggests that more members of two groups share intimate relations. Social psychologists Lalonde and Uskul (Chapter 7) explore attitudes toward inter-ethnic dating among young people in Toronto. They found different levels of acceptance of inter-dating among groups. They suggest that a stronger sense of Canadian identity is associated with a more positive view of inter-ethnic dating. A stronger sense of Canadian identity reflects the adoption of the multicultural values of the country. However, they also found ethnic group and gender differences in levels of openness. Their findings highlight the importance of public discourse, partly related to government policies, in affecting group relations in a multi-ethnic society.

Ho (Chapter 8) directly picks up the topic of how government policies affect intergroup relations, specifically integration. She argues that immigration policies are a double-edged sword. Using the experiences of Chinese immigrants in Canada, she shows that most immigrants appreciate the multiculturalism policies because they encourage groups to retain their own cultural activities. The environment helps new immigrants in adapting to the new country, as they can easily find support in their own communities. Yet, at the same, the multiculturalism policies foster in-group interaction that makes immigrants feel isolated from the wider society. These immigrants also feel that the policies do not provide practical help in job search or transfer of credentials to the new country. In short, Ho has demonstrated that policies, particularly multiculturalism policies, can have both positive and negative effects on group relations and immigrant adaptation.

Chen and Yi (Chapter 9) explore the attitudes of local residents toward immigrants in Taiwan. They found that local residents have more favorable attitudes toward immigrants from Japan, Europe, and North America. Their analysis further shows that cultural ideology in Taiwan is an important factor in the differential attitudes toward different groups.

Though their findings are based on another country, they echo the arguments of Lalonde and Uskul that the public discourse of a society shapes group relations.

IMMIGRANT ADAPTATION IN MULTI-ETHNIC CITIES

Today's immigrants not only are faced with more racially and ethnically diversified cities, but they themselves are no longer homogenous. There is diversity in the place of origin of immigrants and in their socioeconomic background (Portes and Rumbaut 2006). As others have documented, there is considerable variation in education level and language ability within groups. The variations in socioeconomic background have considerable impact on the integration of groups. Studies have documented that individuals with limited socioeconomic resources will have a lower starting point in the integration process (Zhou 1997). It will take them longer to narrow the gap between themselves and others. In addition, their socioeconomic status may limit their social and economic attainments, such as choice of neighborhood or quality of schools (Massey and Mullan 1984).

Most studies have documented the diverse paths of integration among immigrants with different socioeconomic resources (Portes and Min 1993; Zhou 1997). However, Wang and Du (Chapter 10) focus on the contribution of Asians in Canada and point out that, although Asians as a group are diverse in terms of place of origin and socioeconomic background, they have made considerable social, political, and cultural contributions to Canadian society. These contributions have shaped existing institutions and processes. Instead of exploring the extent to which immigrants of minority groups need to catch up with the larger society, the discussion focuses on how much they contribute to that society. Wang argues that the integration process should not be seen simply as the one-sided integration of a minority into a majority. Instead, minority and majority groups are constantly influencing each other and shaping the social structures.

Liao and Özcan (Chapter 11) explore the retention of family structure over generations to understand the effects of demographic and socioeconomic diversity on the integration of immigrants and their children. The family is viewed as one of the major social, emotional, and financial supports for immigrants. Family forms can influence immigrant integration. Studies have shown that family forms can affect the well-being of the second generation (Kao 2004). Using U.S. censuses and current population surveys, the authors show that the diverse background of immigrants may have affected the likelihood of retaining horizontal extended family living among Asian and Hispanic second generations. However, the effect is not found for retaining the vertical extended family living arrangement. Their findings suggest that differences in socioeconomic background, such as owning a business or female headship, can affect the retention of vertical and horizontal family forms among members of these groups.

Chiang (Chapter 12) addresses the important issue that the political climate at the place of origin interacting with ethnic identity can affect the integration process of immigrants. Through in-depth interviews of early Taiwanese immigrants in Vancouver and Toronto, Chiang found that those who arrived in Canada in different time periods had different political experiences at their place of origin. These experiences have affected their integration patterns. Therefore, the study of immigrant adaptation should be aware of possible subgroup differences and take into consideration immigrants' experiences before immigration. Her findings remind us that there can be considerable subgroup differences within groups.

In short, the chapters in this edited volume help us to appreciate the complexity of understanding immigrant adaptation in multi-ethnic cities. With studies from Canada, Taiwan, and the United States, and by exploring the topic from the perspectives of ecology, intergroup relations, and intragroup diversity, the book allows us to identify some common issues and patterns for immigrant adaptation in multi-ethnic cities.

NOTES

1. The population of Taiwan is represented by five main [social] groups that differ in terms of time of arrival, size, and language of use. The Taiwan indigenous population, the "aborigines," constitutes about 2% of the population. The Hoklos and Hakka, who are often referred to as "native Taiwanese," are ethnic Han Chinese who were in Taiwan before 1945 and their descendants, and they form about 70% and 12%, respectively. The fourth group consists of the "Mainlanders" and their descendants, who came to Taiwan from 1946 to 1950 when the Mainland fell to the communists. The fifth group is constituted by marriage migrants mainly from Mainland China, Vietnam, Indonesia and Cambodia.

REFERENCES

Alba, Richard. 2005. "Bright vs. Blurred Boundaries: Second-Generation Assimilation and Exclusion in France, Germany, and the United States." *Ethnic and Racial Studies* 28(1):20–49.
Alba, Richard D., and John R. Logan. 1991. "Variations on Two Themes: Racial and Ethnic Patterns in the Attainment of Suburban Residence." *Demography* 28:431–53.
Alba, Richard, and Victor Nee. 2003. *Remaking the American Mainstream: Assimilation and Contemporary Immigration.* Cambridge, MA: Harvard University Press.

Castles, Stephen, and Mark J. Miller. 1998. *The Age of Migration: International Population Movements in the Modern World.* New York: Guilford Press.
Citizenship and Immigration Canada. 2011. *Canada-Facts and Figures 2010: Immigration Overview—Permanent and Temporary Residents.* Ottawa: Minster of Public Works and Government Services Canada.
Employment and Immigration Canada. 1989. *Immigration Statistics.* Ottawa: Ministry of Supply and Services Canada.
Fong, Eric, and Kumiko Shibuya. 2005. "Multiethnic Cities in North America." *Annual Review of Sociology* 31:285–84.
Hao, Lingxin, and Eric Fong. 2011. "Linking Dichotomous Segregation with Multi-group Segregation: Weighted Segregation Ratios in Selected U.S. Metropolitan Areas." *Social Science Research* 40(1):379–91.
Iceland, John, and Melissa Scopilliti. 2008. "Immigrant Residential Segregation in U.S. Metropolitan Areas, 1990–2000." *Demography* 45(1):79–94.
Kao, Grace. 2004. "Parental Influences on the Educational Outcomes of Immigrant Youth." *International Migration Review* 38(2):427–49.
Lichter, Daniel T., and Kenneth M. Johnson. 2009. "Immigrant Gateways and Hispanic Migration to New Destinations." *International Migration Review* 43(3):496–518.
Lieberson, Stanley. 1980. *A Piece of the Pie: Black and White Immigrants since 1880.* Berkeley: University of California Press.
Logan, John R., and Richard D. Alba. 1993. "Locational returns to human capital: minority access to suburban community resources." *Demography* 30:243–68.
Massey, Douglas S., and Nancy A. Denton. 1993. *American apartheid : segregation and the making of the underclass.* Cambridge, MA: Harvard University Press.
Massey, Douglas S., and Eric Fong. 1990. "Segregation and neighborhood quality: blacks, Hispanics, and Asians in the San Francisco metropolitan area." *Social Forces* 69:15–137.
Massey, Douglas S., and Brendan P. Mullan. 1984. "Processes of Hispanic and black spatial assimilation." *American Journal of Sociology* 89:836–73.
Park, Robert Ezra, Ernest Watson Burgess, and Roderick Duncan McKenzie. 1967. *The city [by] Robert E. Park, Ernest W. Burgess [and] Roderick D. McKenzie. With an introduction by Morris Janowitz.* Chicago,: University of Chicago Press.
Portes, Alejandro, and Josh DeWind. 2004. "A Cross-Atlantic Dialogue: The Progress of Research and Theory in the Study of International Migration." *International Migration Review* 38(3):828–51.
Portes, Alejandro, and Zhou Min. 1993. "The New Second Generation: Segmented Assimilation." *Annals of the American Academy of Political and Social Science* 530:74–96.
Portes, Alejandro, and Ruben G. Rumbaut. 2006. *Immigrant America: A Portrait* Los Angeles: University of California Press.
Schiller, Nina Glick, Linda Basch, and Cristina Szaton-Blanc. 1992. *Towards a Transnational Perspective on Migration: Race, Class, Ethnicity, and Nationalism Reconsidered.* New York: New York Academy of Science.
Statistics Canada. 1996. *1996 Census Table: Selected demographic, cultural, educational, labour force and income characteristics (207) of the total population by age groups (6) and sex (3), showing visible minority population (14) (20% sample)(94F0009XDB96003).*
Statistics Canada. 2008. "2006 Census Table: Visible Minority Groups (15) X Age Groups (10) and Sex (3) (97–562-xcb2006009)."
Telles, Edward E., and Vilma Ortiz. 2008. *Generations of Exclusion: Mexican Americans, Assimilation and Race.* New York: Russell Sage Foundation.

United States Department of Homeland Security. 2011. *Yearbook of Immigration Statistics: 2010*: U.S. Department of Homeland Security, Office of Immigration Statistics.

White, Michael J., and Jennifer E. Glick. 2009. *Achieving Anew: How New Immigrants Do in American Schools, Jobs, and Neighborhoods*. New York: Russell Sage Foundation.

Zhou, Min. 1997. "Segmented Assimilation: Issues, Controversies, and Recent Research on the New Second Generation." *International Migration Review* 31(4):825–58.

Immigrant/Racial/Ethnic Residential Patterns in Multi-ethnic Cities

2 The Dynamics of Immigrant Residential Incorporation in the United States
Theoretical Issues and Empirical Challenges
John Iceland

INTRODUCTION

Migration is a global phenomenon, with few societies untouched by either the departure of their citizens to other nations or by the influx of newcomers. Many commentators in immigrant-receiving countries have expressed concern about whether immigration will permanently change the character of their country or result in new social divisions. There is particular apprehension about whether the divide between new ethnic minorities and the majority ethnic group will eventually result in race-based stratification reflected by, and preserved in, "ethnic ghettos" (Johnston, Poulsen, and Forrest 2002; Peach 1996). The long-run effects of immigration will be contingent on how successfully immigrants and their children are incorporated in their new destinations.

Much of the literature on immigrant integration in a variety of settings (e.g., United States, Canada, and Western Europe) is fraught with ambiguity about how to best assess the extent of integration in host societies. The goal of this chapter is to discuss some of the theoretical and empirical issues that underpin this ambiguity, including: (1) temporal issues, (2) the choice of groups and reference group, (3) whether assimilation is an individual or group-level process, and (4) challenges in adjudicating between alternative theories. I illustrate these issues with an examination of patterns and trends in racial, ethnic, and immigrant residential segregation in U.S. metropolitan areas in recent decades. In doing so, I will also highlight areas in which ambiguity remains and provide some thoughts on moving theoretical and empirical debates forward.

THEORIES OF IMMIGRANT INCORPORATION

Three theoretical perspectives commonly used to explain how immigrants and minority groups become incorporated into a society are assimilation, segmented assimilation, and ethnic stratification (Alba and Nee 2003;

Portes and Zhou 1993). Classic spatial assimilation theory posits that immigrant groups experience a process toward integration with a society's majority group through the adoption of mainstream attitudes, culture, and human capital attributes. Early in this process, groups may live apart from the native majority and in more disadvantaged neighborhoods for a number of reasons. The low socioeconomic status of many immigrant groups means that such individuals may simply not be able to afford to live in the same neighborhoods as the more affluent native majority. People with low levels of human capital may also be dependent on their ethnic communities to gain access to jobs, housing, and credit (Alba and Nee 2003; Portes and Rumbaut 2006). Social networks—both kin and community—are key factors shaping where immigrants live. However, immigrant group members are more likely to move into residential areas outside ethnic enclaves if and as they acculturate and become more socioeconomically similar to the native majority. Over the long run, this process of decreasing social distance results in a convergence in residential patterns and outcomes across groups over time. Alba and Nee (2003) emphasize that assimilation is often a process that occurs across generations. While immigrants themselves might assimilate to some extent, progress is predicted to be more evident among their children, who presumably grow up fully acculturated.

The segmented assimilation perspective, as principally discussed in the U.S. immigrant incorporation literature, focuses on divergent patterns of incorporation among contemporary immigrants and their descendents (Portes and Zhou 1993). According to this theory, the host society offers uneven possibilities to different groups based on social factors, including ethnic origin. Recent immigrants become absorbed by different segments of the "native society," ranging from, in the U.S. context, affluent and predominantly Anglo middle-class suburbs to impoverished predominantly African American inner-city ghettos. Structural factors that affect patterns of incorporation include racial stratification and the range of economic opportunities available in a particular place at a particular time. Racial discrimination in particular may diminish the opportunities available to non-white immigrants (Zhou 1999).

Thus, according to the segmented assimilation model, we should expect to see considerable differences in levels of residential segregation among different groups. For example, black immigrants may be much more segregated from the native white population in the United States than Asian immigrants because discrimination against blacks in general is more prevalent there (Ross and Turner 2005). The segmented assimilation perspective may have salience in other countries too. For example, in Great Britain, immigrant groups vary widely in their outcomes, with Bangladeshis and Pakistanis often appearing to be among the most disadvantaged, while other groups, such as Caribbean immigrants, are experiencing some level of upward mobility and less residential segregation (Finney and Simpson 2009).

In contrast to the residential convergence of groups predicted by spatial assimilation theory, or even the divergence in outcomes across immigrant groups, the ethnic stratification perspective emphasizes the widespread retention of ethnic ties and ethnic communities over time and across generations (Charles 2006). Ethnic group members often have preferences to maintain residence within their traditional ethnic communities even when they could afford to live in other areas. Some also argue that prejudice and discrimination by the majority group (e.g., whites in the U.S. context) serve to maintain their social distance from other minority groups (Massey and Denton 1993). The effects of structural barriers are thought to be greatest for blacks in the United States because blacks have historically been perceived in the most unfavorable terms (Charles 2006). Despite some declines in discrimination in recent years, many believe that both its effects and white avoidance of racially mixed or minority neighborhoods still play central roles in shaping the residential patterns of minority group members in the United States (Ross and Turner 2005). In other countries, the ethnic pecking order may of course differ. Again, in Great Britain, black immigrants, predominantly from the Caribbean, fare relatively well, while some Asian groups do less well (Iceland, Mateos, and Sharp 2011; Peach 1999).

DEBATES AND AMBIGUITIES IN THE LITERATURE

Testable hypotheses can be assigned to each of the three theories described above. In terms of residential segregation, assimilation theory would predict declines in segregation over time and across generations, with group characteristics (such as socioeconomic status and English language ability) playing significant roles. According to segmented assimilation theory, we would see divergent patterns of assimilation across groups, with race likely playing an important role in this divergence. According to ethnic retention, we would be expected to see little convergence in residential patterns for most immigrant groups.

While I have tested these types of theories in my previous work on residential segregation (e.g., Iceland 2009; Iceland and Scopilliti 2008), debates continue about whether residential (and other kinds of) assimilation are occurring. In the following, I will discuss a series of factors that are at the source of these debates, including: (1) temporal issues, (2) the choice of groups and reference group in a study, (3) whether assimilation is an individual or group-level process, and (4) challenges in adjudicating between alternative theories.

Temporal Issues

Immigrant integration, if it happens at all, occurs only across a significant amount of time and usually across generations. One therefore has to proceed with caution when drawing conclusions based on data that are not truly longitudinal. Take, for example, the following information on black-white, Hispanic-white, and Asian-white segregation, as measured by the dissimilarity index, over the 1980 to 2000 period. The dissimilarity index measures how evenly groups are distributed across neighborhoods in a given metropolitan area. It ranges from 0 (complete integration) to 1 (complete segregation). The general rule of thumb is that scores above 0.6 are considered high in absolute terms, a score between 0.3 and 0.6 indicates moderate segregation, and scores below 0.3 are quite low.

Figure 2.1 indicates that that the average black-white dissimilarity score averaged across all U.S. metropolitan areas declined from 0.727 in 1980 to 0.640 in 2000.[1] The 0.640 figure can be interpreted as indicating that about 64% of African Americans (or whites) would have to move for all neighborhoods in the metropolitan area to have an equal proportion of African Americans (or whites). Hispanic-white dissimilarity increased very slightly from 0.502 to 0.509 over the same period, while the scores for Asians likewise increased slightly from 0.405 to 0.411. Thus, while African American-white dissimilarity dropped by 12.0% from 1980 to 2000, Hispanic-white dissimilarity increased by 1.5% and Asian-white dissimilarity increased by 1.4% over the period.

From these trends we infer that while blacks are the residentially most segregated minority group in the United States, there are signs pointing toward their greater integration over time. In contrast, while Hispanic and Asian segregation is more moderate, these groups are showing no signs of assimilating. In fact, one could conclude from this figure alone that Asian and Hispanic enclaves are likely fortifying themselves, which will perhaps result in growing long-term ethnic distinctions and, especially in the Hispanic case, residential disadvantage and social isolation.

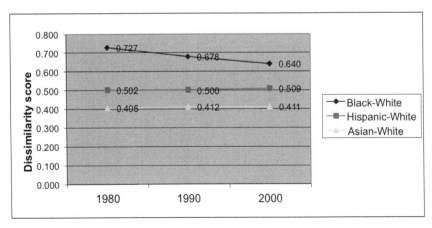

Figure 2.1 Dissimilarity scores by race, Hispanic origin, and year: 1980–2000.

The Dynamics of Immigrant Residential Incorporation

The weakness of this conclusion is that the data are based on overall population snapshots at three points in time; they do not address potential generational differences in segregation. Table 2.1 shows patterns of segregation by year, ethnic group, nativity, and, among immigrants, year of entry. The table not only shows differences in segregation by nativity, but it allows one to see the experience of different "cohorts" of immigrants from 1990 to 2000. It shows, for example, levels of segregation of Hispanic immigrants who arrived in the United States between 1980 and 1990 as observed in the 1990 census and then levels of segregation of this group 10 years later as observed in the 2000 census.

Among Hispanics and Asians as whole, we see a pattern of little change in dissimilarity from native-born non-Hispanic whites (more simply referred to as "whites" or "Anglos" below) from the 1990 census to 2000, consistent with results in Figure 2.1.[2] However, we also see that among all groups (Hispanics, Asians, and blacks), the foreign-born are more segregated from whites than the native-born of these groups. This finding is consistent with the predictions of spatial assimilation theory. We also see that that recent Hispanic and Asian immigrants tend to have higher levels of segregation from whites than Hispanics and Asians who have been in the United States longer—this is also consistent with assimilation. Segregation declined modestly for most cohorts of Hispanics in the 10 years between the 1990 and 2000 censuses, though changes for Asians are not statistically significant.

Table 2.1 Dissimilarity from Native-Born Non-Hispanic Whites by Race, Hispanic Origin, Nativity, and Year of Entry: 1990 and 2000

	Number of Metro Areas	1990	2000
All foreign-born people	187	0.411	0.443
All foreign-born people 1990–2000	187	-	0.517
All foreign-born people 1980–1989	187	0.514	0.493
All foreign-born people 1970–1979	187	0.462	0.443
All foreign-born people < 1970	187	0.302	0.313
All Hispanics	170	0.514	0.522
Native-born Hispanics	170	0.480	0.481
Foreign-born Hispanics	170	0.598	0.599
All foreign-born Hispanics	84	0.600	0.602
Foreign-born Hispanics 1990–2000	84	-	0.651
Foreign-born Hispanics 1980–1989	84	0.650	0.623
Foreign-born Hispanics 1970–1979	84	0.628	0.600
Foreign-born Hispanics < 1970	84	0.530	0.514

(continued)

Table 2.1 (continued)

	Number of Metro Areas	1990	2000
All Asians and Pacific Islanders	157	0.434	0.434
Native-born Asians and Pacific Islanders	157	0.402	0.394
Foreign-born Asians and Pacific Islanders	157	0.475	0.477
All foreign-born Asians and Pacific Islanders	63	0.475	0.482
Foreign-born Asians and Pacific Islanders 1990–2000	63	-	0.545
Foreign-born Asians and Pacific Islanders 1980–1989	63	0.534	0.520
Foreign-born Asians and Pacific Islanders 1970–1979	63	0.484	0.475
Foreign-born Asians and Pacific Islanders < 1970	63	0.498	0.507
All blacks	84	0.713	0.674
Native-born blacks	84	0.716	0.675
Foreign-born blacks	84	0.747	0.712
All foreign-born blacks	24	0.754	0.727
Foreign-born blacks 1990–2000	24	-	0.751
Foreign-born blacks 1980–1989	24	0.775	0.751
Foreign-born blacks 1970–1979	24	0.778	0.754
Foreign-born blacks < 1970	24	0.784	0.772
Foreign-born non-Hispanic whites	91	0.271	0.305
Foreign-born non-Hispanic whites 1990–2000	91	-	0.470
Foreign-born non-Hispanic whites 1980–1989	91	0.451	0.420
Foreign-born non-Hispanic whites 1970-1979	91	0.408	0.403
Foreign-born non-Hispanic whites < 1970	91	0.247	0.270

Note: Includes metropolitan areas with at least 1,000 members of the group in question. Means are weighted by the size of the group in question. Higher values indicate more segregation.
Source: Iceland and Scopilliti (2008).

The pattern for foreign-born blacks differs in some important respects from that of Hispanics and Asians. We see that the segregation from whites of all blacks, native-born blacks, and foreign-born blacks generally declined between the 1990 and 2000 censuses. However, when we look at data from either census, more recent arrivals do not have statistically significant higher dissimilarity scores than earlier arrivals. In addition, the small declines in dissimilarity for cohorts from 1990 to 2000 are not statistically significant either. These latter findings are not consistent with spatial assimilation.

The pattern for foreign-born white immigrants is actually quite similar to patterns for Hispanic and Asian immigrants, though the overall level of segregation for this group from native-born non-Hispanic whites is appreciably lower. More recent white immigrants have higher levels of segregation than those who have been in the United States longer. We also see declines in segregation for the recent cohort, though little change for those who came from 1970 to 1979 and actually increases among those arriving before 1970.[3]

Overall, these figures provide some support for the spatial assimilation perspective, though a few patterns are equivocal, and there is some variation across racial and ethnic groups. Spatial assimilation appears to be less prevalent among black immigrants than other groups, and foreign-born whites display the lowest levels of segregation from native-born non-Hispanic whites than others.

Of note, these more detailed data provide a different interpretation on patterns of assimilation for Hispanics and Asians than Figure 2.1. The findings strongly suggest that Hispanic and Asian segregation increased slightly in recent decades mainly because a larger proportion of those groups are recent immigrants who are more segregated than immigrants who have lived in the United States for longer, and especially higher segregation than the native-born of the respective ethnic groups, who appear to be less likely to live in ethnic enclaves and more likely to share neighborhood with the native white population.

The Choice of Groups and Reference Group

The range of immigrant groups included in a given study and the choice of the reference group (i.e., the comparison group) can affect a study's conclusions, and thus its theoretical implications. For example, if a study of residential segregation examined only the patterns of Hispanics and Asians, the conclusions point fairly clearly toward support for spatial assimilation. Both groups display strong differences in segregation by nativity, where the native-born members are less segregated from whites than the foreign-born. However, the inclusion of blacks in the study provides greater ambiguity about the theoretical implications. Since the evidence on black assimilation is mixed, it would not be unreasonable to conclude that segmented assimilation receives some significant support (i.e., assimilation trajectories vary by group). In fact, if one examined residential patterns of blacks alone (and not included other groups), then a conclusion supporting ethnic disadvantage (declines in black-white segregation in recent decades notwithstanding) could be warranted. Thus, the range of groups included in a study can produce different conclusions about assimilation and related theories across studies. Generally, we would expect that the greater the number of groups considered (such as even within panethnic groups), the greater the variation in outcomes.

The issue of the "reference group" is also an important one. Studies that have used the dissimilarity and isolation indexes generally compare the residential patterns of two groups at a time. In the United States, studies have typically measured the segregation of various groups from non-Hispanic whites—the traditional reference group. This is based on the notion that whites are the demographically and politically dominant group in society. Residential distance from whites implies disadvantage, which in turn could extend to other spheres (e.g., economic, educational). This has historically been the case for African Americans, who for much of the 20th century were confined to poor ghettos and experienced multiple forms of social, economic, and political disadvantages (Massey and Denton 1993).

Over the past decade, researchers have increasingly calculated additional indexes (often supplementing traditional indexes) for all groups with alternative reference groups—such as all people not in the group of interest or the the segregation of two minority groups from each other (e.g., the segregation of African Americans from Hispanics) (Lewis Mumford Center 2001). Along these lines, there is growing interest in multi-group segregation measures that allow researchers to consider the joint distribution of multiple racial and ethnic groups (Iceland 2004; Reardon and Firebaugh 2002).

Studies in the United States that have examined multi-group segregation have found declines in such segregation, generally fueled by the decline in black segregation from all other groups and white segregation from all other groups (Iceland 2004). Figure 2.2 illustrates this decline using the multi-group information theory index (or Thiel's H), which is one common segregation measure of evenness. Like dissimilarity, it ranges from 0 (low segregation) to 1 (high segregation). In addition to the multi-group H, the figure also shows dual-group Hs, where the reference group consists of all people not in the group in question. For example, the "African American" H indicates the level of segregation of African Americans from all people who are not African American. Research that relies on a multi-group measure of segregation generally also looks at detailed pair-wise segregation indexes to understand global figure.

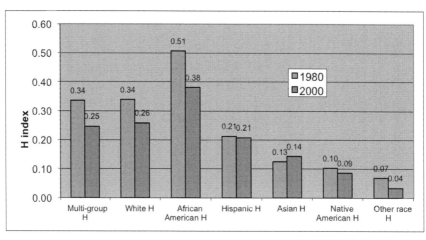

Figure 2.2 Information theory index (H) values: 1980–2000.

In other work, I have explored how examining the segregation of Hispanics from multiple reference groups sheds further insight on the assimilation process. Specifically, in one study (Iceland and Nelson 2008), we examined the segregation of Hispanics from U.S.-born Anglos and U.S.-born African Americans. By using more than one reference group, we can investigate the possibility that Hispanic groups might experience multiple forms of assimilation. That is, if we adopt a definition of assimilation that denotes a reduction of group differences over time, it is possible, for example, that Hispanics may be assimilating with Anglos or African Americans, or even both. In this vein, White, Kim, and Glick (2005) argue that in very diverse societies it has become increasingly important to recognize that groups can become spatially proximate with a number of other ethnic groups or, conversely, remain highly segregated from them.

Figures 2.3a and 2.3b illustrate this theme. They present mean dissimilarity scores of Hispanics, by race and nativity, from native-born Anglos and African Americans. Figure 2.3a indicates that native-born Hispanics are less segregated from Anglos than the foreign-born—consistent with the predictions of spatial assimilation theory. However, we also see distinct differences in Hispanic-white segregation by race. White Hispanics are much less segregated from Anglos (0.47) than black Hispanics (0.74). The dissimilarity score for other-race Hispanics (0.57) falls between the two groups, though closer to the white Hispanic score. Among all groups, the foreign-born are more segregated than the native-born.

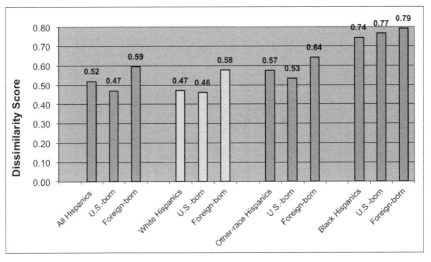

Figure 2.3a Dissimilarity of Hispanics, by race and nativity, from Anglos: 2000.

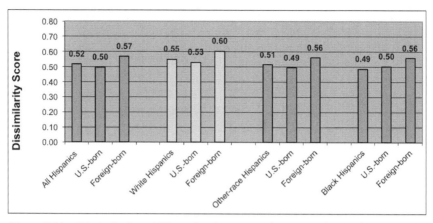

Figure 2.3b Dissimilarity of Hispanics, by race and nativity, from African Americans: 2000.

Figure 2.3b, where the reference group is African Americans, shares some similarities with Figure 2.3a. In particular, U.S.-born Hispanics of all groups are less segregated from African Americans than the foreign-born. This pattern—specifically, where we see a generational assimilation of Hispanics as a whole with Anglos (Figure 2.3a) and African Americans (Figure 2.3b)—is consistent with the notion of multiple forms of assimilation. A further comparison of Figure 2.3a with Figure 2.3b also indicates that white Hispanics, particularly the native-born, are less segregated from Anglos than African Americans, but black Hispanics are considerably less segregated from African Americans than Anglos. Other-race Hispanics are fairly similarly segregated from both African Americans and Anglos. We will return to the somewhat unique residential patterns of black Hispanics later.

Assimilation as an Individual vs. Group-Level Process

As noted above, the possibility of assimilation with multiple groups has not received extended discussion in the literature. Part of the issue might be traced to a lack of clarity about what is the appropriate unit of analysis when studying assimilation: is it the individual or group? Assimilation is often considered at the individual level. An immigrant individual can be said to assimilate in various ways, such as by moving out of an ethnic enclave, working in the mainstream economy, or perhaps marrying outside of his or her ethnic group. In this vein, Alba and Nee (2003) discussed how individuals sometimes "cross" color lines in these ways. For example, historically there are examples of individual African Americans crossing color lines by "passing" as white.

However, it is more fruitful to consider assimilation as a group-level process. Certainly, individuals may or may not assimilate. Some experience upward mobility, others downward mobility (the same can be said of the native-born population). Of principal importance, however, are aggregate-level patterns. What are overall levels of segregation by generation? What is the distribution of incomes among an immigrant group compared to the native-born population? In the example of Hispanic "multiple forms of assimilation" discussed above, individual decisions about moving into, say, a black or white neighborhood outside of an ethnic enclave may obscure the fact that some Hispanics are moving into white neighborhoods and others are moving into more African American ones, such that, in the aggregate, we have greater dispersion of Hispanics into all sorts of neighborhoods over time and across generations. In this case, an aggregate-level analysis could be considered more informative than an individual-based one. Having said that, often times the same conclusion can by arrived at by different analytical approaches (i.e., with individual or aggregate data) provided that the studies are designed to allow broad group-level generalizations.

Challenges in Adjudicating Between Alternative Theories

A common challenge in immigration research lies in deciding whether the evidence at hand is more consistent with one theoretical perspective or another. I have grappled with this in my own research on residential segregation, where there is often mixed evidence supporting spatial assimilation vs. segmented assimilation. Take again the example of black Hispanics. Table 2.2 shows regression results indicating the extent to which nativity and other group characteristics are associated with levels of black Hispanic segregation from Anglos and from African Americans (Iceland and Nelson 2008). According to spatial assimilation theory, we should see generational differences in segregation (e.g., the native-born should be less segregated than the foreign-born), and group characteristics such as income should also matter (greater income parity between groups should be associated with less segregation). According to segmented assimilation, we might expect to see black Hispanics assimilating with native-born non-Hispanic African Americans but not with Anglos.

In many respects, the results shown in the table are consistent with spatial assimilation and, in fact, with the aforementioned multiple forms of assimilation. Specifically, the negative coefficient for the native-born dummy variable indicates that native-born black Hispanics are less segregated from both Anglos and African Americans than foreign-born black Hispanics. The significant income coefficient in the Anglo regression (Model 2) also indicates that a higher ratio in black Hispanic income to Anglo income (i.e., greater parity) is associated with less segregation between the two groups. Nevertheless, as indicated by the high intercept in the Anglo regressions (and as shown in Figure 2.3a), overall levels of black Hispanic-Anglo segregation are very high in absolute terms, and the nativity difference in this context seems modest. So which is it? Assimilation or segmented assimilation? The best we can do is describe the evidence and provide our best professional judgment, which for us in this case meant concluding that spatial assimilation received the strongest support but also equivocating by noting that segmented assimilation is not an unreasonable conclusion either.

Table 2.2 Generalized Linear Regressions with Levels of Dissimilarity of Black Hispanics, by Reference Group: 2000

	Segregation from Anglos				Segregation from blacks			
	Model 1		Model 2		Model 1		Model 2	
	coef.	std. err.	coef.	std. err.	coef.	std. err.	coef.	std. err.
Intercept	0.803**	0.016	0.768**	0.198	0.659**	0.020	0.319	0.308
Nativity								
Native-born	−0.054**	0.014	−0.068*	0.029	−0.106**	0.018	−0.123**	0.042
Foreign-born (omitted)								
Other group-specific characteristics								
Hispanic group/Anglo ratio of median household income			−0.111**	0.041			0.048	0.037
% speaking English very well/well			0.020	0.093			−0.012	0.133
% owning a home			−0.027	0.057			−0.058	0.091
Log Likelihood	109.593		174.204		93.262		135.586	
DF	97		78		97		78	

**p<0.01 *p<0.05

Notes: The unit of analysis is the segregation score for a black Hispanic nativity group in a given metropolitan area. The analysis includes metropolitan areas with at least 1,000 black Hispanics. Model 2 also contains controls for country of origin, group size, region, and the following metropolitan characteristics: log of total population, % minority, % in manufacturing, % in government, % in the military, % over 65 years old, % enrolled in college, % of housing units built in last 10 years, % of population in the suburbs.

CONCLUSION

In this chapter, I discussed four issues that affect debates over immigrant assimilation, and particularly how they apply to studies of immigrant residential segregation. These are: (1) temporal issues, (2) the choice of groups and reference group in a study, (3) whether assimilation is an individual or group-level process, and (4) challenges in adjudicating between alternative theories. Regarding the first issue, I have argued that of key importance in assessing immigrant integration is an examination of generational trajectories. Early studies that examined the adaptation of post-1965 immigrants to the United States were limited in the amount of data on the second and greater generations. It is unsurprising that immigrants often remain disadvantaged relative to the native-born population, even if they immigrated many years ago. Many immigrants never become fully acculturated. Educational credentials earned in the country of origin also may not be assigned the same value by U.S. employers as those earned in the United States. In terms of understanding long-term trajectories of incorporation, however, one needs to examine the well-being of the second and subsequent generations. Results regarding residential segregation suggest that Asians and Hispanics are residentially assimilating, while the evidence for African Americans is mixed.

The choice of the groups analyzed and reference group used in a given study has consequences for that study's conclusions and theoretical implications. A study that focuses on Asian socioeconomic outcomes is likely to conclude that economic assimilation aptly characterizes Asian patterns of incorporation. However, a study that includes a wider set of groups (such as within panethnic groups) may be more likely to conclude that segmented assimilation has the most explanatory power, as there will likely be some measure of variation in outcomes across the groups considered. With regard to the reference group issue, what is the "American mainstream"? Should it still be Anglos—by far the most commonly used reference group in immigration research in the United States—even though the group is declining in relative size and increasingly no longer the sole holder of political power, especially in multi-ethnic areas? In their study of immigrant incorporation in New York City, Kasinitz and his co-authors (2008) point out that their second-generation respondents often feel not so much like white Americans, who are a distinct minority in their city and often not present in their everyday lives, but they feel comfortable as multi-ethnic "New Yorkers." This fact points to the importance of considering multiple reference groups in studies of incorporation—at least in such multi-ethnic contexts.

I also highlighted the importance of considering assimilation as a group-level process rather than an individual process. While any particular person may choose (and be able to) cross group boundaries, of principal importance is what happens at the aggregate level. In particular, as Alba and Nee (2003) discuss, assimilation refers to the extent to which group differences decline over time. In other words, assimilation is not simply an additive compilation of individual-level trajectories, but rather the process by which group boundaries blur and eventually dissolve.

Finally, I considered the challenges in adjudicating between alternative assimilation-related theories. Results are often ambiguous, and it takes a careful reading of the evidence and professional judgment to discern whether results are more consistent with one perspective over another. I raised the example of black Hispanics, who in many respects are assimilating with both Anglos and African Americans (or are experiencing "multiple forms of assimilation"), though to some extent the overall very high levels of segregation between black Hispanics and Anglos overshadow the generational decline. All these issues considered, evidence presented above indicates that immigrants are by-and-large becoming residentially assimilated in American metropolitan areas, even as race remains an important construct in American life. While race clearly helps shape where different groups live, long-term declines in black segregation, along with evidence of Asian and Hispanic spatial assimilation, suggests that race will play an increasingly smaller role in residential patterns in the future.

As a final note, it is important to acknowledge that other prominent issues often color debates on immigrant assimilation, even if they are perhaps less salient in an examination of residential patterns. One is selection, whereby immigrants are usually positively selected on unobservable characteristics (e.g., ambition). Selection issues are often paramount when trying to understand health disparities, such as the Hispanic health "paradox," where Hispanic immigrants, despite being of low socioeconomic status on average, are healthy relative to the native population according to many indicators. A second issue that the existing literature has perhaps not fully come to grips with is ascertaining the extent of assimilation among immigrant groups who arrive with an initial advantage over the native population, such as in education or income. For these groups, what does assimilation mean? Does it mean some kind of attenuation of difference with the native population across generations, which in some sense means relative downward mobility? Or does it involve persisting immigrant group advantage across generations?

This is an important and exciting time to be studying immigrant incorporation. Because international migration to all parts of the globe has dramatically increased over the past few decades, both sending and receiving countries are trying to understand the implications of this mass movement of people for their national identity, social cohesiveness, and economic well-being. Future research should continue to try to illuminate these issues.

NOTES

1. All segregation scores in the tables are weighted by the size of the minority group in question. The scores therefore represent the experience of the average minority group individual rather than the average metropolitan area.

2. Figure 2.1 reports means for all metropolitan areas while Table 2.1 includes a slightly narrower range of metropolitan areas that contain at least 1,000 group members in both 1990 and 2000.
3. That segregation increased between 1990 and 2000 for those who entered the United States before 1970 could reflect a compositional change in that group: in 1990, a higher proportion of those immigrants came from the pre-1920s immigration boom, whereas by 2000, a number of those immigrants had died, and the population therefore consisted more of immigrants who arrived in later years.

REFERENCES

Alba, Richard, and Victor Nee. 2003. *Remaking the American Mainstream: Assimilation and Contemporary Immigration.* Cambridge, MA: Harvard University Press.

Charles, Camille Zubrinsky. 2006. *Won't You Be My Neighbor: Race, Class, and Residence in Los Angeles.* New York: Russell Sage Foundation.

Finney, Nissa, and Ludi Simpson. 2009. "Population Dynamics: The Roles of Natural Change and Migration in Producing the Ethnic Mosaic." *Journal of Ethnic and Migration Studies* 35(9):1479–96.

Iceland, John. 2009. *Where We Live Now: Immigration and Race in the United States.* Berkeley, CA: University of California Press.

Iceland, John. 2004. "Beyond Black and White: Metropolitan Residential Segregation in Multi-ethnic America." *Social Science Research* 33:248–71.

Iceland, John, Pablo Mateos, and Gregory Sharp. 2011. "Ethnic Residential Segregation by Nativity in Great Britain and the United States." *Journal of Urban Affairs* 33(4):409–429.

Iceland, John, and Kyle Anne Nelson. 2008. "Hispanic Segregation in Metropolitan America: Exploring the Multiple Forms of Spatial Assimilation." *American Sociological Review* 73(5):741–65.

Iceland, John, and Melissa Scopilliti. 2008. "Immigrant Residential Segregation in U.S. Metropolitan Areas, 1990–2000." *Demography* 45(1):79–94.

Iceland, John, Daniel H. Weinberg, and Erika Steinmetz. 2002. *Racial and Ethnic Residential Segregation in the United States: 1980–2000.* U.S. Census Bureau, Census Special Report, CENSR-3. Washington, DC: U.S. Government Printing Office.

Johnston, Ron, Michael Poulsen, and James Forrest. 2002. "Are There Ethnic Enclaves/Ghettos in English Cities?" *Urban Studies* 39(4):591–618.

Kasinitz, Philip, John H. Mollenkopf, Mary C. Waters, and Jennifer Holdaway. 2008. *Inheriting the City: The Children of Immigrants Come of Age.* Cambridge, MA: Harvard University Press.

Lewis Mumford Center. 2001. "Ethnic Diversity Grows, Neighborhood Integration Lags Behind." Report by the Lewis Mumford Center, State University of New York at Albany (December).

Massey, Douglas S., and Nancy Denton. 1993. *American Apartheid: Segregation and the Making of the Underclass.* Cambridge, MA: Harvard University Press.

Peach, Ceri. 1996. "Does Britain Have Ghettos?" *Transactions of the Institute of British Geographers* 21:216–35.

Peach, Ceri. 1999. "London and New York: Contrasts in British and American Models of Segregation." *International Journal of Population Geography* 5:319–51.

Portes, Alejandro and Min Zhou. 1993. "The New Second Generation: Segmented Assimilation and Its Variants Among Post-1965 Immigrant Youth." *Annals of the American Academy of Political and Social Science* 530 (November):74–96.

Portes, Alejandro, and Ruben G. Rumbaut. 2006. *Immigrant America: A Portrait*, 3rd ed. Berkeley, CA: University of California Press.
Reardon, Sean F., and Glenn Firebaugh. 2002. "Measures of MultiGroup Segregation." *Sociological Methodology* 32(1):33–67.
Ross, Stephen L., and Margery Austin Turner. 2005. "Housing Discrimination in Metropolitan America: Explaining Changes between 1989 and 2000." *Social Problems* 52(2):152–80.
White, Michael J., Ann H. Kim, and Jennifer E. Glick. 2005. "Mapping Social Distance: Ethnic Residential Segregation in a Multiethnic Metro." *Sociological Methods and Research* 34(2):173–203.
Zhou, Min. 1999. "Segmented Assimilation: Issues, Controversies, and Recent Research on the New Second Generation." In *The Handbook of International Migration: The American Experience*, edited by Charles Hirschman, Philip Kasinitz, and Josh DeWind. 196–211. New York: Russell Sage Foundation.

3 Partial Residential Integration
Suburban Residential Patterns of New Immigrant Groups in a Multi-ethnic Context[1]

Eric Fong

INTRODUCTION

There was a time in North America when the typical urban settlement pattern of immigrants was considered to have two stages: first, immigrants shared a neighborhood, usually in the central city, with members of their own ethnic group; then, with time, they gradually moved out of these ethnic neighborhoods to suburban neighborhoods where they were more exposed to other established groups (Burgess 1925). However, this traditional thinking has been challenged in recent years, with growing evidence of anomalies (Alba and Logan 1993; Alba, Logan, Stults, Marzan, and Zhang 1999; Logan, Alba, and Zhang 2002; Wright, Ellis, and Parks 2005).

Studies now document that more immigrants are choosing to settle in suburban areas very soon after their arrival. For example, Alba, Logan, Stults, Marzan, and Zhang (1999) reported that about 10% of all recent major immigrant groups in the United States settled in suburban areas within 5 years of their arrival. This pattern applies to the other major immigrant-receiving country on the same continent, Canada, where a considerable proportion of new immigrants are now settling in major suburban municipalities (Fong, Luk, and Ooka 2005; Teixeira and Murdie 1997).

Some members of new immigrant groups cluster in suburban areas, where they generally experience less segregation from other groups (Clark and Blue 2004). More importantly, their growing presence in the suburbs contributes to the increasing racial and ethnic diversity of suburban neighborhoods (Fong and Shibuya 2005). Consequently, the study of residential patterns should no longer concentrate solely on the sharing of neighborhoods between the majority group and a particular minority group. Rather, it is important to develop a detailed delineation of the various groups in neighborhoods, including their immigration status.

Surprisingly, despite marked changes in the suburbanization patterns of immigrants and the increasingly multi-ethnic metropolitan context, most studies of immigrant residential patterns in suburban areas have not taken these changes into consideration. Instead, studies still tend to focus on two groups in a shared neighborhood (usually a minority group and whites) or on the concentration of a minority group (Alba and Logan 1991; Alba et al. 1999; Massey and Denton 1988). Most studies look at new immigrant groups with respect to the multi-ethnic composition of, or immigrant representation in, city neighborhoods (Maly 2005; Modarres 2004). Few focus on suburban residential patterns of recent immigrant groups. Thus, there is a certain urgency to developing an understanding of the multi-ethnic nature of suburbs, and of the foreign-born composition of suburban residential patterns among different new immigrant groups.

In this study, we use 1996 census tract data from Toronto to explore the racial and ethnic composition of suburban neighborhoods in relation to four new immigrant groups: Eastern Europeans, South Asians, East and Southeast Asians, and blacks. Toronto was chosen because it is a common destination for immigrants to Canada, and immigrants comprise 42% of the city's total population. Of these immigrants, 46% arrived between 1981 and 1996 (Statistics Canada 1998). Our findings show that among these four new immigrant groups, only Eastern Europeans demonstrate a clear sign of residential integration in suburbs. At the same time, the data further show that the proportions of new immigrant groups are positively related to other groups' immigrants in suburban neighborhoods. Thus is created the partially integrated situation of recent new immigrant groups in suburban areas. This development is particularly obvious for blacks. Eastern Europeans, despite partial residential integration in suburban areas, are more likely to share neighborhoods with the charter groups (i.e., British and French) than with the other three new immigrant groups.

LITERATURE REVIEW

In recent years, the spatial assimilation perspective has influenced the understanding of residential patterns of new immigrant groups (Charles 2003; Rosenbaum and Friedman 2001). Proponents of this approach argue that in any city, there inevitably will be neighborhoods with higher ethnic representation, because recently arrived immigrants require residential proximity to maintain their relationships with co-ethnic members from whom they seek economic and social support (Charles 2003; Clark and Blue 2004; Massey 1985). However, as they stay longer in the country, they extend their social networks and improve their socioeconomic resources. Ethnic support becomes less important to them. They move out of their ethnic neighborhoods into other areas, particularly suburban neighborhoods, where they share neighborhoods with other groups (Fong and Wilkes 1999; Iceland, Sharpe, and Steinmetz 2005; Mesch 2002). However, recent studies indicate that new immigrant groups have diverse socioeconomic resources (Clark 1999; Portes and Zhou 1993; Zhou 1997). Only those with sufficient resources will translate their economic gains into suburban locations (Rosenbaum and Friedman 2004).

Although most studies based on the spatial assimilation perspective include the entire metropolitan area, recent studies have begun to focus on the suburban residential patterns of immigrant groups. According to the spatial assimilation perspective, suburbanization occurs as groups translate their socioeconomic resources into better neighborhoods, which usually are located in suburban areas where neighborhoods are characterized as racially and ethnically mixed. This view of the suburban residential pattern of immigrant groups highlights two important processes. First, new immigrant groups, like previous immigrant groups, are less likely to cluster in suburban neighborhoods than in city neighborhoods (Massey and Denton 1988). Second, residing in suburban areas reflects the socioeconomic advancement of immigrant groups (Charles 2003; Logan, Alba, and Zhang 2002; Massey and Denton 1988; Orfield 2002).

Drawing from the discussion, we hypothesize that:

Hypothesis 1: New immigrant groups have lower proportions in suburban neighborhoods than in city neighborhoods, controlling for various factors.

Hypothesis 2: The effects of the socioeconomic resources of new immigrant groups are strongly related to their proportion in suburban neighborhoods.

A number of findings support the assertion that groups with higher socioeconomic resources are associated with smaller proportions of recent immigrant groups in suburban areas. A recent study by Clark and Blue (2004) echoes previous findings that socioeconomic resources are important to new immigrant groups achieving higher status residential locations. In addition, these studies show that residing in suburban areas usually increases immigrants' exposure to majority groups (Charles 2003; Massey 1985). However, these studies tend to focus on immigrants sharing suburban neighborhoods with whites, and usually they do not provide information about the diverse racial and ethnic composition now found in these neighborhoods (Massey and Denton 1988; South, Crowder, and Chavez 2005; White 1987). This omission limits the understanding of the dynamics in suburban areas, specifically with respect to the multi-ethnic context. Given the evidence suggesting that groups differ in their ability to translate socioeconomic resources into better neighborhood amenities (Logan, Alba, and Leung 1996), it is quite possible that, in a multi-ethnic context, groups have more opportunities to share neighborhoods with some groups but less with others (Iceland 2003, 2004; Iceland et al. 2005; Logan, Alba, and Leung 1996; Massey and Denton 1988; Rosenbaum and Friedman 2001, 2004, 2006;).

To better understand the multi-ethnic group composition of suburban neighborhoods, we draw further discussion from the place stratification perspective, developed from the dual segmented housing market perspective

(Alba and Logan 1991). Here, the racial and ethnic composition of neighborhoods is considered to be a reflection of the structural stratification of society. Given that resources and prestige are unevenly associated with neighborhoods, advantaged groups, seeking to maintain the status quo, are reluctant to share neighborhoods with disadvantaged groups (Rosenbaum and Friedman 2004). As a result, through various agents, including financial institutions, real estate agents, and local community groups, disadvantaged groups encounter difficulty moving into the neighborhoods of the advantaged groups (Charles 2000, 2003; Fong and Shibuya 2000). In other words, despite an increase in their socioeconomic resources, some groups are less likely to share neighborhoods with the advantaged groups (Iceland, Sharpe and Steinmetz 2005; Iceland and Wilkes 2006; Price-Spratlen and Guest 2002; Wilkes and Iceland 2004). This perspective seems to explain black residential patterns in the United States very well. Iceland, Sharpe, and Steinmetz (2005) have documented that blacks are less likely to move into neighborhoods with more whites, even in suburban areas, despite an increase in socioeconomic resources. Rosenbaum and Friedman (2004, 2006) showed that even when compared with the foreign-born black population, native-born blacks do not show any improvement in their likelihood of sharing neighborhoods with whites.

The implications of the place stratification perspective on the suburban residential patterns of new immigrant groups are obvious (Adelman, Tsao, Tolnay, and Crowder 2001). The proportion of established groups in a neighborhood will be lower when there is a higher proportion of new immigrant groups (Alba and Logan 1991). Given that new immigrant groups usually retain a high level of attachment to their own groups because of their distinct cultural practices and ethnic languages, and that established groups prefer to maintain the status quo, the established groups may be reluctant to share neighborhoods with new immigrant groups. This relationship will apply in both city and suburban neighborhoods, because established groups in either location will prefer to keep things as they are.

When we incorporate nativity status into the picture, we expect that the proportions of the native-born population (regardless of ethnicity) will be positively related to new immigrant groups in neighborhoods, especially in suburban areas (Zavodny 1999). As native-born residents seek a suburban life that emphasizes integration, they may avoid sharing neighborhoods with immigrants from different backgrounds (Horton 1995; Rose 2000; Saito 1998). Consequently, instead of sharing neighborhoods with the native-born population of other groups, new immigrant groups are more likely to share with immigrants from other groups.

This unique pattern created by the arrival of new immigrant groups in the suburbs may have significant implications. The social dynamics of sharing neighborhoods with immigrants from other groups can be different from sharing neighborhoods with a native-born population or co-ethnic members. For one thing, immigrants belonging to other groups are also learning the ways of the new society and may still be in the process of adapting to the new country. In addition, given the usually strong cultural attachments among immigrants, the interaction of immigrants across groups may be superficial. As Suttles (1972) noted in his ethnographic work on the intergroup relations of a few immigrant groups in Addams, "Ethnicity is the major basis of division within the Addams area, but practically every resident has at least one acquaintance in another ethnic group. These relationships are usually rather superficial and often consist of little more than a nod between adults living in adjoining buildings" (p. 61). Intergroup social dynamics, such as trust and reciprocal relations, can take longer to develop among immigrant groups with shallow relationships. In a recent study of a suburban community in California, the findings echoed Suttle's observation of limited interaction of immigrants across groups (Saito 1998).

Nevertheless, because of the presence of other groups in their neighborhoods, new immigrant groups may consider themselves to have achieved spatial integration, even if there are few native-born members of the other groups and their interaction with immigrants from these groups is superficial. Partial residential integration may develop among new immigrant groups.

In short, the above discussion of the place stratification perspective leads us to two hypotheses related to the racial and ethnic composition of neighborhoods with respect to new immigrant groups:

Hypothesis 3: The negative relationship between the proportion of new immigrant groups and the proportion of other groups is stronger in suburban neighborhoods than in city neighborhoods.
Hypothesis 4: The proportion of new immigrant groups is positively related to the immigrant proportion of other ethnic groups in suburban neighborhoods.

Before presenting results based on the Canadian census for Toronto, we provide a context for interpreting the results with a brief discussion of the racial and ethnic composition of that city, and the changes therein.

Multi-ethnic Toronto

Toronto has always been a major immigrant gateway city in Canada. Population growth has been largely the result of immigrant settlement. Although the early immigrants settling in Toronto were overwhelmingly British, about 87% in 1911, this proportion gradually decreased. By the middle of the last century, the major increase in immigration was from Southern and Eastern Europe. For example, between 1951 and 1961, the percentage of Italians rose 400%, from 3% to 12% of the city population, and the Hungarian population increased by 33%, from 3% to 4% of the city population (Lemon 1985).

Since the changes in Canadian immigration policies in 1967, whereby the selection of immigrants was based on market demand, Toronto has become more diverse. There has been a sharp increase in newcomers from Asia, Africa, and the West Indies (Badets and Chui 1994). In 1960, the ten leading source countries of immigrants to Canada, other than the United States, were European countries. Thirteen years later, in 1973, five of the ten leading source countries were in Asia or the West Indies. In 1984, seven of the ten leading source countries were Asian, West Indian, and Latin American (McVey and Kalbach 1995). The majority of immigrants from these countries settled in Toronto.

By 1996, the British representation in Toronto had dropped to only 11%, compared with 52% in 1961. At the same time, the Asian and black populations jumped. Asians and blacks rose from a negligible representation of the city population in 1961 to 8% and 6%, respectively, in 1996[2] (Lemon 1985; Statistics Canada 1996a, 1996b). In 1996, 61% of Asians were of East and Southeast Asian origin, and 39% were South Asian[3] (Statistics Canada 1996a, 1996b). The majority of blacks were of Caribbean origin. As a result of these changing immigration patterns, the term "visible minorities" began to be used in the late 1970s in reference to blacks and Asians and gradually has gained acceptance (Driedger 1996).[4] The term is used to differentiate blacks and Asians from European minority groups (Europeans other than British and French).

These new immigrant groups have diverse socioeconomic backgrounds. In 1996, about 22% of South Asians in Canada had completed university, compared with only 11% of British, one of the charter groups in Canada. Within the black population, about 55% of whom are immigrants, only 11% had completed university (Statistics Canada 1996a, 1996b). Similarly, the income levels of the new immigrant groups are diverse. In 1996, the total median individual income of blacks and various Asian groups ranged from $14,430 to $21,334.[5] The language ability of these new immigrants varies. About 14% of East and Southeast Asians, but only 1% of blacks, do not speak either English or French (Statistics Canada 1996a, 1996b).

Recent studies in North America have documented that society's reception of these new immigrant groups is varied (Reitz and Breton 1994; Smedley 1993). Most studies show that visible minority groups, South Asians and blacks in particular, have experienced discrimination (Driedger 1999; Fong and Wilkes 2003; Owusu 1999). Reitz and Breton (1994) reviewed survey results on race and ethnic attitude and concluded that blacks have experienced a higher level of discrimination than other new immigrant groups. Henry (1994) studied blacks in Toronto and also documented that as a group they have experienced discrimination in the housing and job markets.

With its growing ethnic diversity, and the different socioeconomic resources and experiences of its new immigrant groups, Toronto provides a unique context in which to explore the racial and ethnic composition of new immigrant groups in suburban neighborhoods.

DATA

Data for this study come from specially tabulated 1996 Canadian census tract data. These tables contain detailed information about groups at the tract level. We include all 808 census tracts in the Toronto census metropolitan area. Although our study focuses on suburban neighborhoods, we include city census tracts for comparison.

We focus our study on Toronto, the largest Canadian metropolitan area, which has the largest percentage of immigrants in the country. The immigrant population of Toronto reached 44% in 1991, as compared with 25% in Los Angeles-Long Beach, 39% in Miami, and 24% in New York in 1990 (Reitz 1998). Without doubt, Toronto provides a unique multi-ethnic context in which to study neighborhoods (Fong and Wilkes 2003).

We focus our analysis on four major new immigrant groups: Eastern Europeans, East and Southeast Asians, South Asians, and blacks. Except for blacks, we use broad geographic regions to define groups, because a larger grouping can avoid the data suppression that may occur if specific ethnic groups, usually with a smaller size, are used. "Black" is a racial category while the other groups are based on ethnicity. The term "blacks" is used because it is one of the categories of racial and ethnic groups provided by Statistics Canada. In addition, this grouping will allow us to compare our findings with those obtained from American data. Eastern Europeans, East and Southeast Asians, South Asians, and blacks comprise, respectively, 8%, 32%, 13%, and 8% of immigrants who arrived in Canada between 1981 and 1996 (Statistics Canada 1996a, 1996b). They also represent the diverse racial backgrounds of recent immigrants. To be as inclusive as possible, and to capture the multi-ethnic composition of neighborhoods, we focus on the composition of nine racial and ethnic groups in neighborhoods: the two charter groups (i.e., British and French); Eastern, Northern, Southern, and Western Europeans; South, East, and Southeast Asians; and blacks. Individuals included in these groups are mutually exclusive. Altogether, they represent on average about 71% of the population in the census tracts. The approach is similar to other studies that also used census data (Darden 2004; Fong and Shibuya 2005). In our analysis, we ran two models for each new immigrant group. The first model explores how the distribution of each new immigrant group is related to the distribution of multi-groups in the neighborhood. The second model further includes the proportion of immigrants of all these groups in the neighborhood. To avoid a possible correlation between the total and immigrant proportions of the group, the model includes the total immigrant proportion of all these groups in the neighborhood, instead of the individual immigrant proportion of each group.

The unit of analysis of the study is neighborhood. As a proxy for neighborhood, we use the census tract, the geostatistical area defined by Statistics Canada, to highlight the common socioeconomic characteristics of its residents. Similar to the census tract defined in the United States, Canadian census tracts typically range from 2,500 to 8,000 with an average of about 4,000 persons. Census tracts are divided so that the socioeconomic backgrounds of residents are as homogenous as possible. Tract boundaries are usually determined by major streets, landmarks, or geographic landscape.

One of the tasks of the study is to classify city and suburban areas. Given that Statistics Canada does not define city and suburban boundaries, we classify census tracts in the former city of Toronto as city neighborhoods.[6] The remaining tracts in the Toronto census metropolitan area are classified as suburban neighborhoods. We further code census tracts in the five former cities outside the former city of Toronto (East York, Etobicoke, North York, Scarborough, and York) as inner suburban neighborhoods. Tracts beyond these former cities are classified as outer suburban neighborhoods. However, some of the outer areas of the five former cities were developed in recent decades. Therefore, areas in the five former cities where the percentage of housing built before 1946 is at least one standard deviation below the mean are also classified as outer suburbs. Most of these tracts are located near the outer areas of the cities.

Patterns of Suburbanization Among Groups in Toronto

Table 3.1 shows the population of blacks, South Asians, East and Southeast Asians, and Eastern Europeans residing in city and suburban areas. We present two sets of percentages to describe their location patterns. The first set, the percentage of a group in the suburban area, shows the level of the group's suburbanization. The second set, the percentage of a group in relation to the total suburban population, illustrates the suburban representation of a group relative to other groups. Although we provide information about the city residential patterns of each group, it is for reference only. Our discussion focuses on suburban patterns.

The patterns of suburbanization among all four groups paint an optimistic picture. Despite their recent arrival, most members of these four groups reside in suburban neighborhoods. In addition, there are similar percentages in suburban areas, ranging from 81% to 93%. The results may simply reflect the rapid suburban development of Toronto since the 1950s, as in other major cities in North America. Among the four groups, blacks and South Asians have the highest suburbanization rates in Toronto. The patterns of blacks in Canada are sharply different from those of blacks in the United States, and they may reflect the fact that most blacks have arrived in Canada since the 1970s and do not share the unique history of blacks in the United States.

The last two columns report the percentages of group populations within the total city and suburban populations. They reveal additional information about suburbanization patterns. Although East and Southeast Asians

Table 3.1 City and Suburban Distribution of Blacks, South Asians, East and Southeast Asians, and Eastern Europeans, 1996

	Population Counts			Within-group Proportions		Proportions of Total Population	
	City	Suburbs	Total	City	Suburbs	City	Suburbs
Total							
Blacks	33,335	240,900	274,235	12.16%	87.84%	5.18%	6.72%
South Asians	23,995	304,775	328,770	7.30%	92.70%	3.73%	8.50%
East and Southeast Asians	95,745	429,900	525,645	18.21%	81.79%	14.88%	12.00%
Eastern Europeans	40,235	173,385	213,620	18.83%	81.17%	6.25%	4.84%
Immigrants							
Blacks	20,440	144,305	164,745	12.41%	87.59%	3.18%	4.03%
South Asians	18,035	222,700	240,735	7.49%	92.51%	2.80%	6.21%
East and Southeast Asians	70,190	325,715	395,905	17.73%	82.27%	10.91%	9.09%
Eastern Europeans	25,075	103,475	128,550	19.51%	80.49%	3.90%	2.89%

Source: 1996 Canadian Census.

40   *Eric Fong*

and Eastern Europeans have high rates of suburbanization, their representation is lower in the suburbs than in the city. The results suggest that the representation of these groups in city and suburbs is affected by the presence of other groups. Therefore, the understanding of their representation in suburban neighborhoods should take other groups into consideration.

Distribution of New Immigrant Groups in City and Suburban Neighborhoods

To further explore the suburban residential patterns of new immigrant groups, we compare their levels of clustering in suburban and city neighborhoods in Table 3.2. We report the percentage of each group residing in suburban and city neighborhoods of different levels of ethnic concentration. Information about city neighborhoods is included because it helps us compare suburban patterns. Residing in suburban areas does not necessarily lead to residential integration. Both blacks and South Asians have higher percentages living in suburban neighborhoods with higher co-ethnic

Table 3.2   Distribution of Blacks, South Asians, East and Southeast Asians, and Eastern Europeans in Neighborhoods with Different Levels of Concentration by Location, 1996

Levels of Co-Ethnic Concentration in Neighborhoods	Blacks %	N	South Asians %	N	East and Southeast Asians %	N	Eastern Europeans %	N
City								
0%–2.9%	43.4	62	62.2	89	6.3	9	31.5	45
3%–5.9%	28.0	40	20.3	29	20.3	29	32.9	47
6%–9.9%	14.0	20	11.2	16	17.5	25	18.2	26
10%–14.9%	7.7	11	4.2	6	20.3	29	4.9	7
15%–19.9%	2.8	4	0.0	0	13.3	19	0.7	1
20% of more	1.4	2	1.4	2	20.3	29	6.3	9
Suburbs								
0%–2.9%	39.9	264	36.5	241	19.8	131	39.8	263
3%–5.9%	20.7	137	19.1	126	21.5	142	32.4	214
6%–9.9%	20.4	135	16.9	112	19.7	130	12.1	80
10%–14.9%	7.3	48	10.0	66	14.2	94	7.7	51
15%–19.9%	5.1	34	6.8	45	7.26	48	2.6	17
20% of more	4.8	32	8.8	58	15.3	101	1.8	12

Source: 1996 Canadian Census.

concentration than in city neighborhoods (i.e., 15% or more of co-ethnic members in tracts). The percentage of blacks and South Asians residing in neighborhoods with more than 15% of co-ethnic members rises from 4.2% in the city to 9.9% in suburban areas for blacks and from 1.4% to 15.6% for South Asians. These findings echo Darden's (2002, 2004) findings on the residential segregation patterns of blacks and South Asians in Toronto.

There are indications of residential integration in suburban areas for East and Southeast Asians and Eastern Europeans. They have lower representation in suburban neighborhoods with higher co-ethnic concentration than in city neighborhoods. However, despite signs of residential integration, it is important to point out that there are still substantial clusters of East and Southeast Asians in neighborhoods with high concentrations of co-ethnic members. About 23% of East and Southeast Asians reside in suburban neighborhoods with 15% or more of their own group.

In short, although the percentage of groups in suburban neighborhoods can be affected by their overall percentage there, the results show substantial variations of concentration among groups. Only Eastern Europeans show a clear sign of residential integration in suburban neighborhoods with a smaller percentage of group members clustered in neighborhoods with higher co-ethnic concentration. Though the percentage of East and Southeast Asians residing in co-ethnic concentrated neighborhoods in the suburbs is lower than in the city, there is still a large percentage residing in suburban ethnic concentrated neighborhoods. Considerable percentages of blacks and South Asians do not experience residential integration. They live in suburban ethnic concentrated neighborhoods.[7]

Sharing Neighborhoods in City and Suburbs

The results thus far indicate that a high percentage of each of the four groups resides in suburban areas. The results also demonstrate variations in these groups sharing neighborhoods with other groups in suburbs and city. To assess the racial and ethnic composition of tracts where the four new immigrant groups live, and how the patterns are related to their socioeconomic resources, we ran a series of OLS regression models. The dependent variable in each of these models is the group proportion of one of the new immigrant groups in the tract. We ran two models for each group. The first model includes the total proportion of various major groups in the tract (including the charter groups, Northern Europeans, Western Europeans, Southern Europeans, Eastern Europeans, South Asians, East and Southeast Asians, and blacks) and the group's socioeconomic characteristics (including the group's median household income, the proportion of members who completed university, and the proportion of members not knowing English or French). The second model also includes the total immigrant proportion of all these groups. The immigrant proportion of all the groups helps us to evaluate how the presence of the new immigrant groups is related to the immigrant proportion of other groups. We combine the immigrant proportion of all groups to avoid possible correlation between the total proportion of a specific group and its immigrant proportion in the tract.

We ran one model including only tracts in the city and another with only tracts in the suburbs. Results from the city model are used as reference for the suburban model. We further control for inner and outer suburban areas for possible ecological differences in the suburban model. Most neighborhoods in suburban areas have been developed recently. As developers will not restrict their sales to any group of buyers, and government policies are opposed to any discriminatory sales practices, these neighborhoods are more conducive to residential integration. In short, these models are set up to take into consideration the multi-ethnic nature and immigrant characteristics of suburban neighborhoods with reference to city models. Specifically, they estimate how the shares of each European and visible minority group, as well as the nativity of these groups, are related to the presence of new immigrant groups, controlling for the effects of socioeconomic resources.

Drawing from the first hypothesis, we expect that the four new immigrant groups will have lower proportions in suburban neighborhoods than in city neighborhoods, controlling for other factors. This pattern would reflect the expectation that these new immigrant groups will have higher exposure to other groups in suburban neighborhoods. If this pattern occurs among the four new immigrant groups, the intercept of their suburban models should be lower than the intercept of their city models, controlling for other factors. Intercepts of the models can be interpreted as the "typical" proportion of new immigrant groups in suburban or city neighborhoods, controlling for the proportion of other groups and the socioeconomic characteristics of the recent immigrant group under study.

The results show that the intercepts of the suburban model for blacks, South Asians, and East and Southeast Asians are slightly higher than those of the city model, other things being equal. However, the intercept of the suburban model for Eastern Europeans, controlling for immigrant proportion in tract, is drastically reduced by half. These results suggest that only Eastern Europeans experience residential integration in the suburbs, controlling for other factors.

The second hypothesis leads us to expect that the income, educational level, and language ability of a new immigrant group will be strongly related to its suburban neighborhood proportion. The results support the hypothesis. For all groups, a higher proportion of the group not knowing English or French is related to a higher level of suburban ethnic clustering, while educational level is related only for blacks and South Asians. The language ability of blacks is particularly strongly related to suburban ethnic clustering. The stronger effect when comparing the language coefficient of the black model with corresponding coefficients of the models of other groups is statistically significant. The patterns reflect that blacks in particular have a strong tendency to move out of their clustered neighborhoods when they have higher education and better language ability. The finding that income does not relate to suburban ethnic clustering is consistent with other Canadian studies. It may reflect the progressive nature of the Canadian tax structure that redistributes resources. It may also reflect that immigrant families commonly pool resources from relatives beyond their own households to improve their living arrangements. Taken together, socioeconomic resources, except income, are related to the proportion of new immigrant groups in suburban neighborhoods, particularly blacks.

The third hypothesis suggests that the negative relationship of the total proportion of all other groups and the proportion of the new immigrant group under study will be stronger in suburban neighborhoods than in city neighborhoods. The results confirm the hypothesis. With the exception of the proportion of Northern Europeans in the East and Southeast Asian model, the proportion of other groups is always statistically significant in the suburban neighborhoods, but it is not always so in the city neighborhoods.

A careful comparison of the coefficients of the four new immigrant groups reveals an important pattern. Eastern European suburban residential patterns are unique. In comparison to the other three new immigrant groups, this group experiences substantial residential integration with the charter groups in the suburbs. The negative coefficients of the charter group proportions with the other three new immigrant groups are stronger than the coefficient of the Eastern European suburban model. In other words, Eastern Europeans in the suburbs are more likely than the other three new immigrant groups to share neighborhoods with the charter groups. Further reinforcing the arguments, the negative coefficient of the charter group proportion in suburban neighborhoods is lower than in the city in the Eastern European models.

The final hypothesis suggests that the immigrant proportions of other groups will be positively related to the proportions of new immigrant groups in suburban neighborhoods. The results show mixed patterns. The relationships are significant only for blacks and Eastern Europeans in the suburban neighborhoods. However, it is important to point out that the immigrant proportion does not relate to the presence of any new immigrant group in city neighborhoods.

Sharing Neighborhoods with Immigrants in City and Suburbs

To further explore the patterns of immigrants of the new immigrant groups, we ran a series of models in which the dependent variables are the immigrant proportions of the four new immigrant groups. We included the same set of independent variables as reported in Table 3.3. The results of the regression models are summarized in Table 3.4. The discussion particularly focuses on whether foreign-born members of the new immigrant groups are more likely to share neighborhoods with immigrants of other groups. It is noteworthy that, in general, the variance shown by the models presented in Table 3.4 is less than the variance shown by the models reported in Table 3.3. This difference suggests that the residential patterns of the immigrant portion of the new immigrant groups are less easily explained by the set of variables used to explain the patterns of the new immigrant groups in their entirety. Thus, we are cautious when discussing the results.

Table 3.3 OLS Regression of Group Composition and Immigrant Composition on Proportion of Blacks, South Asians, East and Southeast Asians, and Eastern Europeans in Neighborhoods by Location, 1996

City	Blacks		South Asians		East and Southeast Asians		Eastern Europeans	
Prop. Charter Groups	-0.226**	-0.212**	-0.12**	-0.118**	-0.545**	-0.552**	-0.374**	-0.382**
Prop. Northern Europeans	-0.801	0.450	-0.57	-0.668	0.297	0.772	0.855	1.054
Prop. Western Europeans	-0.131	-0.072	-0.13	-0.115	-0.846*	-0.885**	0.486	0.456
Prop. Southern Europeans	-0.160**	0.152**	-0.09**	-0.085**	-0.543**	-0.540**	-0.305**	-0.309**
Prop. Easter Europeans	-0.223**	-0.221**	-0.05	-0.058	-0.561**	-0.550**		
Prop East and Southeastern Asians	-0.137**	-0.127**	-0.04	-0.041			-0.334**	-0.339**
Prop. South Asians	0.252**	0.231**			-0.117	-0.098	-0.165	-0.159
Prop. Blacks			0.139*	0.130*	-0.388**	-0.359**	-0.479**	-0.472**
Prop. Immigrants		0.008		0.003		-0.010		-0.006
Group median income	0.000	-0.000	-0.000	-0.000	-0.000	-0.000	0.000	0.000
Prop. completed university	-0.057**	-0.058**	-0.011	-0.011	0.020	0.024	-0.082**	-0.083**
Prop. not knowing English or French	0.600**	0.610**	0.138**	0.133**	0.462**	0.458**	0.262**	0.257**
Intercept	0.175**	0.142**	0.090	0.077**	0.402**	0.431**	0.297	0.320**
N	143	143	143	143	143	143	143	143
Adjusted R^2	0.436	0.441	0.340	0.338	0.785	0.786	0.467	0.466

Suburbs								
Prop. Charter Groups	-0.250**	-0.236**	-0.298**	-0.294**	-0.614**	-0.619**	-0.19**	-0.177**
Prop. Northern Europeans	-1.416**	-1.786**	-1.446**	-1.568*	-1.200	-0.990	-1.01**	-1.463**
Prop. Western Europeans	-0.602**	-0.575**	-0.753**	-0.747**	-1.040**	-1.048**	-0.31**	-0.274*
Prop. Southern Europeans	-0.390**	-0.193**	-0.272**	-0.271**	-0.524**	-0.526**	-0.19**	-0.179**
Prop. Eastern Europeans	-0.200**	-0.411**	-0.386**	-0.394**	-0.707**	-0.692**		
Prop. East and Southeast Asians	-0.235**	-0.234**	-0.179**	-0.180**			-0.210**	-0.211**
Prop. South Asians	-0.090**	0.085**	0.111**	0.106	-0.338**	-0.335**	-0.190**	-0.192**
Prop. Blacks				0.002	-0.604**	-0.597**	-0.283**	-0.287**
Prop. Immigrants		0.008**		0.000		-0.004		0.009**
Group median income	0.000*	-0.000*	0.000	0.000	0.000	0.000	-0.000	-0.000
Prop. completed university	-0.054**	-0.053**	-0.036**	-0.37**	0.006	0.007	-0.016	-0.018
Prop. not knowing English or French	0.825**	0.805**	0.166**	0.165**	0.348**	0.351**	0.000**	0.210**
Prop. not knowing English	0.010**	0.011**	-0.013**	-0.01**	0.001	0.001	0.010**	0.011**
Intercept	0.228	0.197**	0.262**	0.254**	0.468**	0.480**	0.201**	0.164**
N	658	658	658	658	658	658	658	658
Adjusted R²	0.541	0.545	0.527	0.526	0.665	0.665	0.322	0.335

Note: p** < 0.05; p* < 0.1
Source: 1996 Canadian Census

Table 3.4 OLS Regression of Group Composition and Immigrant Composition on Immigrant Proportion of Blacks, South Asians, East and Southeast Asians, and Eastern Europeans in Neighborhoods by Location, 1996

	Blacks		South Asians		East and Southeast Asians		Eastern Europeans	
City								
Prop. Charter Groups	−0.505**	−0.472**	−0.146	−0.11	−0.432**	−0.405**	−0.404**	−0.392**
Prop. Northern Europeans	−7.119	−7.920	0.863	0.041	−4.131	−6.289**	3.346*	3.022
Prop. Western Europeans	2.422**	2.558*	−3.679**	−3.59**	−1.273	−1.097	−0.431	−0.383
Prop. Southern Europeans	0.050	0.068	−0.018	−0.01	−0.138	−0.154*	−0.112	−0.106
Prop. Eastern Europeans	−0.076	−0.071	−0.313	−0.34	−0.059	−0.106		
Prop. East and Southeast Asians	−0.124	−0.101	0.153	0.175			−0.487**	−0.480**
Prop. South Asians	1.081**	1.047			0.248	0.164	0.812*	0.803*
Prop. Blacks			1.153**	1.093**	0.036	−0.094	−0.133	−0.146
Prop. Immigrants		0.018		0.026		0.045**		0.053
Group median income	0.001	0.001	0.001*	0.001*	−0.000	−0.000	−0.000	0.000
Prop. completed university	0.081	0.079	0.541**	0.539**	0.241**	0.219**	−0.117	−0.115
Prop. not knowing English or French	−0.801	−0.777	0.638**	0.605**	0.310**	0.329**	0.505*	0.512
Intercept	0.637**	0.562**	0.543**	0.453*	0.789	0.655**	0.771**	0.733**
N	143	143	143	143	143	143	143	143
Adjusted R²	0.165	0.161	0.279	0.276	0.388	0.416	0.143	0.137

Suburbs								
Prop. Charter Groups	-0.377**	-0.231**	-0.218**	-0.12	-0.303**	-0.280**	-0.647**	-0.575**
Prop. Northern Europeans	5.628**	1.706	0.5	2.618	-0.630	-0.396	2.956	0.616
Prop. Western Europeans	-1.474**	-1.186**	-0.794	-0.62	-1.593**	-1.554**	-1.141**	-0.963**
Prop. Southern Europeans	-0.041	0.039	-0.142*	-0.11	-0.165**	-0.158**	-0.402**	-0.361**
Prop. Eastern Europeans	0.112	-0.121	-0.024	-0.22	0.021	-0.051		
Prop. East and Southeast Asians	-0.113	-0.093	-0.028	-0.03			-0.582**	-0.585**
Prop. South Asians	0.054	0.000			-0.067	-0.080	0.172	-0.184*
Prop. Blacks			0.422**	0.319**	0.163	0.127	0.167	0.147
Prop. Immigrants		0.083**		0.06**		0.020**		0.049**
Group median income	0.003**	0.003**	0	0.001**	-0.000	-0.000	-0.001**	-0.001**
Prop. completed university	-0.109	-0.094	0.301**	0.29**	0.303**	0.301**	0.088	0.080
Prop. not knowing English or French	0.413	0.198	0.548**	0.517**	0.466**	0.452**	1.192**	1.120**
Inner suburban area	0.021	0.023	0.009	0.006	-0.019*	-0.018*	0.001	0.002
Intercept	0.589	0.263**	0.658**	0.449**	0.750**	0.687**	0.865**	0.672**
N	658	658	658	658	658	658	658	658
Adjusted R²	0.221	0.270	0.166	0.194	0.294	0.298	0.332	0.353

Note: p** < 0.05; p* < 0.1
Source: 1996 Canadian Census

To address the issue, we first explore the intercepts of the models. The results indicate two patterns. First, the intercept of the full model shows that the immigrant clustering of these groups remains at similar levels in the suburbs and city, except for blacks. Second, the value for the intercepts of the full model, which includes both specific group and immigrant proportions, is smaller than the value for the intercepts of models where only proportions of groups are documented, especially among the suburban models. These results taken together suggest that among the four groups, the clustering of immigrants in the suburbs is to a considerable extent associated with the immigrant proportions of other groups.

Unlike the findings in the previous tables, the clustering of immigrants of the four groups is positively and consistently related to the immigrant proportion of other groups. However, the association with the immigrant proportion of other groups varies among all four groups. The coefficients clearly show that black immigrants in suburban areas are more likely to share their neighborhoods with immigrants of other groups. However, the relationship of Eastern European immigrants and the immigrant proportion of other groups is the weakest among all new immigrant groups. In other words, Eastern European immigrants experience residential integration in suburban neighborhoods with a small increase in the immigrant proportion of other groups.

Finally, although group socioeconomic resources generally are related to other new immigrant groups, we found that the coefficients of the socioeconomic resources of blacks do not relate to their immigrant proportion in either city or suburban neighborhoods, with the exception of income (which is weakly related to the proportion of black immigrants in suburban neighborhoods). Importantly, these findings all point to the fact that the suburban residential patterns of black immigrants are uniquely different from those of other new immigrant groups.

CONCLUSION

Most major cities in North America are becoming multi-ethnic, with a growing representation of immigrants. Studies have begun to explore the residential patterns of new immigrant groups in suburban neighborhoods within this multi-ethnic context. In this study, we extend the existing literature by utilizing both the spatial assimilation and the place stratification perspectives and differentiating the nativity of group members.

We argue that the understanding of the suburban residential patterns of new immigrant groups should consider the composition and nativity of other major racial and ethnic groups. Though we suggest that new immigrant groups experience lower segregation in suburban neighborhoods than in city neighborhoods, these new immigrant groups are more likely to share neighborhoods with immigrants of other groups. Subsequently, the documented "spatial integration" of new immigrant groups is also about sharing neighborhoods with immigrants from other groups. It gives rise to the partial integration of new immigrant groups in suburban areas.

Using 1996 Canadian census data on Toronto, we explored the suburban residential patterns of four new immigrant groups: Eastern Europeans, South Asians, East and Southeast Asians, and blacks. These groups together represent about 66% of immigrants who arrived in Canada after 1980. We proposed four hypotheses to understand the suburban residential patterns of the new immigrant groups. The findings only partially support the hypotheses. First, results show that only Eastern Europeans have significantly lower clustering in suburban neighborhoods than in city neighborhoods. Second, findings clearly show that the clustering levels in suburban neighborhoods of all new immigrant groups are related to their socioeconomic resources. Specifically, language ability is especially crucial, but income is not, to the clustering level of new immigrant groups in suburban neighborhoods. However, socioeconomic resources are strongly related for blacks only when their group proportion, but not their immigrant proportion, is used as the dependent variable. Third, the presence of the new immigrant groups is negatively related to the proportion of other groups in suburban neighborhoods. However, this relationship is weaker for Eastern Europeans and the charter groups in suburban areas. Finally, when the analysis focuses on the immigrant proportions of these new immigrant groups, the results clearly show the partial residential integration of all new immigrant groups, as they are more likely to share neighborhoods with immigrants of other groups. This relationship is much weaker for Eastern European immigrants. In other words, Eastern European immigrants are able to experience more residential integration in suburban areas without a significant increase in the immigrant proportion of other groups.

Taken together, the results suggest three important implications for the suburban residential patterns of new immigrant groups. First, our findings suggest that, just as they were for previous generations of immigrants, socioeconomic resources are still important for the residential integration of new immigrant groups in suburban areas. Like those earlier immigrants, these new immigrants reside in more ethnically and racially diverse neighborhoods as their socioeconomic resources improve (Clark and Blue 2004). Second, the differential residential experiences of groups in the suburbs, divided along racial lines, also apply to new immigrant groups. Eastern Europeans are able to reside in suburban neighborhoods with lower proportions of their own group and are more likely to share neighborhoods with the charter groups. Visible minorities do not share this experience. In particular, blacks do not lower their residential concentration in suburban areas. Regardless of cause, the differences in the suburban residential patterns of new immigrant groups, which can be defined along racial lines, reflect the long-standing racial hierarchy in North American cities. Finally, the presence of immigrants living in suburban neighborhoods does not necessarily relate to full spatial integration.

Even when they share neighborhoods with other groups, these immigrants are more likely to share with immigrants of other groups, while the relationship is weakest for Eastern Europeans. Given the usually strong attachment among co-ethnic immigrants, the interaction of immigrants across groups can be superficial. In addition, since these immigrants are learning the ways of the new country, interaction with immigrants of other groups does not necessarily help other aspects of integration. Thus, the patterns described can create a situation of only partial residential integration among new immigrant groups in suburban areas.

Our results suggest avenues for future research on multi-ethnic neighborhoods. They highlight the importance of differentiating nativity when examining multi-ethnic neighborhoods. They also suggest that future studies should explore how the socioeconomic resources of new immigrant groups are related to the native-born and foreign-born populations of other groups. Although our results are consistent among the new immigrant groups in one particular city, the study could be extended to other cities to verify the findings. It is possible that results obtained from other major cities in Canada or the United States may differ from the results presented here. In addition, future studies should further update the results with more recent census data. They also should include more cities to explore multi-ethnic neighborhoods at the metropolitan level.

NOTES

1. This research was supported by Social Sciences and Humanities Research Council of Canada. Direct correspondence to Eric Fong, Department of Sociology, 725 Spadina Avenue, University of Toronto, Toronto, Ontario, Canada M5S 2J4. Email: fong@chass.utoronto.ca
2. No information about Asians and blacks was available in 1961. Based on data provided by Lemon (1985), Chinese and Japanese, the two largest Asian groups, comprised 1.7% in 1961, while Africans consisted of 0.5%.
3. According to the 1996 Canadian census, East and Southeast Asians include Chinese, Filipino, Indo-Chinese, Indonesian, Japanese, Korean, Malay, Mongolian, Taiwanese, and Tibetan. South Asians include Bangladeshi, Bengali, East Indian, Goan, Gujarati, Pakistani, Punjabi, Sinhalese, Sri Lankan, and Tamil (Statistics Canada 1996a, 1996b).
4. Driedger (1996) suggested that the term was first used by Ujimoto and Hirabayashi (1980) to describe Asian groups in their book, *Visible Minorities and Multiculturalism: Asians in Canada*. Later it was expanded to include blacks.
5. These figures include South Asians, East and Southeast Asians, and blacks.
6. The former city of Toronto was amalgamated with five other cities: East York, Etobicoke, North York, Scarborough, and York.
7. The concentration of blacks in Canada is relatively low in comparison with blacks in the United States. The difference is partly related to the unique history of blacks in the United States. It is also related to demographic differences. A large proportion of blacks in Canada are foreign-born with less difference from other groups in socioeconomic resources.

REFERENCES

Adelman, Robert M., Hui-Shen Tsao, Stewart E. Tolnay, and Kyle D. Crowder. 2001. "Neighborhood Disadvantage among Racial Groups: Residential Location in 1970 and 1980." *The Sociological Quarterly* 42:603-32.

Alba Richard D., and John R. Logan. 1991. "Variations on Two Themes: Racial and Ethnic Patterns in the Attainment of Suburban Residence." *Demography* 28:431-53.

Alba, Richard D., and John R. Logan. 1993. "Minority Proximity to Whites in Suburbs." *American Journal of Sociology* 98:1388-1427.

Alba, Richard D., John R. Logan, Brian J. Stults, Gilbert Marzan, and Wenquan Zhang. 1999. "Immigrant Groups in the Suburbs: A Reexamination of Suburbanization and Spatial Assimilation." *American Sociological Review* 64:446-60.

Badets, Jane, and Tina W. L. Chui. 1994. *Canada's Changing Immigrant Population*. Ottawa: Prentice Hall Canada.

Burgess, Ernest W. 1925. "The Growth of the City: An Introduction to a Research Project." In *The City*, edited by Robert E. Park, Ernest W Burgess, and R. D. McKenzie, 47-62. Chicago: University of Chicago Press

Charles, Camille Zubrinsky. 2003. "The Dynamics of Racial Residential Segregation." *Annual Review of Sociology* 29:167-207.

Charles, Camille Zubrinsky. 2000. "Neighborhood Racial-Composition Preferences: Evidence from a Multiethnic Metropolis." *Social Problems* 47:379-407.

Clark, William A. V. 1999. *The California Cauldron*. New York: Guilford Publications.

Clark, William A. V., and Sarah A. Blue. 2004. "Race, Class, and Segregation Patterns in U.S. Immigrant Gateway Cities." *Urban Affairs Review* 39:667-88.

Darden, Joe. 2004. *The Significance of White Supremacy in the Canadian Metropolis of Toronto*. Edwin Mellen Press.

Darden, Joe. 2002. "Residential Segregation and Neighborhood Socioeconomic Inequality." In *Urban Ethnic Encounters: The Spatial Consequences*, edited by Freek Colombign and Aygen Erdentug, 27-43. London: Routledge.

Driedger, Leo. 1999. "Immigrant/Ethnic/Racial Segregation: Canadian Big Three and Prairie Metropolitan Comparison." *Canadian Journal of Sociology* 24:485-509.

Driedger, Leo. 1996. *Multi-Ethnic Canada*. Toronto: Oxford University Press.

Fong, Eric, Chiu Luk, and Emi Ooka. 2005. "Spatial Distribution of Suburban Ethnic Businesses." *Social Science Research* 34:215-35.

Fong, Eric, and Kumiko Shibuya. 2000. "The Spatial Separation of the Poor in Canadian Cities." *Demography* 37:449-59.

Fong, Eric, and Kumiko Shibuya. 2005. "Multiethnic Cities in North America." *Annual Review of Sociology* 31:285-304.

Fong, Eric, and Rima Wilkes. 1999. "The Spatial Assimilation Model Reexamined: An Assessment by Canadian Data." *International Migration Review* 33:594-620.

Fong, Eric, and Rima Wilkes. 2003. "Racial and Ethnic Residential Patterns in Canada." *Sociological Forum* 18:577-602.

Henry, Frances. 1994. *The Caribbean Diaspora in Toronto: Learning to Live with Racism*. Toronto: University of Toronto Press.

Horton, John. 1995. *The Politics of Diversity: Immigration, Resistance, and Change in Monterey Park, California*. Philadelphia: Temple University Press.

Iceland, John. 2003. *Poverty in America: A Handbook*. Berkeley: University of California Press.

Iceland, John. 2004. "Beyond Black and White: Metropolitan Residential Segregation in Multi-Ethnic America." *Social Science Research* 33:248-71.
Iceland, John, Cicely Sharpe, and Erika Steinmetz. 2005. "Class Differences in African American Residential Patterns in US Metropolitan Areas: 1990-2000." *Social Science Research* 34:252-66.
Iceland, John, and Wilkes, Rima. 2006. "Does Socioeconomic Status Matter? Race, Class and Residential Segregation." *Social Problems* 53:248-73.
Lemon, James. 1985. *Toronto Since 1918: An Illustrated History.* Toronto: James Lorimer & Company, Publishers and National Museum of Man, National Museums of Canada.
Logan, John, Richard D. Alba, and Shu-Yin Leung. 1996. "Minority Access to White Suburbs: A Multiregional Comparison." *Social Forces* 74:851-82.
Logan, John R., Richard Alba, and Wenquan Zhang. 2002. "Immigrant Enclaves and Ethnic Communities in New York and Los Angeles." *American Sociological Review* 67:299-322.
Maly, Michael T. 2005. *Beyond Segregation: Multiracial and Multiethnic Neighborhoods in the United States.* Philadelphia: Temple University Press.
Massey, Douglas S. 1985. "Ethnic Residential Segregation: A Theoretical Synthesis and Empirical Review." *Sociology and Social Research* 69:315-50.
Massey Douglas S., and Denton Nancy A. 1988. "Suburbanization and Segregation in United-States Metropolitan Areas." *American Journal of Sociology* 94:592-626.
McVey, Wayne W., and Warren E. Kalbach. 1995. *Canadian Population.* Toronto: Nelson.
Mesch, Gustavo S. 2002. "Between Spatial and Social Segregation among Immigrants: The Case of Immigrants from the FSU in Israel." *International Migration Review* 36:923-34.
Modarres. Ali. 2004. "Neighborhood Integration: Temporality and Social Fracture." *Journal of Urban Affairs* 26:351-77.
Orfield, Myron. 2002. *American Metropolitics: The New Suburban Reality.* Washington, DC: Brookings Institution Press.
Owusu, Thomas Y. 1999. "Residential Patterns and Housing Choices of Ghanaian Immigrants in Toronto, Canada." *Housing Studies* 14:77-97.
Portes, Alejandro, and Min Zhou. 1993. "The New Second Generation: Segmented Assimilation and Its Variants." *Annals* 530:74-96.
Price-Spratlen, Townsand, and Avery M. Guest. 20002. "Race and Population Change: A Longitudinal Look at Cleveland Neighborhoods." *Sociological Forum* 17:105-36.
Reitz, Jeffrey G. 1998. *Warmth of the Welcome: The Social Causes of Economic Success for Immigrants in Different Nations and Cities.* New York: Westview Press.
Reitz, Jeffrey G., and Raymond Breton. 1994. *The Illusion of Difference: Realities of Ethnicity in Canada and the United States.* Toronto: C. D. Howe Institute.
Rose, John. 2000. "Contexts of Interpretation: Assessing Immigrant Reception in Richmond, Canada." *The Canadian Geographer* 45:474-93.
Rosenbaum, Emily, and Samantha Friedman. 2001. "Differences in the Locational Attainment of Immigrant and Native-Born Households with Children in New York City." *Demography* 38: 337-48.
Rosenbaum, Emily, and Samantha Friedman. 2004. "Generational Patterns in Home Ownership and Housing Quality among Racial/Ethnic Groups in New York City, 1999." *International Migration Review* 38:1492-1533.
Rosenbaum, Emily, and Samantha Friedman. 2006. *The Housing Divide.* New York: New York University Press.
Saito, Leland T. 1998. *Race and Politics: Asian Americans, Latinos, and Whites in a Los Angeles Suburb.* Urbana: University of Illinois Press.

Smedley, Audrey. 1993. *Race in North America: Origin and Evolution of a Worldview*. Boulder, CO: Westview Press.
South, Scott, Kyle Crowder, and Erick Chavez. 2005. "Migration and Spatial Assimilation among U.S. Latinos: Classical versus Segmented Trajectories." *Demography* 42:497–521.
Statistics Canada.1996a. Selected demographic, cultural, educational, labour force and income characteristics (170) of the population by selected ethnic categories (15), age groups (6) and sex (3), showing single and multiple ethnic origin responses (3) (20% sample) (94F0009XDB96011)
Statistics Canada. 1996b. Selected demographic, cultural, educational, labour force and income characteristics (207) of the total population by age groups (6) and sex (3), showing visible minority population (14) (20% sample) (94F0009XDB96003)
Statistics Canada. 1998. Special Requested Tables: Total non-Institutional Population by User-Defined Ethnic Origin (28) Showing Selected Characteristics (38).
Suttles, Gerald. 1972. *The Social Construction of Communities*. Chicago: University Of Chicago Press.
Teixeira, Carlos, and Robert A. Murdie. 1997. "The Role of Ethnic Sources of Information in the Residential Relocation Process: A Case Study of Portuguese Homebuyers in Suburban Toronto." *Urban Geography* 18:497–520.
Ujimoto, K. Victor, and Gordon Hirabayashi. 1980. *Visible Minorities and Multiculturalism: Asians in Canada*. Toronto: Butterworths.
White, Michael J. 1987. *American Neighborhoods and Residential Differentiation*. New York: Russell Sage Foundation.
Wilkes, Rima, and John Iceland. 2004. "Hypersegregation in the Twenty-First Century." *Demography* 41:23–36.
Wright, Richard, Mark Ellis, and Virginia Parks. 2005. "Re-Placing Whiteness in Spatial Assimilation Research." *City & Community* 4:111–35.
Zavodny, Madeline. 1999. "Determinants of Recent Immigrants' Locational Choices." *International Migration Review* 33:1014–30.
Zhou, Min. 1997. "Segmented Assimilation: Issues, Controversies, and Recent Research on the New Second Generation." *International Migration Review* 31(4):975–1008.

4 Asian Immigrants in Vancouver
From Caste to Class in Socio-Spatial Segregation?

David Ley

INTRODUCTION

This chapter emerges from my research on the spatial imprint of immigrants and other minorities in the city. I ask the question, how do we conceptualise the difference that immigrant socio-spatial segregation makes? My approach is to use a comparative method through time, examining the effects of three distinctive historical regimes in the same city—Vancouver, Canada—and for the same broad ethnic group—members of the Chinese diaspora. My concern is to consider what ethno-spatial segregation means in the micro-narratives of immigrant lives when shaped by the meta-narratives of three distinctive regimes of hegemonic ideology, ideologies borne and deployed by both the state and civil society. I shall interpret these meta-narratives against immigrant landscapes that both reflect and reproduce them.

In this manner, conceptualisation may begin with immigrant segregation but does not end there. The objective is to theorise what ethno-spatial segregation *means* in the daily life of immigrants in terms of the enveloping cultural politics and political economy of receiving societies. I employ a comparative method examining the contexts of Asian immigration to Canada through three periods of hegemonic belief and practice at the level of the state and civil society. The discussion begins in an unequal colonial plural society, giving way to the rise of multicultural impulses and policies from the mid-1960s onward, which collided in the mid-1980s with the rise of a neoliberal governance that has dominated the period up to the present.

COLONIAL VANCOUVER

British Columbia ceased to be a colony of the British Crown in 1867 but continued to display colonial attributes and attitudes for another hundred years (Ley 1995). Colonial ideology, as we shall see, established a well-defined social and cultural hierarchy that imposed a tenacious gradient of social distance between majority and minority populations.

Our discussion begins in Vancouver's Old Chinatown, among the oldest and largest in North America (Lai 1988). Its very naming as an ethnic place confirms the segregated spatial experience of its inhabitants, and indeed this compact isolation is reproduced in a genre of Chinatown novels like Wayson Choy's (1995) *Jade Peony*, which explores this bounded lifeworld of a few city blocks on the edge of downtown. Nearby, until the 1940s, was Japantown, a similarly enclosed immigrant neighbourhood, separate and institutionally complete. Scattered through the young industrial city were a number of Indian reserves, the legally contained settlement forms of the formerly mobile First Nations bands (Harris 2002). East from Chinatown and Japantown was a mixed working-class population, Canadian, American, and European, with local spatial concentrations of southern and eastern Europeans. Westward was an Anglo-Canadian elite in spacious mansions built in neocolonial styles. This segregated population spoke to a society of parallel lives, with meticulous personal and institutional lines of separation along class, ethnic, and racial divisions. Its connection to empire was nonetheless clear. The 1921 Census showed that 80% of the population claimed British heritage, and as two world wars and several royal visits made patently clear, it was a population defined by a strong measure of imperial fealty.

How to conceptualise this social geography of ethno-spatial difference? The dominant conceptualisation in young industrial cities for many decades followed Robert Park and the Chicago School, a tradition from which we have learned much. In the methodology developed in Chicago, segregation was measured in a series of segregation and dissimilarity indices whose refinement continues to the present (Walks and Bourne 2006). In this manner, a grid of measurable spatial relationships could be established between ethno-cultural groups. And what underlay these spatial patterns? Two principal mechanisms were identified. First was the micro-economic capacity of a household to bid for space in a competitive property market that sorted individuals according to their incomes. Second, and accounting for the spatial grouping of ethnically similar households, was the social distance that one ethnicity expressed from another. These two processes of spatial sorting emerged from individual and group preferences and ability to pay. But overseeing the micro-processes was a more ambiguous Darwinian version of Adam Smith's invisible hand, directing individual actions toward a dynamic spatial equilibrium. Competition in the city had a pervasively Darwinian teleology, and Park's language of natural areas, habitats, the processes of invasion and succession, were all part of a paradigm of human ecology (McKenzie 1968) or, as Park (1936) sometimes put it, biological economics. The natural area was an expression of a natural order.

But was it? The naturalisation of spatial patterns and social distance in human ecology has been challenged on several grounds and perhaps most robustly by the development of a neo-Marxist social science in the 1970s. David Harvey (1973), in his celebrated *Social Justice and the City*, commented, "It seems a pity that contemporary geographers have looked to Burgess and Park rather than to Engels for their inspiration" (133). I do not want to pursue this neo-Marxist problematic further here, but I do note that it introduces the dimension of *political* power to the relations between groups on the map of the city—albeit a very narrow version of power in the classic two-class model. And what a difference the addition of political power adds to the effects of human ecology in socio-spatial relations! With the incorporation of political power, we understand the slow death of Old Chinatown during the period of the xenophobic Chinese Immigration Act from 1923 to 1947, which, like parallel legislation in the United States, effectively blocked legal immigration from China for a quarter century. We note too, as we build in power, the elimination of Japantown during the 1940s from the face of the city with the internment of Canadian nationals of Japanese origin during the moral panic precipitated during the 1939–45 war. It was of course no different in the United States, where similar legal innovations aggressively othered immigrants from Asia—though it was not only immigrants from Asia who suffered in this manner, for Nancy Foner (2000) and others have described the extraordinary resistance to immigrants from Southern and Eastern Europe in the United States during the 1880–1930 period.

A series of theoretical approaches are now at our disposal, all of them insisting that the power that places immigrant groups into spatial niches in the city, with highly differential life chances, is much more human than the social Darwinian variation on the invisible hand employed by the Chicago human ecologists. To highlight the deployment of power, one might turn, in addition to neo-Marxists like David Harvey, to whiteness studies, critical race studies, or postcolonial authors, all of whom see political power itself as emanating from all-pervasive ideologies of racial hierarchy. An under-appreciated author I have found helpful is J. S. Furnivall (1939, 1956), who wrote from the 1930s to the 1950s as a colonial administrator in the territories of Southeast Asia toward the end of empire, where he identified what he called *plural societies*. The plural society comprised segregated ethnic groups of Europeans and Asians who lived separate social and cultural lives and came together only for economic self-advancement. As such, wrote Furnivall (1956), "In the plural society the highest common factor is the economic factor, and the only test that all apply in common is the test of cheapness" (310).

The colony of Singapore established by Stamford Raffles was one such plural society, and like other colonial societies, these lines of stratification were not quickly extinguished in the postcolonial period (Demaine 1984). Jackson's 1822 town plan for Singapore employed by Raffles was itself based on the model of colonial Calcutta (Goh 2005) and was a design that enforced the separation of minorities and their domination by a colonial elite. Much later the Group Areas Act in South Africa perfected this spatial design of separation for domination during the final four decades of apartheid (Western 1997). What was true of Singapore and Cape Town was true to a lesser degree of many of the colonial port cities of Europe overseas, including, I would argue, Vancouver. The logic of a plural society incorporated segregation as both an expression and a reinforcement of asymmetric power and life chances.

For it was not ability to pay that separated minority groups in early Vancouver but something altogether more invidious—race-coloured hegemony. The malfeasant union of race and space reproduced racial hierarchies in which different Asian groups were marginalised with minimal entitlements (Ley 2010a). In Vancouver's early 20th-century society, the historical geographer, Cole Harris (1997), identified "a particularly virulent racism . . . race became the pre-eminent symbol. It defined simply and effectively, with no need to go into details, who was acceptable and who was not" (p268). The spatialization of difference in segregated districts gave a sharp edge to the contours of race. Popular racism was fanned by groups like the abominably named Asiatic Exclusion League, an outfit formed in San Francisco in 1905, with a satellite group established in Vancouver in 1907. After its inaugural meeting led by various dignitaries, a mob rampaged through nearby Chinatown and Japantown, attacking property and roughing up residents. This was not merely popular prejudice but extended into political and legal institutions, most notably the Head Tax and the subsequent Chinese exclusion legislation passed by the federal government (Anderson 1991). What was at stake here was not class but caste: through racist blinders, Asian immigrants were neither white, nor civilised, nor Christian, but a stigmatised and outcast other.

Extraordinary efforts were justified to hold the race line. If segregation broke down and Chinese immigrants moved in any numbers outside the demarcated holding area of Chinatown, then Councillor Hoskins told the daily Vancouver *Province* newspaper in 1919, the only alternative would be "to take up arms to drive them into the sea" (Anderson 1991, 123).

MULTICULTURAL VANCOUVER

We can remain in Chinatown for our second moment of reflection on the meaning of immigrant segregation. The landscape of Chinatown has changed little in the more liberal era since 1945, although the status of minorities in Canada has been significantly redefined. And stability has reigned supreme since 1971, when, in the first flourish of multiculturalism, the district was designated by the provincial government as the Chinatown Historic Area. In that year, people of Chinese ancestry were still significantly confined within the district's historic boundaries, although diffusion was already occurring south and east into other neighbourhoods. An enigma of multiculturalism is that it has made a premium of the former penalty of ethnic difference. The diversity that led formerly to abjection leads now to multicultural engagement. In a magical twist, landscapes like the Chinatowns that once evoked rejection and exclusion are now re-presented as a source of pride and enrichment.

How did this transformation come about? One can trace a progression of liberalizing events from the 1960s onward, with the steady rise of civil rights, the welfare state, and immigration reform that removed former preferences favouring European source countries. A new cultural hegemony was taking shape. There was recognition that Canada was already a more complex society than the old model of the English and French charter groups. The intervention of Jewish and Ukrainian stakeholders in the public process around the 1960s Royal Commission on Bilingualism and Biculturalism proclaimed a more plural set of identities, and it aided a final outcome the commissioners did not foresee, when Prime Minister Trudeau announced to Parliament in 1971 that Canada's destiny was to be not bicultural but multicultural.

By the 1990s, multiculturalism had been adopted in Australia, New Zealand, and a number of western European states, though as it fused with different national contexts, it came to mean different things in different places and moreover evolved significantly through time (Vertovec and Wessendorf, 2010). In Canada, multiculturalism's principal objective today is the protection of the civil rights of recognizable cultural groups against unfair treatment from the state or in civil society (Ley 2010b). But multiculturalism began as a small-budget program in the 1970s to preserve and promote heritage cultures, and many accounts still treat it in these terms. Certainly the preservation of a historic Chinatown engineered by different levels of government in the 1970s fell into this policy envelope.

It was government action that defined Chinatown as a historic area in 1971, and that bounded it on the map, containing and even amplifying its difference. It was prescribed to continue to be what it had always been—a facsimile of a townscape in South China in the late 19th century. In fact the role of the state was stronger, for in detailed regulations and design specifications, the streetscape was embellished in the image of a Western-defined *chinoiserie* (Anderson 1991). New structures, with considerable state funding, added to the effect: a classical Chinese garden, built by labourers from China, and a Chinese Cultural Centre to preserve cultural memories and practices. Most recently, a Chinese arch has been added to the urban landscape, providing a precise demarcation of ethnic turf as one enters through this ornamental gateway.

A profound irony is at work here. The liberal state through its multicultural practices is perfecting what the colonial state accomplished through racist badgering and spatial confinement. Geographical containment was part of the colonial strategy of management and control of a marginalised group that was to be set apart; now the multicultural state wishes to bound and embalm the territory that helped constitute that marginalisation. What we see is the continuing essentialization of a cultural heritage in a restricted space, where landscape and identity conspire together to emphasize diversity and difference while simultaneously concealing the crude perceptions and practices that defined Chinatown in the first place. This aesthetic parade is all there for our viewing. Walk today westward along Pender Street, the spine of Chinatown, past memory-filled buildings like the Chinese Benevolent Society (1909) and the Chinese Freemasons' Building (1901), temporary home of the itinerant Dr. Sun Yat-sen, and one passes the site, abundantly signposted as a historic trail, of the one-time warren of tenements and bunkhouses along Canton and Shanghai Alleys, the original core of Chinese settlement on land scavenged from tidal marshes. The coherence of the landscape narrative along the trail reminds us that we are in an outdoor museum, meticulously orientalized by a bookish multiculturalism, with design, color, and landscape texture now prescribed by bureaucratic guidelines.

Vancouver is not alone in such socio-spatial practices. I mentioned earlier colonial Singapore and the Jackson Plan of 1822 employed by Raffles and colonial administrators to divide and manage the diverse cultural groups in a precisely segregated plural society. After a generation of mindless modernization characterised by urban clear cutting, the postcolonial state in Singapore has found some uses for its multicultural heritage. Malay Village, Little India, areas of Chinese shophouses, even the colonial Civic District are now all dutifully deployed about their business of reproducing ethnic difference. That task, Robbie Goh (2005) informs us, is to tie multiculturalism, in a neoliberal era, squarely into an urbanity that nurtures the commodity culture of domestic leisure and foreign tourism.

But the relationship between multiculturalism and ethnic segregation has become fraught in Western immigrant-receiving nations in recent years. Trevor Phillips' anxious speculation about multicultural Britain, "sleepwalking toward segregation" in his celebrated words, provided quite literally a wake-up call (Phillips 2005). To the extent that multiculturalism essentializes heritage cultures, it has been chastised for encouraging segregated neighborhoods that become hot beds of hostile difference and even blamed for nurturing terrorist cells (Ley 2010b). But in fact there are few differences in immigrant segregation between states, for example, Britain and France or Canada and the United States, that do or do not have a multicultural policy. Rather, it is the high level of immigration into gateway cities like Vancouver in the past 25 years that has led to an increase in segregation, just as it did in Chicago a century ago, a time when the melting pot not the mosaic was the metaphor and assimilation the accompanying expectation. While it may aid cultural preservation and the *appearance* of differences in places like Old Chinatown, multiculturalism, unlike an earlier racism, is rarely a robust enough ideology to shape immigrant residential patterns.

NEOLIBERAL VANCOUVER

With the rise of neoliberalism in the 1980s, we move into our third and final historic context of immigrant settlement, and for this third moment of reflection, we need only walk another two hundred metres west along

Pender Street, for suddenly we move from the preserved landscape of Old Chinatown, redeemed by the multicultural state, to the vital cosmopolitan energy of International Village, built by Hong Kong tycoons, where raw global capitalism has a very different project in mind. We are on the edge of the vast Concord Pacific development of high-rise condominium towers on former industrial and railway lands on the edge of downtown, a site used for the Expo 86 World's Fair.

The fair was a transparent attempt by a neoliberal provincial government to prime international tourism and investment through the global extravaganza of an urban spectacle. It was fully in keeping with this political economy that privatization should follow at the end of Expo 86. The vast downtown site, along two kilometres of waterfront, has a 25-year build-out plan, and it is the creative work of its purchaser, Li Ka-shing, and two other Hong Kong tycoons. The land, owned by the British Columbia provincial government, was auctioned to the highest bidder at the end of Expo 86, itself an advertisement to global investment, by a neoliberal government firmly committed to Mrs. Thatcher's aphorism that "there is no alternative" (Harvey 2005) when it comes to privatization and the global rule of the market.

As I was told by a real estate agent who serviced new immigrants from East Asia, "Where the big fish swim, the small fish follow" (Ley 2010a). The desire for portfolio diversification that brought the three Hong Kong tycoons to Vancouver created a scenario ripe for imitation, and an extraordinary flood of capital entered the Vancouver land market from East Asia in the decade following the Expo purchase in spring 1988. Much of the capital came from absentee investors, but a significant pool—I estimate $35–$40 billion over a ten-year period—was available to wealthy immigrants who landed through Canada's business immigration program, minted it might seem for their convenience (Ley 2003). For in the commodification of everything in the 1980s, immigration and citizenship itself became available to entrepreneurs from overseas with substantial business experience and financial capital. The new business program fitted to a tee the geopolitics of East Asia and aspirations there for passport insurance, Western education, and Canadian quality of life. Between 1980 and 2001, some 35% of the 330,000 business immigrants entering Canada came to Vancouver, with more than two-thirds originating in Hong Kong and Taiwan. Vancouver also received the wealthiest members of this cohort.

How has this recent migration cohort inserted itself into the social geography of Vancouver? It is an ethnic Chinese population that is on the whole cosmopolitan and well travelled. Their model of urbanity is not the parochialism of a preserved Chinatown. They know the East Asian rules of the game when it comes to urban property; in the creative destruction of Hong Kong, Shanghai, and Taipei land booms, there is no room for sentimental *chinoiserie*; a progressive modernity eschews such backward-looking tendencies in favor of the vigorous returns earned on new urban development (Abbas 1997; Forrest and Lee 2004).

And so the protected charms of multicultural Chinatown are unattractive to the new immigrants. How else to explain the fact that in 1970, when there were 30,000 ethnic Chinese in Vancouver, Chinatown was booming, but today with more than 400,000 ethnic Chinese in the metropolitan area, Old Chinatown has lost its allure and become a problem for city planners to solve? The map of newly arrived Chinese Canadians is more fully defined by their financial capital. Rather than being sequestered in a tightly segregated inner city district, the 37,000 Chinese-origin households who landed in Vancouver from 1986 to 1996 are widely scattered, living in 85% of all the metropolitan census tracts. It is middle-class consumption in new houses and suburban malls that new East Asian immigrants seek, not the outmoded charms of Old Chinatown.

Nonetheless, some concentration of the new immigrants does exist. Populations are concentrated in the southern neighborhoods of Vancouver and the northern section of Richmond, a Chinese ethnoburb. What is immediately notable about these clusters is their proximity to the Vancouver International Airport, with its frequent flights to the principal cities of East Asia and especially to Hong Kong. This relationship unsettles the discourse of segregation. For the name of the game now is movement not stasis. Segregation suggests a sedentary population, a population somewhat rooted in place. But the millionaire migrants from East Asia are frequently on the move, transnational businessmen with revenue streams in the hot and humid coastal plains of East Asia while their families are living in the cool temperate hill station of Vancouver (Ley 2010a). Their concentration near the airport facilitates a style of middle-class everyday life that is shaped by transnational mobility.

As such, the millionaire migrant from East Asia is the global neoliberal subject *par excellence*. Crossing boundaries, seeking profit, and on the move, there seems to be no impediment to this space of flows of capital and entrepreneurs (Hamilton 1999; Ong 1999). Our third moment of socio-spatial reflection reveals a novel symmetry of enterprising immigrant agency and neoliberal state structure, factors that are indispensible to interpret diasporic Chinese insertion into the social geography of the city. The outcome is a map of unsettled segregation occupied largely by a cosmopolitan immigrant class.

CONCLUSION

In this chapter, I have sought to locate immigrant settlement from East Asia within the cultural politics and political economy of the destination country. Through a comparative method that works with three separate historic periods, I have argued that the *meaning* of segregation has changed through each era regardless of trends in the *measure* of segregation. Pressing the argument to its limit, we see the movement from a colonial society with segregation defined by the caste system of racial hierarchy, through the transition of multiculturalism, which looked back at essentialized cultural difference but also forward to the cultural commodification of the present global neoliberal era, our third era, where a market mandate creates a new stratification of migrants defined primarily by class advantage. In presenting this generalization, I have minimized in this short chapter qualifiers that should be added and that I will not pause to itemize here. The principal case I wish to make is to advance a richer conceptualization of the society that contextualizes immigrant segregation, telling us more about both the experience of everyday life in these districts as well as the broader contours of cultural politics and political economy in the receiving society that shape a life experience. Allowing for local contingencies, what we see in Vancouver I suspect can be repeated elsewhere around the Pacific Basin in other former colonial port cities such as Singapore or Sydney.

REFERENCES

Abbas, A. 1997. *Hong Kong and the Politics of Disappearance*. Hong Kong: University of Hong Kong Press.
Anderson, K. 1991. *Vancouver's Chinatown: Racial Discourse in Canada, 1875–1980*. Montreal: McGill-Queen's University Press.
Choy, Wayson. 1995. *Jade Peony*. Vancouver: Douglas and McIntyre.
Foner, N. 2000. *From Ellis Island to JFK: New York's Two Great Waves of Immigration*. New Haven, CT: Yale University Press.
Demaine, H. 1984. "Furnivall Reconsidered: Plural Societies in South-East Asia in the Post-Colonial Period." In *Geography and Ethnic Pluralism*, edited by C. Clarke, D. Ley, and C. Peach, 23–50. London: Allen & Unwin.
Forrest, R., and Lee, J. 2004. "Cohort Effects, Differential Accumulation and Hong Kong's Volatile Housing Market." *Urban Studies* 41(11):2181–96.
Furnivall, J. S. 1939. *Netherlands India*. Cambridge: Cambridge University Press.
Furnivall, J. S. 1956. *Colonial Policy and Practice*. New York: New York University Press.
Goh, R. B. H. 2005. *Contours of Culture: Space and Social Difference in Singapore*. Hong Kong: Hong Kong University Press.
Hamilton, G. (ed.) 1999. *Cosmopolitan Capitalists: Hong Kong and the Chinese Diaspora at the end of the Twentieth Century*. Seattle: University of Washington Press.
Harris, R. C. 2002. *Making Native Space: Colonialism, Resistance and Reserves in British Columbia*. Vancouver: UBC Press.
Harris, R. C. 1997. *The Resettlement of British Columbia*. Vancouver: UBC Press.
Harvey, D. 1973. *Social Justice and the City*. London: Arnold.
Harvey, D. 2005. *A Brief History of Neoliberalism*. Oxford: Oxford University Press.
Lai, D. 1988. *Chinatowns: Towns within Cities in Canada*. Vancouver: UBC Press.
Ley, D. 1995. "Between Europe and Asia: The Case of the Missing Sequoias." *Ecumene* 2:187–212.
Ley, D. 2003. "Seeking *homo economicus*: The Strange Story of Canada's Business Immigration Program." *Annals, Association of American Geographers* 93:426–41.

Ley, D. 2010a. *Millionaire Migrants: Trans-Pacific Life Lines*. Oxford: Wiley-Blackwell.

Ley, D. 2010b. "Multiculturalism: A Canadian Defence." In *The Multiculturalism Backlash: European Discourses, Policies and Practices*, edited by S. Vertovec and S. Wessendorf, 190–206. Abingdon, UK: Routledge.

McKenzie, R. 1968. *On Human Ecology*, edited by A. Hawley. Chicago: University of Chicago Press.

Ong, A. 1999. *Flexible Citizenship: The Cultural Logics of Transnationality*. Durham, NC: Duke University Press.

Park, R.1936. "Human Ecology." *American Journal of Sociology* 42:1–15.

Phillips, T. 2005. "After 7/7: Sleepwalking to Segregation", Speech to the Manchester Council for Community Relations, UK, 22 September.

Vertovec, S., and Wessendorf, S., eds. 2010. *The Multiculturalism Backlash: European Discourses, Policies and Practices*. Abingdon, UK: Routledge.

Walks, A., and Bourne, L. 2006. "Ghettoes in Canada's Cities? Racial Segregation, Ethnic Enclaves and Poverty Concentration in Canadian Urban Areas." *The Canadian Geographer* 50:273–97.

Western, J. C. 1997. *Outcast Cape Town*, 2nd ed. Berkeley: University of California Press.

5 Are Native "Flights" from Immigration "Port of Entry" Pushed by Immigrants?
Evidence from Taiwan

Ji-Ping Lin

INTRODUCTION

In light of the persistence and the emerging trend of international migration in the world, debates on immigration impact have never ceased and are becoming even more contentious in immigration-receiving countries (Borjas 2001; Massey and Taylor 2004; Smith and Edmonston 1998; Stahl 2003). The most addressed issues by relevant studies comprise two broad aspects. The first one focuses on immigration impact on the employment opportunities of domestic labor market and thus the resulted impact on the wage level of native workers. The other, within the spatial context, studies immigration impact on internal migration of the native-born populations (hereafter the native-borns). Either from the supply or demand side of manpower, both aspects of study are interrelated but hard to accommodate simultaneously except for a few studies (e.g., Borjas 2006; Card 2001).

The theme of research in this study is the impact of immigrant labor on internal migration of native-born labor force (hereafter native labor), aiming at ascertaining the relationship between immigration and internal migration of native labor and assessing the extent to which immigrants affect redistribution of domestic manpower. The study is inspired by the observed association between internal migration and immigration and the relationship of skill differentials between native populations and immigrants that have long been noted by a number of studies from major immigrants-receiving countries, particularly the United States (Bogue and Liegel 2009; Borjas 1987a; Card 1990; Filer 1992; Frey 1996, 2005; Frey and Speare 1988; Long 1988; Walker et al. 1992; Wright et al. 1997). Take the past trends in the United States for example, Frey (1996, 2005) finds (1) that based on the 1990 and 2000 U.S. censuses, in the 1985–1990 the large metropolitan areas served as major immigration ports of entry which were characterized by a "flight" of low-skilled internal migrants, and (2) that metropolitan areas that received modest gains from internal migrants attracted relatively few immigrants and were selective of the well-educated internal migrants; in 1995–2000 although there were some changes from earlier patterns, there is a continued out-migration of internal migrants with less education from most high immigration metropolitan areas. Bogue and Liegel (2009) also indicate that the main losers of internal migration are metropolitan areas or states that are least attractive to natives with lower education and more attractive to those with college education, but these trends of improving educational composition are largely reversed by low-skilled immigrants. By contrast, the major gainers of internal migration are intermediate-size metropolitan areas that enjoy various growths due to regional restructuring and economic growth.

In this regard, immigration has both advantages and disadvantages for receiving countries. Since it may help create or foster an existing "dual" economy, low-skilled immigrants tend to complement natives with higher educations or native professionals/managers, but they also compete for low-paying and informal jobs against and even substitute for low-skilled native workers (Piore 1979; Walker et al. 1992). It is thus generally hypothesized that a large and sustained influx of low-skilled foreign labor into a few immigration "ports of entry" might not only push out native labor within these "ports" but also tend to discourage in-migration flows of native labor from other domestic labor markets, leading to an essential population redistribution within the internal labor market. In the context of linked migration system between internal migration and immigration, it is theoretically expected that if the impact of low-skilled immigration on internal migration of native labor is distinct, the corresponding pushing effect on out-migration and discouraging effect on in-migration will be stronger for the low-skilled and less-educated native labor. However, because of the complementary effect of low-skilled immigration for the professionals and managers who in turn may intensify the in-flows of low-skilled immigrants into professionals/manager preferred destinations to provide the needs for personal services, the major immigration "ports of entry" are expected to have a retention effect on out-migration for native labor with higher educations and a pulling effect on in-migration for the comparable native labor outside these ports (Walker et al. 1992).

Relevant studies on the context of immigration impact on the geographic migration of the native-borns are mostly seen in the United States. Because scholars so far have not reached a consensus on whether immigration affects the native-born internal migration, the existing research findings turn out to be mixed or controversial. For examples, an earlier study by Manson and his associates (1985) on Mexican immigrants in southern California lends support to the notion that Mexican immigrants serve as complements to skilled in-migrants and as substitutes for the less-skilled local workers; Filer (1992) studies internal migration of 272 metropolitan areas in the United States, finding that the level of attractiveness for a specific metropolitan area is negatively associated with the concentration level of immigration; Walker et al. (1992) find that native blue-collar workers have been spatially displaced by immigration, but there is no evidence supporting the argument that the growth in white-collar employment in major large metros have stimulated a complementary immigrant in-flow to satisfy service needs from the expanding professional class posited by Sassen (1988); and the study by Winter-Ebmer and Zweimüller (1999) indicates that the displacement impact of immigrants on Austrian young native workers does exist but turns out to be minor.

Other empirical research stratifying the population in study by educational and skill level has lent support to the pushing effect of immigration on internal migration. For example, Frey (1996) and Frey et al. (1996) find that internal migration of American workers does respond to the presence of immigration. Frey and Liaw (1998), using the 1990 U.S. census data, find that low-skilled immigrants do affect the interstate migration of the U.S.-born low-skilled Americans. Their findings indicate that the pushing effects of low-skilled immigration on the departure process is much stronger than the corresponding discouraging and complementary effects in the destination choice process, and that the pushing effects of low-skilled immigration are selectively stronger on the low-skilled, the poor, the whites, and the older age groups. Bogue and Liegel (2009) suggest that low-skilled immigration is a key plausible explanation for unskilled Americans with a low rate of arrival and higher rate of departure from main losers of internal migration. Brücker, Fachin, and Venturini (2011) take another route for immigration impact study in Italy. Instead of focusing on immigration impact on the out-migration of the natives from main immigration gateway cities, they study whether immigrants "discourage" the in-migration of the natives from other regions into gateway cities. Their findings suggest that by controlling for the effects of unemployment and wage differentials, immigrant labor does discourage internal labor mobility significantly.

Nevertheless, empirical research reports no significant impact of immigration on native internal migration. Using the 1990 U.S. population census, Card (2001) explores the effects of immigrant in-flows on the labor market opportunities of natives and older immigrants. He finds that even after controlling for endogenous mobility decisions, inter-city migration flows of natives and older immigrants are largely unaffected by new immigrants. He further finds that immigration between 1985 and 1990 depressed the employment rate of low-skilled natives in major U.S. cities by 1% to 2% on average, and this negative impact becomes substantial in high-immigrant cities. White and Liang (1998) examine the impact of immigration on the labor market opportunities of the native-borns based on the U.S. Current Population Survey (CPS), finding that the states with high levels of recent immigration are less likely to retain Anglo workers or receive new Anglo interstate migrants, but this apparent substitution effect is partially offset by the presence of long-term immigrant stock. White and Imai (1994) indicate that there is no significant effect of immigrants on internal migration in the United States. By applying the 1980 and 1990 U.S. Census Bureau microsamples to three sets of regression models, Wright et al. (1997) find that net migration of the native-borns for metropolitan areas is either positively related or unrelated to immigration, and the net loss of native labor from large metropolitan areas is more likely the result of industrial restructuring instead of immigration. Thus, they claim no solid evidence in support of an effect of immigration on internal migration. Using the same data, Ellis and Wright (1999) subdivide native- and foreign-born migrants of metropolitan Los Angeles by national origin and ethnicity, finding that native- and foreign-born groups do channel into particular industrial sectors of metropolitan Los Angeles in 1985–1990. Moreover, based on the U.S. population census and using 94 metropolitan areas as the labor markets, Fairlie and Meyer (1997) examine whether the levels of black self-employment are lower in labor markets with a higher share of immigrants. Their findings suggest that immigration has no effect or only a small negative but statistically insignificant effect on black male or female self-employment.

Kritz and Gurak (2001), based on the 1990 5% Public Use Microdata Sample (PUMS), studied whether the native- and foreign-borns differ in their migratory response to high immigration in the United States. After taking the migratory response of the foreign-borns to immigration into consideration and controlling for state economic and regional context, their research results do not support the claim that internal migration of the U.S. native-borns is the response to recent immigration. Using the 1996 and 2001 New Zealand Censuses and being closely based on the empirical approach of Card (2001), Maré and Stillman (2010) find little support for the displacement effect of migrant in-flows on either the native-borns or earlier immigrants with similar skills. They further suggest that given the similarities between New Zealand and Australia with regard to immigration systems and migration behavior (Hugo 2006), the immigration impact in Australia should resemble that observed in New Zealand.

Because the aforementioned empirical results are inclusive, Ley (2007) stresses the spatial regularity of countervailing immigration, and net domestic migration flows may not be exclusively explained by labor market effects. He extends the analysis to Australian and Canadian main immigration "port-of-entry" cities of Sydney and Toronto, finding that the two flows of immigrants and domestic migrants are responding to different drivers. He stresses that domestic migrants leaving gateway cities are mainly triggered by housing market effects, although cultural avoidance of the natives can't be denied. In contrast, in-flows of immigrants into gateway cities are mainly related to co-ethnic networks, national immigration policy, and business cycle effects. Based on the Panel Study of Income Dynamics (PSID), Crowder, Hall, and Tolnay (2011) study the causal relationship between neighborhood immigration and native out-migration, suggesting that the association between neighborhood immigration and native out-migration can be attributed to the fact that immigrants tend to settle in neighborhoods in which natives are conducive to make out-migration. Ethnic flight thesis and local housing market competition are mediating factors in explaining the out-migration of whites and blacks, respectively.

In spite of inconclusive empirical findings, the research recognizes that the migration system of Taiwan during the period of 1996–2000 is very suitable for research in this regard. The main reasons are as follows. First, like the development history of the United States in the 17th to 19th centuries, Taiwan had a long historical tradition of migration, and the Taiwanese were seen to be as footloose as Americans (Campbell 1903; Knapp 1980). However, the population system and domestic labor market of Taiwan were closed to the world systems for nearly a century from the beginning of Japanese jurisdiction in 1895 until the early 1990s. Except for voluminous influxes of Chinese diasporas in the late 1940s due to the civil war of China, international migration was not crucial in affecting Taiwan's population system by the 1950s (Barclay 1954; Clark 1989). For the sake of economic development since the 1960s, Taiwan did not restrict immigration of ordinary foreigners, mostly professionals and managers, as well as their dependents from America and Japan and partly from Europe, but strictly banned low-skilled immigration from other countries. As a result of democratization and the onset of internal development toward a pluralistic system (Clark 1989; Copper 1988), Taiwan's domestic labor market started reopening to the world systems in the late 1980s. Moreover, because of the economic boom in the late 1980s that led to the formation of a dual economy (Ranis 1992), the economy of Taiwan was increasingly hampered by rising wage levels and shortages of native labor in the early 1990s. These endogenous changes finally forced the Taiwanese government to open up the domestic labor market to low-skilled immigrants (Lee and Wang 1996; Selya 1992; Tsai and Tsay 2004).

Second, the low-skilled foreign laborers are contract workers mostly from the ASEAN countries (Tsai and Tsay 2004). It is worth highlighting that the contract immigrant workers are selected from the lower tail of income distribution and from the lower hierarchy of socioeconomic status in the sending countries. When moving to Taiwan for work, they are paid by Taiwanese employers slighter higher than the legal level of minimum wage. Similar to Borjas (1987b), the migration process of low-skilled immigrants into Taiwan is negative selection. Moreover, it is worthy of stressing that the immigration destinations of contract workers in Taiwan were predetermined by their Taiwanese employers before their immigration (Tseng 2004; Tsai and Tsay 2004). In other words, low-skilled foreign laborers do not have any privilege to choose destinations before immigrating into Taiwan. In addition, they were not allowed to change their Taiwanese employers once moving to Taiwan until the year of 2007 due to the concern of human rights, suggesting that they were not able to make internal migration. As a result, the joint effects of destination choice before immigration and the internal migration after immigration for contract immigrant workers can be ignored in the selected period of research.

Native "Flights" from Immigration "Port of Entry" 69

Third, before immigration grew in importance, it is worth highlighting a drastic change of internal migration in Taiwan in the early 1990s. Mainly because of regional economic restructuring and economic globalization in the late 1980s and early 1990s, the internal labor migration in Taiwan experienced a salient transition from a long-lasting net transfer of native labor into the dual north-south regions to a unidirectional net transfer into northern metropolitan areas (Lin and Liaw 2000). The effect of international migration was not crucial to this dramatic change. As illustrated by Figure 5.1, Taiwan officially opened up the domestic labor market for low-skilled immigrants in 1992. The number of low-skilled foreign laborers in Taiwan rose to about 350,000 by 2010, and the share of low-skilled foreign labor to native labor and to low-skilled native labor keeps at a rate of about 3.3% and 5.5% on average since the year of 2000, respectively. It is observed that the period of 1996–2000 had the most noteworthy growth in terms of volume and rate that was only a few years after the aforementioned prominent transition in native destination choice preference. By the end of 2011, contract foreign workers amount to around 426 thousands. In terms of the racial and ethnic background, they mostly come from Indonesia, the Philippines, and Thailand before the year of 2000; but Vietnam starts becoming a new source of immigration after 2001. For example, in 2000 23.8% of immigrant workers came from Indonesia, 30.1% from the Philippines, 43.7% from Thailand, and only 2.4% from Vietnam; in 2011 the corresponding share is 41.2% for Indonesia, 19.5% for the Philippines, 16.9% for Thailand, and 22.5% for Vietnam.

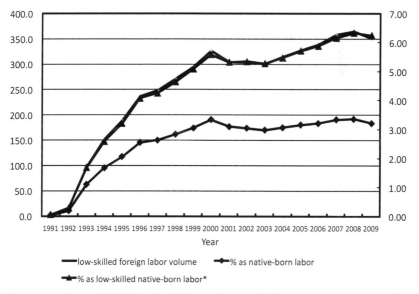

Figure 5.1 Low-skilled foreign labor volume and share as Taiwan native-born labor.

Fourth, the heterogeneity in the native and foreign populations in Taiwan is not as enormous as that observed in the United States. The reasons are as follows. Because the ordinary immigrants are not voluminous, a crucial note by Kritz and Gurak (2001) about the need to differentiate between the migratory response of the foreign-borns and the native-borns turns out to be unnecessary in the context of Taiwan. In addition, the study recognizes that a key methodological problem that is common in all such studies is the modeling of immigrant location decisions as exogenous. As a matter of fact, it is important to stress that the location decisions of immigrants are not exogenous, but instead are mostly determined by the same factors (e.g., income, employment opportunity, environmental amenity, social structure, cultural similarity, etc.) that determine migration of native populations. This problem suggests that the destination choice of immigrant arrivals needs to be properly instrumented while conducting immigration impact on the internal migration of the natives. Because low-skilled immigrants were not allowed to make internal migration and their destinations were predetermined during the selected study period, the aforementioned problem in this study can be ignored.

In effect, similar to the experiences in America (Massey 1995), recent immigration into Taiwan has three distinct features, i.e., a rapid increase in volume in a short period of time, being selective of the less-educated and the low-skilled labor, and being concentrated in a few immigration "ports of entry," mainly in the capital area and the economic heartlands of the country. The aforementioned development of migration systems suggests that Taiwan is an ideal "laboratory," and the period of 1996–2000 is a suitable period for studying immigration impact on native internal migration.

METHODOLOGY: A MICRO-MACRO LINK APPROACH

To assess the extent to which native labor responds to immigration and the extent to which domestic manpower redistributes due to immigration impact, the study contributes to derive the statistical distributions of aggregate out-migration, in-migration, and thus net flows of migration across domestic labor markets by linking them with individual-level migration probabilities that are estimated functions of a set of explanatory variables. First of all, suppose a domestic labor market consisting of I regions has N workers. For a specific region i within the labor market, the number of workers is N_i that can be further classified by G_i groups of labor. Workers between different subgroups of G_i are heterogeneous in individual characteristics and face different conditions of labor market, but workers within the same subgroup of G_i, say g, that has N_i^g workers share the same features in individual characteristics and labor market conditions, thus

$$N = \sum_{i=1}^{I} N_i = \sum_{i=1}^{I} \sum_{g=1}^{G_i} N_i^g.\text{[1]}$$

Statistical Distributions of Aggregate Out-migration Flows

Because the N_i^g individuals in the group of labor g within region i are identical in individual characteristics and labor market conditions, let the shared common feature be represented by $\mathbf{X}_i^g$, and they are thus expected to have the same probability of making out-migration $Pr(\mathbf{X}_i^g)$. Thus, for a given i and g, let Y_i^g represent the number of N_i^g individuals departing from i, apparently $Y_i^g \sim b(N_i^g, Pr(\mathbf{X}_i^g))$. On the basis of neo-classical school of migration theories that acknowledge individual decisions of labor migration are mutually independent (Massey et al. 1993), the statistical distributions of $\{Y_i^g\}$ are thus mutually independent, although not identical for all i and g; in other words, $Y_i^g \overset{ind.}{\sim} b(N_i^g, Pr(\mathbf{X}_i^g))$ for all i and g. Apparently, the expectation of Y_i^g is $E(Y_i^g) = N_i^g Pr(\mathbf{X}_i^g) = \mu_i^g$ and variance is $Var(Y_i^g) = N_i^g Pr(\mathbf{X}_i^g)(1 - Pr(\mathbf{X}_i^g)) = \sigma_i^{g2}$.

According to the *Central Limit Theorem* (CLT), if N_i^g is not very small, Y_i^g can be accepted to have a normal distribution with expectation and variance μ_i^g and σ_i^{g2}, respectively; or alternatively, $Y_i^g \overset{ind.}{\sim} N(\mu_i^g, \sigma_i^{g2})$, and

$$\frac{Y_i^g}{N_i^g} \overset{ind.}{\sim} N(\frac{\mu_i^g}{N_i^g}, \frac{\sigma_i^{g2}}{N_i^{g2}}), \forall i,j.$$

Because any linear combination of normal random variables remains normally distributed, the number of workers departing region i,

$$Y_i^+ = \sum_{g=1}^{G_i} Y_i^g$$

is still normally distributed, leading to

$$Y_i^+ \overset{ind.}{\sim} N(\mu_i^+, \sigma_i^{+2}), \forall i,$$

with the departure rate corresponding to i being distributed as

$$\frac{Y_i^+}{N_i^+} \overset{ind.}{\sim} N(\frac{\mu_i^+}{N_i^+}, \frac{\sigma_i^{+2}}{N_i^{+2}}), \quad N_i^+ = \sum_{g=1}^{G_i} N_i^g, \forall i.$$

Similarly, the total number of labor migrants

$$Y_+^+ = \sum_{i=1}^{I} Y_i^+$$

in the labor market can be inferred to be statistically distributed by

$$Y_+^+ \sim N(\mu_+^+, \sigma_+^{+2}),$$

where

$$\mu_+^+ = \sum_{i=1}^{I} \mu_i^+, \quad \sigma_+^{+2} = \sum_{i=1}^{I} \sigma_i^{+2},$$

72 Ji-Ping Lin

and the aggregate out-migration rate of the labor market in study,

$$\frac{Y_+^+}{N},$$

is thus distributed as

$$\frac{Y_+^+}{N} \sim N(\frac{\mu_+^+}{N}, \frac{\sigma_+^{+2}}{N^2}).$$

Statistical Distributions of Aggregate In-migration and Net Migration Flows

Only deriving the statistical distributions corresponding to the volume and rate of out-migration from a specific region is not sufficient. It is also important to derive the statistical distributions of in- and net migration flows among a set of potential destinations. First of all, let Y_{ij}^g represent the number of individuals who decide to move from region i to region j; note that

$$Y_i^g = \sum_{\substack{i=1 \\ j \neq i}}^{I} Y_{ij}^g.$$

Because any migrant from i has $I-1$ potential destinations to choose from (note that the choice set of potential destinations may vary with migrants; only those migrating from the same region have the same set of choices of potential destinations), let $P_{ij}^g = Pr(\mathbf{X}_{ij}^g)$ represent the probability of Y_i^g migrants from labor group g and region i deciding to move into region $j \neq i$, with

$$\sum_{\substack{j=1 \\ j \neq i}}^{I} P_{ij}^g = 1.$$

Thus, with Y_i^g given, say, $y_i^g (y_i^g = 0,1,2,\ldots N_i^g)$, the conditional distribution of Y_{ij}^g given $Y_i^g = y_i^g$ has a multinomial distribution as:

$$Pr(Y_{ij}^g = y_{ij}^g; j=1,2,\cdots I, j \neq i \mid Y_i^g = y_i^g) = \frac{y_i^g!}{\prod_{\substack{j=1 \\ j \neq i}}^{I} Y_{ij}^g!} \prod_{\substack{j=1 \\ j \neq i}}^{I} P_{ij}^g.$$

Note that if $i \neq i'$ or $j \neq j'$ or $g \neq g'$, then Y_{ij}^g and $Y_{i'j'}^{g'}$ are mutually independent, Y_{ij}^g and $Y_{ij'}^{g'}$ are also mutually independent, but $\{Y_{ij}^g\}$ are correlated for a given i and g. For simplicity, let Y_i^g and Y_j^g, $j \neq i$, respectively, represent the i-th and the j-th element of $\mathbf{Y}_i^g = (Y_{i,1}^g \ldots Y_{i,i-1}^g \quad Y_i^g \quad Y_{i,I+1}^g \ldots Y_{i,I}^g)$; let $\mathbf{\mu}_i^g$ and $\mathbf{\Sigma}_i^g$ be the expectation and covariance matrix of $\mathbf{Y}_i^g$, respectively. According to the *CLT*, $\mathbf{Y}_i^g$ has an asymptotic multinormal distribution as N_i^g approaches infinity. Empirically, if N_i^g is large enough, the probability density function of $\mathbf{Y}_i^g$ can be regarded to be multinormally distributed by

$$\mathbf{Y}_i^g \underset{N_i^g \to \infty}{\overset{ind}{\sim}} N(\boldsymbol{\mu}_i^g, \boldsymbol{\Sigma}_i^g), \forall i, g.$$

Again, let

$$\mathbf{Y}_i^+ = \sum_{g=1}^{G_i} \mathbf{Y}_i^g, \quad \boldsymbol{\mu}_i^+ = \sum_{g=1}^{G_i} \boldsymbol{\mu}_i^g, \quad \boldsymbol{\Sigma}_i^+ = \sum_{g=1}^{G_i} \boldsymbol{\Sigma}_i^g,$$

the CLT tells us that $\mathbf{Y}_i^+ \overset{ind}{\sim} N(\boldsymbol{\mu}_i^+, \boldsymbol{\Sigma}_i^+), \forall i$ as $N_i^+ \to \infty$. Although deriving the distributions of $\mathbf{Y}_i^g$ and $\mathbf{Y}_i^+$ is not empirically useful, it serves as the base in deriving the statistical distribution for net migration volume and rate. Since the marginal distribution of a multinormal distribution remains normally distributed, suggesting that for a given j, $Y_{ij}^+ \sim N(\mu_{ij}^+, \sigma_{ij}^{+2}), \forall i, j \neq i$, where

$$\mu_{ij}^+ = \sum_{g=1}^{G_i} \mu_{ij}^g, \quad \sigma_{ij}^{+2} = \sum_{g=1}^{G_i} \sigma_{ij}^{g2}.$$

Thus, the volume of migrants moving into region j,

$$Y_{+j}^+ = \sum_{\substack{i=1 \\ i \neq j}}^{I} Y_{ij}^+, \text{ is } Y_{+j}^+ \sim N(\mu_{+j}^+, \sigma_{+j}^{+2}), \forall j, \mu_{+j}^+ = \sum_{i=1}^{I} \mu_{ij}^+,$$

and

$$\sigma_{+j}^{+2} = \sum_{\substack{i=1 \\ i \neq j}}^{I} \sigma_{ij}^{+2},$$

leading to the net migration rate of region j having the form of

$$\frac{Y_{+j}^+}{N_{+j}^+} \sim N\left(\frac{\mu_{+j}^+}{N_j^+}, \frac{\sigma_{+j}^{+2}}{N_j^{+2}}\right).$$

Procedures of Implementing Immigration Impact Analysis

The study has shown that the aggregate volumes and rates of out-migration, in-migration, and net migration, as derived from individual departure probabilities and individual conditional probabilities of choosing potential destinations, are essentially normally distributed. The above-mentioned statistical inferences indicate that two micro-models of migration must be constructed at first before implementing impact analysis on the migratory response of native labor to immigration. The first is the model dealing with the decision to migrate, and the other is the one dealing with destination choice behavior given a native worker decides to move. The first and the second micro-models in migration studies are called "departure model" and "destination choice model," respectively, and have been widely used in a number of studies (e.g., see Clark and Onaka 1985; Kanaroglou and

Ferguson 1996; Liaw 1990; Newbold and Liaw 1995; Pellegrini and Fotheringham 1999, 2002).

The research utilizes a two-level nested logit model based on discrete choice theory (Ben-Akiva and Lerman 1985; McFadden 1974) to formulate individual migration decision, with $P_i(o)$ denoting the probability of worker i departing from origin o and $P_i(d|o)$ representing the probability of i choosing d from the choice set D (the set of all possible destinations). The coefficient vectors of both models are estimated by the maximum likelihood method. The goodness-of-fit for a given specification of model is assessed by the statistic ρ^2 defined as $\rho^2 = 1 - L / L_o$, where L is the maximum loglikelihood of the specification in question and L_o is the maximum loglikelihood of the null model. Note that although this statistic is theoretically bounded between 0 and 1, a value of 0.2 can represent a very good fit (McFadden 1974).

Before conducting immigration impact analysis, a prerequisite is to determine the empirical specification of the preferred departure and destination choice models. The "preferred model" in the study refers to the model in which the estimated coefficients of explanatory variables are not only statistically significant but are also required to be substantively meaningful and consistent with existing theories. Given that the preferred models for departure and destination choice have been properly constructed, if immigration is found to be crucial in explaining both/either models, two steps are taken to assess the extent to which native labor respond to immigration impact. First, the study systematically increases and decreases the level of immigration in the departure and destination model by, e.g., 5%, 10%, 15%, etc., with the remaining explanatory variables being fixed. For each given level of change in immigration, the study then computes the departure probability and destination choice probabilities for each individual in the micro-data. Second, the study computes the expected volumes and rates of out-migration, in-migration, and thus net migration by integrating all individual probabilities of departure and destination choice based on the method of impact analysis mentioned above.

DATA AND SPECIFICATION

Data

The estimation of the models and the exercise of immigration impact analysis described earlier are mainly based on two broad categories of data sources. The first are compiled from the 1996–2000 micro-data of Taiwan Manpower Utilization Surveys (MUSs) that are utilized to control for the effects of individual characteristics. The MUS is a well-established large-scale survey conducted by the Taiwan Census Bureau in May of each year since 1978. Each MUS of 1996–2000, comprising around 60,000 individuals aged 15 and over, records abundant personal information on demographic characteristics, human capital, socioeconomic status, labor market participation and work experience, place of work and residence, labor mobility and job turnover, wage, etc. In contrast to the census data that use a five-year period to record migration, one advantage of using MUSs is that the definition of migration can be based on consecutive years, allowing us to avoid the risk of entailing return migration and multiple moves in a longer period. The MUS datasets are cross-sectional in nature and have been widely used in research undertaken throughout the Taiwanese academic community in general. It is worth emphasizing that in terms of the questionnaire design and sampling framework, MUSs are essentially similar to the U.S. CPS and the Canadian Labor Force Survey (LFS). Therefore, our research results are, to a large extent, internationally comparable. The second are collected from a number of official aggregate statistics ranging from the year of 1995 through 1999 that are used to control for the contexture effects of regional labor market. It is worth stressing that the measured time point of aggregate regional statistics is one year earlier than the micro-data of MUSs, aiming at controlling for the causal effect of labor market conditions preceding the incidence of individual migration and thus at avoiding confounding estimation results. The aggregate statistics of labor market conditions are termed as ecological attributes in the study.

The study adopts prefecture, similar to the U.S. county, as the spatial unit for defining individual migration and measuring ecological attributes (there are 23 prefectures in total, including 21 prefectures and pities, and 2 metropolises; see Figure 5.2). Reasons for utilizing a prefecture-level unit are twofold. One is that the ecological attributes that are theoretically important as controlled variables are only available at the prefecture level, while the other and most important is that each prefecture has its own distinctive labor market feature (e.g. urban, semi-urban, or rural) and that prefecture is the most suitable regional unit that enables us to eliminate most short-distance moves like residential mobility. Thus, an individual is defined as a migrant if her or his prefecture of work at the time of the survey is not identical to that of a year preceding the survey, otherwise as a stayer.

It is worth noting that migration has long been found to be a highly selective process in the sense that migrants are distinctly different from non-migrants in terms of demographic characteristics, human capital, socioeconomic and psychosocial status, etc. (e.g. Model 1997; Rogers 1979; Sjaastad 1962). The selective feature embedded in the migration process was formally noted at first by Thomas (1938) that migration selectivity is the differential responses of demographic structure of population to the spatial variation in utility, say, wage. Thus, as stressed by Greenwood (1975) and Greenwood and Hunt (2003), the study on migration differential, or migration selectivity, is an indispensible step for any migration research.

76 *Ji-Ping Lin*

Northern Region
1 Keelung City
2 Taipei City
3 Hsinchu City
4 Taipei Pref.
5 Yilan Pref.
6 Taoyuan Pref.
7 Hsinchu Pref.

Central Region
8 Taichung City
9 Miaoli Pref.
10 Taichung Pref.
11 Changhwa Pref.
12 Nantou Pref.
13 Yunlin Pref.

Southern Region
14 Chiayi City
15 Tainan City
16 Kaohsiung City
17 Chiayi Pref.
18 Tainan Pref.
19 Kaohsiung Pref.
20 Pingtung Pref.
21 Penghu Pref.

Eastern Region
22 Hualien Pref.
23 Taitung Pref.

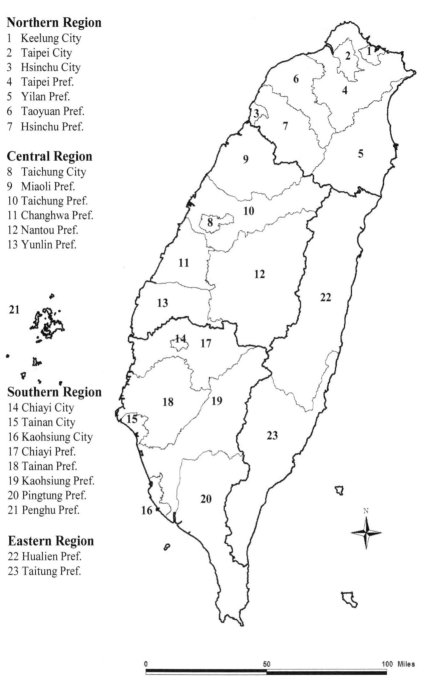

Figure 5.2 Regions and prefectures/cities.

The strategy of adopting a two-level nested logit model to realize the migration process is convenient for research, but the study also recognizes it may be associated with the problems of migration self-selection. The underlying reason is that the potential differences in latent individual characteristics between migrants and stayers may affect the propensity to migrate and that migrants are a self-selected subset of the population who might differ in many respects from those deciding not to migrate. It is thus important to deal with migrant self-selection problem, otherwise we may encounter the problem of biased estimated coefficients generated from, e.g., the idiosyncratic elements of origin and potential destination wage structures (Borjas et al. 1992; Detang-Dessendre et al. 2004; Nakosteen et al. 2008). It is not easy to accommodate this problem for empirical analysis. But as noted by Nakosteen et al. (2008) that migrant selection is by definition a phenomenon that takes place before or concurrent with the process of migration, it is problematic to use postmigration data such as earnings, suggesting that the realistic way to avoid the potential entanglement of migrant selection with labor market outcomes that occur after migration is to abandon postmigration information. As a result, the study avoids using postmigration information in the MUSs micro-data (e.g., individual wage), and the measured time point of ecological attributes must be one year preceding the corresponding MUSs.

Specification

Previous studies of native migratory response to immigration vary to a large extent in the specifications of the populations that respond to in-flows of foreigners. Since the study focuses on the impact associated with low-skilled foreign labor who are recruited by Taiwanese employers, the study recognizes the importance that the native population in study must be restricted to those whose worker status are the same as their foreign counterparts. As a result, the samples applied to the departure model are restricted to native-born individuals aged 16–64 who participate in the civilian labor force, with employers and the self-employed being excluded. Unfortunately, because the MUSs do not record information on the previous place of work for the unemployed and those not in the labor market a year preceding the survey, the study thus excludes both subsets from the MUS samples.

By definition, the qualified observations are further dichotomized into migrants and stayers. Using the variable of workplace a year preceding the survey as linkage variable, each qualified individual regardless of migrant/stayer status in the data of a given survey year is linked with the ecological attributes that are a year preceding the survey. As summarized in Table 5.1, the number of selected samples for research amounts to about 161,000, of which 2,827 individuals are observed to make labor migration. It is worth emphasizing that migration by definition in the study is based on the comparison between concurrent and previous workplace of prefecture,

78 Ji-Ping Lin

Table 5.1 Size of Samples Selected from the 1996–2000 MUSs for Study

		Selected Samples		Excluded Samples		
Year	Total Samples	Workers	Migrant Workers	Workers	Unemployed	Not in the LF
Pooled 1996–2000	303,033	161,169	(2,827)	2,185	4,036	135,643
1996	60,371	32,264	(631)	806	736	26,565
1997	60,044	32,127	(534)	440	765	26,712
1998	61,142	32,585	(562)	422	733	27,402
1999	60,619	32,225	(551)	225	991	27,178
2000	60,857	31,968	(549)	292	811	27,786

suggesting that most local job-change moves and other types of migration due to residential consideration and schooling are not counted as migrant, and it is not surprising to see a relatively low proportion of migrants in the qualified samples for study. Table 5.2 provides some basic statistics derived from the sample utilized in the study by a few crucial individual characteristics by each year of the MUSs.

Table 5.2 Sample Statistics by Some Selected Variables Derived from the 1996–2000 MUSs

	Stayers			Migrants		
Variable	n	mean	std. dev.	n	mean	std. dev.
Pooled 1996–2000 MUSs						
Gender	161,169	1.4	0.5	2,827	1.4	0.5
Age (years)	161,169	38.5	12.0	2,827	30.9	9.0
Marital status	161,169	1.8	0.6	2,827	1.5	0.6
Child-rearing status	161,169	0.2	0.4	2,827	0.1	0.3
Educational level	161,169	5.0	1.8	2,827	5.8	1.6
Monthly wage (thousands NT$)	143,924	33.7	22.6	2,742	30.8	16.1
1996 MUS						
Gender	32,264	1.4	0.5	631	1.4	0.5
Age (years)	32,264	38.3	12.1	631	30.3	9.2
Marital status	32,264	1.8	0.6	631	1.5	0.6
Child-rearing status	32,264	0.2	0.4	631	0.1	0.3
Educational level	32,264	4.9	1.8	631	5.7	1.6

(continued)

Table 5.2 (continued)

Variable	Stayers n	Stayers mean	Stayers std. dev.	Migrants n	Migrants mean	Migrants std. dev.
Monthly wage (thousands NT$)	28,775	32.3	21.1	604	29.0	13.0
1997 MUS						
Gender	32,127	1.4	0.5	534	1.4	0.5
Age (years)	32,127	38.4	12.0	534	30.7	8.4
Marital status	32,127	1.8	0.6	534	1.5	0.6
Child-rearing status	32,127	0.2	0.4	534	0.1	0.3
Educational level	32,127	5.0	1.8	534	5.8	1.6
Monthly wage (thousands NT$)	28,648	32.8	21.6	516	30.1	13.3
1998 MUS						
Gender	32,585	1.4	0.5	562	1.4	0.5
Age (years)	32,585	38.5	11.9	562	31.2	9.1
Marital status	32,585	1.8	0.6	562	1.5	0.6
Child-rearing status	32,585	0.2	0.4	562	0.1	0.3
Educational level	32,585	5.1	1.8	562	5.8	1.6
Monthly wage (thousands NT$)	29,223	34.3	23.6	550	31.6	19.1
1999 MUS						
Gender	32,225	1.4	0.5	551	1.3	0.5
Age (years)	32,225	38.6	12.0	551	31.3	8.9
Marital status	32,225	1.8	0.6	551	1.5	0.6
Child-rearing status	32,225	0.2	0.4	551	0.1	0.3
Educational level	32,225	5.1	1.8	551	5.9	1.6
Monthly wage (thousands NT$)	28,601	34.2	24.1	541	31.9	18.1
2000 MUS						
Gender	31,968	1.4	0.5	549	1.3	0.5
Age (years)	31,968	38.7	12.0	549	31.3	9.1
Marital status	31,968	1.8	0.6	549	1.5	0.6
Child-rearing status	31,968	0.2	0.4	549	0.1	0.3
Educational level	31,968	5.2	1.8	549	5.9	1.6
Monthly wage (thousands NT$)	28,677	34.8	22.5	531	31.8	16.2

Notes:
Gender: male=1, female=2;
Marital status: 1=single, 2: married/cohabited; 3:divorced/separated; 4:widowed;
Child-rearing status: 0=no child, 1=with at-least one child;
Education: 1-3=primary schooling or less, 4=junior high, 5-6=senior high, 7=college; 8=university; 9=graduate

The data applied to the destination choice model are labor migrants who, as mentioned above, amount to 2,827 individuals. It is important to stress that in addition to internal migration, emigration is a reasonable alternative for a native-born migrant in response to immigration impact. Because such tremendous immigration impact is barely seen in the real world and our research data do not record information regarding international migration, the study thus does not take emigration into consideration, suggesting the number of potential destinations is 22 when an individual decides to move. The data applied to the destination choice model are constructed by pooling the linked data of each observed migrant's individual characteristics with the ecological attributes one year before migration for each of the 22 potential destinations. Since we must construct 22 records with respect to each potential destination for each observed migrant, the number of records applied to the destination choice model is thus equal to 62,194 (= 22 × 2,827). Moreover, two variables are included in order to control for the effects of migration costs and origin-destination migration barriers. The first is the Euclidean distance between population centers of the origin and a potential destination. The other is the indicator of contiguity, which assumes the value of 1, otherwise 0, if a specific origin and a potential destination share a common border.

The study in particular recognizes the importance regarding the selection of the measurement of key explanatory variables in assessing immigration impact. A number of studies utilize the absolute volume of immigrants within a domestic labor market to assess the extent of immigration impact (e.g., Frey 1996; Walker et al. 1992). However, some scholars like Wright et al. (1997), Card (2001), and Borjas (2006) et al. have questioned the appropriateness of this measurement, because the absolute count of immigrants is highly correlated with the size of the native labor force and the economic scale of the labor market. Thus, the measurement of the quantity of immigrant labor relative to native labor might be a more meaningful measurement. In addition, utilizing only the absolute volume of immigrants without regard to the size of the location could be odd, since it means that, for example, 1,000 foreigners amounting to 2% of a location's population of 50,000 in the departure model are expected to influence native departures in the same way as 1,000 foreigners in a location where they make up 5% of a population of 20,000. It suggests the need to consider the effect of immigration stock relative to that of the native-borns. The share of immigrants to the native-borns has been widely used in many studies to assess immigration impact (e.g., Altonji and Card 1991; Borjas 1987a; Card 1990; Grossman 1982; LaLonde and Topel 1991; Pischke and Velling 1997). In contrast, using immigration share is not without its shortcomings. For example, Card (2001) also notes that given the enormous heterogeneity between immigrants and natives, the share of immigrants in a locality may be too crude an index of immigrant competition for any particular subgroups of natives.

In effect, findings from the existing literature tell us that using either absolute or relative counts of immigrants has its own niches in study. Here the study uses a simple metaphor to highlight that both measurements might be potentially crucial in explaining immigration impact. If we consider the immigration impact on the migratory response of native labor as being analogous to the meteorite impact on the Earth, the scale of impact depends on both the mass and velocity of the meteorite that hits the Earth. Neither a tiny meteorite with surprising high-hitting speed nor a massive meteorite with very low-hitting speed will produce noticeable impact. As such, immigrant volume is analogous to meteorite mass and immigrant volume relative to native labor analogous to the impact speed. As a result, the study takes both immigrant volume and share of low-skilled immigrants to native labor into consideration as major explanatory variables.

The strategy of defining the geographic dimension for the labor market is another crucial dimension of concern for the study on immigration impact. Various studies have figured out that the measured impact of immigration intimately depends on the geographic definition of the labor market (e.g., Borjas 2006; Card 2001; Frey 2005).[2] To distinguish immigration impact, the study not only uses the categories of region and metropolitan area,[3] but also utilizes a category specified by the study is called the foreign labor intensity (FLI) region. The FLI regions are determined by the following steps. First of all, since immigration impact is an outcome of immigration, it is more plausible to use postmigration than premigration data to identify the spatial scale of impact. As a result, the study utilizes the micro-data of the 2000 Taiwan Population Census to classify various types of FLI regions based on the following steps: (1) the study computes the share of total low-skilled foreign labor to the total population of Taiwan μ_{fs}, and the share of low-skilled foreign labor to the population for each of the all 7,728 smallest administrative localities, $\{m_{fs}\}$, called "Chun-Li"; and (2) let σ_{fs} denote the standard deviation of $\{m_{fs}\}$ and $z_{fs} = (m_{fs} - \mu_{fs})/\sigma_{fs}$, the calculated $\mu_{fs} = 0.014$ and $\sigma_{fs} = 0.072$ in the study. A Chun-Li is categorized as low immigration intensity if its $z_{fs} < 0$, as some immigration intensity if $0 < z_{fs} < 1.96$, and as significant immigration intensity if $z_{fs} > 1.96$. Figure 5.3 illustrates the spatial pattern of Chun-Li by the level of z_{fs}.

By excluding the central mountain areas, the study thereafter uses Geographic Information Systems (GIS) to overlay the categorized Chun-Li's with the boundaries of metropolitan areas and prefectures, as demonstrated in Figure 5.3, which suggests that (1) the Taipei metropolitan area in northern Taiwan is characterized by having the highest volume of low-skilled foreign labor and having the highest proportion of Chun-Li's that are categorized as "some" and "significant" immigration intensity within the same

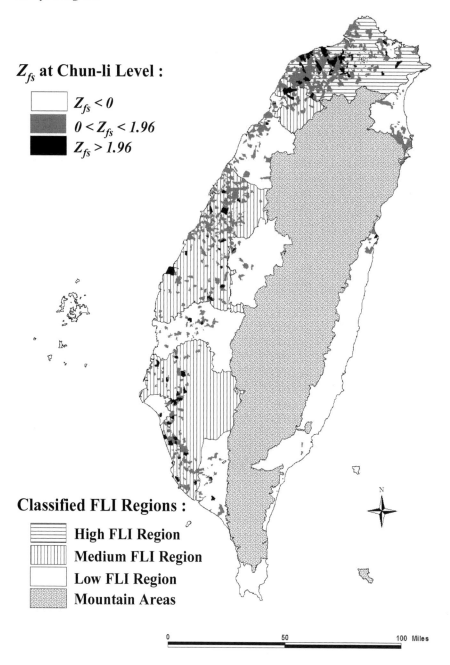

Figure 5.3 Distribution of low-skilled foreign labor relative quantity and classified regions of FLI.

area; and (2) Hsinchu City/Prefecture (known as Taiwan's Silicon Valley in the global information and communication technology [ICT] industry) in northern Taiwan, Taichung, and Kaohsiung metropolitan areas in central and southern Taiwan are classified by having the second highest volume of low-skilled immigrant and the proportion of Chun-Li's with "some" and "significant" immigrant intensity next to that in Taipei metropolitan area. Since the above-mentioned geographic areas can be classified by a prefecture-level unit that is used as a spatial unit of migration, the study consequently uses a prefecture-level unit to divide the domestic labor market of Taiwan into three broad categories: high FLI, medium FLI, and low FLI, as shown by Figure 5.3.[4]

In addition to controlling for the effects associated with the volume and relative quantity of low-skilled foreign labor and the FLI dummies, the study also controls for effects associated with other noteworthy ecological attributes, including population size as proxy for economic scale, population density as proxy for environmental amenity, rate of employment growth and unemployment as employment opportunities, prefectural government expenditure per capita termed as local finance level in the study and household disposable income level as proxy of regional income level, non-agricultural share of total employment as proxy for regional employment structure and urbanization level, and share of housing cost to total household income as proxy of living quality and amenity.

The data used for the estimation of departure model are the 161,169 individual samples in the data for study, while the data used for estimating destination choice model are the 2,827 individuals categorized as labor migrant by definition. The original weights are set at a level that will allow the sum of weights be equal to the size of the population in study. It is worth stressing that while estimating the model, if these weights were directly applied in estimation procedure, the magnitudes of the t-ratio would be artificially inflated, and the resulting statistical significance turns out to be meaningless. To avoid the artificial inflation, it is highly needed to use rescaled sample weights so that their sum is made to be equal to the sample size. In the study, rescaled sample weights are utilized while estimating the departure and destination choice models. For each sample, its rescaled weight Wrs is the original sample weight Ws scaled by a factor of $n/\Sigma Ws$ (i.e., $Wrs = Ws * n/\Sigma Ws$), where n is the sample size for study (161,169), and ΣWs is the sum of all original sample weights in the study data. Note that the sum of all rescaled sample weights is equal to the sample size n. The advantage of applying rescaled sample weight for model estimation is that information regarding original sample weight and sample size can be simultaneously incorporated into model estimation.

FINDINGS

Observed Patterns

Based on the pooled samples selected from the 1996–2000 MUSs, Table 5.3 summarizes the corresponding volumes and rates of out-, in-, and net migration of native labor and relative quantity of low-skilled foreign labor in the domestic market of Taiwan.[5] Taken as a whole, Table 5.3 uses three alternative definitions for the geographic areas encompassed by the labor market: regions, metropolitan areas, and FLI areas. Table 5.3 indicates that the weighted 1996–2000 average number of labor force in study amounts to 9.3 million that are about 95% of Taiwan's total labor force in the comparable period, and that the share of low-skilled foreign labor to native labor is of about 2.9%.

The first panel of Table 5.3 using region (see Figure 5.2) as the labor market indicates that northern region, the largest regional labor market, had the highest share of native labor (48.2%) and the highest share of low-skilled foreign labor within it (3.5%). In comparison with other regions, northern region is not only associated with higher out- and in-migration in terms of volume and rate but also associated with a net loss of native labor. Central and southern regions had a similar labor stock, with the central region having a higher share of low-skilled foreign labor than its southern counterpart. In spite of this, the rates of in-, out-, and net migration for the central regions resembled those observed in the southern region. The eastern region that serves as the marginal labor market had the lowest stock of labor force and the highest rate of net migration.

Using metropolitan areas as the labor market (see Figure 5.4), the second panel of Table 5.3 suggests that in general the share of low-skilled foreign labor within a metropolitan was negatively associated with the net migration rate of the metropolitan area, with the exception of the Hsinchu sub-metropolitan area. The observed pattern in the Hsinchu sub-metro was very noteworthy. The Hsinchu sub-metro has long been known as "Taiwan's Silicon Valley" and is one of the most crucial manufacturing and R&D centers of ICT industries in the world (Rubinstein 2007; Shih et al. 2007). Its stock of labor constituted only 4.0% of the Taiwan total labor force, but the share of low-skilled foreign labor within it was of 5.10%, which was higher than any other metropolitan areas. Moreover, it was also observed to be associated with the highest rate of net migration.

By contrast, the third panel of Table 5.3 presents results by the labor market classified by the level of low-skilled foreign labor intensity (see Figure 5.3). The results suggest that the share of local labor to total labor force and the share of low-skilled foreign labor within a local labor market derived from the labor market classified by the level of FLI are not as varied as those using the scale of either regions or metropolitan areas.

Table 5.3 Relative Quantity of Low-skilled Foreign Labor to Native-born Labor and Internal Migration of Native-born Labor by Region, Metropolitan Area, and Regional Level of FLI: Average in 1996–2000

Labor Market	Native-born Labor (persons)[a] Volume (persons) A	Share of Labor Market (%)	Ratio of Lowskilled Foreign Labor to Native-born Labor (×100)[b]	Volume of Internal Migrants (persons)[a] Out-migration B	In-migration C	Net Migration C - B	Rate of Internal Migration (%) Out-migration B/A	In-migration C/A	Net Migration (C - B)/A
Taiwan Overall	9,323,407	100.00	2.92	168,512	168,512	0	1.81	1.81	0.00
Region[c]									
Northern	4,494,140	48.20	3.48	88,325	84,849	-3476	1.97	1.89	-0.08
Central	2,046,010	21.94	2.94	34,833	36,252	1419	1.70	1.77	0.07
Southern	2,578,673	27.66	2.02	42,217	44,113	1896	1.64	1.71	0.07
Eastern	204,583	2.19	1.82	3,137	3,298	161	1.53	1.61	0.08
Metropolitan Area[d]									
Taipei MA	3,749,152	40.21	3.38	76,037	71,836	-4201	2.03	1.92	-0.11
Hsinchu Sub-MA	372,222	3.99	5.10	10,184	11,326	1142	2.74	3.04	0.31
Taichung MA	1,084,837	11.64	2.65	23,406	22,759	-647	2.16	2.10	-0.06
Tainan MA	781,605	8.38	2.34	13,359	13,424	65	1.71	1.72	0.01
Kaohsiung MA	1,141,644	12.24	2.07	20,808	20,754	-54	1.82	1.82	0.00
Non-metropolitan areas	2,193,946	23.53	2.56	24,718	28,413	3695	1.13	1.30	0.17
Region by Level of Foreign Labor Intensity (FLI)[e]									
High FLI	3,613,819	38.76	3.66	73,272	69,619	-3,653	2.03	1.93	-0.10
Medium FLI	3,040,781	32.61	3.33	45,430	49,844	4,414	1.49	1.64	0.15
Low FLI	2,668,807	28.62	2.08	49,810	49,049	-761	1.87	1.84	-0.03

(a) Compiled from the selected samples in Table 1, with sample weight being applied
(b) Volume of low-skilled Foreign Labor comes from the 1996-2000 Annual Report on Labor Statistics, Ministry of Labor Affairs, Taiwan
(c) see Figure 5.2
(d) see Figure 5.3
(e) see Figure 5.1

86 *Ji-Ping Lin*

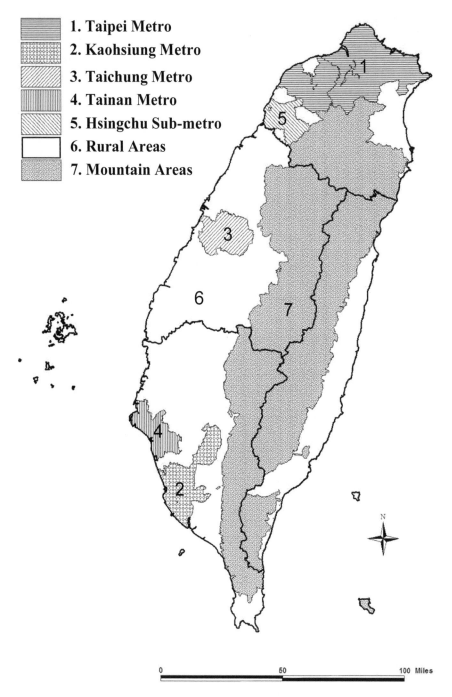

Figure 5.4 Metropolitan areas.

In terms of net migration volume and rate, the high FLI and medium FLI areas had the most noteworthy net loss and net gain of native labor migrants. The net gain of migrants in the medium FLI areas appeared to be at the expense of the net loss of migrants from the high FLI areas, and the observed pattern in the low FLI areas turns out to be minor.

Since low-skilled foreign labor is hypothesized to compete with and/or even substitute for native labor with similar skills, it is thus crucial to examine the migration pattern of native labor by educational level. Table 5.4 demonstrates the observed out-, in-, and net migration of native labor with different education in the labor market classified by the three categories of high, medium, and low FLI areas. In Table 5.4, "less education" refers to those with at most junior high education, "middle

Table 5.4 Internal Migration of Native-born Labor by Level of FLI: Average in 1996–2000

Labor Market	Native-born Labor (persons)[a] Volume (persons) A	Volume of Internal Migrants (persons)[a] Out-migration B	In-migration C	Net Migration C - B	Rate of Internal Migration (%) Out-migration B / A	In-migration C / A	Net Migration (C - B) / A
Taiwan Overall	9,323,407	168,512	168,512	0	1.81	1.81	0.00
High FLI Overall[e]	3,613,819	73,272	69,619	-3,653	2.03	1.93	-0.10
Less Education	1,175,379	32,095	28,577	-3,518	2.73	2.43	-0.30
Middle Education	1,269,376	27,298	27,398	100	2.15	2.16	0.01
High Education	1,169,064	13,879	13,644	-235	1.19	1.17	-0.02
Medium FLI Overall	3,040,780	45,431	49,844	4,413	1.49	1.64	0.15
Less Education	1,432,123	14,333	18,433	4,100	1.00	1.29	0.29
Middle Education	1,051,414	18,691	18,621	-70	1.78	1.77	-0.01
High Education	557,243	12,407	12,790	383	2.23	2.30	0.07
Low FLI Overall	2,668,807	49,810	49,049	-761	1.87	1.84	-0.03
Less Education	1,172,136	16,769	16,187	-582	1.43	1.38	-0.05
Middle Education	921,021	19,917	19,887	-30	2.16	2.16	0.00
High Education	575,650	13,124	12,975	-149	2.28	2.25	-0.03

Note: Less eduction: at-most junior high education; middle education: senior high education; high education: at-least college education (a) and (e), see Table 5.3

education" to those with senior high education, and "high education" to those having at least college education. The results suggest that (1) the observed net loss of migrants in the high FLI area (3,653 in volume and 0.10 in rate) were mostly due to net loss of those with less education (3,518 in volume and 0.30 in rate), and (2) the observed net gain of migrants in the medium FLI areas (4,413 in volume and 0.15 in rate) were mostly due to the gain from those with less education (4,100 in volume and 0.29 in rate). In sum, although the high FLI areas that serve as the political and socioeconomic heartlands in Taiwan have long been fairly attractive for all nationals in general, the less educated migrants were more prone to make out-migration from the high FLI areas, particularly those with less education.

Estimation Results of Micro-Migration Models

Preferred Departure Model

The estimation of departure model aims at testing the hypothesized pushing effect of low-skilled foreign labor on native labor with similar skill and the hypothesized retention effect on native professionals/managers or native labor with higher education, with a set of crucial factors in theories and substance in explaining departure behavior being controlled. As stressed above, the study avoids using postmigration information such as personal wage in the hope of reducing biased estimation results. Variables of individual characteristics taken into consideration include gender, age, marital status, education, and other variables such as industry, occupation, and firm size that are measured one year before the survey. Attributes of origin include volume of low-skilled foreign labor, share of low-skilled foreign labor to native labor, economic scale, employment structure, income level, and employment opportunities. The study also utilizes a number interaction terms of individual characteristics with origin attributes, hoping to distinguish the differentials of individual response to a given labor market condition of origin. Through a rigorous process of model selection, Table 5.5 presents the estimation results of the preferred departure model.

We present the estimation results irrelevant to low-skilled immigration at first, then turn to discuss results regarding immigration effects. Regarding the effects of individual characteristics, Table 5.5 suggests that males are more migratory than females (0.3404 for the dummy variable *Male*), and the single and the separated (0.3162 for the dummy variable *Single* and 0.5995 for the dummy *Separated*) are more prone to making migration than the married and the widowed natives. The estimated results regarding age and educational effects are very reasonable and fall within theoretical expectation. The estimated coefficients for the variables *Ln(Age)* and *Age* (1.3304 and −0.9682, respectively) suggest that the age pattern of departure probability is convex.[6] The estimated age pattern is consistent with the so-called migration schedule pattern (Rogers 1979). Since the estimated coefficients increase with educational level (0.8888 for college and 1.0774 for university and above), it is also consistent with the well-known educational selectivity of migration in the sense that migration in general is selective of the better educated. In short, the effects of individual characteristics reasonably fall within theoretical expectations, suggesting that individual factors have been properly controlled in the preferred model.

Other individual variables including industry, occupation, job seniority, and firm size that are measured one year before the MUS are all taken into consideration while estimating the departure model. The separate estimated result with respect to each of these variables exhibits reasonable pattern and significant effect. For examples, workers in the tertiary sector are more footloose than those in secondary and primary sectors; professionals and managers are the most migratory sub-group in occupational hierarchy; job seniority exhibits an expected negative effect on the likelihood of departure, and workers of smaller firms are more prone to move than their counterparts working for larger firms. Because these variables are highly related to age and education, the incorporation of the aforementioned variables tend to produce perplexed educational and/or age effects. Since educational selectivity and age pattern of migration are the most fundamental variables to the departure model, they are not included in the preferred departure model.

As for the effects of origin attributes, the estimated results in Table 5.5 indicate that explanatory variables that are used to control for labor market conditions of origin have substantial effects on the departure probability for native labor. As stated above, the study utilizes volume of low-skilled foreign labor and their share to native labor to assess immigration impact of low-skilled foreign labor. It is worth noting that the variable for volume of low-skilled foreign labor and the variable for low-skilled foreign labor share to native labor are found to be highly correlated with respect to population size and local finance level. The variable for population size serves as the proxy variable for origin economic scale and the one for local finance level as the proxy for origin income level. When conducting modeling estimation, some estimation results, although significant, become odd or unreasonable when the aforementioned four highly inter-correlated variables are incorporated simultaneously into the departure model.

In light of the theoretical importance of origin economic scale and income level in accounting for departure decision of the natives and location distribution of foreigners, the study acknowledges that the variables of origin population size and local finance level must have higher priority of being selected into the model than the variables for volume and relative share of low-skilled foreign labor. As a result, we report the estimated results associated with the effects of origin economic scale and income at first.

First of all, the most noteworthy is the effect of origin income. Using the variable of local finance level (NT$10,000 per capita) as the proxy for origin

Table 5.5 Estimation Results of the Most Preferred Departure Model

Explanatory Variables	Coefficient	t-ratio	P-value	Variable Name
Constant term	-5.0383	-21.8	< 0.0001	Const
I. Personal Characteristics of Native-born Labor				
Gender effect (refe. group : female)				
Male (if Gender = 1)	0.3404	8.6	< 0.0001	Male
Marital status effect (refe. group : married/widowed)				
The single (if marital status = 1)	0.3162	6.3	< 0.0001	Single
The separated (if marital status = 3)	0.5995	5.6	< 0.0001	Separated
Age effect (unit: 10 years of age)				
Ln (Age)	1.3304	3.4	0.0008	LnAge
Age	-0.9682	-7.6	< 0.0001	Age
Educational effect (refe. group : senior high and below)				
Vocational college (if education = 7)	0.8886	9.8	< 0.0001	College
University and graduate (if education >= 8)	1.0774	10.9	< 0.0001	Univ-Grad
II. Ecological Attributes of Origin				
Effect of Foreign Labor				
Professional and managerial native-born labor*Low-skilled foreign labor volume	-0.1772	-4.9	< 0.0001	PMTP-PFor
Agricultural workers (dummy) *Low-skilled foreign labor volume	0.1162	2.4	0.0162	AgriFor
Native-born labor of Taipei Metro *Low-skilled foreign labor volume	0.0966	4.7	< 0.0001	TPPFor
Effect of Housing Cost				
Share of housing cost to total household incomes	10.6473	9.1	< 0.0001	HusCostR
Effect of Income				
Local finance level (unit:10,000 NT$/per person)	-0.0978	-4.1	< 0.0001	LocalFin
Primary education and below (dummy) *Local finance level	0.1549	4.4	< 0.0001	PriLFin
Junior high education (dummy) *Local finance level	0.1673	6.0	< 0.0001	JHiLFin

(continued)

Table 5.5 (continued)

Explanatory Variables	Most Preferred Specification			Variable Name
	Coefficient	t-ratio	P-value	
Senior high education (dummy) *Local finance level	0.1783	7.2	< 0.0001	SHiLFin
Effect of Economic Scale				
Ln (Population size) (unit: million persons)	−0.2406	−6.1	< 0.0001	LnPopn
Effect of Employment Opportunity				
Unemployment rate (unit:%)	0.0789	2.6	0.0102	UnempR

Summary Statistics:
1. Number of samples for estimation = 161,169, including 2,827 migrants and 158,342 stayers
2. Loglikelihood: null model = −14,833, most preferred model = −13,990
3. d.f. = 17, Rho-square = 0.0568

income, the negative coefficient for the variable of local finance (−0.0978 for *LocalFin*) and the estimated coefficients for the interaction terms of local finance with various educational levels indicate that the effect of origin income level differs by educational level. Because the sums of its coefficient (−0.0978) with respect to the estimated coefficient for its interaction terms with primary education (0.1549 for *PriLFin*), junior high education (0.1673 for *JHiLFin*), and senior high education (0.1783 for *SHiLFin*) are all positive, the retention effect of origin income is limited to native labor with education of college and above, whereas the less educated native labor are more likely to leave high income areas. These findings are consistent with the observed patterns presented above. In accordance with theoretical expectation, the variable of origin population size as the proxy for origin economic scale exhibits negative effect on departure probability of the natives (−0.2406 for *LnPopn*).

The remaining origin attributes of origin housing costs and unemployment are all associated with substantively meaningful and significant positive effects for the departure process (10.6473 for *HuscostR* and 0.0789 for *UnempR*). In addition, the variable for employment growth and the theoretical inclusive variable derived from the preferred destination choice model are also included in the model for estimation. The estimated coefficients for both variables exhibit the expected effect but are not statistically significant. They are thus excluded from the preferred departure model.

With the most fundamental origin attributes being controlled in the departure model, the study now discusses the estimated results regarding immigration impact. Taken as a whole, probably due to the low proportion of individuals who are classified as labor migrants in the study data, the effects of low-skilled foreign labor are not as prominent as those associated with other explanatory variables. According to the estimated coefficients shown in Table 5.5 for the interaction terms of native professionals and managerial workers and agricultural workers with respect to the variable of low-skilled foreign labor volume (–0.1772 for *PMTPPFor* and 0.1162 for *AgriFor*, respectively), native professionals and managerial workers are significantly associated with less likelihood of making departure, whereas agricultural workers are more likely to depart from areas with a higher level of low-skilled foreign labor. Moreover, it is found that native labor for the Taipei metropolitan area is more likely to make out-migration than native labor outside theTaipei metropolitan area (0.0966 for *TPPFor*).

The estimated coefficients for both variables of the volume and relative share of low-skilled foreign labor are negative but not significant. The model also estimates the coefficients for the interaction terms of manufacturing workers and workers of various occupational skill levels with the variable for low-skilled foreign labor, finding that the estimated coefficients are either substantively meaningful but not significant or at times substantively odd but significant. These results thus are not considered to be included in the preferred departure. Findings from the preferred departed model suggest that the probability of a certain type of low- or less skilled native worker is more subject to the impact of low-skilled immigration, but the estimated results are not significant. This finding is mainly because the explanatory power has already been taken by the variable for the local finance level.

Preferred Destination-choice Model

The major categories of destination attributes taken into consideration to account for the destination choice behavior of native labor migrants include potential destinations' volume of low-skilled foreign labor, share of low-skilled foreign labor to native labor, economic scale, employment structure, income level, employment opportunities, and costs of moving to each potential destination. The study also utilizes a number of interaction terms of migrant individual characteristics with destination attributes to rationalize the destination choice preference of migrants. Through a rigorous process of model selection, the estimation results of the preferred destination choice model are summarized in Table 5.6. It is worth stressing that the estimation results regarding the share of low-skilled foreign labor to native labor and its interactions with migrant characteristics are not included in the preferred model. The main reason is that it is highly correlated with the variable representing destination income level.

Regarding the effect of low-skilled foreign labor, native labor migrants as a whole are less likely to move into destinations with a higher volume of low-skilled foreign labor, as suggested by the negative estimated coefficient for the volume of low-skilled foreign labor in at destination (–0.0420

Native "Flights" from Immigration "Port of Entry" 93

Table 5.6 Estimation Results of the Most Preferred Destination-choice Model

Explanatory Variables	Coefficient	t-ratio	P-value	Variable Name
Effect of Foreign Labor				
Volume of low-skilled foreign labor in a potential destination (unit: 10,000 persons)	-0.0420	-1.5	0.0668	ForNoDest
Native-born labor migrants choosing to move to Taipei Metro (dummy) *Volume of foreign labor in Taipei Metro	-0.1694	-7.7	< 0.0001	TPPFor
Native-born labor migrants in social services (dummy) *ForNoDest	-0.1040	-2.8	0.0026	SclsFor
Native-born labor migrants in tradtional manufacturing (dummy) *ForNoDest	0.1418	2.6	0.0047	TradFor
Native-born labor migrants with at-least college education (dummy) *ForNoDest	0.0576	2.0	0.0228	CUGFor
Effect of Migration Costs				
Ln(Distance between Origin and a specific potential destination; unit: kilometer)	-0.9172	-28.8	< 0.0001	LnDist
Native-born labor migrants with at-least university education (dummny) *LnDist	0.3416	6.9	< 0.0001	UnivDist
Contiguity indicator between origin and a specific potential destination (dummy)	0.4100	5.6	< 0.0001	ContInd
Effect of Regional Economic Scale				
Ln (Population size in a specific potential destination; unit: million persons)	0.7324	14.3	< 0.0001	LnPopn
Effect of Regional Employment Stucture				
Share of the labor force not in the primary sector for a specific potential destination (unit: %)	4.4534	9.2	< 0.0001	NonAgriR
Native-born agricultural migrant worker (dummy) *NonAgriR	-13.4138	-11.3	< 0.0001	AgrNAgr
Native-born manufacturing migrant worker (dummy) *NonAgriR	-4.3351	-4.0	< 0.0001	ManuNAgr
Native-born construction migrant worker (dummy) *NonAgriR	-3.7075	-3.7	0.0001	ConsNAgr

(continued)

Table 5.6 (continued)

Explanatory Variables	Most Preferred Specification			Variable Name
	Coefficient	t-ratio	P-value	
Native-born migrant workwer in persoanl/social service (dummy) *NonAgriR*	-2.2395	-3.1	0.0010	*SclsNAgr*
Effect of Regional Income Level				
Native-born migrant worker with college education (dummy) *local finance level per capita for a specific potential destination	0.1249	3.1	0.0010	*ColLFin*
Native-born migrant worker with at-least university education (dummy) *local finance level per capita for a specific potential destination	0.2022	4.6	< 0.0001	*UniLFin*
Effect of Employment Opportunity				
Unemployment rate of a specific potential destination (unit: %)	-0.0759	-1.5	0.0668	*UnempR*
Native-born migrant worker searching for job search via government agency(dummy)* employment growth rate of a specific potential destination (unit: %)	0.0785	3.5	0.0002	*AdsEmpG*

Summary Statistics:
1. No. of native-born migrants = 2,827; No. of potential destinations for each migrants = 22
2. Log-likelihood of the null model = -7,625; Log-likelihood of the most preferred model = -5,630; d.f. = 18
3. Rho-square = 0.2617

for *ForNoDest*). It thus lends support to the hypothesized discouraging effect of immigration on the destination choice for native labor migrants. Moreover, the associated discouraging effect becomes further intensified in the Taipei metropolitan area, as indicated by the negative estimated coefficient (−0.1694) for the variable of *TPPFor* (Taipei Prefecture**ForNoDest*). However, native migrants with higher education are more capable of overcoming the discouraging effect associated with foreign labor volume than migrants with less education, as suggested by the positive estimated coefficient of the interaction term of migrants with at least a college education with foreign labor volume (0.0576 for *CUGFor*). However, it lends support to the attractive effect of low-skilled immigration on the in-migration of native migrants with higher educations.

Because a substantial proportion of low-skilled foreign labor is employed in manufacturing and social/personal services, it is reasonable to hypothesize that immigration impact is expected to be particularly significant for native labor in these industries. However, the findings in Table 5.6 do not fully support this hypothesis. The estimated coefficient for the interaction term of migrants in traditional manufacturing with low-skilled foreign labor volume has a positive coefficient (0.1418 for *TradFor*), suggesting that low-skilled foreign labor does not discourage in-migration of native labor in the traditional manufacturing industry. On the contrary, native migrants in the social and personal service industry are less prone to choosing destinations with a high volume of low-skilled labor (−0.1040 for *SclsFor*), lending support to the discouraging effect of low-skilled immigration on the in-migration likelihood of native workers in the social and personal service industry, mostly native servants providing elementary personal services like housekeeping, nursing care, etc.

In addition to the effects associated with low-skilled foreign labor, the most noteworthy are variables representing migration costs. As expected, the estimated coefficient for the logarithm of moving distance is not only negative (−0.9172 for *LnDist*), but it is also associated with a very significant t-ratio (−28.8). Besides, the estimated coefficient for contiguity is positive (0.4100), and the better-educated migrants are less subject to migration constraints (0.3416 for *UnivDist*). Another crucial variable in explaining destination choice is the economic scale of destination (*LnPopn*). As expected, the estimated coefficient is not only positive, but it is also very significant.

The model utilizes the variable of the share of the labor force not in the primary sector (*NonAgriR*) as the proxy variable to control for the effect of destination employment structure and urbanization level. The estimation results in Table 5.6 indicate that it is not only associated with a significant positive effect for the destination choice of migrant in general (4.4534 for *NonAgriR*, with a t-ratio of 9.2), but it also exhibits the differential effects in selecting migrants from different economic sectors, as suggested by the negative value (−8.9604) of the sum of its estimated coefficient (4.4534) with the coefficient for its interaction with agricultural migrant workers (−13.4138), and the sum of its coefficient with respect to the coefficient for its interaction with migrant workers in the manufacturing (*ManuNAgr*), construction (*ConsNAgr*), and social/personal service (*SclsNAgr*) industries (0.1184, 0.7459, and 2.2139, respectively).

The remaining crucial factors in the preferred model are income level and employment opportunity at destination. The model uses local finance level per capita as the proxy variable for the level of destination income. In accordance with theoretical expectation, the positive destination income effect increases with the educational level of migrants, as suggested by the estimated coefficients for its interaction with college-educated migrants (0.1249 for *ColLFin*) and university-educated migrants (0.2022 for *UniLFin*). In terms of the effects associated with destination employment opportunity, the unemployment rate at destination exhibits the expected negative effect, and labor migrants searching for a job through the assistance of a government agency are more prone to move to destinations with higher employment growth.

Aggregate Outcomes of Immigration Impact Analysis

This subsection demonstrates the extent to which native labor responds to low-skilled immigration derived from the aggregate outcomes of immigration impact analysis that uses the domestic labor market encompassed by the three categories of FLI areas. Based on the estimation results of the preferred departure and destination choice models, we calculate the individual probability of making migration and the conditional individual probabilities of choosing potential destinations for each sample in the data for study. After that, we thus compute the probability of moving to a specific destination for each sample in the data. The expected volumes for out-, in-, and thus net migration are thus derived by aggregating all individual probabilities of making migration and all individual probabilities of moving to a specific destination from all samples in the data.[7] To assess the extent to which native labor responds to a specific level of low-skilled foreign labor, the study at first rescales the volume of low-skilled foreign labor by a fixed factor, with the remaining explanatory variables in both micro-models of migration being held constant, then computes the resulting volumes and rates of out-, in-, and net migration of native labor.

Table 5.7 Migratory Responses of Native-born Labor to Changing Levels of Low-skilled Foreign Labor

Percentage Change in Low-skilled Foreign Labor Volume (%)	Out-migration Rate (%) High FLI (O1)	Out-migration Rate (%) Med FLI (O2)	Out-migration Rate (%) Low FLI (O3)	In-migration Rate (%) High FLI (I1)	In-migration Rate (%) Med FLI (I2)	In-migration Rate (%) Low FLI (I3)	Net Migration Rate (%) High FLI (I1)-(O1)	Net Migration Rate (%) Med FLI (I2)-(O2)	Net Migration Rate (%) Low FLI (I3)-(O3)
-80	2.2282	1.5891	1.8916	2.1737	1.6392	1.7236	-0.0545	0.0501	-0.1680
-70	2.2015	1.5735	1.8916	2.1406	1.6392	1.7375	-0.0610	0.0657	-0.1541
-60	2.1744	1.5650	1.8880	2.1070	1.6407	1.7444	-0.0674	0.0757	-0.1436
-50	2.1492	1.5508	1.8844	2.0754	1.6436	1.7686	-0.0739	0.0928	-0.1158
-40	2.1231	1.5380	1.8808	2.0437	1.6407	1.7756	-0.0794	0.1026	-0.1052
-30	2.0985	1.5281	1.8808	2.0136	1.6421	1.7963	-0.0849	0.1140	-0.0845
-20	2.0748	1.5139	1.8664	1.9839	1.6392	1.8102	-0.0909	0.1253	-0.0562
-10	2.0507	1.5040	1.8664	1.9547	1.6421	1.8240	-0.0960	0.1381	-0.0424
0	2.0276	1.4941	1.8664	1.9265	1.6392	1.8379	-0.1011	0.1451	-0.0285
+10	2.0049	1.4799	1.8628	1.8992	1.6362	1.8517	-0.1057	0.1564	-0.0111
+20	1.9833	1.4685	1.8556	1.8715	1.6318	1.8690	-0.1118	0.1633	0.0134
+30	1.9617	1.4557	1.8520	1.8452	1.6289	1.8794	-0.1165	0.1731	0.0274
+40	1.9406	1.4472	1.8448	1.8204	1.6274	1.8898	-0.1202	0.1802	0.0450
+50	1.9209	1.4345	1.8412	1.7965	1.6245	1.9036	-0.1244	0.1900	0.0625
+60	1.9008	1.4245	1.8376	1.7722	1.6171	1.9140	-0.1286	0.1926	0.0765
+70	1.8812	1.4132	1.8376	1.7493	1.6156	1.9313	-0.1319	0.2024	0.0938
+80	1.8626	1.4033	1.8267	1.7270	1.6112	1.9417	-0.1357	0.2080	0.1150

Native "Flights" from Immigration "Port of Entry" 97

In order to manifest the dynamic features of the migratory response of native labor to low-skilled foreign labor, the study conducts a series of simulation scenarios by systematically decreasing and increasing low-skilled foreign labor volume by 10%, 20%, 30%, 40%, 50%, 60%, 70%, and 80%, respectively. Based on the results of various simulation scenarios, the research then examines and compare how in-, out-, and net migrations of native labor change with different levels of low-skilled immigration. The detailed aggregate results of all simulation scenarios are summarized in Table 5.7. The study uses Figure 5.5.1, 5.5.2, and 5.5.3 to illustrate how native labor in the three categories of FLI areas respond to different levels of low-skilled foreign labor with respect to the rate of out-, in-, and net migration, respectively.

As demonstrated by Figure 5.5.1, the aggregate out-migration rate of native labor is negatively associated with low-skilled immigration volume for the high, medium, and low FLI areas. It is worth stressing that increasing immigration volume in the study shows no evidence of impact on lifting the out-migration of native labor. The negative association of low-skilled immigration on out-migration is mainly because the retention effect of low-skilled foreign labor on professional and managerial native labor outweighs

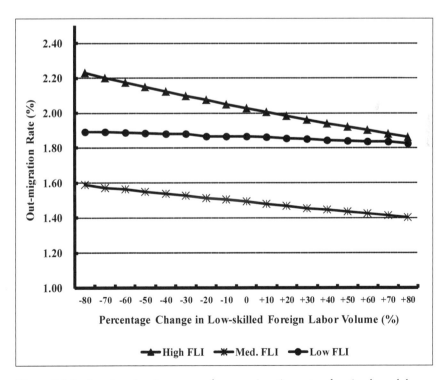

Figure 5.5.1 Immigration impact on the out-migration rate of native-born labor.
Source: see Table 5.7.

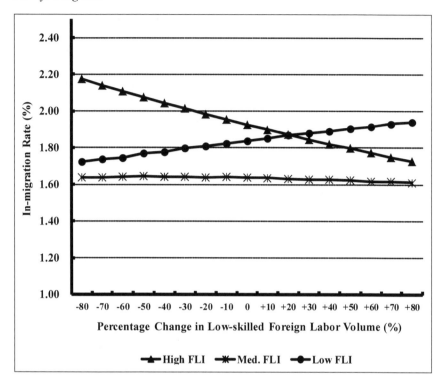

Figure 5.5.2 Immigration impact on the in-migration rate of native-born labor.
Source: see Table 5.7.

the associated pushing effect on low-skilled native workers in the departure process. In addition, although the preferred departure model does not exhibit a distinct effect of immigration for different FLI areas, the simulation results reveal a phenomenon that the aggregate negative association of low-skilled immigration on out-migration is more remarkable in the high and medium FLI areas, but it turns out to be minor in the low FLI areas. For examples, an increase of 10% of low-skilled foreign labor averagely leads to about 0.0228% decrease in out-migration rate for the high FLI areas, about 0.0116% decrease for the medium FLI areas, but only 0.0041% decrease for the low FLI areas.

Regarding the impact on the in-migration rate of native labor, Figure 5.5.2 illustrates that the aggregate in-migration rate of native labor is negatively and positively associated with low-skilled immigration volume for the high and low FLI areas, respectively. The most noticeable is that low-skilled immigration exhibits nearly no impact for the medium FLI areas. For example, an increase of the low-skilled immigration volume by 10% on average results in about 0.0279% decrease in the in-migration rate for the high FLI areas, about 0.0136% increase in in-migration for the low

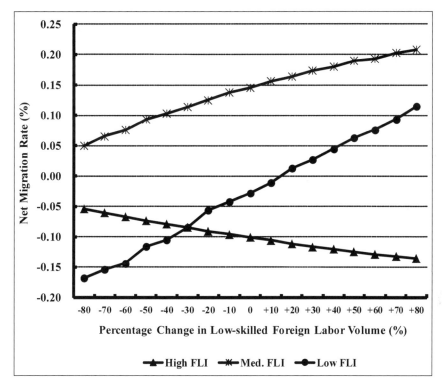

Figure 5.5.3 Immigration impact on the net migration rate of native-born labor.
Source: see Table 5.7.

FLI areas, but only 0.0017% decrease in in-migration for the medium FLI areas. In essence, the above pattern of impact is intimately related to the joint estimation results from the departure and destination choice models, particularly the results from the destination choice model, which suggests the low-skilled immigration volume exhibits an overall discouraging effect in the destination choice process for native labor migrants, and the corresponding discouraging effect is particularly salient in Taipei metropolitan area.

The overall impact of low-skilled immigration on the net migration rate of native labor is demonstrated by Figure 5.5.3, which is derived from the results of immigration impact on out-migration and in-migration. Figure 5.5.3 suggests that the overall immigration impact on the net migration of native labor is quite different for the high FLI areas and for the medium and low FLI areas: the aggregate net migration rate of native labor is positively associated with low-skilled immigration volume for the medium and low FLI areas but negatively associated with low-skilled immigration volume for the high FLI areas. Taken as a whole, it is found that an increase of 10% in low-skilled immigration volume on average will lead to about 0.0177%

and 0.0099% increase in net migration rate for the low and medium FLI areas, respectively, but about 0.005% decrease in net migration rate for the high FLI areas.

CONCLUSION

Based on various sources of datasets and the proposed method, the study has assessed the hypothesized effects of immigration on the redistribution of domestic manpower. Taken as a whole, research findings suggest that low-skilled immigration into Taiwan does influence the internal migration of native labor and the redistribution of domestic manpower. The research at first examines the observed patterns of internal migration, which show that areas with high concentration of low-skilled immigration were associated with a net loss of native labor, mostly the natives with less education, whereas areas with less concentrated low-skilled immigration were internal migration gainers that seemed at the expense of the net loss from high immigration concentration areas.

Findings from the departure model lend support to the retention effect of low-skilled immigration for native professionals and managers, whereas it only shows signs but insignificant pushing effect for native low-skilled labor; low-skilled immigration as a whole had a discouraging effect for all native labor migrants, and this discouraging effect was further intensified in the Taipei metropolitan area. Findings from the destination choice model also support the attractive effect of low-skilled immigration on the in-migration of native migrants with higher educations. The research does not find support that low-skilled foreign labor discourages in-migration of native labor in the traditional manufacturing industry, whereas a significant discouraging effect was found on in-migration likelihood of native workers in the industry of social and personal service who were mostly native servants providing elementary personal services such as housekeeping and nursing care.

The results of immigration impact analysis help illuminate the dynamic relationship between domestic manpower redistribution and immigration. Findings of immigration impact on native net migration are consistent with the conventional way of what we have been used to thinking about, but the underlying mechanisms derived from findings of immigration impact analysis tell us a story that is somewhat different from the conventional wisdom about immigration impact on native migratory responses. It looks plausible as a whole to find a negative association between the net migration of the native-borns and low-skilled immigration for the high FLI areas and a corresponding positive association for the low and medium FLI areas. In light of findings suggested by immigration impact analysis, it is worth emphasizing that for the high FLI areas, the positive association between immigration level and net migration of native labor is not produced by the pushing effect of immigrants on native labor; rather it mainly resulted from the negative impact of immigration on the in-migration that outweighs the corresponding negative impact on out-migration for native labor. On the contrary, the strong positive association between the net migration and immigration for the low FLI areas is mainly shaped by the positive immigration impact on in-migration and the negative immigration impact on out-migration, and the corresponding positive association for the medium FLI areas is the result of a fixed level of in-migration irrelevant to immigration impact and the negative immigration impact on out-migration.

In the end, although we observe a similar pattern of "flights" of native labor, mostly native migrants with less education, from major immigration "port of entry" on both sides of Taiwan and the United States, the underlying forces shaping immigration impact are somewhat different on both settings. For Taiwan, immigration tends to have more impact on native destination choice than on departure decision, which is different from the findings in the United States. In effect, immigration impact analysis regarding the impact on the net migration of native labor suggests "flights" of native labor are caused by immigration "pushes." But by jointly examining both impacts of immigration on native out-migration and in-migration, the research finds this is not the case in Taiwan. The observed native "flights" from high immigration concentration areas essentially are not mainly triggered by immigration pushing force; instead it mainly resulted from the negative impact of immigration on the in-migration, which outweighs the corresponding negative impact on out-migration for native labor.

ACKNOWLEDGMENTS

The research is funded by the National Science Council (grant no. NSC 99-2410-H-001-077-MY2). The author is grateful to Taiwan's Census Bureau of DGBAS for kindly providing research data. A previous version of this chapter was presented at the conference on "Immigration in Multi-ethnic Contexts: An International Comparison, December 8–10, 2010, Taipei." The author would like to express special thanks to David Ley, Richard Wanner, and Suzanne Model for their constructive criticisms and suggestions.

NOTES

1. N_i^g varies in magnitude with source of data. For example, N_i^g is equal to 1 if research data are the raw data of census, while N_i^g represents the weight of an individual respondent in a survey data. Another example is that N_i^g may represent the number of records for a sample of housing units with information on the characteristics of each unit and each person in it in the U.S. PUMS files.
2. For example, Borjas (2006) finds the so-called mirror-image patterns of immigration impact in the sense that as one expands labor market size, the

wage impact of immigration becomes larger, but on the other hand, the corresponding impact on native migration rate becomes smaller.
3. There are four officially defined categories of region, including northern, central, southern, and eastern. Taiwan's regions are legal administrative divisions (see Figure 5.2) similar to the U.S. census divisions. Originally defined by Taiwan's Directorate-General of Budget, Accounting, and Statistics (DGBAS) following the framework proposed by Speare et al. (1988), the metropolitan areas in the study are geographic entities that essentially resemble the United States' metropolitan statistical areas (MSAs) in definition. The main metropolitan areas by the order of scale are Taipei, Kaohsiung, Taichung, Tainan, and Hsinchu (see Figure 5.4)
4. With mountain areas being excluded, the high FLI area comprises Taipei City, Taipei Prefecture, and Taoyuan Prefecture; the medium FLI area consists of Taichung City, Taichung Prefecture, Changhwa Prefecture, Tainan Prefecture, Kaohsiung City, Kaohsiung Prefecture, Yunlin Prefecture, and Hsinchu City/Prefecture; and the low FLI area is the remaining prefectures (see Figure 5.3).
5. The sum of all sample weights for a specific year of MUS is equal to the number of population aged 15 and above. Since the samples for study (161,169) mentioned in "DATA AND SPECIFICATION" are selected and pooled from the 1996–2000 MUSs, the weight of each observation in the selected samples for study is thus scaled by a factor of one-fifth. The rescaled sample weights are utilized to derive the observed migration patterns of native labor. As a result, the presented figures in Tables 5.1–5.4 represent the average over the period of 1996–2000.
6. To allow for testing non-monotonic effect associated with an explanatory variable x, the study adopts the form $f(x) = a*Ln(x) + b*x$, where a and b are coefficients associated with $Ln(x)$ and x, respectively. The shapes of this function are much more flexible than those of the commonly used quadratic function. The qualitative properties of this function are as follows. First, if either a or b is zero with the other being non-zero, the effect of x is either positive or negative, depending on the sign of the non-zero parameter. Second, the effect of x is positive if both a and b are positive, whereas the effect of x is negative if both a and b are negative. Third, the effect of x becomes convex if $a > 0$ and $b < 0$ and concave if $a < 0$ and $b > 0$. Graphically, the exponential of $a*Ln(x) + b*x$ resembles a Gamma function.
7. The immigration impact analysis mentioned in "METHODOLOGY" is implemented by a set of complex Gauss programs developed by the author. Along with the aggregates of all individual expected probabilities of migration and all individual probabilities of choosing potential destinations, all relevant statistics derived in "METHODOLOGY" are also computed simultaneously while conducting the analyses. For the sake of simplicity, they are not presented in the study.

REFERENCES

Altonji, Joseph G., and David Card. 1991. "The Effects of Immigration on the Labor Market Outcomes of Less-Skilled Natives." In *Immigration, Trade, and the Labor Market*. Chicago, edited by John M. Abowd and Richard B. Freeman, 201–34. Chicago: University of Chicago Press.

Barclay, George W. 1954. *Colonial Development and Population in Taiwan*. Princeton, NJ: Princeton University Press.

Ben-Akiva, Moshe, and Steven Lerman. 1985. *Discrete Choice Analysis: Theory and Application to Travel Demand.* Cambridge, MA: MIT Press.

Bogue, Donald J., and Gregory Liegel. 2009. "Mobility Dynamic of Metro Areas with Large Net Internal Migration Losses and Gains." In *Immigration, Internal Migration, and Local Mobility in the U.S. Northampton*, edited by Donald J. Bogue, Gregory Liegel, and Michael Kozloski, 73–109. Northampton, MA: Edward Elgar.

Borjas, George J. 1987a. "Immigrants, Minorities, and Labor Market Competition." *Industrial and Labor Relations Review* 40(3):382–92.

Borjas, George J. 1987b. "Self-Selection and the Earnings of Immigrants." *American Economic Review* 77(4):531–53.

Borjas, George J. 2001. *Heaven's Door: Immigration Policy and the American Economy.* Princeton, NJ: Princeton University Press.

Borjas, George J. 2006. "Native Internal Migration and the Labor Market Impact of Immigration." *Journal of Human Resources* 41(2):221–58.

Borjas, George J., Stephen G. Bronars, and Stephen J. Trejo. 1992. "Self Selection and Internal Migration in the United States." *Journal of Urban Economics* 32:159–85.

Brücker, Herbert, Stefano Fachin, and Alessandra Venturini. 2011. "Do Foreigners Replace Native Immigrants? A Panel Cointegration Analysis of Internal Migration in Italy." *Economic Modeling* 28(3):1078–89.

Campbell, William, eds. 1903. *Formosa under the Dutch: Description from Contemporary Records.* London: Kegan Paul, Trench, Trubner and Co.

Card, David. 1990. "The Impact of the Mariel Boatlift on the Miami Labor Market." *Industrial and Labor Relations Review* 43(2):245–57.

Card, David. 2001. "Immigrant Inflows, Native Outflows, and the Local Labor Market Impacts of Higher Immigration." *Journal of Labor Economics* 19(1):22–64.

Clark, Cal. 1989. *Taiwan's Development: Implications for Contending Political Economy Paradigms.* Westport, CT: Greenwood Press.

Clark, William A. V., and Jun. L. Onaka. 1985. "An Empirical Test of a Joint Model of Residential Mobility and Housing Choice." *Environment and Planning A* 17(7):915–30.

Copper, John F. 1988. *A Quiet Revolution: Political Development in the Republic of China.* Washington, DC: Ethics and Public Policy Center.

Crowder, Kyle, Matthew Hall, and Stewart E. Tolnay. 2011. "Neighborhood Immigration and Native Out-Migration." *American Sociological Review* 76(1):25–47.

Detang-Dessendre, Cecile, Carine Drapier, and Hubert Jayet. 2004. "The Impact of Migration on Wages: Empirical Evidence from French Youth." *Journal of Regional Science* 44:661–91.

Ellis, Mark, and Richard Wright. 1999. "The Industrial Division of Labor Among Immigrants and Internal Migrants to the Los Angeles Economy." *International Migration Review* 33:26–54.

Fairlie, Robert W., and Bruce D. Meyer. 1997. "Does Immigration Hurt African-American Self-employment?" Working Paper No. 6265. Cambridge, MA: National Bureau of Economic Research.

Filer, Randall K. 1992. "The Effect of Immigration Arrivals on Migratory Patterns of Native Workers." In *Immigration and the Work Force*, edited by G. J. Borjas and R. B. Freeman, 245–70. Chicago: University of Chicago Press.

Frey, William H. 1996. "Immigration, Internal Migration and Demographic Balkanization in America: New Evidence for the 1990s." *Population and Development Review* 22:741–63.

Frey, William H. 2005. *Immigration and Domestic Migration in U.S. Metro Areas: 2000 and 1990 Census Findings by Education and Race.* Ann Arbor: University of Michigan Population Studies Center.

Frey, William H., and Kao-Lee Liaw. 1998. "The Impact of Recent Immigration on Population Redistribution in the United States." In *The Immigration Debate: Studies on the Economic, Demographic, and Fiscal Effects of immigration*, edited by J. P. Smith and B. Edmonston. Washington, DC: National Academy Press.

Frey, William H., Kao-Lee Liaw, Yu Xie, and Marcia J. Carlson. 1996. "Interstate Migration of the US Poverty Population: Immigration 'Pushes' and Welfare Magnet 'Pulls'." *Population and Environment* 17:491–536.

Frey, William H., and Alden Speare. 1988. *Regional and Metropolitan Growth and Decline in the United States*. New York: Russell Sage Foundation.

Greenwood, Michael J. 1975. "Research on Internal Migration in the United States: A Survey." *Journal of Economic Literature* 13(2):397–433.

Greenwood, Michael J., and Gary L. Hunt. 2003. "The Early History of Migration Research." *International Regional Science Review* 26(1):3–37.

Grossman, Jean Baldwin. 1982. "The Substitutability of Natives and Immigrants in Production." *Review of Economics and Statistics* 54(4):596–603.

Hugo, Graeme. 2006. "An Australian Diaspora?" *International Migration* 44(1):105–33.

Kanaroglou, Pavlos S., and Mark R. Ferguson. 1996. "Discrete Spatial Choice Models for Aggregate Destinations." *Journal of Regional Science* 36(2):271–90.

Knapp, Ronald G., eds. 1980. *China's Island Frontier: Studies in the Historical Geography of Taiwan*. Honolulu: The University Press of Hawaii.

Kritz, Mary M., and Douglas T. Gurak. 2001. "The Impact of Immigration on the Internal Migration of Natives and Immigrants." *Demography* 38(1):133–45.

LaLonde, Robert J., and Robert H. Topel. 1991. "Labor Market Adjustments to Increased Immigration." In *Immigration, Trade, and the Labor Market*, edited by John M. Abowd and Richard B. Freeman, 167–99. Chicago: University of Chicago Press.

Lee, Joseph S., and Su-Wan Wang. 1996. "Recruiting and Managing of Foreign Workers in Taiwan." *Asian and Pacific Migration Journal* 5:281–301.

Ley, David. 2007. "Countervailing Immigration and Domestic Migration in Gateway Cities: Australian and Canadian Variations on an American Theme." *Economic Geography* 83(3):231–54.

Liaw, Kao-Lee. 1990. "Joint Effects of Personal Factors and Ecological Variables on the Interprovincial Migration Pattern of Young Adults in Canada." *Geographical Analysis* 22:189–208.

Lin, Ji-Ping, and Kao-Lee Liaw. 2000. "Labor Migrations in Taiwan: Characterization and Interpretation Based on the Data of the1990 Census." *Environment and Planning A* 32(9):1689–709.

Long, Lary. 1988. *Migration and Residential Mobility in the United States*. New York: Russell Sage Foundation.

Manson, Donald M., Thomas J. Espenshade, and Thomas Muller. 1985. "Mexican Immigration to Southern California: The Issue of Job Competition and Worker Mobility." *Review of Regional Studies* 15:21–33.

Maré, David C., and Steven Stillman. 2010. "The Impact of Immigration on the Geographic Mobility of New Zealanders." *Economic Record* 86(273):247–59.

Massey, Douglas S. 1995. "The New Immigration and Ethnicity in the United States." *Population and Development Review* 21:631–52.

Massey, Douglas S., and Edward Taylor. 2004. *International Migration: Prospects and Policies in a Global Market*. Oxford: Oxford University Press.

Massey, Douglas S., et al. 1993. "Theories of International Migration: A Review and Appraisal." *Population and Development Review* 19(3):431–66.

McFadden, Daniel. 1974. "Conditional Logit Analysis of Qualitative Choice Behavior." In *Frontiers in Econometrics*, edited by P. Zarembka. New York: Academic Press.
Model, Suzanne. 1997. "An Occupational Tale of Two Cities: Minorities in London and New York." *Demography* 34(4):539–50.
Nakosteen, Robert A., Olle Westerlund, and Michael Zimmer. 2008. "Migration and Self-selection: Measured Earnings and Latent Characteristics." *Journal of Regional Science* 48(4):76988.
Newbold, K. Bruce, and Kao-Lee Liaw. 1995. "Return and Onward Migration in Canada, 1976–1981: An Explanation Based on Personal and Ecological Variables." *The Canadian Geographer* 39(1):16–30.
Pellegrini, Pasquale A., and A. Stewart Fotheringham. 1999. "Intermetropolitan Migration and Hierarchical Destination Choice: A Disaggregate Analysis from the US Public Use Microdata Samples." *Environment and Planning A* 31:1093–118.
Pellegrini, Pasquale A., and A. Stewart Fotheringham. 2002. "Modelling Spatial Choice: A Review and Synthesis in A Migration Context." *Progress in Human Geography* 26(4):487–510.
Piore, Michael J. 1979. *Birds of Passage: Migrant Labor in Industrial Societies*. Cambridge: Cambridge University Press.
Pischke, Jörn-Steffen, and Johannes Velling. 1997. "Employment Effects of Immigration to Germany: An Analysis Based on Local Labor Markets." *Review of Economics and Statistics* 79(4):594–604.
Ranis, Gustav. 1992. *Taiwan: From Developing to Mature Economy*. Boulder, CO: Westview Press.
Rogers, Andrei. 1979. "Migration Patterns and Population Redistribution." *Regional Science and Urban Economics* 9(4):275–310.
Rubinstein, Murray A. 2007. "Taiwan's Socioeconomic Modernization, 1971–1996." In *Taiwan: A New History (Expanded Edition)*, edited by Murray A. Rubinstein, 366–402. New York: M. E. Sharpe, Inc.
Sassen, Saskia. 1988. *The Mobility of Labor and Capital: A Study in International Investment and Labor Flow*. London: Cambridge University Press.
Selya, Roger M. 1992. "Illegal Migration in Taiwan: A Preliminary Overview." *International Migration Review* 26(3):787–805.
Shih, Chintay, Kung Wang, and Yi-Ling Wei. 2007. "Hsinchu, Taiwan: Asia's Pioneering High-tech Park." In *Making IT: The Rise of Asia in High Tech*, edited by Henry S. Rowen, Marguerite Gong Hancock, and William F. Miller, 101–22. Stanford, CA: Stanford University Press.
Sjaastad, Larry A. (1962). "The Costs and Returns of Human Migration." *Journal of Political Economy* 70(5)80–93.
Smith, James P., and Barry Edmonston, eds. 1998. *The Immigration Debate: Studies on the Economic, Demographic, and Fiscal Effects of Immigration*. Washington, DC: National Academy Press.
Speare, Alden, Kezhi Liu, and Ching-lung Tsay. 1988. *Urbanization and Development: The Rural-urban Transition in Taiwan*. Boulder, CO: Westview Press.
Stahl, Charles W. 2003. "International Labour Migration in East Asia: Trends and Policy Issues." In *Migration in the Asia Pacific: Population, Settlement and Citizenship Issues*, edited by Robyn R. Iredale, Charles Hawksley, and Stephen Castles. Northampton, MA: Edward Elgar Publishing.
Thomas, Dorothy S. 1938. *Research Memorandum on Migration Differential*. New York: Social Science Research Council.
Tsai, Pan-Long, and Ching-Lung Tsay. 2004. "Foreign Direct Investment and International Labour Migration in Economic Development: Indonesia, Malaysia, Philippines and Thailand." In *International Migration in Southeast Asia*,

edited by Aris Ananta and Evi Nurvidya Arifin, 94–136. Singapore: Institute of Southeast Asian Studies.

Tseng, Yen-Fen. 2004. "Politics of Importing Foreigners: Foreign Labour Policy in Taiwan." In *Migration Between States and Markets*, edited by Han Entzinger, Marco Martiniello, and Catherine Wihtol de Wenden, 100–18. Burlington, VT: Ashgate Publishing Company.

Walker, Robert, Mark Ellis, and Richard Barff. 1992. "Linked Migration Systems: Immigration and Internal Labor Flows in the United States." *Economic Geography* 68(3):234–48.

White, Michael J., and Yoshie Imai. 1994. "The Impact of U.S. Immigration upon Internal Migration." *Population and Environment* 15(3):189–209.

White, Michael J., and Zai Liang. 1998. "The Effect of Immigration on the Internal Migration of the Native-born Population, 1981–1990." *Population Research and Policy Review* 17(2):141–66.

Winter-Ebmer, Rudolf, and Josef Zweimüller. 1999. "Do Immigrants Displace Young Native Workers: The Austrian Experience." *Journal of Population Economics* 12(2):327–40.

Wright, Richard A., Mark Ellis, and Michael Reibel. 1997. "The Linkage between Immigration and Internal Migration in Large Metropolitan Areas in the United States." *Economic Geography* 73(2):234–54.

Group Relations in Multi-ethnic Cities

6 Diversity in People and Places
Multiracial People in U.S. Society

Nancy Denton

INTRODUCTION

In this era of mass immigration, or *Worlds in Motion* as one notable book called it (Massey et al. 2005), societies around the world are becoming more and more racially and ethnically diverse. One result of this increasing diversity is an increase in the multiracial population, reflecting either children of intermarriage or greater precision in identifying one's ancestry, or both. With Census 2000, the United States began officially counting the multiracial population, marking a new era in terms of measuring race. For the first time ever, people were allowed to choose as many races as they wanted on the Census form.

Nearly seven million people chose more than one race in 2000, or about 2.4% of the population. Since then their number has increased by almost one-third, to more than nine million people, 2.9% of the population. So multiracial is a rapidly growing population subgroup. It is important to understand who the multiracial people are, where they live, and what their ties are to other racial and ethnic groups in U.S. society. This chapter will analyze the multiracial population as a whole, and specific combinations of multiple races, with particular emphasis on examining how their location differs by age and race/ethnicity. Though there has been much research on the multiracial population in general and children in particular, there has been less research on specific sub-groups of the population, in particular specific multiracial combinations, adult members of the multiracial population, the geographic location of the multiracial population, and its location with respect to other groups in American society.

Data for this chapter comes from Census 2000 and Census 2010. Though detailed data on multiple race combinations are available for all levels of geography for both years, this analysis will concentrate on the state level in order to examine a greater number of specific combinations of races. Though the chapter will certainly include the children who have featured so prominently in earlier studies of the multiracial population, I will be asking different questions about the present and future multiracial population in the United States. The first question relates to the multiracial population as a whole: Are some particular racial combinations growing more quickly than others? Dominated by children or adults? Next the focus is on geography: Where in the United States do these multiracial people live? Does the location of specific multiple race combinations vary? Does the geographic distribution across states vary by age—are children living in different places than adults? Last, the chapter looks at how the locations of the multiracial population are related to the location of single race populations using a measure of residential segregation. Are children or adults in greater contact with single race non-Hispanic whites and non-Hispanic blacks? What about specific combinations—which of them are more likely to live in states with more single race people? To the extent that race matters in U.S. society, then multiracial identification most likely plays a role in determining spatial location, and thus the residential distance between groups. The analyses in this chapter will not only provide an overview of the location of multiracial and monoracial people in U.S. society, but it will also suggest future research questions about this important and growing population.

LITERATURE REVIEW

Other than the more descriptive reports issued shortly after Census 2000 (Grieco and Cassidy 2001; Jones 2005; Jones and Smith 2001; Tafoya, Johnson, and Hill 2004) and Census 2010 (Humes et al. 2011), research on the multiracial population can be divided into two categories: methodological research and research on the determinants of multiracial children's identification. There was also a single study of the racial segregation of the multiracial population (Frey and Myers 2002), and though Frey (2011) includes some data on the multiracial population, it is not detailed. In addition, a series of papers from a conference held just as the 2000 data were beginning to come out (Perlmann and Waters 2002) explored many other issues related to the multiracial population, including legal implications, effect on population projections, and how the multiracial population was going to be fitted into, as well as change, the federal statistical system. Very little attention has been paid to the adult multiracial population or specific combinations of races. At a more general level, the whole issue of measuring race is seen as problematic by some (Zuberi 2001) and reflective of white rather than black methodology (Zuberi and Bonilla-Silva 2008).

Methodological Issues

The methodological issues raised by the option to select more than one race began with efforts to estimate how many people were likely to report more than one race on the Census. Initial estimates, based in large part on data from the 1996 RAETT, were too high, at 3.1% to 6.6% (Goldstein and Morning 2000; Hirschman et al. 2000). These studies also documented sensitivity to question order, as well as suggested that the concept of origins may be better than race, since Hispanics seem to identify themselves as a racial group.

Allowing people to choose more than one race immediately raised tabulation problems as well, particularly since the race data are used to meet Civil Rights requirements (Goldstein and Morning 2002; Harrison 2002). Once the 1997 committee recommendations and revisions to the racial classification system were announced (Office of Management and Budget 1997a, 1997b), they were followed in 2001 by another Office of Management and Budget (OMB) report. It outlined several methods for assigning multiple race responses into single race categories: Deterministic Whole Assignment, Deterministic Fractional Assignment, and Probabilistic Whole Assignment. The distinction among these bridging methods is whether an individual's responses are assigned to a single racial category (termed whole assignment) or to multiple categories (termed fractional assignment), with whole assignment based on a set of deterministic rules such as smallest or group, and largest group other than white, or based on some probabilistic distribution (Office of Management and Budget 2001). These methods all have advantages, but they also have consequences in terms of changing the racial distribution of the population (Parker and Makuc 2002). Comparing the old and new race data is not easy (Tucker et al. 2002), and context is important even on the Census (Martin et al. 1990).

Deane has recently proposed a statistical method whereby persons contribute as many observations to the sample as necessary to exhaust their multiple racial identifications, effectively shifting the observational unit from a respondent to an identification, and then apply a post hoc correction based on well-established principles used to correct biases occurring as a result of cluster sampling (Denton and Deane 2010). This method avoids the problem that different analysts using the same data can obtain different answers if they use different allocation schemes for the multiple race data. Another well-known multivariate bridging method is the NCHS regression method (Parker and Makuc 2002), but it is difficult for researchers to implement with publicly available data, so a modified version of this method has been developed by Liebler and Halpern-Manners (2008). Their results show that using the regression methodology provides better estimates linking the multiple to single race populations.

In closing, it is important to emphasize the role of the data collectors and the rules of OMB in determining multiple races. As Snipp (2002, 2003) summarized, the categories allowed or mandated on Census forms shape not only the data available for analysis, but the choices that people responding to the data collection make. Hitlin et al. (2007) clearly demonstrate that the Census separation between race and ethnicity is not shared by a lot of Hispanics, to the point that they recommend including Hispanic as a race in the Census question. This was not done in 2010, so we will have to wait to see what happens on the 2020 Census.

Research on Children and Adolescents

Research on the population under age 18 and members of specific multiracial groups such as Native Americans, Alaskan Natives, Native Hawaiians, and Other Pacific Islanders, as well as blacks and whites followed the 2000 Census. Kanaiupuni and Liebler (2005) found that among those with both Hawaiian and another racial heritage, stronger ties to the islands of Hawaii led parents to identify their children as Hawaiian. Liebler (2010) found that living on an American Indian homeland is a strong predictor of parents' choosing a single race Native American identity for their children. Intergenerational transmission of strong single race identities is robust to controls for poverty, geographic isolation, and area racial composition. Using ECCLES data, Brunsma (2005) found great variety in how children are racially identified. There is some evidence of hypodescent (the minority race is chosen), but evidence also indicates that parents are trying to move their children away from the minority designation toward the white or some more neutral one, a shift that is influenced by the socioeconomic status of the parents. Xie and Goyette (1997) find that children with one Asian and one non-Asian parent are 30% to 50% likely to be identified as Asian, which they interpret as indicating that choosing their child's race is an option for these parents, and that parents with more education are more likely to choose an Asian race (cf. Waters 1990, 1999).

Literature on adolescent racial identity has consistently shown that the context of where the race question is being answered—school or home—makes a difference to the answer (Harris 2002; Harris and Sim 2002). In a study of students in nine high schools in Wisconsin and California—multiracial adolescents most often report their minority race, especially if black and white (Herman 2004). But those who appear white are more likely to report white, and what they report is influenced by family, neighborhood, and school contexts (Doyle and Kao 2007). This research on adolescents is of particular interest since in the ten years since Census 2000, roughly half of the multiracial children will now be over age 18 and presumably filling out their own Census forms.

DATA AND METHODS

As noted above, data for this chapter come from the 2000 and 2010 Censuses of Population and Housing, which contains the detailed combinations of races for levels of geography smaller than the nation as a whole on Summary File 1. Since the multiracial population is not large, segregation indices are calculated at the state level. The index used is the well-known Index of Dissimilarity, which can be interpreted as the proportion of either group that would have to change states in order to be evenly distributed across states. The formula for the index is $D_{ab} = .5 * \text{sum} \; | \, (a_i/A - b_i/B) \, |$, where a_i and b_i are the populations of groups a and b in state i, and A and B are the national totals of the populations of these groups. The index thus

Diversity in People and Places 113

compares two groups at a time, and it uses the overall proportions in each racial group as the standard. The data to compute the indices come from tables P4 and P6 of Summary File 1 in 2000 and tables P9 and P11 in 2010. Hispanics are removed from the multiple and single race populations and treated as a separate group. So the white, black, and Asian populations are all non-Hispanic, though for ease of reading, the modifier "non-Hispanic" will not be added every time.

RESULTS

Growth of the Multiracial Population

Table 6.1 summarizes the growth of the U.S. population between 2000 and 2010. Overall, the U.S. population increased by 9.7%, but substantial variation exists across racial/ethnic subgroups. The non-Hispanic population grew just under 5% while the Hispanic population grew by 43%.[1] Among single race non-Hispanic groups, growth varies from a very low 1.2% among non-Hispanic whites to a high of 42.9% for those choosing Asian alone. So Hispanics and Asians are the fastest growing groups, followed by Native Hawaiian and Other Pacific Islanders, who grew 36.2%. The American Indian and Alaska Native populations, as well as the Black

Table 6.1 Growth of the U.S. Population by Race and Hispanic Origin, 2000–2010

	2000	2010	% Change
Total:	281,421,906	308,745,538	9.7
Not Hispanic or Latino:	246,116,088	258,287,944	4.9
White alone	194,552,774	196,817,552	1.2
Black or African American alone	33,947,837	37,685,848	11.0
American Indian and Alaska Native alone	2,068,883	2,247,098	8.6
Asian alone	10,123,169	14,465,124	42.9
Native Hawaiian and Other Pacific Islander alone	353,509	481,576	36.2
Some other race alone	467,770	604,265	29.2
Two or more races	4,602,146	5,966,481	29.6
Hispanic or Latino	35,305,818	50,477,594	43.0

Sources:
Census 2010 - C2010BR-02 - "Overview of Race and Hispanic Origin"
Census 2000 - P4 HISPANIC OR LATINO, and NOT HISPANIC OR LATINO, by RACE

population, groups with long-standing residence in the United States, grew much more slowly, at 8.6% and 11%, respectively. The multiple race population, the focus of this chapter, grew 29.6%, making them among the faster growing populations.

Who Is Multiracial in the United States?

At the conceptual level, it seems obvious that people who identify (or are identified by someone else) with multiple races would by definition have parents who are of different races or at least one parent who identifies with more than one race (Stephan and Stephan 1989). It is also possible that more distant ancestors may influence a person's racial choice as well. But these statements assume that the option of identifying with more than one race has always been available. If, however, as happened in the United States in 2000, the option of identifying with more than one race abruptly becomes available for the first time after decades of being told to "choose only one," then the people who choose more than one race can clearly be divided into two groups: children under age 18, still living with their different race parents (or at least one multiracial parent); and adults. In the former case, it is probably parents who chose more than one race for their children, reflecting the parents' union and their desire to have their child reflect them, to say nothing of the fact that the parents would usually fill out the Census form. Adults, in contrast, may have chosen more than one race for themselves, though if the Census form is filled out by only one person in the household, then multiple races may be selected for them as well, though more likely with some knowledge of their own choice of a racial identity.

Parents of different races who had borne children and who wanted to identify them on the Census were the driving force behind the change in Census procedures (Farley 2002, 2004). Yet when the 2000 Census data were released, just over 40% of the multiple race population was below the age of 18, the usual age for children living with their parents (Jones 2005; Jones and Smith 2001). In 2010, that number increased, but to just over 50%. So significantly more than half of the multiracial population was adults in 2000, while just under half (49.51%) were adults in 2010. As a result of the distinct ages of the people who identified as being of more of than one race, we argue that allowing people to select more than one race has tapped two different groups of people who may differ by more than their age. At the same time, most of the research on the multiple race population has focused on the children and not on the adults. While this is understandable, as the children allow for the estimation of models of what characteristics of parents, other than their own race, enhance or inhibit their identification of their child as being of more than one race, it still means that more than half of the multiple race population identified in Census 2000 has been largely ignored by researchers. About half of the people whose parents chose their multiple race identity in 2000 aged into the adult category by 2010, where they presumably chose their own race, a pattern that will continue with future censuses. So an examination of the adult multiracial population is increasingly important.

Moving from the conceptual level, studying the multiple race population involves understanding how the U.S. Census Bureau tabulates multiracial data. For a variety of reasons, Hispanics are not considered a race in the Census but are counted in a separate question that precedes the race question (cf. Cresce et al. 2004; Denton and Deane 2010, among many others, for a more detailed explanation). As a result, when the Census defines multiracial, it does not include Hispanics as a race. Only whites, blacks, Asians, American Indians and Alaskan Natives (AIAN), Native Hawaiians and Other Pacific Islanders (NHOPI), and Some Other Race (SOR) are considered races. In both censuses, 97% of those who selected SOR as their sole race were Hispanic. Tabulating all possible single, two, three, four, five, and six race combinations of these groups results in 63 separate racial categories, and further classifying them by Hispanic origin results in 126 categories. Data for each of these 126 combinations are provided down to the block level. For many (if not most) jurisdictions, many of these categories contain few people at the same time as the number of categories complicates analysis (Farley 2004).

A second issue with the multiracial classification is that only combinations of the major race groups, plus some other race, are considered multiracial. Other races identified by name on the Census form are not tabulated as multiple races. So the marriage between a Chinese and a Vietnamese does not produce multiracial children, but one between a Native Hawaiian and Other Pacific Islander and a Chinese does. Native American Tribes are specified on the Census form as well, but different tribal affiliations are not tabulated as multiracial. For Hispanics, this means that their multiracial identity is confined to the six major race groups and does not include specific groups such as Cuban or Mexican, though parents may consider their children multiracial as well. In short, the definition of multiracial in the U.S. Census may not agree with what people think of when they hear the term or what researchers necessarily want to analyze. Still, given the growth rate and increasing importance of this population, it is important to study them and understand how they are part of U.S. society.

Combinations and More Combinations!!!

As noted above, the Census tabulates the multiracial population into all possible combinations of the six major race groups, separately for non-Hispanics and Hispanics. Table 6.2 shows all 63 detailed racial combinations for the non-Hispanic population of the United States in 2000 and 2010, as well as the total Hispanic population. The first thing to notice is how quickly the numbers of people in each racial combination drop off: by the time one gets to three race combinations, there are only 461,000 persons out of 309 million.

Table 6.2 Growth in Specific Combinations of Races, 2000–2010

	2000	2010	% Change
Total:	281,421,906	308,745,538	9.7
Hispanic or Latino	35,305,818	50,477,594	43.0
Not Hispanic or Latino	246,116,088	258,267,944	4.9
Population of one race:	241,513,942	252,301,463	4.5
White alone	194,552,774	196,817,552	1.2
Black or African American alone	33,947,837	37,685,848	11.0
American Indian and Alaska Native alone	2,068,883	2,247,098	8.6
Asian alone	10,123,169	14,465,124	42.9
Native Hawaiian and Other Pacific Islander alone	353,509	481,576	36.2
Some other race alone	467,770	604,265	29.2
Population of two or more races:	4,602,146	5,966,481	29.6
Population of two races:	4,257,110	5,465,681	28.4
White; Black or African American	697,077	1,588,362	127.9
White; American Indian and Alaska Native	969,238	1,205,924	24.4
White; Asian	811,240	1,487,712	83.4
White; Native Hawaiian and Other Pacific Islander	100,702	147,804	46.8
White; Some other race	731,719	139,799	−80.9
Black or African American; American Indian and Alaska Native	168,022	237,850	41.6
Black or African American; Asian	99,513	170,144	71.0
Black or African American; Native Hawaiian & Other Pacific Islander	27,479	45,395	65.2

Diversity in People and Places 117

Black or African American; Some other race	255,966	86,923	-66.0
American Indian and Alaska Native; Asian	43,052	46,572	8.2
American Indian and Alaska Native; Native Hawaiian & Other Pacific Islander	5,453	7,544	38.3
American Indian and Alaska Native; Some other race	21,477	9,148	-57.4
Asian; Native Hawaiian and Other Pacific Islander	129,130	149,561	15.8
Asian; Some other race	185,754	130,871	-29.5
Native Hawaiian and Other Pacific Islander; Some other race	11,288	12,072	6.9
Population of three races:	311,029	460,911	48.2
White; Black or African American; American Indian & Alaska Native	94,161	180,848	92.1
White; Black or African American; Asian	18,229	51,346	181.7
White; Black or African American; Native Hawaiian & Other Pacific Islander	2,527	7,827	209.7
White; Black or African American; Some other race	27,691	13,087	-52.7
White; American Indian and Alaska Native; Asian	18,405	33,596	82.5
White; Am. Indian & Alaska Native; Native Hawaiian & Other Pacific Islander	3,884	6,483	66.9
White; American Indian and Alaska Native; Some other race	13,796	5,082	-63.2
White; Asian; Native Hawaiian & Other Pacific Islander	77,616	120,327	55.0
White; Asian; Some other race	21,964	10,277	-53.2
White; Native Hawaiian & Other Pacific Islander; Some other race	4,741	1,563	-67.0

(continued)

Table 6.2 (continued)

	2000	2010	% Change
Population of three races (continued):			
Black or African American; American Indian and Alaska Native; Asian	4,849	7,565	56.0
Black or African American; American Indian & Alaska Native; Native Hawaiian & Other Pacific Islander	753	1,692	124.7
Black or African American; American Indian & Alaska Native; Some other race	4,648	3,227	−30.6
Black or African American; Asian; Native Hawaiian & Other Pacific Islander	4,501	5,986	33.0
Black or African American; Asian; Some other race	6,217	4,452	−28.4
Black or African American; Native Hawaiian & Other Pacific Islander; Some other race	1,289	2,194	70.2
American Indian & Alaska Native; Asian; Native Hawaiian & Other Pacific Islander	2,131	2,235	4.9
American Indian and Alaska Native; Asian; Some other race	955	765	−19.9
American Indian & Alaska Native; Native Hawaiian & Other Pacific Islander; Some other race	200	265	32.5
Asian; Native Hawaiian & Other Pacific Islander; Some other race	2,472	2,094	−15.3
Population of four races:	27,155	34,556	27.3
White; Black or African American; American Indian & Alaska Native; Asian	8,912	14,300	60.5
White; Black or African American; American Indian & Alaska Native; Native Hawaiian & Other Pacific Islander	740	1,963	165.3
White; Black or African American; American Indian & Alaska Native; Some other race	2,576	3,385	31.4

White; Black or African American; Asian; Native Hawaiian & Other Pacific Islander	1,635	3,509	114.6
White; Black or African American; Asian; Some other race	848	944	11.3
White; Black or African American; Native Hawaiian & Other Pacific Islander; Some other race	157	192	22.3
White; American Indian & Alaska Native; Asian; Native Hawaiian & Other Pacific Islander	4,411	7,460	69.1
White; American Indian & Alaska Native; Asian; Some other race	491	317	−35.4
White; American Indian & Alaska Native; Native Hawaiian & Other Pacific Islander; Some other race	160	105	−34.4
White; Asian; Native Hawaiian & Other Pacific Islander; Some other race	5,493	1,055	−80.8
Black or African American; American Indian & Alaska Native; Asian; Native Hawaiian & Other Pacific Islander	530	664	25.3
Black or African American; American Indian & Alaska Native; Asian; Some other race	223	225	0.9
Black or African American; American Indian & Alaska Native; Native Hawaiian & Other Pacific Islander; Some other race	45	93	106.7
Black or African American; Asian; Native Hawaiian & Other Pacific Islander; Some other race	854	298	−65.1
American Indian & Alaska Native; Asian; Native Hawaiian & Other Pacific Islander; Some other race	80	46	−42.5
Population of five races:	6,342	5,008	−21.0
White; African American; American Indian & Alaska Native; Asian; Native Hawaiian & Other Pacific Islander	5,081	4,211	−17.1

(continued)

Table 6.2 (continued)

	2000	2010	% Change
Population of five races (continued):			
White; African American; American Indian & Alaska Native; Asian; Some other race	483	448	−7.2
White; African American; American Indian & Alaska Native; Native Hawaiian & Other Pacific Islander; Some other race	32	68	112.5
White; African American; Asian; Native Hawaiian & Other Pacific Islander; Some other race	227	110	−51.5
White; American Indian & Alaska Native; Asian; Native Hawaiian & Other Pacific Islander; Some other race	380	127	−66.6
African American; American Indian & Alaska Native; Asian; Native Hawaiian & Other Pacific Islander; Some other race	139	44	−68.3
Population of six races:	510	325	−36.3
White; Black or African American; American Indian & Alaska Native; Asian; Native Hawaiian & Other Pacific Islander; Some other race	510	325	−36.3

Sources:
Census 2000: P4. HISPANIC AND LATINO BY RACE [73] - Universe: Total population
Census 2010: PL 94-171 - P2 HISPANIC AND LATINO BY RACE [73] - Universe: Total population
Shaded lines are the six largest multiple race combinations that do not include Some Other Race.
* indicates Multiple race combinations that will be analyzed in more detail.

Diversity in People and Places 121

There are just over 35,000 combinations of four races, just over 5,000 for five race combinations, and only 325 persons who report six races. Even among the two race combinations, which 5.5 million persons reported, two combinations, American Indian and Alaskan Native with Native Hawaiian and Other Pacific Islander (AIAN + NHOPI) and American Indian and Alaskan Native with Some Other Race (AIAN + SOR), are under 10,000 persons. Four of the four race and five race combinations were chosen by fewer than 100 persons. It is clear that even at the level of the nation as a whole, many racial combinations may exist in theory but barely do so in reality.

A related issue with data this detailed is shown in the percent change column. Given that the 2000 Census was the first one to allow the reporting of multiple races, it would be expected that there would be more multiple race persons in 2010 as people became more familiar with the option, as well as because more multiple race children were born during the last decade. Two numerically large multiple race groups, white and black or African American (W + B) and white and Asian (W + A), more than doubled or almost doubled, increasing by 127.9% and 83.4%, respectively. However, 23 of the 57 multiple race categories, 40%, show declines, suggesting variability in reporting of multiple race combinations rather than increasing adoption of multiple race identity. A closer look shows that all but one of these categories involves SOR, the category where the Census Bureau admits a tabulation error in 2000.[2] Overall, however, the data in Table 6.2 show that two race combinations are the most often chosen, with a handful of three-race combinations (W + B + AIAN, W + A + NHOPI, W + B + A, W + AIAN + A, W + B + SOR, W + A + SOR) and one four race combination (W + B + AIAN + A) chosen by at least 10,000 persons.

Given the large number of possible combinations, it is interesting to ask whether the choice of more than one race is more common among some groups than others. More than half of Native Hawaiian and Other Pacific Islanders chose that race in combination with some other race, and more than 40% of those who chose American Indian and Alaska Native did as well. About 13% of Asians chose that race in combination with another race (Grieco et al. 2011).

Is the Multiracial Population Primarily Children or Adults?

As noted above, despite the fact that it was parents of multiracial children who organized the social movement that ultimately resulted in Census 2000 including the multiple race option, only about two-fifths of the multiracial population counted in Census 2000 was under the age of 18 and just half was in 2010. To the extent that the multiracial population is young, there is the potential for increasing population growth if these young people continue their multiracial identification into their own adulthood and assign it to their own children. Table 6.3 shows how the percentage of the population that is under age 18 varies by racial combination chosen in 2000 and 2010.

Table 6.3 Age Variation in Specific Combinations of Races, 2000–2010

	2000	% Children	2010	% Children
Total:	281,421,906	25.7	308,745,538	24.0
Hispanic or Latino	35,305,818	35.0	50,477,594	33.9
Not Hispanic or Latino	246,116,088	24.4	258,267,944	22.1
Population of one race:	241,513,942	24.0	252,301,463	21.5
White alone	194,552,774	22.6	196,817,552	20.2
Black or African American alone	33,947,837	31.3	37,685,848	27.5
American Indian and Alaska Native alone	2,068,883	33.2	2,247,098	28.8
Asian alone	10,123,169	23.9	14,465,124	22.0
Native Hawaiian and Other Pacific Islander alone	353,509	31.0	481,576	28.2
Some other race alone	467,770	41.1	604,265	36.9
Population of two or more races:	4,602,146	41.4	5,966,481	46.8
Population of two races:	4,257,110	41.0	5,465,681	46.8
White; Black or African American	697,077	74.0	1,588,362	69.2
White; American Indian and Alaska Native	969,238	29.4	1,205,924	28.3
White; Asian	811,240	50.8	1,487,712	49.6
White; Native Hawaiian and Other Pacific Islander	100,702	39.8	147,804	37.7
White; Some other race	731,719	25.7	139,799	31.1
Black or African American; American Indian & Alaska Native	168,022	30.5	237,850	29.7
Black or African American; Asian	99,513	45.7	170,144	45.4
Black or African American; Native Hawaiian & Other Pacific Islander	27,479	37.2	45,395	36.3
Black or African American; Some other race	255,966	31.7	86,923	31.5

American Indian and Alaska Native; Asian	43,052	30.3	46,572	29.5
American Indian & Alaska Native; Native Hawaiian & Other Pacific Islander	5,453	36.0	7,544	37.1
American Indian and Alaska Native; Some other race	21,477	30.9	9,148	27.3
Asian; Native Hawaiian and Other Pacific Islander	129,130	27.6	149,561	25.4
Asian; Some other race	185,754	30.3	130,871	22.2
Native Hawaiian & Other Pacific Islander; Some other race	11,288	34.2	12,072	25.8
Population of three races:	311,029	46.6	460,911	46.3
White; Black or African American; American Indian & Alaska Native	94,161	41.5	180,848	41.8
White; Black or African American; Asian	18,229	67.6	51,346	69.4
White; Black or African American; Some other race	27,691	63.8	13,087	49.7
White; American Indian and Alaska Native; Asian	18,405	52.2	33,596	50.9
White; Asian; Native Hawaiian & Other Pacific Islander	77,616	87.1	120,327	44.3
White; Asian; Some other race	21,964	59.9	10,277	40.0
Population of four races:	27,155	44.8	34,556	48.9
Population of five races:	6,342	29.1	5,008	31.4
Population of six races:	510	33.5	325	25.2

Sources:
Census 2000: P4. HISPANIC OR LATINO, AND NOT HISPANIC OR LATINO, BY RACE
Census 2000: P6. HISPANIC OR LATINO, AND NOT HISPANIC OR LATINO, BY RACE FOR THE POPULATION 18 YEARS AND OVER
Census 2010: P9. HISPANIC OR LATINO, AND NOT HISPANIC OR LATINO, BY RACE
Census 2010: P11. HISPANIC OR LATINO, AND NOT HISPANIC OR LATINO, BY RACE FOR THE POPULATION 18 YEARS OR OVER

It is clear that the multiracial population is much more youthful than the total population. Overall, the youthfulness of the entire population declined between 2000 and 2010, from 25.7% to 24.0%, while that of the multiracial population increased, from 41.4% to 46.8%. The percentage of children remains at about 47% among those who are identified with three races or four races in 2010 and then declines with the larger numbers of races included. Of particular interest is the youthfulness of two specific combinations: 69.2% of the white, black, or African American combination is children, as are 69.4% of the white, black, African American, and Asian groups. These findings suggest that these groups are experiencing higher intermarriage rates and thus producing more multiracial children.

Though many combinations are about 40% to 50% children, some combinations are primarily adults. Among the two race combinations, those that involve American Indian and Alaska Native, and to a lesser extent Native Hawaiian and Other Pacific Islanders, are more likely to be dominated by adults.[3] This result may in part reflect that some people are using the ability to acknowledge parts of their ancestry that they long knew about, for example, the mixture of American Indian with whites and blacks.

Where in the United States Do Multiracial People Live?

Now that the various combinations of races and their relative frequencies have been described, the next question is, where do multiracial people live? Figure 6.1 shows the percentage of each state population that was of two or more races in 2010.[4] The populations of Hawaii and Alaska were the most multiracial in 2000, at 19.5% and 5.1%, respectively, and this trend continued in 2010, when they were 19.4% and 6.4% multiracial, respectively. However, in terms of numbers of multiracial people, these two states do not dominate because they are relatively small. Hawaii ranks fifth in terms of numbers of multiracial persons, after California, New York, Texas, and Florida, while Alaska ranks 35th (data not shown). In terms of numbers, California is home to nearly a million multiracial people, but the numbers drop off sharply as New York has only 326,000 and Hawaii 264,000. While it may seem to many that multiracial people are a result of the high immigration to the United States, it is noteworthy that other than Alaska and Hawaii, only one of the other two states with a large number of multiracial people is an immigrant gateway, California; the fourth is Oklahoma, suggesting the importance of the American Indian population in the multiracial group. Overall, the multiracial population is concentrated in the West and Southwest, with Florida, New York, and states near New York having much smaller concentrations, though some multiracial people live in every state.

Diversity in People and Places   125

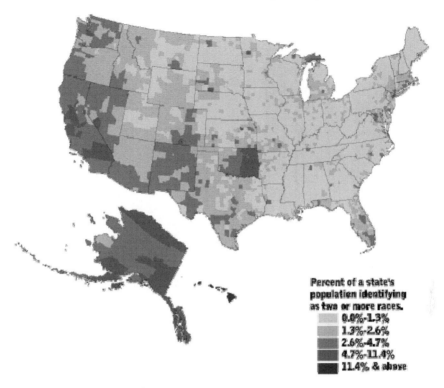

Figure 6.1 Population of two or more races, 2010.
Source: www.CensusScope.org; http://www.censusscope.org/us/print_map_multiracial.html

Do Specific Multiracial Groups Live in Different Places?

More specific information about the multiracial population by state is found in Table 6.4, which shows the percentage of each state's multiracial population that was in each of six specific categories in 2010, as well as the percentage of the multiracial combination these six groups cover. The ten states with the highest and the ten states with the lowest percentage are presented for each specific combination. Looking at the first combination, white and African American, of whom there were almost 1.6 million in 2010, we see that they comprise the largest portion of a state's population mainly in the interior states in the South and Midwest, areas that traditionally had large black populations. The next group, white and American Indian and Alaska Native, was the third largest two race category in 2010, at 1.2 million. They are found in states that were the destination of the Native American population when they were moved from the southeastern part of the country in the mid-19th century. Whites and Asians, the third combination, make up substantial portions of the multiracial population in

Table 6.4 Percentage of Total Multiple Race Population in Each of Six Specific Combinations, by State, 2010

White; Black or African American		White; American Indian and Alaska Native		White; Asian		Black or African American; American Indian and Alaska Native		Black or African American; Asian		White; Black or African American; American Indian and Alaska Native		These 6 Groups as Percent of Total Two or More Races Population	
Top Ten													
Kentucky	46.7	Oklahoma	67.2	California	40.5	D.C.	13.3	D.C.	6.6	D.C.	7.7	Oklahoma	95.5
Ohio	46.5	Montana	62.1	Washington	32.2	Delaware	8.7	New York	5.9	Maryland	4.9	West Virginia	93.0
Indiana	46.4	Alaska	54.5	Virginia	31.0	North Carolina	8.1	Florida	5.1	Minnesota	4.8	South Dakota	92.5
West Virginia	45.2	South Dakota	53.6	Nevada	31.0	Rhode Island	7.6	Maryland	4.9	Ohio	4.6	Vermont	92.2
Delaware	43.6	North Dakota	49.8	Utah	30.4	Maryland	7.6	Georgia	4.8	Rhode Island	4.6	Montana	91.7
Iowa	43.5	Wyoming	46.0	Colorado	29.4	Mississippi	7.5	Nevada	4.1	North Carolina	4.5	Ohio	91.6
Pennsylvania	43.1	Vermont	44.8	Idaho	28.8	Louisiana	7.2	New Jersey	3.9	Michigan	4.5	Kansas	91.5
South Carolina	40.5	Maine	44.5	Illinois	28.5	Georgia	6.8	California	3.8	Delaware	4.3	Arkansas	91.3
Tennessee	38.4	Arkansas	43.6	D.C.	28.2	Oklahoma	6.3	Virginia	3.7	Pennsylvania	4.2	North Dakota	91.0
Mississippi	38.0	Idaho	39.5	New Jersey	28.1	Connecticut	6.1	Delaware	3.5	Connecticut	4.1	Wisconsin	91.0
Bottom Ten													
Washington	19.1	Connecticut	13.4	Louisiana	14.6	Washington	1.9	Utah	0.9	Maine	2.4	Connecticut	81.9
New Mexico	17.2	Virginia	12.4	Mississippi	14.4	Montana	1.7	New Hampshire	0.7	Nevada	2.3	Florida	79.1
Utah	17.0	Rhode Island	12.0	Alaska	14.3	Oregon	1.4	South Dakota	0.7	Florida	2.2	California	78.9
Oregon	15.8	Delaware	11.8	Montana	14.3	Wyoming	1.1	West Virginia	0.7	Arkansas	2.2	Nevada	75.7
California	15.1	Massachusetts	11.6	Alabama	14.1	New Hampshire	1.1	Wyoming	0.7	Montana	2.1	New Jersey	75.7
Idaho	14.6	Maryland	10.1	Kentucky	13.9	Utah	1.0	Oklahoma	0.6	North Dakota	2.0	New York	75.5
Oklahoma	12.2	New York	9.9	Arkansas	12.5	Vermont	1.0	Idaho	0.6	Idaho	1.7	Utah	71.1
Montana	11.2	New Jersey	8.2	South Dakota	12.3	Maine	0.9	Vermont	0.5	Wyoming	1.6	Massachusetts	70.8
Alaska	9.2	D.C.	5.1	West Virginia	12.0	Idaho	0.9	Maine	0.4	Utah	1.2	Rhode Island	70.4
Hawaii	1.2	Hawaii	2.4	Oklahoma	6.1	Hawaii	0.3	Montana	0.3	Hawaii	0.4	Hawaii	27.7

states that are associated with immigration, such as California, where they are two-fifths of the multiracial population, or Washington, where they are almost one-third. They were the second largest two race group in 2010, and at almost 1.5 million, they are nearly as numerous as the white-black combination. The other three multiple race combinations shown, black and Native American, black and Asian, and white, black, and Native American are smaller in size, and so they do not make up as substantial a portion of the multiracial population of their states. What is interesting, however, is that when you look at the states in the top ten for each of the six combinations, there are relatively few repetitions, with many states appearing on the list only once or twice. In fact, only two states appear four times, Delaware and the District of Columbia, and Maryland appears three times. So these specific combinations are quite geographically dispersed at the same time as the locations reflect historical population locations.

It is noteworthy that the groups are substantial proportions of the multiracial population of their respective states: the W+B combination is almost half of the multiracial population in Kentucky, Ohio, Indiana, and West Virginia, while the W+AIAN combination is more than half of the multiracial population in North and South Dakota, Alaska, and Montana, and almost 70% in Oklahoma. Even the third combination, white and Asian, is more than 40% of the multiracial population in California. So it makes sense to think of these populations as distinctive, at least at the state level, though how they are distinctive is beyond the scope of this chapter. For most of the combinations shown, no matter how high their representation in the states in the top ten, in the state where they are the least represented they comprise a very small percentage of the population.

The final column in Table 6.4 shows the percentage of the state's total multiracial population that these six combinations represent. The numbers range from 95.5% in Oklahoma to 70.4% in Rhode Island, with the low of 27.7% in Hawaii. The low number for Hawaii is because none of the six largest combinations included the Native Hawaiian and Other Pacific Islander group. But leaving Hawaii aside, it is very interesting that we can capture almost three-quarters of the multiracial population with just six categories, making the usefulness of the detail provided by the Census Bureau questionable. This point is important because we get very little information about specific combinations, and it would be nice to know more about those that are more numerous, such as those shown in Table 6.4, such as their education, income, occupation, family status, etc. Though it is obvious that they cannot provide this detail on all the groups listed in Table 6.2, confidentiality would be much less of an issue for just these six groups.

A related question is the geographic distribution of children in these specific combinations. Looking at the percentage of each of the six specific multiple race combinations shown in Table 6.4 that is children by state (data not shown), it is very interesting that with the exception of the District of Columbia, more than half of the W + B group is children in every single state, rising to nearly 80% in Arkansas, Kentucky, Alabama, and Mississippi. The W + AIAN group is least likely to be children, with the other groups falling in between. If one compares the states listed in Table 6.4 with those in Table 6.5, considerable overlap exists for the W + B and W + AIAN categories, but less for the other combinations, suggesting that in some states a particular combination is more likely to be children. For the total multiracial population, the states with the highest proportions children tend to be states that are in the middle of the country and not very diverse. For example, in Iowa, 59% of the multiracial population is children, and in Nebraska and Utah, it is about 57%, falling to 56% in Minnesota, Indiana, and Wisconsin. The states where the multiracial population is least likely to be children are the District of Columbia, Hawaii, New York, and Vermont, which range from 25% to 40% children. This finding suggests that the multiracial population is the result of intermarriage in states that are not very diverse. However, it is true that in every state there are substantial proportions of both children and adults in the multiracial population, so children and adults are part of the population throughout the county even though one age dominates more in some places than in others.

Table 6.5 Dissimilarity of People of Two or More Races vs. Non-Hispanic Single Race Groups, 2000–2010

Panel A. 2000

	Whites	Blacks	American Indians	Asians	NHOPI	SOR	Hispanics
Total	0.228	0.361	0.451	0.223	0.434	0.211	0.334
Adults	0.239	0.358	0.436	0.211	0.422	0.225	0.319
Children	0.225	0.373	0.495	0.246	0.465	0.223	0.360

Panel B. 2010

	Whites	Blacks	American Indians	Asians	NHOPI	SOR	Hispanics
Total	0.191	0.344	0.436	0.263	0.449	0.249	0.351
Adults	0.213	0.356	0.420	0.249	0.421	0.274	0.338
Children	0.183	0.334	0.488	0.269	0.491	0.214	0.358

Panel C. Change 2000–2010

	Whites	Blacks	American Indians	Asians	NHOPI	SOR	Hispanics
Total	0.037	0.017	0.015	−0.040	−0.015	−0.038	−0.017
Adults	0.026	0.002	0.016	−0.038	0.001	−0.049	−0.019
Children	0.042	0.039	0.007	−0.023	−0.026	0.009	0.002

Source: Author's calculation from Census 2000 SF1 Tables P4 and P6 and Census 2010 SF1 Tables 9 and 11.

Which Single Race Groups Are Multiracial Adults and Children Near?

One way of conceptualizing where multiracial people live and who they potentially associate with is to calculate how evenly they are distributed across the United States in relation to single race populations. If multiracial people are found primarily in states with large populations of the groups that define them as multiracial, that implies a different scenario for integration than if they are found in states where their component single race groups are scarce. Using the Index of Dissimilarity, Table 6.5 shows the segregation of the multiracial population as a whole, and separately for children and adults, from each of the non-Hispanic single race categories as well as from all Hispanics. The top panel reports the scores from 2000, the middle panel the 2010 scores, and the bottom panel the difference between the two years.

Looking at the first column, the low segregation of the multiracial population from non-Hispanic whites is particularly interesting: the score of .228 in 2000 implies that only 23% of either non-Hispanic whites or the multiracial population would have to move to be evenly distributed across the states. By 2010, this number declined to .191, implying the multiracial population became more evenly distributed during the decade. For both multiracial children and adults, segregation from non-Hispanic whites is low and declined by three to four points over the decade. Since the non-Hispanic white population is found in all states of the United States, these segregation scores suggest that the multiracial population is not unevenly distributed across states.[5]

The multiracial population is much more segregated at the state level from all the non-white single race groups, with 2010 scores of .436 and .449 for American Indians and NHOPIs and .344 and .351 for blacks and Hispanics. Scores for the segregation of multiracial people from Asians and those of SOR are lower but still higher than those for the multiracial population and non-Hispanic whites. The segregation of multiracial people from blacks and Native American and Alaskan Natives declined by a couple of points over the decade, but it increased by four points for Asians and a couple of points for the other groups.

Comparing the segregation of adults to children reveals that multiracial children are slightly less segregated from whites than adults (.225 vs. .239 in 2000 and .213 vs. .183 in 2010). In both years, multiracial children are more segregated than adults from the other racial groups, as well as from Hispanics, though in 2010 they are less segregated from blacks than adults are. A possible interpretation of this result is that the multiracial children are more likely to have at least one white parent, and hence live closer to whites than to minorities. Still, these segregation scores are generally lower than what we might expect given research on single racial groups (Logan and Stults 2011; Logan et al. 2004; Massey and Denton 1993).

What About Specific Combinations of Races?

Turning now to a more detailed examination of specific combinations of races, Table 6.6 presents, separately for adults and children, the segregation of 14 specific multiracial combinations from four single race groups, each defined as non-Hispanic: whites, blacks, American Indian and Alaskan Natives, and Asians.[6] Given relatively small changes between 2000 and 2010, Table 6.6 contains 2010 information only. Several patterns stand out in the table. First, for both children and adults, segregation of specific multiracial combinations tends to be lowest from non-Hispanic whites. Though there is quite a range of scores, from .093 to .709 for W + B and A + NHOPI, respectively, the segregation of multiracial children is generally lowest from whites, as is the segregation of adults. Second, regardless of the initial level of segregation from whites, the scores are uniformly higher between the multiracial combination and blacks. Given the influence of the rule of hypodescent in the United States, this is a bit of a surprise. Third, segregation is also generally higher from American Indians and Alaskan Natives than from whites. The pattern of changes between segregation from blacks and that from AIANs is not as easily described; sometimes the multiracial group is more segregated from AIANs than from blacks, sometimes less. Last, the segregation of the multiracial groups from Asians is generally lower than their segregation from either blacks or AIANs, often lower than their segregation from whites for both children and adults.

Examining specific combinations of races in Table 6.6 reveals that combinations that include Native Hawaiians or Other Pacific Islanders tend to be more highly segregated, no doubt because this group is so heavily concentrated in Hawaii. Combinations that include American Indians and Alaskan Natives are also quite highly segregated compared with those that include whites, blacks, or Asians, again most likely because of the geographical concentration of the AIAN group. While it is clear that there is great variety in terms of how the multiracial combinations are distributed across the states with regard to the single race groups, no clear pattern relating to specific combinations is easily discerned.

Since Table 6.5 suggested that, as a group, multiracial children were less segregated from non-Hispanic whites but more segregated from other races, the third panel of Table 6.6 compares the segregation for children and adults by subtracting the children's segregation score from the adults'. Negative scores therefore mean that children are *more* segregated than adults, while positive ones mean that adults are more segregated. The numbers in this panel of the table are uniformly quite small, with only five of them being .1 or more, so the difference in percentage points between the segregation of children and adults is usually less than ten points. In another 11 cases, it is between five and ten points, so for

Table 6.6 Dissimilarity of Children and Adults in Specific Multiple Race Combinations from Non-Hispanic Single Race People, 2010

Panel A. Children

From Non-Hispanic

Two Race Groups:	White Alone:	Black alone:	AIAN alone:	Asian alone:
WH_BL	0.093	0.259	0.515	0.359
WH_AIAN	0.290	0.469	0.310	0.453
WH_AS	0.297	0.417	0.548	0.155
WH_NHOPI	0.487	0.608	0.559	0.387
BL_AIAN	0.226	0.270	0.431	0.355
BL_AS	0.327	0.315	0.582	0.169
BL_NHOPI	0.349	0.376	0.578	0.249
AIAN_AS	0.366	0.473	0.494	0.191
AIAN_NHOPI	0.578	0.682	0.407	0.526
AS_NHOPI	0.709	0.775	0.703	0.536

Three Race Groups:

WH_BL_AIAN	0.185	0.338	0.456	0.342
WH_BL_AS	0.295	0.361	0.548	0.242
WH_AIAN_AS	0.406	0.532	0.476	0.308
WH_AS_NHOPI	0.698	0.785	0.693	0.617

Panel B. Adults

From Non-Hispanic

Two Race Groups:	White Alone:	Black alone:	AIAN alone:	Asian alone:
WH_BL	0.113	0.274	0.454	0.306
WH_AIAN	0.227	0.403	0.313	0.420
WH_AS	0.304	0.419	0.481	0.158
WH_NHOPI	0.472	0.588	0.504	0.346
BL_AIAN	0.208	0.212	0.451	0.331
BL_AS	0.332	0.323	0.536	0.235
BL_NHOPI	0.381	0.372	0.584	0.356
AIAN_AS	0.342	0.422	0.493	0.165
AIAN_NHOPI	0.458	0.571	0.387	0.387
AS_NHOPI	0.613	0.695	0.611	0.408
WH_BL_AIAN	0.172	0.274	0.445	0.306
WH_BL_AS	0.306	0.338	0.510	0.215
WH_AIAN_AS	0.378	0.507	0.444	0.275
WH_AS_NHOPI	0.692	0.778	0.673	0.601

(continued)

Table 6.6 (continued)

Panel C. Adults–Children

	From Non-Hispanic			
Two Race Groups:	White Alone:	Black alone:	AIAN alone:	Asian alone:
WH_BL	0.02	0.015	−0.061	−0.053
WH_AIAN	−0.063	−0.066	0.003	−0.033
WH_AS	0.007	0.002	−0.067	0.003
WH_NHOPI	−0.015	−0.02	−0.055	−0.041
BL_AIAN	−0.018	−0.058	0.02	−0.024
BL_AS	0.005	0.008	−0.046	0.066
BL_NHOPI	0.032	−0.004	0.006	0.107
AIAN_AS	−0.024	−0.051	−0.001	−0.026
AIAN_NHOPI	−0.12	−0.111	−0.02	−0.139
AS_NHOPI	−0.096	−0.08	−0.092	−0.128
Three Race Groups:				
WH_BL_AIAN	−0.013	−0.064	−0.011	−0.036
WH_BL_AS	0.011	−0.023	−0.038	−0.027
WH_AIAN_AS	−0.028	−0.025	−0.032	−0.033
WH_AS_NHOPI	−0.006	−0.007	−0.02	−0.016

Source:
Author's Calculations from Census 2010 SF1 Tables P9 and P 11.

the majority of scores in panel c, children and adults are about equally segregated from the single race groups. What is more interesting is that in combinations that contain Native Hawaiian and Other Pacific Islanders (NHOPI) or American Indian or Alaska Native (AIAN), children tend to be more segregated than adults. All of the cases where children are ten points more segregated than adults contain NHOPI as one of the combinations, with AIAN-NHOPI children being much more segregated from whites, blacks, and Asians than the adult members of this group.

In terms of substantive meaning, multiracial children are less segregated from whites, as only half of the combinations in that column are negative and most are quite small. A similar pattern can be seen for segregation of children from blacks and Asians. However, for 10 or the 14 combinations shown, children are more segregated than adults from the AIAN population. While a difference in an index of dissimilarity of a couple of points is not usually important, a difference of eight or ten points is more likely to be meaningful. Since children live with families, the differences in segregation between children and adults are suggestive of differences in who claimed multiple racial identifications or had them claimed for them since if the entire household was multiracial, then they would live in the same state and not be segregated. At the same time, it must be noted that these segregation indices are computed at a very high level of aggregation, namely, the state level, and the actual location of the children and the adults is not really known from these data.

DISCUSSION AND FUTURE RESEARCH

As often happens, this chapter raises almost as many questions as it answers, though it is appropriate to first summarize what has been learned. The expected 20% increase in the multiracial population the 2009 ACS expected for the 2010 Census was too low, and the group actually increased 29.6%, thus confirming the importance of the multiracial population. Focusing at the state level, this chapter has examined the location of the multiracial population in more detail than has been done in past studies. The location of the multiracial population is partly connected to immigration and partly to the location of homelands of indigenous peoples, but these two facts hardly tell the whole story. Particularly with regard to immigration, there is great variation in the presence of the multiracial population across the gateway states. Measured across states, the dissimilarity index, measuring the evenness of population distribution, is in the low to moderate range, though there is considerable variability, especially when specific combinations of multiple races are considered. Children tend to be somewhat more segregated than adults, though mixed white and black children are five points less segregated from whites than adults of the same racial combination.

The most obvious future research needed is to incorporate more characteristics of the multiracial population into the analysis. In order to better understand this group, we need to know more about them in terms of their education, occupation, income, family and household, and homeownership status. In addition, investigation of the multiracial options among the Hispanic population is also warranted. Using micro-data is the only way to do this as the summary data used in this chapter do not contain any socioeconomic data for detailed multiple race combinations. Though an exploration of the characteristics of the multiple race children and adults turned out to be beyond the scope of this chapter, it is an important topic. Other research has shown income, age, and locational differences between multiracial and monoracial American Indian and Alaskan Natives, Native Hawaiian and Pacific Islanders, Asians, and blacks. For the first two groups, the multiracial are advantaged in terms of income, but the opposite is true for the latter two groups (Liebler and Halpern-Manners 2008). In particular, looking at specific combinations of races in terms of their socioeconomic status would provide a clue as to how the multiple race population will fare in U.S. society in years to come. As they grow more numerous, they may play a role in determining the color line (Alba 2009; Bonilla-Silva 2006; Lee and Bean 2004).

A second path for future investigation is to look at variation in the location of the multiple race population within states, initially across counties, but possibly within metropolitan areas as well. Profiles of neighborhood residence characteristics would also be of interest. Issues of assimilation are very dependent on where one lives (Alba and Nee 2005; Massey and Denton 1993). However, these locational analyses must take into account the sparse distribution of this population. Perhaps a sensible approach is to focus just on a few specific combinations in a few locations to get a sense of their neighborhood environments is the way to begin.

In closing, I must note that while I remain fascinated by the multiracial population, and by the detailed combinations made available in the data, actually working with these data did raise questions as to their usefulness. In particular, it is clear that releasing the results of all 63 combinations, cross classified by Hispanic origin, and separately for those over the age of 18, down to the block level, raises issues of confidentiality. That in turn limits what can be learned about each of the combinations of races. Sacrificing some geographic detail for more characteristics would seem in order. Also, it is fair to ask how much other data could be produced if so much energy were not devoted to producing the race data, much of which is empty cells.

Still, as the world becomes more interconnected in many ways, the importance of people whose background reflects that interconnection can only increase. Immigration from Asia and Africa shows no sign of decreasing, nor does that from Latin and South America. How mulitracial persons, including those of Hispanic ethnicity, integrate into society, where they live, and how socially near or distant they are from monoracial people will in important ways determine the future cohesion of society. So learning how to count the multiracial population in ways that make meaningful study possible is a crucial social science endeavor for the 21st century.

NOTES

1. In the remainder of this chapter, the discussion will pertain to the non-Hispanic multiple race population. While the Hispanic multiple race population is of interest, more than two-thirds of the Hispanics who chose more than one race listed Some Other Race as the other race. Since Hispanics make up 97% of the Some Other Race category, their choice of this most likely reflects the fact that they consider Hispanic to be their race. It is notable, however, that just over 6% of the Hispanic population was of two of more races in 2010 compared with only 2.3% of the non-Hispanic population.
2. Footnote 13 from Grieco et al. (2011) is reprinted here: "In Census 2000, an error in data processing resulted in an overstatement of the Two or More Races population by about 1 million people (about 15 percent) nationally, which almost entirely affected race combinations involving Some Other Race. Therefore, data users should assess observed changes in the Two or More Races population and race combinations involving Some Other Race between Census 2000 and the 2010 Census with caution. Changes in specific multiple- race combinations not involving Some Other Race, such as White and Black or White and Asian, generally, should be more comparable."
3. This is also true of combinations involving SOR, though it is difficult to know how to interpret these answers since Hispanics are not included here.
4. Though the bottom category of the legend in Figure 6.1 is 0.0%, there are actually some multiracial people in all 50 states plus the District of Columbia. However, in some states, they are less than 1% of the population.

5. Given the issues with the SOR data in 2000, the segregation of the multiracial population from them is included in the table for completeness but is not discussed in the text.
6. The location of the NHOPI population is predominately in Hawaii, and the difficulty interpreting the SOR group is the reason for excluding these groups as comparisons. Total segregation scores are not presented as the segregation of adults and children separately is of greater interest and captures the same information.

REFERENCES

Alba, Richard. 2009. *Blurring the Color Line: The New Chance for a More Integrated America.* Cambridge, MA: Harvard University Press.
Alba, Richard, and Victor Nee. 2005. *Remaking the American Mainstream: Assimilation and Contemporary Immigration.* Cambridge, MA: Harvard University Press.
Bonilla-Silva, Eduardo. 2006. *Racism Without Racists: Color-Blind Racism and the Persistence of Racial Inequality in the United States,* 2nd edition. Lanham, MD: Rowman & Littlefield Publishers, Inc.
Brunsma, David L. 2005. "Interracial Families and the Racial Identification of Mixed-Race Children: Evidence from the Early Childhood Longitudinal Study." *Social Forces* 84(2):1131–57.
Cresce, Arthur R., Audrey Dianne Schmidley, and Roberto R. Ramirez. 2004. "Identification of Hispanic Ethnicity in Census 2000: Analysis of Data Quality for the Question on Hispanic Origin." Washington, DC: US Bureau of the Census, Working Paper No. 75. http://www.census.gov/population/www/documentation/twps0075/twps0075.pdf
Denton, Nancy A., and Glenn D. Deane. 2010. "Researching Race and Ethnicity: Methodological Issues." In *Handbook of Race and Ethnic Studies,* edited by Patricia Hill Collins and John Solomos, 66–88. London: Sage Publications.
Doyle, Jamie Mihoko, and Grace Kao. 2007. "Are Racial Identities of Multiracials Stable? Changing Self-Identification Among Single and Multiple Race Individuals." *Social Psychological Quarterly* 70(4):405–23.
Farley, Reynolds. 2002. "Racial Identities in 2000: The Response to the Multiple-Race Response Option." In *The New Race Question: How the Census Counts Multiracial Individuals,* edited by Joel Perlmann and Mary C. Waters, 33–61. New York: Russell Sage Foundation.
Farley, Reynolds. 2004. "Identifying with Multiple Races: A Social Movement That Succeeded but Failed?" In *The Changing Terrain of Race and Ethnicity,* edited by Maria Krysan and Amanda E. Lewis, 123–48. New York: Russell Sage Foundation.
Frey, William H. 2011. "Multiracial Population and Profile." Accessed November 1, 2011. www.censusscope.org.
Frey, William H., and Dowell Myers. 2002, July. "Neighborhood Segregation in Single-Race and Multirace America: A Census 2000 Study of Cities and Metropolitan Areas." Fannie Mae Foundation Working Paper. Washington, DC: Fannie Mae Foundation.
Goldstein, Joshua R., and Ann J. Morning. 2000. "The Multiple-Race Population of the United States: Issues and Estimates." *Proceedings of the National Academy of Science* 97(11):6230–35.
Goldstein, Joshua R., and Ann J. Morning. 2002. "Back in the Box: The Dilemma of Using Multiple-Race Data for Single-Race Laws." In *The New Race Question: How the Census Counts Multiracial Individuals,* edited

by Joel Perlmann and Mary C. Waters, 119–36. New York: Russell Sage Foundation.
Grieco, Elizabeth M., and Rachel C. Cassidy. 2001, March. "Overview of Race and Hispanic Origin." U.S. Bureau of the Census. 2000 Census Briefs, C2KBR/01–1.
Harris, David R. 2002. "Does It Matter How We Measure? Racial Classification and the Characteristics of Multiracial Youth." In *The New Race Question: How the Census Counts Multiracial Individuals*, edited by Joel Perlmann and Mary C. Waters, 62–101. New York: Russell Sage Foundation.
Harris, David, and Jeremiah Sim. 2002. "Who Is Multiracial? Assessing the Complexity of Lived Race." *American Sociological Review* 67:614–27.
Harrison, Roderick J. 2002. "Inadequacies of Multiple-Response Race Data in the Federal Statistical System." In *The New Race Question: How the Census Counts Multiracial Individuals*, edited by Joel Perlmann and Mary C. Waters, 137–60. New York: Russell Sage Foundation.
Herman, Melissa. 2004. "Forced to Choose: Some Determinants of Racial Identification in Multiracial Adolescents." *Child Development* 75(3):730–48.
Hirschman, Charles, Richard Alba, and Reynolds Farley. 2000. "The Meaning and Measurement of Race in the U.S. Census: Glimpses into the Future." *Demography* 37(August):381–93.
Hitlin, Steven, J. Scott Brown, and Glen H. Elder, Jr. 2007. "Measuring Latinos: Racial vs. Ethnic Classification and Self-Understandings." *Social Forces* 86(2):587–611.
Humes, Karen R., Nicholas A. Jones, and Roberto Ramirez. 2011, March. "Overview of Race and Hispanic Origin: 2010." U.S. Bureau of the Census. 2010 Census Briefs, C2010BR-02.
Jones, Nicholas A. 2005. "We the People of More Than One Race in the United States." In *Census 2000 Special Reports*, 1–19. Washington, DC: The U.S. Bureau of the Census.
Jones, Nicholas A., and Amy Symens Smith. 2001. "The Two or More Races Population: 2000." In *Census 2000 Brief*, 1–10. Washington, DC: The U.S. Bureau of the Census.
Kanaiupuni, Shawn Malia, and Carolyn A. Liebler. 2005. "Pondering Poi Dog: The Importance of Place to the Racial Identification of Mixed-Race Native Hawaiians." *Ethnic and Racial Studies* 28(4):687–721.
Lee, Jennifer, and Frank D. Bean. 2004. "America's Changing Color Lines: Immigration, Race/Ethnicity, and Multiracial Identification." *Annual Review of Sociology* 30:221–42.
Liebler, Carolyn A. 2010. "Homelands and Indigenous Identities in a Multiracial Era." *Social Science Research* 39:596–609.
Liebler, Carolyn A., and Andrew Halpern-Manners. 2008. "A Practical Approach to Using Multiple-Race Response Data: A Bridging Methodology for Public Use Microdata." *Demography* 45(1):143–55.
Logan, John R., and Brian J. Stults. 2011. "The Persistence of Segregation in the Metropolis: New Findings from the 2010 Census." Accessed March 24, 2011. http://www.s4.brown.edu/us2010/Data/Report/report2.pdf
Logan, John R., Brian J. Stults, and Reynolds Farley. 2004. "Segregation of Minorities in the Metropolis: Two Decades of Change." *Demography* 41(1):1–22.
Martin, Elizabeth, Theresa J. DeMaio, and Pamela C. Campanelli. 1990. "Context Effects for Census: Measures of Race and Hispanic Origin." *Public Opinion Quarterly* 54:551–66.
Massey, Douglas S., Joaquin Arango, Graeme Hugo, Ali Kouaouci, Adela Pellegrino, and J. Edward Taylor. 2005. *Worlds in Motion: Understanding International Migration at the End of the Millennium*. London: Oxford University Press.

Massey, Douglas S., and Nancy A. Denton. 1993. *American Apartheid: Segregation and the Making of the Underclass*. Cambridge, MA: Harvard University Press.

Office of Management and Budget, Executive Office of the President. 1997a. "Revisions to the Standards for the Classification of Federal Data on Race and Ethnicity." *Federal Register* 62(10):58782–790.

Office of Management and Budget, Executive Office of the President. 1997b. "Recommendations From the Interagency Committee for the Review of the Race and Ethnic Standards to the Office of Management and Budget Concerning Changes to the Standards for the Classification of Federal Data on Race and Ethnicity." *Federal Register* 62(131): 36873–6946.

Office of Management and Budget, Executive Office of the President. 2001. "Provisional Guidance on the Implementation of the 1997 Standards for Federal Data on Race and Ethnicity." *Federal Register* (because of its length, this document is not reproduced in the Federal Register, but is available electronically from the OMB web site: www.whitehouse.gov/omb/fedreg/index.html).

Parker, J. D., and Makuc, D. M. 2002. "Methodologic Implications of Allocating Multiple-Race Data to Single-Race Categories." *Health Services Research* 37(1):201–13.

Perlmann, Joel, and Mary C. Waters, eds. 2002. *The New Race Question: How the Census Counts Multiracial Individuals*. New York: Russell Sage Foundation.

Snipp, C. Matthew. 2002. "American Indians: Clues to the Future of Other Racial Groups." In *The New Race Question: How the Census Counts Multiracial Individuals*, edited by Joel Perlmann and Mary C. Waters, 189–214. New York: Russell Sage Foundation.

Snipp, C. Matthew. 2003. "Racial Measurement in the American Census: Past Practices and Implications for the Future." *Annual Review of Sociology* 29:563–88.

Stephan, Cookie White, and Walter G. Stephan. 1989. "After Intermarriage: Ethnic Identity among Mixed-heritage Japanese-Americans and Hispanics." *Journal of Marriage and the Family* 51:507–19.

Tafoya, Sonya M., Hans Johnson, and Laura E. Hill. 2004. *Who Chooses to Choose Two?* New York: Russell Sage Foundation; Washington, DC: Population Reference Bureau.

Tucker, Clyde, Steve Miller, and Jennifer Parker. 2002. "Comparing Census Race Data Under the Old and the New Standards." In *The New Race Question: How the Census Counts Multiracial Individuals*, edited by Joel Perlmann and Mary C. Waters, 365–90. New York: Russell Sage Foundation.

Waters, Mary C. 1990. *Ethnic Options: Choosing Identities in America*. Berkeley: University of California Press.

Waters, Mary C. 1999. *Black Identities: West Indian Immigrant Dreams and American Realities*. Cambridge and New York: Harvard and Russell Sage.

Xie, Yu, and Kimberly Goyette. 1997. "The Racial Identification of Biracial Children with One Asian Parent: Evidence from the 1990 Census." *Social Forces* 76:547–57.

Zuberi, Tukufu. 2001. *Thicker Than Blood: How Racial Statistics Lie*. Minneapolis: University of Minnesota Press.

Zuberi, Tukufu, and Eduardo Bonilla-Silva, eds. 2008. *White Logic, White Methods: Racism and Methodology*. Lanham, MD: Rowman and Littlefield.

7 Openness to Inter-ethnic Relationships for Chinese and South Asian Canadians
The Role of Canadian Identity

Richard N. Lalonde and Ayse K. Uskul

INTRODUCTION

Social scientists have a long-standing interest in the study of intimate interpersonal relationships. Historically, intimate relationships have usually been endogamous in nature. Endogamy is the practice of marrying within one's social groups (e.g., ethnicity, race, social class, religion). In fact, there have been social prescriptions, past and present, against exogamy (out-marriage). For example, an anti-miscegenation law was passed in the United States in 1880, which prohibited marriage between whites and "Mongolians," and it was not overturned until 1948 (Fujino 2000). Whereas endogamy in intimate relationships has been the universal norm, a number of situational and psychological factors can lead individuals to engage in interracial or inter-ethnic relationships. Immigration and the creation of multicultural states clearly provide opportunities for forming inter-ethnic relationships. From an intergroup relations perspective, intimate inter-ethnic relationships can be viewed as exemplars of relationships where the social distance between two members of different ethnic groups has been fully bridged. Moreover, the greater the number of inter-ethnic couples in a multi-ethnic society, the more the boundaries between groups will be seen as permeable.

In the first part of this chapter, we will review the existing literature on immigration and intermarriage, with a particular focus on Asian immigration in a North American context. In the second part of this chapter, one factor in particular, national or Canadian identity, will be examined in relation to attitudes toward interracial dating among second-generation immigrants within the multicultural context of Canada. Attitudes toward inter-ethnic and interracial relationships as well as intergroup dating experiences can be seen as important psychological precursors to exogamy (e.g., King and Bratter 2007). Moreover, such intimate intergroup relationships meet the criteria for facilitating positive intergroup contact; when these relationships are successful, they should foster prejudice reduction within a society because they can impact the extended family and friends of the individuals involved in the relationships (i.e., the extended-contact hypothesis; Wright, Aron, McLaughlin-Volpe, and Ropp 1997).

The Social Norm of Endogamy

Prior to the industrial revolution of the 19th century and large-scale migration to cities, individuals within villages shared similar social features (e.g., ethnicity, language, religion), and thus their relationships with each other were endogamous. With the advent of the industrial revolution and rural migration to urban centers, the homogeneity of social networks began to dissipate. These changes impacted the structure and nature of families. Thornton and Fricke (1987) offered a comparative analysis of the West, China, and South Asia regarding social change and the family. They argued that many of the changes that took place across these three settings were quite similar (e.g., separation of workplace from the home). Other aspects of change, however, varied across settings. One of these was the importance of maintaining kinships and alliances through marriage (i.e., endogamy). In some South Asian settings, for example, arranged marriages or even consanguineous marriages (i.e., between relatives) continued to be relatively common (e.g., Hussain 1999) while Western norms regarding marriage have changed quite rapidly.

Many of the social-psychological factors that are conducive to friendship and relationship formation help to buttress the norm of endogamy. Dwyer (2000) outlined three of these factors in her book, *Interpersonal Relationships*. First among them is the concept of *propinquity* or *proximity*. We tend to form relationships with the people we are more likely to encounter; these people are in close physical proximity and surround us. The second factor she described is *similarity*. A number of studies have shown that we tend to like individuals who are similar to ourselves in terms of ethnicity, personality, attitudes, and values. A third factor influencing relationship formation is *physical attraction*. Given that attractiveness is in part culturally relative, we would expect individuals to find individuals from their in-groups as somewhat more attractive than individuals from out-groups. Let us now examine the nature of endogamy in the North American immigration context and see how some of the above factors play out in this context.

The Immigration Experience and Intermarriage

Individuals in Western settlement societies typically pair off with someone they have previously met. These potential partners usually come from a pool delineated by their neighborhoods, schools, places of work, and recreational activities. Immigrants arriving in the new host Western country will encounter greater ethnic, racial, and religious diversity in their places of residence and work than they did in their country of origin. This greater exposure to out-group members should impact the likelihood of individuals engaging in intergroup unions of an intimate nature (particularly for the children of immigrants) and having mixed background children. In Canada, the percentage of individuals indicating more than one ethnic ancestry is ever increasing (36% in 1996, 38% in 2001, 41% in 2006; Statistics Canada, 2008). These rather large percentages can be attributed to Canadians whose European ancestors came in earlier immigration periods (e.g., French, Scots, Germans, Ukrainians) and who subsequently intermarried. With the rapid rise of immigrants coming from the East to North America, recent studies have focused on examining Asian intermarriages in North America (e.g., Okamoto 2007; Qian, Blair, and Ruf 2001). We now turn to a summary of this literature.

A study by Lee and Boyd (2008) compared levels of endogamy for Asians in the United States and Canada on the basis of the 2000 U.S. census and the 2001 Canadian census. Results indicated that overall rates of endogamy were about 80% for Asian American couples and 92% for Asian Canadian couples. Of the couples who engaged in exogamy, the majority involved intermarriage with a white partner (65% in the United States and 73% in Canada), and Asian women were more likely to intermarry than Asian men. Exogamy rates, moreover, were not the same for all Asian ethnic groups. Whereas exogamy was quite high for the Japanese (41% in the United States and 49% in Canada), it was much lower for individuals of Chinese (14% in United States and 6% in Canada) and South Asian (9% in the United States and 5% in Canada) ancestries. In addition to gender, immigrant generational status also played a role. For all Asian ethnic groups (except for the Japanese), the longer the exposure to the Western culture, the more likely they were to intermarry. For example, whereas the percentage of intermarriage was about 48% for native-born Chinese Americans, it was only about 10% for foreign-born Chinese Americans (44% vs. 5% in Canada). Lee and Boyd (2008) concluded their comparative analysis by stating that Asians in Canada and United States are more similar than different in their patterns of intermarriages. The one key difference was that rates of Asian exogamy were lower in Canada than in the United States, which may be attributed to the fact that Asian immigrants, dominated by two ethnic groups (Chinese and South Asians), are geographically more concentrated in urban centers in Canada (e.g., the metropolitan areas of Vancouver and Toronto) than in the United States.

Two recent studies, one from Canada (Milan, Maheux, and Chui 2010) and one from the United States (Kalmijn and van Tubergen 2010), help us further understand some of the influences on intermarriage for immigrants. Milan and colleagues (2010) used data from the 2006 Canadian census and reported a number of statistics illustrating that the norm of endogamy is strong, at least along racial lines. Only 4% of Canadian couples involved one partner who was a member of a visible minority and one who was not. Among visible minority groups, the Japanese, particularly second-generation

Canadians, were most likely to intermarry. Chinese and South Asians, the two largest visible minority groups in Canada, had the lowest proportions of exogamy, thus providing indirect evidence for a propinquity effect; given the geographic concentration of large numbers of Chinese and South Asian immigrant families in urban centers (see Fong Chapter 3; Wang and Du Chapter 9), they would have ample opportunities to meet a prospective partner from their respective ethnic groups. Finally, three additional factors were associated with a higher probability of a mixed union: age (younger compared to older adults), education (more educated compared to less educated), and area of residence (Vancouver and Toronto had the most mixed unions).

In the United States, Kalmijn and van Tubergen (2010) used pooled population surveys (1994–2006) to examine intermarriage patterns of 94 different ethnic groups. They replicated the pattern of results for Asian immigrants found by Lee and Boyd (2008), such that Japanese Americans were most likely to intermarry whereas South Asians (Indian and Pakistani origin) were most likely to be endogamous. The Chinese-speaking national origin groups (China, Hong Kong, Taiwan) fell between the Japanese and the South Asians in their intermarriage rates. Moreover, the generational status of immigrants had a strong effect; endogamy was stronger for first-generation than for second-generation immigrants. Kalmijn and van Tubergen (2010) further explored the roles of structural and cultural influences on intermarriage. From a structural perspective, they found a substantial effect for in-group size; the larger the size of the in-group, the more likely the children of immigrants would marry endogamously (see also Okamoto 2007). This is further evidence for the role of propinquity in relationship formation. From a cultural perspective, intermarriage with a white partner was more common for immigrant groups that came from nations that share characteristics of the host Western society: (1) a Christian background, (2) English as an official language, and (3) a higher rate of globalization (e.g., greater importing and exporting of books). These three cultural factors are related to the similarity factor that Dwyer (2000) reported as being a key variable in relationship formation.

Social-Psychological Research on Interracial and Inter-ethnic Dating

When it comes to interracial and inter-ethnic relationships, sociologists and social demographers have focused much of their research on marriage (see above examples). Some social psychologists, in contrast, have placed their attention on dating, which is a normative precursor to marriage in a North American context. While much of the research on interracial dating has examined black–white relationships (e.g., Lalonde, Giguère, Fontaine, & Smith, 2007), increasing attention has been directed toward the dating attitudes and behaviors of Asians in North America. Fujino (1997), for example, compared the dating practices of Chinese, Japanese, and white

American students in Los Angeles and found that, parallel to the marriage literature, Japanese Americans were more likely to have out-dated than Chinese Americans; Chinese Americans, in turn were more likely to have out-dated than white Americans. Fujino also found that propinquity (perceived proportion of whites in their home community) was a significant predictor for interracial dating with whites among both Asian women and men. Moreover, Asian women were more likely to date whites when they valued attractiveness in a dating partner.

In line with the marriage data, Levin, Taylor, and Caudle (2007) found in a large sample of California university students that Asians, African Americans, Latinos, and whites were more likely to intra-date (i.e., with in-group members) throughout their first three years of college compared with later years. Of the groups, Asian Americans were the least likely to inter-date, and this difference was more pronounced for Asian men than for Asian women. For all groups, intra-dating was related to having more close in-group friends in high school, thus providing further evidence for a propinquity effect. Finally, it was found that Asian Americans, Latinos, and whites were more likely to inter-date when they reported less pre-college in-group bias and less pre-college intergroup anxiety. For Asian American students, this latter effect was moderated by their ingroup identification; low pre-college intergroup anxiety was associated with inter-dating only for those who also had weaker pre-college Asian in-group identification.

Mok (1999) further explored the role of in-group identification in her study of interracial dating attitudes of Asian American students. She tapped into the three factors that Dwyer (2000) had identified as being important in relationship formation using a number of variables: in-group density and percentage of in-group friends as indicators of propinquity, acculturation that can be construed as an index of similarity to Americans, and perceptions of attractiveness of Asian and white Americans. Mok also assessed cultural variables such as in-group identity and parental influence. She found that the three best predictors of Asian Americans' openness to dating white Americans were being more strongly acculturated to American society, perceiving greater heterosexual attractiveness in whites, and having fewer Asian American friends.

Current Studies

Our research (Uskul, Lalonde, and Cheng 2007; Uskul, Lalonde, and Konanur 2011) has followed the social-psychological tradition of examining attitudes toward inter-ethnic or interracial dating relationships. This research was conducted in Canada, where the norm of endogamy is somewhat stronger for Asians Canadians when compared with Asian Americans (Lee and Boyd 2008). We have focused on Canada's two largest visible minority groups, Chinese Canadians and South Asian Canadians (see Wang and Du Chapter 9); both of these groups have very high rates of endogamy

(Milan et al. 2010). Finally, we have a particular interest in the attitudes of second-generation Canadians, who represent an interesting group as they have access to two sets of potentially contradictory cultural norms (heritage and mainstream Canadian) regarding dating and marriage.

Second-generation immigrants have been socialized by their family to value their heritage cultural identity by their parents and other family members, who tend to emphasize the continuation of their own heritage values and norms through their children. In a study of parenting goals among South Asian Canadian mothers, Maiter and George (2003) found that *identity formation* appeared as one of the most important parenting goals in this group. Mothers felt that not educating their children about South Asian culture would leave them without a sense of belongingness and without a strong heritage identity.

While heritage cultural identity may play an important role in the shaping of immigrants' overall identity and ensuring cultural continuity, first- and second-generation immigrants also acquire a mainstream cultural identity. Moreover, heritage and mainstream cultural identities have been shown to be independent from each other in their influence on the acculturation process among different Chinese immigrant samples in Canada (Ryder, Alden, and Paulhus 2000) and the United States (Tsai, Ying, and Lee 2000). Ryder et al. (2000) found that identification with the mainstream culture was a significant positive predictor of psychosocial adjustment for Chinese Canadians, whereas heritage culture identification was unrelated to adjustment. Lalonde, Hynie, Pannu, and Tatla (2004) found that heritage cultural identity was related to South Asian Canadians' preference for traditional attributes in a mate, but not mainstream cultural identity.

Immigrants are likely to be pulled and pushed by their heritage and mainstream identities and each culture's norms when engaging in their close interpersonal relationships. Integration, the most popular acculturation strategy (e.g., Phinney, Berry, Vedder, and Liebkind 2006), involves simultaneous identification with the heritage culture and participation in the mainstream culture (Berry 1980). With respect to views toward intergroup dating, both heritage and mainstream identities may play a role in the shaping of these views, albeit in opposite directions. In-group identification would be expected to drive stronger preferences and dating norms for endogamy (i.e., preference for traditional attributes in a mate; marrying or dating within one's heritage ethnic group), whereas identification with the majority culture would be expected to drive greater openness to exogamy (dating or marrying outside one's ethnic group). Given that Canadian identity and pride have been associated with greater acceptance and encouragement of ethnic diversity (Cameron and Berry, 2008; Lalonde 2002), Canadian national identification should be related to one's openness to inter-ethnic relationships. Moreover, Canadian identity can be construed as a superordinate or common identity for all Canadians regardless of ethnicity. Thus, it should facilitate more openness to out-group members (cf., common ingroup identity model; Gaertner and Dovidio 2000). West, Pearson, Dovidio, Shelton, and Trail (2009), for example, found that perceptions of a common identity among randomly assigned college roommates facilitated the development of cross-group friendships.

Selected findings from two of our recent studies will be reported in this chapter. The first study (Uskul et al. 2007) involved a cross-cultural comparison of young Chinese and European Canadians and their views on interracial dating. The second study (Uskul et al. 2011) involved a cross-cultural comparison of both younger and older South Asian and European Canadians and their views on interracial dating. Details of the statistical analyses (i.e., inferential statistics regarding comparisons of group means) can be found in these articles. Selected aspects of the data from these studies will be examined to explicitly focus on a cultural (heritage and Canadian) identity hypothesis.

It was predicted that the superordinate national Canadian identity, rather than heritage identity, would drive the views of first- and second-generation Canadians about interracial dating. The assumption is that whereas in-group identification may be associated with an ethnic in-group orientation in interpersonal relationships (i.e., intragroup dating), identification with the national culture would be more likely to lead individuals to contemplate others who belong to the larger national in-group, and this would include others who are not necessarily members of the ethnic ingroup. Stronger endorsement of Canadian identity, therefore, was expected to be associated with more favorable attitudes toward interracial dating (i.e., *superordinate identity hypothesis*).

Study 1—A Comparison of Young Chinese Canadians and European Canadian Participants

Participants were 61 Chinese Canadian (30 women and 31 men) and 59 European Canadian (30 women and 29 men) students from a large multicultural university in Toronto. Their average age was 22 years. The sample, therefore, was at an age where dating is acceptable by Canadian norms. All European Canadians self-identified as white, and all Chinese Canadians self-identified as Asian. The majority of the European Canadians were born in Canada (80%). The percentage of Canadian-born Chinese was 39.3%, while the bulk of the remaining sample was born in China or Hong Kong (44.3%). The mean age of arrival to Canada for those born outside of Canada was 11.5 years for the European Canadians and 12.6 years for the Chinese Canadians.

The demographic split on country of birth for Chinese Canadians (i.e., those born outside and inside Canada) permitted us to examine differences in the views on interracial dating between first- and second-generation immigrants. Chinese Canadians born in Canada tended to be more personally open to interracial dating ($M = 5.70$) than Chinese Canadians born in Asia ($M = 4.95$). Second-generation Chinese Canadians also endorsed a stronger Canadian identity ($M = 5.70$) than first-generation respondents ($M = 4.76$), but the two groups did not differ in level of heritage culture identity. Chinese Canadians who had spent more of their lives in Canada, therefore, were more likely to be open to the norms of that society, but they still maintained stable levels of identification with their heritage culture (see Cheung, Chudek, and Heine 2011).

In terms of interracial dating, 51% of the European Canadians (13 men, 17 women) reported being currently in or having previously been in an interracial relationship, in comparison with 28% of the Chinese Canadians (6 men, 11 women). This differential pattern of greater interracial dating for European Canadians compared with Chinese Canadians was significant.

Measures

All scale items were assessed with seven-point Likert-type scales, ranging from 1 (*strongly disagree*) to 7 (*strongly agree*). All participants completed the questionnaire in English.

Social Identifications

Cameron's (2004) 12-item measure of social identity assessed the degree of both Canadian and heritage culture identification (e.g., "In general, I'm glad to be Canadian" and "I feel strong ties to other heritage group members"). Participants were asked to reiterate their ethnic identity before completing items relating to their heritage culture. The Cronbach alpha reliability coefficients for Canadian identity and heritage identities, respectively, were all equal to or above .82 for both samples.

Attitudes toward Interracial Dating

Fifteen items were adapted from a study on interracial dating between European Canadian and Black Canadians (Lalonde et al. 2007). This measure assessed two distinct components of dating attitudes that loaded onto separate factors in a factor analysis: one tapped general attitudes toward interracial dating (nine items, e.g., "It does not bother me if Chinese [white] people date white [Chinese] people"), and the other assessed personal openness to interracial dating (six items, e.g., "I would date a Chinese [white] person"). Items were adjusted such that the European Canadians were asked about dating Chinese, and the Chinese Canadians were asked about dating whites. The Cronbach alpha reliability coefficients for the general attitude and for personal openness to interracial dating, respectively, were all equal to or above .88 for both samples.

Results and Discussion

A Group (Chinese Canadian, European Canadian) by Gender ANOVA was first conducted for each interracial dating attitude measure. General attitude toward interracial dating was associated with significant main effects for Group and Gender, as well as a Group by Gender interaction. The personal openness to interracial dating measure was associated with a significant Group effect, as well as a significant Group by Gender interaction. Both Group effects indicated that European Canadians had a more favorable attitude and were more open to interracial dating than Chinese Canadians.

An examination of the Group by Gender interactions indicated that the responses of male Chinese Canadians were driving the interaction effects. In their general attitudes toward interracial dating, Chinese Canadian females ($M = 6.52$) were very similar to European Canadian females ($M = 6.68$) and European Canadian males ($M = 6.58$). In their personal openness to interracial dating, Chinese Canadian females ($M = 5.54$) were again similar to European Canadian females ($M = 5.53$), both of whom were less personally open to interracial dating than were European Canadian males ($M = 6.19$). Chinese Canadian males, however, were less favorable than European Canadian males both in their general attitudes toward interracial dating ($M = 5.60$) and in their personal openness to interracial dating ($M = 5.08$). Chinese Canadian males also had significantly less favorable general attitudes toward interracial dating than did Chinese Canadian females.

Relationship between Social Identities and Views on Interracial Relationships

Correlations between general and personal views on interracial dating and the two identity measures provided clear support for our hypothesis (see Table 7.1). Heritage culture identity was not significantly associated with either of the measures of interracial dating for either cultural group, whereas Canadian cultural identity was a significant correlate of both dating measures for Chinese Canadians. The more Chinese Canadians identified themselves as Canadian, the more likely they were to have a positive attitude toward interracial dating and to be open to interracial dating.

Table 7.1 Correlations between Cultural Identity Variables and Attitude Measures

		Heritage Identity	Canadian Identity
General attitude—interracial dating	Chinese Canadians	.13	.33**
	European Canadians	−.05	.18
Personal openness—interracial dating	Chinese Canadians	−.01	.44**
	European Canadians	−.15	.12

In order to rigorously test the hypothesis that Canadian identity, compared with heritage identity, is a better predictor of the interracial dating views of Chinese Canadians, one-tailed comparisons of correlation coefficients representing these associations were conducted following the method proposed by Meng, Rosenthal, and Rubin (1992). Both of these comparisons proved to be significant or near significant. For Chinese Canadians, Canadian identity was a stronger predictor of the general attitude toward interracial dating ($z = 1.35$, $p < .09$) and personal openness to interracial dating ($z = 2.50$, $p = .006$), compared with Chinese identity.

The *superordinate identity hypothesis* predicted that Canadian identity, rather than heritage identity, would drive the views of Chinese Canadians with regard to interracial dating. Among Chinese Canadians, Canadian identity, but not heritage identity, was associated with more favorable attitudes toward and greater personal openness to interracial dating. This finding replicates previous research findings that have found that mainstream and heritage culture identities play different roles in the acculturation process (Lalonde et al. 2004; Remennick 2005; Ryder et al. 2000). This finding is also in line with Mok's (1999) finding that among Asian American students, higher acculturation to an American/Western way of living was associated with greater likelihood of dating white Americans. Our contention is that mainstream (i.e., Canadian) identity, rather than heritage identity, plays a contributing role in interracial dating attitudes because, from a Chinese Canadian perspective, such views are more out-group-focused than in-group-focused. Canadian identity, moreover, has been specifically associated with greater acceptance and encouragement of ethnic diversity (e.g., Cameron and Berry 2008).

The Role of Interracial Dating Experience

The two interracial dating attitude measures were also related to participants' interracial dating *experience*, but only for Chinese Canadians. Group (Chinese Canadian, European Canadian) by Dating history (no, yes) ANOVAs revealed significant interaction effects for general attitude and personal openness. Simple effects analyses indicated that interracial dating history made no difference for European Canadians. Chinese Canadians with interracial dating experience, in contrast, reported significantly more positive general attitudes ($M = 6.56$) and higher levels of personal openness to interracial dating ($M = 6.46$) in comparison with those with no history ($M = 5.72$, $M = 4.75$, respectively). It is worth noting that Chinese Canadians with interracial dating experience also reported significantly higher Canadian identity scores ($M = 5.46$) than those with no such experience ($M = 4.96$).

This differential effect of interracial dating history on the two cultural groups suggests that having dated someone of a different racial background may help second-generation immigrants become more familiar with the norms of the mainstream culture, in this case a Canadian culture that encourages ethnic diversity. These are correlational data, however, and it may well be that Chinese Canadians who have more internalized Canadian norms are more willing to experiment with interracial dating.

Study 2—A Comparison of South Asian Canadians and European Canadian Participants

The sample consisted of 118 South Asian Canadians (60 women and 58 men) and 120 European Canadians (60 women and 60 men). Approximately half of the sample in each cultural group consisted of an older generation (60 European Canadians, 58 South Asian Canadians), and the other half consisted of university students representing the younger generation (60 university students in each cultural group). Younger participants were recruited primarily on campus and through social networks, and older participants were recruited using convenience sampling in the Greater Toronto Area. The mean ages of each sample were as follows: older South Asian Canadians (M = 51.70), older European Canadians (M = 47.50), South Asian Canadian students (M = 24.10), and European Canadian students (M = 24.31).

All participants were either Canadian citizens or had permanent residency. European Canadians self-identified as White and South Asian Canadians as South Asian. The majority of the European Canadians (80%) were born in Canada; participants not born in Canada were primarily from the older generation (79%) and reported European countries as their birth place. All of the older South Asian Canadians were born outside of Canada and can be clearly identified as first-generation immigrants. Within the younger generation South Asian Canadian sample, the majority were born in Canada (78%), and of those who were not, the mean age of arrival in Canada was 13.36 years (SD = 7.06). The younger South Asian Canadian sample, therefore, was largely composed of second-generation immigrants. The majority of South Asian participants born outside of Canada came from India (80%), while the rest indicated countries such as Sri Lanka, Pakistan, Zambia, and Kenya. Almost all of the participants in the older generation samples were married (84%) or divorced (10%), and most of them had children (88% of the European Canadians and 98% of the South Asian Canadian sample). All participants in the younger generation samples were unmarried.

In terms of interracial dating among the student sample, 53% of the European Canadians (19 men and 13 women) reported that they were in or have been in an interracial dating relationship, in comparison with 50% of the South Asian Canadians (13 men and 17 women).

Measures

All scale items were associated with seven-point Likert-type scales, ranging from one (*strongly disagree*) to seven (*strongly agree*). All participants completed the questionnaire in English.

Cultural Identifications

Cameron's (2004) measure of social identity was again used to measure the strength of both mainstream (Canadian) and heritage culture identifications. The Cronbach alpha reliability coefficients were acceptable for all samples (from .78 to .88).

Intergroup Dating Items

Ten of the items used in Study 1 were selected to examine views on intergroup dating. Four items tapping general attitudes toward intergroup dating were phrased without specifying particular groups (e.g., "Persons of different races should not become seriously involved"). Six items tapping personal openness toward intergroup dating were phrased such that the younger generation European Canadian sample was asked about dating South Asians (e.g., "I would happily date a South Asian person"), and the younger generation South Asian sample was asked about dating white European Canadians (e.g., "I am open to involvement in an intergroup relationship with a white person"). Older generation participants responded to the openness items by thinking of their child dating a member of the opposite cultural group (e.g., "I am open to my child's involvement in an intergroup relationship with a South Asian person"). The Cronbach alpha reliability coefficients were acceptable for all for samples (from .75 to .96).

Results and Discussion

A Group by Generation by Gender ANOVA was conducted for the general attitude toward intergroup dating measure. Significant main effects for Group and Generation, as well as a Group by Generation interaction, were found. South Asian Canadians ($M = 5.25$) had less favorable attitudes toward intergroup dating than did European Canadians ($M = 5.75$), and participants in the older generation group ($M = 5.28$) had less favorable attitudes toward intergroup dating than did younger generation participants ($M = 5.72$). The Group by Generation interaction indicated that the older generation South Asians' responses were driving the interaction effect. Specifically, older generation South Asian Canadians ($M = 4.80$) had less positive general attitudes toward intergroup dating than did older generation European Canadians ($M = 5.76$), younger generation South Asian Canadians ($M = 5.25$), and younger generation European Canadians ($M = 5.74$). The latter three groups did not differ from each other on this measure. There is evidence of a generational divide on the issue of generational dating, but this gap is only present for South Asian Canadians, suggesting that second-generation South Asian Canadians have access to two different cultural views and are acculturating to the majority Canadian view.

Given that the personal openness toward intergroup dating measure was phrased differently for the older and younger generation samples, this measure was examined separately for the older and younger samples in Group by Gender ANOVAs. For the older sample, the openness measure was only associated with a significant main effect of Group, such that the European Canadians ($M = 5.79$) exhibited a higher level of openness toward their child dating a South Asian compared with South Asian Canadians' openness ($M = 4.28$) toward their child dating a white Canadian. For the younger sample, the openness measure was also associated with a significant main effect of Group, with European Canadians ($M = 5.54$) showing a greater level of personal openness toward intergroup dating than did South Asian Canadians ($M = 4.48$). This main effect of Group was qualified by a marginally significant interaction with Gender. Male South Asian Canadian participants ($M = 4.26$) showed significantly less favorable personal openness toward intergroup dating than European Canadian males ($M = 5.79$) and females ($M = 5.28$). Female South Asian Canadians ($M = 4.71$) differed significantly from European Canadian men, but not from European Canadian women on the personal openness measure.

These results again provide evidence of a cultural gap between European Canadians and South Asian Canadians on the issue of openness to interracial dating. The gap is clear for the older generation of respondents, with European Canadians being more open than South Asian Canadians. The gap is more nuanced for the younger group of respondents, where male South Asians appear to be less willing to share the views of their majority European Canadian peers.

Identity Measures and Intergroup Dating

The identity hypothesis predicted that mainstream cultural identity, rather than heritage identity, would be associated with the views of both younger and older generation South Asian Canadians about intergroup dating. Correlations between the two indices of views on intergroup dating and the two cultural identity measures are reported in Table 7.2. Support was found for our hypothesis. On the one hand, heritage culture identity was not significantly correlated with any of the measures of intergroup dating for any of the groups except for the older generation South Asian Canadian sample, where stronger endorsement of heritage cultural identity was associated with lower levels of openness toward intergroup dating of children. In contrast, Canadian cultural identity was significantly correlated with both dating measures for the younger generation South Asian Canadians as well as for the older generation South Asian Canadians. More interestingly, Canadian identity was a significant or marginally significant correlate for the older generation but not the younger generation European Canadians. Thus, in all groups, except the younger generation European Canadians, the more participants identified themselves as Canadian, the more likely they were to have a more positive attitude toward intergroup dating and to be more open to intergroup dating.

Table 7.2 Correlations between Cultural Identity Variables and Study Measures

			Cultural Identity Variables		
Measures	Group	Generation	Heritage Identity	Canadian Identity	z value
General attitude toward intergroup dating	South Asian Canadians	Older	–.16	.31*	3.57***
		Younger	.16	.38**	1.80*
	European Canadians	Older	–.03	.28*	2.40**
		Younger	–.25+	–.14	ns
Openness toward intergroup dating	South Asian Canadians	Older	–.27*	.32*	4.51***
		Younger	–.002	.40**	3.21***
	European Canadians	Older	–.12	.26+	2.92**
		Younger	–.16	–.11	ns

***$p < .001$, **$p < .01$, *$p < .05$, + $p < .08$.

In order to more rigorously test the hypothesis that mainstream cultural identity would be a better predictor of the views of South Asian Canadians on intergroup dating compared with heritage identity, one-tailed comparisons of correlation coefficients representing these associations were conducted. All of these comparisons proved to be significant (see z values in the last column of Table 7.2). It thus appears that the more South Asians identify themselves as Canadians, the more accepting they become of intergroup relationships of an intimate nature.

The Role of Interracial Dating Experience

The two interracial dating attitude measures were also examined in relation to the younger respondents' previous interracial dating experiences. A Group (South Asian Canadian, European Canadian) by Dating history (no, yes) ANOVA revealed a significant dating history main effect for general attitude. Those with current or prior interracial dating experience reported a more positive general attitude ($M = 5.69$) compared with those with no experience ($M = 5.43$). For personal openness to interracial dating, significant effects were found for Dating history and Group. These effects were qualified by a significant Dating history by Group interaction. Simple effects analyses indicated that interracial Dating history made no difference for European Canadians. South Asian Canadians with interracial dating experience, however, reported significantly higher levels of personal openness to interracial dating ($M = 5.55$) in comparison with those with no history ($M = 3.41$). This differential effect of interracial dating history on the two cultural groups can be interpreted in different ways, but it is clear that South Asian Canadians who have not dated interracially have aligned their behavior with their attitude.

GENERAL DISCUSSION

The present chapter has reviewed the literature on Asian immigrants and intermarriage in the North American context, and it has described empirical data examining attitudes toward interracial dating for Canadians with Chinese, South Asian, and European backgrounds. The census data from both Canada and the United States are clear. When it comes to marriage, the norm of endogamy along ethno-racial lines is strong. It does become weaker, however, with the passage of time. A number of structural (e.g., number and density of in-group members) and cultural factors (e.g., cultural similarity in terms of language, level of education) have been linked to the norm of endogamy and to the increasing prevalence of exogamy. Given that immigration has fueled more multicultural settings in North America, opportunities for contact between individuals from different cultures is on the rise, and mixed unions and multiracial children will be one of the consequences of this ever increasing contact (see Denton Chapter 6). It is therefore important for social scientists to explore the structural, cultural, and psychological factors that may underlie inter-ethnic and interracial relationships.

Our own research has focused on dating attitudes and behaviors, as these are typical precursors to marriage in a North American context. When we examine the rates of interracial dating that took place for the respondents in our samples, we found them to be quite high (e.g., 50% for the South Asian Canadian sample). These rates are clearly discrepant from the rates of intermarriage in the general population. There is, of course, considerable sampling bias in our studies as these were convenience samples that were obtained from a very multicultural university where there is ample opportunity for intergroup contact. Dating, which is a common precursor to marriage, helps individuals explore and experiment with the intricacies of intimate relationships. If most of these experimental relationships are positive, then research on the contact hypothesis would suggest that they will be beneficial in the long term for positive intergroup relations (see Pettigrew and Tropp 2006).

The Positive Role of National Identity and Its Geographical Limits

The central hypothesis explored in our studies was that Canadian identity would be a positive predictor of positive views on interracial dating. There was clear support for this hypothesis. The second-generation samples in our studies have been educated and socialized in an atmosphere that tries to promote diversity. Some may interpret our data as providing evidence of success of the Canadian experiment in multiculturalism (e.g., Adams 2007; but see Ho Chapter 8). The results of our studies, however, may be limited in their generalizability. The relationship between national identity and inter-ethnic dating attitudes would likely hold in other major Canadian urban centers in addition to Toronto (e.g., Vancouver), but would not necessarily hold in the province of Québec where national identity (i.e., Québecois) and Canadian identity can differ in their meanings (see Cameron and Berry, 2008). In some European contexts, it has been found that a stronger national identity can be associated with more negative views of immigrants or non-majority ethnic groups (e.g., Esses, Wagner, Wolf, Preisser, and Wilbur 2006; González-Castro, Ubillos, and Ibáñez 2009; Verkuyten 1997), and it is quite likely that our findings would not be replicated in these contexts. Nonetheless, promoting superordinate national identities that are inclusive can help attenuate negative responses toward other groups (see Gaertner and Dovidio 2000), and some of this evidence has been found in the Chinese context (Guan, Verkuyten, Fung, Bond, Chan, and Chen 2011).

Cultural Differences in Views on Interracial Dating

When it came to self-report measures of personal openness to and general attitudes toward interracial dating, young Chinese Canadians scored lower than European Canadians on both of these measures in Study 1. A similar pattern of findings was found in Study 2, where the same group differences emerged when comparing the attitudes of older South Asian and European Canadians. For the younger samples in Study 2, the cultural group difference only emerged for the personal openness measure, with younger European Canadians being more open than their South Asian counterparts. We therefore have evidence that second-generation Chinese and South Asian Canadians are still partially holding to their heritage cultural norms regarding dating.

Gender—Another Cultural Layer in the Personal Relationships of Asian Immigrants

There were a few moderating effects of gender in both of our studies. In Study 1, second-generation Chinese Canadian women's views on interracial dating were in line with those of their European Canadian peers, whereas Chinese Canadian males were somewhat more conservative in their views. A similar pattern was found in Study 2, where young South Asian Canadian men were less open to interracial dating than their European Canadian peers. A growing body of literature has highlighted gender differences in the acculturation experiences of East and South Asian immigrants in Western cultures (see Dion and Dion, 2004). Chung (2001) found that female Asian American students reported greater intergenerational conflict about issues of dating and marriage than did male students. Moreover, Huang and Uba (1992) found that Chinese American women were more sexually experienced and more likely to be currently involved in an interracial relationship than were Chinese American men of the same age. Given that sexual restraint and modesty are often viewed as characteristic to a degree of East Asian cultures (see Okazaki 2002), greater sexual experience among bicultural female Chinese Americans may be seen as an indicator of low traditionalism. Suggested reasons for these findings of lower traditionalism among female East Asian immigrants include faster acculturation among females than males (Mok 1999) and female immigrants' rebellion against social pressure to conform to heritage ideals of femininity (Dion and Dion 2004).

Implications for Young Bicultural Canadians

The issue of dating and romantic relationships is a "hot point" of intergenerational conflict for both South Asian (e.g., Talbani and Hasanali 2000) and Chinese (e.g., Tang and Dion 1999) families. In short, dating a person of your choosing at a young age (e.g., 17) is a Western behavior that is non-normative in many Eastern families. A potential for cultural conflict exists between immigrants to the Western world and their adolescent or adult children, particularly when these immigrants come from Asian countries such as China and India (see review by Kwak 2003). First-generation immigrants have usually developed their core cultural ideas, customs, and norms within the distinct political, legal, and educational systems of their heritage culture, as well as through its language, media, and caretaking practices (Fiske, Kitayama, Markus, and Nisbett 1998). In contrast, second-generation immigrants, whose social systems and peers are predominantly Western, access their heritage culture primarily through their families. As a result, these bicultural immigrants (Sung 1985) have access to two potentially distinct sets of cultural values, beliefs, attitudes, and behaviors (Baumeister, Shapiro, and Tice 1985). It is not surprising, therefore, to find that second-generation immigrants experience culturally based intergenerational conflict and internal conflict (LaFromboise, Coleman, and Gerton 1993; Lalonde and Giguère 2008; Tsai, Ying, and Lee 2000).

Cultural conflict, however, is not an omnipresent reality for bicultural individuals. Since an individual's cultural identity is frequently context-driven (Clément and Noels 1992), only one culture of the bicultural individual is typically salient within any given context (e.g., home vs. work). A conflict between the two sets of a bicultural individual's cultural norms, therefore, is more likely to occur when these norms are in opposition to one another and when both social identities are salient (see Giguère, Lalonde, and Lou 2010).

These conditions are often jointly met in the realm of interpersonal relationships, particularly when the dating norms of the two cultures put differential emphasis on individual versus in-group needs or goals. For example, Ahluwalia, Suzuki, and Mir (2008) reported that while marriage is closely associated in Western cultures with romantic love, it is often construed in some East and South Asian cultures primarily as an alliance between two families. Individuals who have access to both of these discourses, such as South and East Asian immigrants in North America and their bicultural children, may therefore experience intergenerational and internal cultural conflict surrounding discrepancies between the two sets of cultural norms. We hope that the insight provided by social science research on this topic can help inform the public about the additional complexities that are involved when romance and relationships cross intergroup boundaries.

REFERENCES

Adams, M. 2007. *Unlikely Utopia: The Surprising Triumph of Canadian Multiculturalism*. Toronto: Penguin.

Ahluwalia, M. K., L. A. Suzuki, and M. Mir. 2008. "Dating, Partnerships, and Arranged Marriages. In *Asian American Psychology: Current Perspectives*, edited by N. Tewari and A. N. Alvarez, 273–94. Mahwah, NJ: Lawrence Erlbaum Associates.

Baumeister, R. F., J. P. Shapiro, and D. M. Tice. 1985. "Two Kinds of Identity Crisis." *Journal of Personality* 53:407–24.

Berry, J. W. 1980. "Acculturation as Varieties of Adaptation." In *Acculturation: Theory, Models and Some New Findings*, edited by A. Padilla, 9–25. Boulder, CO: Westview.

Cameron, J. E. 2004. "A Three-Factor Model of Social Identity." *Self and Identity* 3:239–62.

Cameron, J. E., and J. W. Berry. 2008. "True Patriot Love: Structure and Predictors of Canadian Pride." *Canadian Ethnic Studies* 40(3):17–41.

Cheung, B. Y., M. Chudek, and S. J. Heine. 2011. "Evidence for a Sensitive Period for Acculturation: Younger Immigrants Report Acculturating at a Faster Rate." *Psychological Science* 22:147–52.

Chung, R. H. G. 2001. "Gender, Ethnicity, and Acculturation in Intergenerational Conflict of Asian American College Students." *Cultural Diversity and Ethnic Minority Psychology* 7:376–86.

Clément, R., and K. A. Noels. 1992. "Towards a Situated Approach to Ethnolinguistic Identity: The Effects of Status on Individuals and Groups." *Journal of Language and Social Psychology* 11:203–32.

Dion, K. K., and K. L. Dion. 2004. "Gender, Immigrant Generation, and Ethnocultural Identity." *Sex Roles* 50:347–55.

Dwyer, D. 2000. *Interpersonal relationships*. London: Routledge.

Esses, V. M., U. Wagner, C. Wolf, M. Preisser, and C. J. Wilbur. 2006. "Perceptions of National Identity and Attitudes Towards Immigrants and Immigration in Canada and Germany." *International Journal of Intercultural Relations* 30:671–82.

Fiske, A. P., S. Kitayama, H. R. Markus, and R. E. Nisbett. 1998. "The Cultural Matrix of Social Psychology." In *The Handbook of Social Psychology*, 4th edition, edited by D. T. Gilbert, S. T. Fiske, and G. Lindzey, 915–81. New York: McGraw-Hill.

Fujino, D. C. 1997. "The Rates, Patterns and Reasons for Forming Heterosexual Interracial Dating Relationships among Asian Americans." *Journal of Social and Personal Relationships* 14:809–28.

Fujino, D. C. 2000. "Structural and Individual Influences Affecting Racialized Dating Relationships." In *Relationships among Asian American women. Psychology of Women*, edited by J. L. Chin, 181–209. Washington, DC: American Psychological Association.

Gaertner, S. L., and J. F. Dovidio. 2000. *Reducing Intergroup Bias: The Common Ingroup Identity Model*. Philadelphia, PA: The Psychology Press.

Giguère, B., R. N. Lalonde, and E. Lou. 2010. "Living at the Crossroads of Cultural Worlds: The Experience of Normative Conflicts by Second Generation Youths." *Social and Personality Psychology Compass* 4:14–29.

González-Castro, J. L., S. Ubillos, and J. Ibáñez. 2009. "Predictive Factors of Ethnic Prejudice Toward Immigrants in a Representative Subsample of Spanish Young People." *Journal of Applied Social Psychology* 39:1690–1717.

Guan, Y., M. Verkuyten, H. H. Fung, M. H. Bond, C. C. Chan, and S. X. Chen. 2011. "Outgroup Value Incongruence and Intergroup Attitude: The Roles of Multiculturalism and Common Identity." *International Journal of Intercultural Relations* 35:377–85.

Huang, K., and L. Uba. 1992. "Premarital Sexual Behavior Among Chinese College Students in the United States." *Archives of Sexual Behavior* 21:227–40.

Hussain, R. 1999. "Community Perceptions of Reasons for Preference for Consanguineous Marriages in Pakistan." *Journal of Biosocial Science* 31:449–61.

Kalmijn, M., and F. van Tubergen. 2010. "A Comparative Perspective on Intermarriage: Explaining Differences among National-Origin Groups in the United States." *Demography* 47:459–79.

King, R. B., and J. L. Bratter. 2007. "A Path Toward Interracial Marriage: Women's First Partners and Husbands Across Racial Lines." *Sociological Quarterly* 48:343–69.

Kwak, K. 2003. "Adolescents and Their Parents: A Review of Intergenerational Family Relations for Immigrant and Non-immigrant Families." *Human Development* 45:115–36.

LaFromboise, T., H. K. Coleman, and J. Gerton. 1993. "Psychological Impact of Biculturalism: Evidence and Theory." *Psychological Bulletin* 114:395–412.

Lalonde, R. N. 2002. "Testing the Social Identity-Intergroup Differentiation Hypothesis: We're Not American eh!" *British Journal of Social Psychology* 41:611–30.

Lalonde, R. N., and B. Giguère. 2008. "When Might the Two Cultural Worlds of Second Generation Biculturals Collide?" *Canadian Diversity* (Spring):58–62.

Lalonde, R. N., B. Giguère, M. Fontaine, and A. Smith. 2007. "Social Dominance Orientation and Ideological Asymmetry in Relation to Interracial Dating and Transracial Adoption in Canada." *Journal of Cross Cultural Psychology* 38:559–72.

Lalonde, R. N., M. Hynie, M. Pannu, and S. Tatla. 2004. "The Role of Culture in Interpersonal Relationships: Do Second Generation South Asian Canadians Want a Traditional Partner?" *Journal of Cross-Cultural Psychology* 35:503–24.

Lee, S. M., and M. Boyd. 2008. "Marrying out: Comparing the Marital and Social Integration of Asians in the US and Canada." *Social Science Research* 37:311–29.

Levin, S., P. L. Taylor, and E. Caudle. 2007. "Interethnic and Interracial Dating in College: A Longitudinal Study." *Journal of Social and Personal Relationships* 24:323–41.

Maiter, S., and U. George. 2003. "Understanding Context and Culture in the Parenting Approaches of Immigrant South Asian Mothers." *Affilia* 18:411–28.

Meng, X., R. Rosenthal, and D. R. Rubin. 1992. "Comparing Correlated Correlation Coefficients." *Psychological Bulletin* 111:172–75.

Milan, A., H. Maheux, and T. Chui. 2010. "A Portrait of Couples in Mixed Unions." *Canadian Social Trends* 89:70–80.

Mok, T. A. 1999. "Asian American Dating: Important Factors in Partner Choice." *Cultural Diversity and Ethnic Minority Psychology* 5:103–17.

Okamoto, D. G. 2007. "Marrying out: A Boundary Approach to Understanding the Marital Integration of Asian Americans." *Social Science Research* 36:1391–1414.

Okazaki, S. 2002. "Influences of Culture on Asian Americans' Sexuality." *Journal of Sex Research* 39:34–41.

Pettigrew, T., and L. Tropp. 2006. "A Meta-Analytic Test of Intergroup Contact Theory." *Journal of Personality and Social Psychology* 90:751–83.

Phinney, J. S., J. W. Berry, P. Vedder, P. and K. Liebkind. 2006. The Acculturation Experience:

Attitudes, Identities, and Behaviors of Immigrant Youth. In *Immigrant Youth in Cultural Transition: Acculturation, Identity and Adaptation across National Contexts*, edited by J. W. Berry, J. S. Phinney, D. L. Sam, and P. Vedder, 71–116. London: Lawrence Erlbaum.

Qian, Z., S. L. Blair, and S. Ruf. 2001. "Asian American Interracial and Interethnic Marriages: Differences by Education and Nativity." *International Migration Review* 35:557–86.

Remennick, L. 2005. "Cross-Cultural Dating Patterns on an Israeli Campus: Why Are Russian Immigrant Women More Popular Than Men?" *Journal of Social and Personal Relationships* 22:435–54.

Ryder, A. G., L. E. Alden, and D. L. Paulhus. 2000. "Is Acculturation Unidimensional or Bidimensional? A Head-to-Head Comparison in the Prediction of Personality, Self-Identity, and Adjustment." *Journal of Personality and Social Psychology* 79:49–65.

Statistics Canada. 2008. "Canada's Ethnocultural Mosaic, 2006 Census." Catalogue no. 97–562-X.

Sung, B. L. 1985. "Bicultural Conflicts in Chinese Immigrant Children." *Journal of Comparative Family Studies* 16:255–70.

Tang, T. N., and K. L. Dion. 1999. "Gender and Acculturation in Relation to Traditionalism: Perceptions of Self and Parents Among Chinese Students." *Sex Roles* 41:17–29.

Talbani, A., & P. Hasanali. 2000. "Adolescent Females between Tradition and Modernity: Gender Role Socialization in South Asian Immigrant Culture." *Journal of Adolescence,* 23: 615–627.

Thornton, A., and T. E. Fricke. 1987. "Social Change and the Family: Comparative Perspectives from the West, China, and South Asia." *Sociological Forum* 2:746–79.

Tsai, J. L., Y. W. Ying, and P. A. Lee. 2000. "The Meaning of 'being Chinese' and 'being American'." *Journal of Cross-Cultural Psychology* 31:302–32.

Uskul, A. K., R. N. Lalonde, and L. Cheng. 2007. "Views on Interracial Dating Among Chinese and European Canadians: The Roles of Culture, Gender, and Mainstream Cultural Identity." *Journal of Social and Personal Relationships* 24:891–911.

Uskul, A. K., R. N. Lalonde, and S. Konanur. 2011. "The Role of Culture in Intergenerational Value Discrepancies Regarding Intergroup Dating." *Journal of Cross-Cultural Psychology* 42:1165–78.

Verkuyten, M. 1997. "The Structure of Ethnic Attitudes: The Effects of Target Group, Region, Gender, and National Identity." *Genetic, Social, and General Psychology Monographs* 123:261–84.

West, T. V., A. R. Pearson, J. F. Dovidio, J. N. Shelton, and T. E. Trail. 2009. "Superordinate Identity and Intergroup Roommate Friendship Development." *Journal of Experimental Social Psychology* 45:1266–72.

Wright, S. C., A. Aron, T. McLaughlin-Volpe, and S. A. Ropp. 1997. "The Extended Contact Effect: Knowledge of Cross-Group Friendships and Prejudice." *Journal of Personality and Social Psychology* 73:73–90.

8 The Contradictory Nature of Multiculturalism

Mainland Chinese Immigrants' Perspectives and Their Onward Emigration from Canada

Elaine Lynn-Ee Ho

INTRODUCTION

Theories and practices of multiculturalism have come under considerable debate since its inception and with even greater urgency in recent years. Multicultural citizenship, a concept advanced by Kymlicka (1996), calls for the recognition of minority groups, such as immigrants, and the allocation of rights to their cultural communities so as to facilitate citizenship participation. Abu-Laban (2002) defines multiculturalism as "the freedom to exercise rights as differentiated beings" (p464). Multiculturalism, however, has been criticized by several scholars in different ways. For example, Grillo (2007) regards multiculturalism as a "fuzzy" concept; in other words, it is "difficult, opaque, elusive, and with multiple contested meanings" (p981). More recently, a number of scholars further argue that state-sponsored multiculturalism is in decline (Grillo 2007; Mitchell 2004). Multiculturalism has also come under attack for purportedly contradicting the liberal values underpinning several of the societies that practice it, including Canada. Other scholars claim that multiculturalism treats cultures in an essentializing manner (Abu-Laban 2002) and reinforces power hierarchies within cultural groups, making some such as women more vulnerable to oppression (Shachar 2000). As we will see in this chapter, these scholarly arguments resonate with media debates on multiculturalism and immigration adaptation in Canada, a multi-ethnic society. These media debates draw attention to concerns over migrant employability and failed expectations, the formation of ethnic enclaves, the limits to migrant integration, and, of particular interest to the empirical study in this chapter on Mainland Chinese migration, the resilience of intergroup social distance between cultural groups in multi-ethnic societies.

The variety of perspectives on multiculturalism suggests that it is "a concept that differs by context and writer," as Bloemraad, Korteweg, and Yurdakul (2008, 159) argue, leading them to further urge for more studies on "actually existing multiculturalism," particularly from the perspective of immigrants themselves. Indeed while some studies consider multiculturalism through the lenses of identity negotiations or belonging (Lobo 2010; Thomas 2008), few focus on immigrant attitudes toward multiculturalism. This chapter contributes to the gap in this scholarship by focusing on the experiences of former immigrants who emigrated again eventually, thus extending the scholarship on multiculturalism by approaching migration as a trajectory of changing mobilities over time (Ho 2011a). The chapter considers the case of Mainland Chinese migrants reflecting on their experiences of multiculturalism in the country they have left, namely, Canada, despite their previous immigration histories. They had immigrated to Canada, taken up permanent residency or naturalized as citizens, and, due to settlement difficulties, left the country subsequently and returned to China again (henceforth returnees). Canada is still generally acknowledged as an Anglo-European society despite new immigration from Asia, Africa, and other parts of the world.

In considering this case study, this chapter contributes to conceptual and empirical reflections on immigrant adaptation in multicultural societies and, more specifically, highlights the sustained barriers that prompt subsequent emigration again. Focusing on immigrants who subsequently emigrated provides a fresh perspective on the extent to which multiculturalism enables immigrants to adapt and be accepted into a new multi-ethnic country. Their departure and the reasons leading to that decision provide a troubling view into the inconsistencies and inadequacies inherent in a multicultural approach toward immigrant citizenship and nation-building. In so doing, this chapter focuses on segregation and notions of social distance between groups that come about and are reinforced by multicultural policies despite the good intentions that underpin multiculturalism.

The findings presented in this chapter are drawn from a research project that investigated citizenship attitudes among Mainland Chinese immigrants who had lived in Canada for some years before subsequently leaving to return to China. Thirty interviews were carried out with those who had immigrated to Canada through the skills category, but due to integration barriers, they decided to return to China (henceforth Mainland Chinese returnees). An additional 30 interviews were conducted with Mainland Chinese immigrants still living in Canada, the findings of which help inform the analysis in this chapter. In total, 60 interviews were carried out on this project. Multiculturalism emerged as a significant theme in the interviews conducted with both groups of migrants. Significantly, among the returnees, there were claims that they had left Canada as a result of discrimination and marginalization, which contradicts state-sponsored discourses of multiculturalism as an ethos of acceptance toward cultural difference and equality among cultural groups. Besides fieldwork interviews, a discourse analysis of newspaper articles from 2006 to 2011 in *The Globe and Mail*, one of Canada's prominent national newspapers, was further carried out to contextualize the empirical research. In this chapter, reports and debates concerning multiculturalism will be the subject of discussion. The chapter demonstrates that for these migrants, multiculturalism, as a social compact, results inadvertently in segregation and social distance, thus contributing to eventual decisions to leave the country.

The next section examines discourses of multiculturalism in Canada. Following that, the chapter focuses on the debates on multiculturalism in *The Globe and Mail* so as to provide an indication of the key controversies surrounding multiculturalism that has been the subject of national attention and contextualizes the fieldwork findings in this study. Then the chapter will discuss the interviews exploring migrant attitudes toward multiculturalism in Canada. In so doing, this chapter fleshes out the contradictions within multiculturalism and argues that, despite multiculturalism, migrant experiences of discrimination and marginalization contribute to decisions toward onward emigration. Finally, the conclusion will suggest further areas for consideration in view of the research findings presented.

Multicultural Logics and Policies

For Canada, a British and French settler society, multiculturalism has been a cornerstone of Canadian society since 1971 and made constitutional in 1982. The need to accommodate Quebecois separatism motivated this decision, but multicultural policies helped meet the demands for recognition by indigenous peoples in Canada too. Immigrant groups are also a prominent feature of Canadian society. Immigrants comprise almost one in five of the Canadian population according to the last census in 2006 (Statistics Canada 2006), and a multicultural approach toward integration allows them to retain their ethnic identities. Although Canada once excluded Asians and Africans during the early 20th century, Canada implemented a points-based system in 1967 admitting new immigrants based on criteria such as educational qualifications, professional experience, and income level. Immigrant advocacy and service delivery groups formed quickly in Canada to meet the needs of the newcomers in Canadian society. Public institutions are also expected to "make reasonable accommodation" (Kymlicka 2003, 370–71) toward migrants' ethnic identities.

During the 1980s and 1990s, Hong Kong immigrants were the dominant group in Canada, but from 2006 onward, the volume of immigration from Mainland China surpassed them. However, onward migration, in the form of return to Hong Kong or China, is prominent among both groups of immigrants (see Ho 2011b; Ley and Kobayashi 2005). The efficacy of multiculturalism in Canada has been questioned by several scholars such as P. S. Li (2003), who contends that it "is still immigrants and not Canadian society and its institutions that are required to change" (10). Other scholars such as Mitchell (2004) and Abu-Laban and Gabriel (2002) further argue that multiculturalism in Canada is a diversity tool that is closely aligned to capitalism, thus the state-led promotion of skills-based immigration to the country.

Multiculturalism is enacted as an official Canadian policy for the management of diversity and equality. Canada is also popularly regarded as a country that has successful multicultural policies. Perceptions of state-sponsored multiculturalism may, however, differ "on the ground" when experienced by ethnic minorities with immigrant histories. The remainder of this chapter explores these inconsistencies through the national newspaper reports on multiculturalism and also fieldwork findings on migrant attitudes toward multiculturalism discourses and practices in Canada that lead to their decisions to emigrate once again.

Multiculturalism, a Subject of National Controversy

Multiculturalism has been the subject of significant public debates in Canada (also see Wang and Du, this volume). Media reports on multiculturalism range from positive reviews on the inroads Canada has made in enabling cultural diversity, to critiques of a regressive multicultural climate in the post-9/11 period, and questions over the actual practices of multiculturalism and the lived experience of multiculturalism from the perspective of migrants themselves. On the one hand, Canada is often held up as the poster country for multiculturalism. China and Israel, for example, have both reportedly looked to Canada for insights into ways of managing and integrating plural populations in their respective countries (*The Globe and Mail*, December 18, 2006, and June 25, 2009). A recent international survey, Migrant Integration Policy Index, ranked Canada third in Europe and North American for its efforts in integrating migrants[1] (*The Globe and Mail*, February 28, 2011). The resurgence of religion and accompanying anxieties over the breakdown of multiculturalism in France, Britain, and Germany has led to concomitant concerns over the desirability of a multicultural approach for Canada. However, supporters of a multicultural approach are optimistic that the Canadian brand of multiculturalism is different and will not fall prey to the same perils as its European counterparts.

On the other hand, multicultural policies in Canada have been criticized for the extent to which it has been able, and is willing, to accommodate cultural difference. This is exemplified in the recent national controversy over the ban in Quebec restricting Muslim women from wearing a niqab[2] when accessing some government services and Sikh men from carrying their kirpans when entering legislative buildings (*The Globe and Mail*, January 19, 2011). An earlier niqab-related issue in Quebec had led to similarly fierce public outcry outside of the province, leading one newspaper report to comment that "marshmallow multiculturalism" in Canada, connoting polite tolerance that shuns intense critical scrutiny, actually deters public debate on the complexities of accommodating cultural diversity in the country (*The Globe and Mail*, March 20, 2010).

Related to these critiques on the limits of cultural accommodation is the belief that Canada has not succeeded in instilling "Canadian values" in its immigrant populations. Proponents of this view raised past examples of home-grown Sikh extremism and Muslim terrorism from Canada. However, a set of counter-critiques question: What are these purported "Canadian values" given that "values are always shifting and they do not stay core for long" (*The Globe and Mail*, August 28, 2009)? An attempt to clarify the idea of "Canadian values" was made by Immigration Minister Jason Kenney, who said that values characterizing Canadian society include the supremacy of civil law and gender equality (*The Globe and Mail*, May 9, 2009). Yet the values he named are not unique to Canada and in fact are shared by other liberal democracies. Multiculturalism, others would say, is what defines Canada and thus is worthy of being considered a "Canadian value." Indeed, as this chapter reveals subsequently, many of the Mainland Chinese returnees interviewed take pride in Canada's multicultural approach as did their counterparts who remained in Canada.

Yet multiculturalism, a key component of integration policy in Canada, is not antithetical to assimilation processes despite the oppositional frames set up conventionally in discussions of these policies. Hence, even though Canadians may demonstrate openness to cultural diversity, one can argue that there are unspoken rules expecting immigrants to bridge cultural differences by conforming to Canadian society in order to be deemed acceptable by other Canadians. For example, a survey conducted in 2006 reports that Canadians list multiculturalism second in a list of things that makes them proud of Canada (*The Globe and Mail*, December 10, 2007), but 65% of Canadians are anxious about cultural integration (*The Globe and Mail*, December 8, 2007). In Quebec, where there is a Francophone majority, more than three-quarters of the respondents in a survey (77%) indicated that they believe immigrants should adapt to Quebec and Canadian society (*The Globe and Mail*, October 11, 2007).

These statistics reported by the newspapers suggest that people of diverse cultures are welcomed in Canada, but it does not mean Canadian society will change in accordance with its shifting population composition (*The Globe and Mail*, December 8, 2007). The presence of immigrant-transnationals, like the Hong Kong and Mainland Chinese immigrants, further fuels concerns that Canada is like "the world's best hotel, but where none of the guests make small-talk in the lobby. No getting together in the dining room for meals [and] no gathering in the bar to watch hockey" (*The Globe and Mail*, June 28, 2008). As another study found, Canadians may support immigration, but "they also maintain a 'social distance' from minorities" (*The Globe and Mail*, January 12, 2007). Such social distancing, though supposedly benign, may nonetheless result in immigrants experiencing a sense of exclusion in Canada. The next section of this chapter thus examines the dynamics of social distancing experienced by the Mainland Chinese returnees in spite of the multiculturalism rhetoric in Canada, thus prompting their departure decisions. In so doing, the chapter argues that cultural difference manifests in social distance, but social distancing further accentuates dissimilarity and confers a lack of acceptability that legitimizes the unequal treatment of immigrants.

Mainland Chinese Returnees from Canada: Attitudes Toward Multiculturalism

This section examines the reflections of Mainland Chinese immigrants who left Canada to return to China. During interviews, the Mainland Chinese returnees were asked to name what they thought are some "Canadian values" (if any). Although they struggled initially to come up with a reply, eventually a recurring response given by them was "multiculturalism." In this sense, Canada has to some extent successfully branded itself as a multicultural country to the immigrants from Mainland China. Biao explained his understanding of Canadian multiculturalism this way:

> I explain to my friends [in China] that the Americans have a melting pot; they will slowly make you similar to them but Canada is a mosaic made up of different pieces. You have your own culture, we respect one another but together we are a big picture. I choose to believe that.

In the interviews, Canada's approach to managing ethnic minority groups with immigrant backgrounds was oftentimes contrasted with America. Unlike the American "melting pot," the right to retain one's culture as part of the "mosaic" is an important aspect of being Canadian. Expressing appreciation for Canada's willingness to accommodate culture difference and diversity, Yan said:

> I feel [multiculturalism] is a good thing because you can keep your [culture].... You don't have to change your culture but you accept one another's cultures. It is different from America where you have to adopt American culture; I don't think this is very good. For Canada you can keep your own culture but at the same time you add another layer [as Canadian identity] and everyone follows that.... I think this is stronger.

The anecdotes by Biao and Yan demonstrate that migrants like them invest considerable pride into what they consider the "Canadian identity," made possible by the "Canadian value" of multiculturalism. To them Canada is a mosaic of cultures in which the whole is greater than the sum of its parts. These research findings in the interviews conducted with the returnees resonate with the accompanying set of interviews conducted with Mainland Chinese immigrants who remained in Canada. Both groups expressed appreciation and pride in the Canadian approach toward multiculturalism.

The Contradictory Nature of Multiculturalism   165

However, both groups of migrants also acknowledge the downside of multiculturalism as it materializes in Canadian society. As we will see later in this chapter, for the returnees in particular, the limits to multiculturalism contribute to their onward migration in the form of return to China. For Biao, the issue is:

> I think the multicultural policy results in disparity. If you want to respect another culture you cannot change their culture. A lot of Mainland Chinese migrants I know live in Canada but they have not integrated into the "local" lifestyle. They socialise within their own circles and retain their old ways—they eat Chinese food, go to Chinese restaurants and have their own leisure activities.

In other words, the multicultural approach encouraging plural identities and the preservation of cultural communities results inadvertently in segregation and social distance. Biao's anecdote may be self-essentializing in the way he assumes that the Mainland Chinese community in Canada is a cohesive one despite their regional and linguistic differences. However, the crux of his point is the way that Mainland Chinese migrants experience segregation from the "local lifestyle"[3] in Canada, thus inhibiting migrant integration in several ways, including difficulty for migrants to access the same employment opportunities as "local" Canadians.

There are two dimensions to the employment issue. First, the lack of social interaction with "locals" inhibits new migrants from practicing their English language and social skills (e.g., acquiring common topics of conversation) that will enable them to navigate the Canadian workplace and job interactions. This is, however, a chicken-and-egg issue to them. According to the interviews, the extent to which Mainland Chinese migrants in Canada socialize with "local" Canadians is limited because of language challenges and the lack of common topics of conversation. The second issue pertains to the devaluation of Chinese educational and professional qualifications in Canada, thus leading to deskilling. On this issue, another returnee, Lin, commented:

> Canada shows that it is welcoming to migrants from all over the world but studies have proven that migrant incomes and life quality are lower than the "locals.". I think it is because migrants have not been given a chance. It doesn't mean that putting people together in a room is multiculturalism.

Lin's anecdote echoes media critiques of the lack of intense public scrutiny on the extent to which Canadian society is able and willing to go beyond cultural accomodation and move toward mutual adaptation instead. His metaphor suggests fittingly that proximity does not necessarily bridge social distance. Instead, cultural difference contributes to tangible outcomes such as employers' reluctance to recognize foreign credentials and their insistence on prior Canadian experience, which new immigrants are unlikely to possess. In the workplace, cultural differences may impede meaningful interactions between immigrant employees and their Canadian colleagues, thus exacerbating dissimilarities and also detering immigrants from acquiring socio-cultural competencies that are useful for their career progress. Due to these factors, individually or combined, new immigrants are unlikely to obtain employment in the professional occupations they had worked in previously in China, and they end up working in menial jobs instead after their arrival in Canada.

Such deskilling results in unequal outcomes for ethnic minorities with immigrant backgrounds. For example, Yan said:

> I know a lot of Mainland Chinese migrants have left Canada mainly because they couldn't find jobs. In the factory that my wife worked [in Canada] there were many labourers who had been professors in China, they have a PhD. They joked that this factory is the world's best qualified but there is a problem because these people immigrated to Canada after they became professors. Yet in Canada their credentials are unacknowledged. They experience a great sense of loss. Some have to remain in Canada for the sake of their children. Others choose to return to China.

As Zong Li (2004) argues, Mainland Chinese immigrants in Canada face the problem of transferring credentials internationally, thus resulting in institutional barriers to employment. In fact, 35% of Chinese immigrants reported experiences of discrimination in Canada (*The Globe and Mail*, February 8, 2007). For the Mainland Chinese immigrants who remain in Canada, my research found that their decision is the outcome of weighing competing priorities of personal career progress and better earnings with other important family goals, including children's educational opportunities and lifestyle factors. In such cases, they have chosen to bite the bullet and stay on in Canada for the time being, but the potential of returning to China remains at the backs of their minds. For others, the devaluation of educational and professional qualifications is a deciding factor contributing to onward migration decisions, as expressed above by Lin, himself a return migrant to China (also see Guo and DeVoretz 2007).

The above anecdotes show that while the Mainland Chinese migrants appreciated Canada's multiculturalism ethos, they also challenge the segregation and marginalization that inadvertently comes about from such a policy. They are painfully aware of the limits of multiculturalism in practice. Thomas (2008) argues that multiculturalism provides a normative language for individuals and groups to appreciate and celebrate diversity. In the case of the Mainland Chinese returnees, multiculturalism is spoken about in celebratory tones, but on the level of everyday experience, they still inhabit a racialized subjectivity in Canada that leads to their economic and social marginalization.

Lin's earlier remark on "it doesn't mean that putting people together in a room is multiculturalism" suggests that migrants like him want the Canadian state and Canadians to do more than pay lip service to multiculturalism. As ethnic minorities with immigrant status, they hope for professional recognition and equal opportunities at work, but at the same time, as Biao adds, it is important that migrants and "locals" *mutually* adapt to one another and integrate into the overarching "layer" that is a civic Canadian identity. However, as a news commentator in *The Globe and Mail* (October 3, 2009) argued, migrants are expected to adapt to mainstream society, but cultural groups are "locked into cages of identity" under a multicultural approach, which also prevents "the mainstream culture from changing, evolving and incorporating new thoughts and expressions."

CONCLUSION

Bannerji (2000) and Shachar (2000) have both called multiculturalism a "paradox." The findings in this chapter, on immigrants who have emigrated again, suggest that carving out ethnic groups under the rubric of multiculturalism could solidify social boundaries that become detrimental to the equal treatment of ethnic minorities. Despite state-sponsored claims to multiculturalism in Canada, the interviewees encountered shared experiences of segregation, discrimination, and marginalization; these are arguably processes that result in social distance between ethnic groups that further legitimize unequal treatment toward immigrants. The study discussed here found that social distancing from "local" society contributes to decisions to leave the country for a new start elsewhere despite earlier immigration. This is even though it is contentious into what "local" norms are ethnic minorities with immigrant histories expected to integrate. In Canada, it is a presumed white mainstream society. This chapter thus indicates that there is reason to explore multiculturalism from emigrants' perspective (i.e., the relationship between emigration and multiculturalism). Emigrants, particularly those formerly from immigrant backgrounds, are likely rendered invisible in considerations of multiculturalism within the nation-state, but this chapter demonstrates that examining their experiences actually helps provide valuable insights on the politics and limits of immigrant adaptation in multicultural contexts.

NOTES

1. In the survey, Canada did well in aspects such as its family reunification policy, government initiatives to recognize the qualifications of foreign-born professionals, and other types of educational programs for immigrants, but it scored poorly on the extent to which it engages immigrants politically before they obtain Canadian citizenship status.

2. The niqab is a veil that covers a Muslim woman's face for religious reasons while the kirpan is a ceremonial dagger carried by Sikh men according to a religious commandment.
3. "Local" is commonly used by Mainland Chinese returnees to refer to the white population in Canada, although other ethnic groups are represented in the Canadian population.

REFERENCES

Abu-Laban, Y. 2002. "Liberalism, Multiculturalism and the Problem of Essentialism." *Citizenship Studies* 6(4):459–482.
Abu-Laban, Y., and C. Gabriel. 2002. *Selling Diversity*. Ontario: Broadview Press.
Bannerji, H. 2000. "The Paradox of Diversity: The Construction of a Multicultural Canada and 'Women of Color'." *Women's International Studies Forum* 23(5):537–60.
Bloemraad, I., A. Korteweg, and G. Yurdakul. 2008. "Citizenship and Immigration: Multiculturalism, Assimilation and Challenges to the Nation-State." *Annual Review of Sociology* 34:153–79.
Grillo, R. 2007. "An Excess of Alterity? Debating Difference in a Multicultural Society." *Ethnic and Racial Studies* 30(6):979–98.
Guo, S., and DeVoretz D. 2007. "Chinese Immigrants in Vancouver: Quo Vadis?" *Journal of International Migration and Integration* 7:425–47.
Ho, E. L. E. 2011a. "Migration Trajectories of 'Highly Skilled' Middling Transnationals: Singaporean Transmigrants in London." *Population, Space and Place*. 17(1):116–129.
Ho, E. L. E. 2011b. "Caught Between Two Worlds: Mainland Chinese Return Migration, Hukou Considerations and the Citizenship Dilemma." *Citizenship Studies*. 15(6–7):643–658.
Kymlicka, W. 1996. *A Liberal Theory of Minority Rights*. Oxford: Oxford University Press.
Kymlicka, W. 2003. "Immigration, Citizenship and Multiculturalism: Exploring the Links." *The Political Quarterly* 74:195–208.
Li, P. S. 2003. "Deconstructing Canada's Discourse of Immigrant Integration." *Journal of International Migration and Integration* 4(3):315–33.
Li, Z. 2004. "International Transference of Human Capital and Occupational Attainment of Recent Chinese Professional Immigrations in Canada." *PCERII Working Paper Series*, WP03–04. Accessed November 5, 2010. http://pcerii.metropolis.net/WorkingPapers/WP03–04.pdf.
Lobo, M. 2010. "Interethnic Understanding and Belonging in Suburban Melbourne." *Urban Policy and Research* 28(1):85–99.
Ley, D., and A. Kobayashi. 2005. "Back to Hong Kong: Return Migration or Transnational Sojourn?" *Global Networks* 2:111–17.
Mitchell, K. 2004. "Geographies of Identity: Multiculturalism Unplugged." *Progress in Human Geography* 28(5):641–51.
Shachar, A. 2000. "On Citizenship and Multicultural Vulnerability." *Political Theory* 28(1):64–89.
Statistics Canada. 2006. "Proportion of Foreign Born Highest in 25 years." Accessed November 2, 2010. http://www12.statcan.ca/census-recensement/2006/as-sa/97–557/p2-eng.cfm.
The Globe and Mail. "Canada: China's Muse on Ethnic Harmony; Academics Compare 'Inclusion' Strategies." December 18, 2006.

The Globe and Mail. "How Canadian Are You? Visible-Minority Immigrants and Their Children Identify Less and Less with the Country, Report Says." January 12, 2007.

The Globe and Mail. "Do Ethnic Enclaves Impede Integration?" February 8, 2007.

The Globe and Mail. "Immigration and Identity: A Taste of Things to Come." October 11, 2007.

The Globe and Mail. "When Multi Morphs into Plural; Cultures Can Be Sorted Out; The Hard Part Is Getting Ahead." December 8, 2007.

The Globe and Mail. "Finding Strength in the Ambiguity That Diversity Weaves." December 10, 2007.

The Globe and Mail. "Our Part-Time Home and Native Land; In Canada's Culture of Global Citizens, Millions Live Abroad, Thousands Are Transnationals—and Many More Are Itching to Join Them." June 28, 2008.

The Globe and Mail. "Canadian values boil down to liberal democracy." May 9, 2009.

The Globe and Mail. "Israel Looks to Canada on How to Better Integrate Immigrants." June 25, 2009.

The Globe and Mail. "Down with So-Called Core Values." August 28, 2009.

The Globe and Mail. "Melting Pot or Mosaic? Actually, Neither, Thanks." October 3, 2009.

The Globe and Mail. "The Face of Quebec Revealed in Niqab Debate; English-Speaking Canada Assails Province's Opposition to Headwear; Quebeckers Respond with Cries of 'Marshmallow Multiculturalism.'" March 20, 2010.

The Globe and Mail. "From Niqab to Kirpan: Quebec's Clash over Equality Escalates." January 19, 2011.

The Globe and Mail. "Canada Near Top in Integrating Immigrants, Climbing to Third Place After Sweden, Portugal." February 28, 2011.

Thomas, M. E. 2008. "The Paradoxes of Personhood: Banal Multiculturalism and Racial-Ethnic Identification Among Latina and Armenian Girls at a Los Angeles High School." *Environment and Planning A*:2864–78.

9 The Perception of Social Distance in a Multi-ethnic Society
The Case of Taiwan

Yu-Hua Chen and Chin-Chun Yi

INTRODUCTION

To thrive in an era of globalization, many countries are trying to attract a variety of talented individuals, investors, and skilled workers to contribute to their development. Over the last two decades, Taiwan has become a net receiver of migrants, but the influx has consisted largely of blue-collar guest workers, domestic helpers, and marriage migrants. In fact, 2009 official statistics show that guest workers in the fields of manufacturing and construction accounted for about 75.9% of the total foreign population in Taiwan. Due to the nuclearization of households and rapid aging of the population, policies have been loosened to allow in domestic workers to meet the growing demand for housekeeping and personal care services. Also, there has been a remarkable increase in the number of cross-border marriages since the late 1990s, with marriages between Taiwanese citizens and foreigners accounting for one in five marriages, with 60.7% of foreign spouses coming from Mainland China (including Hong Kong and Macau), 16.7% from Vietnam, 4.1% from Japan, and 3.7% from the United States (Government Information Office 2011).

Inward migration presents many challenges to Taiwanese society, not only with regard to social and political issues, but also potential economic consequences. Some studies have indicated that some hostility exists toward foreign spouses—most of whom come from Mainland China and Southeast Asia (Ming-Chang 2011; Yi and Chang 2006)—and toward their children (Chen 2008). Although migrant workers either fill skill niches in the service economy or do work regarded as socially inappropriate or undesirable by Taiwanese (Lee 2002), it is sometimes claimed that migrant labor exerts a strongly negative pressure on the unemployment rate of the local labor force (Tsay and Lin 2001). Many sensationalistic headlines claim that the costs associated with foreign migrant labor are greater than the rewards, and they urge the government to reconsider a more restrictive policy for allowing in people from less-developed countries. Consequently, stereotypes and prejudice are transmitted through negative portrayals of specific migrants in the media.

Despite increasing public anxiety about inward migration, few studies have investigated the demographic and socioeconomic characteristics that shape perceptions of the impact of migrants on Taiwanese society—particularly guest workers and marriage immigrants from Southeast Asian countries and Mainland China. To explore how open Taiwanese society is, it is our intention to explore more deeply migrants' origins, looking at the linkages of their societies to Taiwan in historical, cultural, economic, and geographic contexts so as to make meaningful comparisons. Drawing on Bogardus' (1959) concept of social distance, we evaluate how the Taiwanese perceive and differentiate their relationships with migrants.

Thus, the first purpose of this study is to investigate variations in Taiwanese attitudes toward acceptance of migrants as co-workers, neighbors, and relatives by marriage. By constructing a typology to represent different attitudes toward immigration, it should also be possible to identify the most crucial and effective determinants, as proposed by previous studies and theoretical explanations, in predicting Taiwanese attitudes toward migrants from specific countries or regions. Thirdly, based on empirical results, we evaluate the utility of self-reported measures in studying attitudes toward migrants and the social context of ethnicity within Taiwanese society.

In the following section, we review major theoretical perspectives and empirical results explaining variations in perceptions of migrant workers and immigrants. The following section provides a detailed description of the data, measurements, and methods used in the analysis. Then we present our results from multinomial logistic regressions of the determinants of attitudes toward people from different countries or regions. In the final section, we summarize major findings and discuss our results and limitations.

BORGADUS' SOCIAL DISTANCE SCALE

Some people easily accept foreigners, but others are highly suspicious or even hostile to people who are not like *us*. Having been a destination for migration at different time periods, Taiwan presents a suitable environment for studying people's perceptions of social distance and exploring what forms their attitudes toward foreign migrants. Proposed by Emory S. Bogardus (1959), the concept of social distance was a construct thought to reflect the degrees of emotional intimacy or social prejudice to outsiders. It has been defined as a willingness to be associated with a certain group or individuals, or with a particular concern in situations of racial integration and equality.

The original social distance scale was designed as a seven-point Guttman scale concerning seven ordinal conditions (marriage, close friend, neighbor, co-worker, citizen, visitor to my country, and excluded from my country). The lower the score, the higher the degree of intimacy a respondent would grant to a particular racial/ethnic group. It was implied that a respondent who agreed with any particular item also agreed with all of the preceding items. As a simple but effective research tool, this scale was replicated by Bogardus himself in four nationwide surveys of American college students from 1926 to 1966 and later by Owen and her colleagues in 1977 (Owen, Eisne, and McFaul 1981). The latest national survey was conducted in 2001, with a few relatively invisible minorities replaced by increasingly visible ones in the list of questionnaire. These studies suggest a growing level of acceptance by an increasingly diverse American society, but race remains the most significant factor in determining personal attitudes toward other racial groups, especially when it comes to intermarriage across a racial boundary (Parrillo and Donoghue 2005). The Bogardus concept was also utilized to measure attitudes toward groups varying by religion, occupation, and nationality (Triandis et al. 1965). Scholars have recognized the applicability of social distance to communities with intellectual disabilities, and the scale has been used as an estimate of discrimination against persons with different limitations in their ability to adapt to everyday situations (Ouellette-Kuntz et al. 2010).

Nevertheless, the ordinal and cumulative nature of the social distance scale has been criticized as too simple to detect the intimacy of intergroup relations. Social interactions and attitudes may differ substantially from close family or friendship relations, to symbolic cultural contacts that occur within and beyond the boundary of one's own country (Sherif 1973). Since the Guttman scale claims there is a cumulative pattern resulting from the social construction of agreement and disagreement, it is an open question whether the ordered situations chosen in Bogardus' original scale indeed represent individuals' perceptions of social distance. Furthermore, as a self-reported attitudinal design, the social distance scale has the potential to be biased by social desirability or political correctness, which in turn may threaten the validity of measurements (Kleg and Yamamoto 1998).

In response to these criticisms, the Borgadus scale has been modified from its original version to fit different social contexts and research purposes. Adopting the concept of social distance, the 2008 Taiwan Social Change Survey focused only on three social situations within which Taiwanese were more likely to interact with foreign immigrants. Using a dichotomous response design, all respondents were asked to answer whether they "approve" or "disapprove" of a foreigner from the six specified countries and regions "being close kin by marriage," "being neighbors in the same street," and "being co-workers in your workplace."

DETERMINANTS OF SOCIAL DISTANCE TOWARD FOREIGN MIGRANTS

Previous studies have been devoted to investigating how the degrees of social distance can vary in ascribed attributes such as age, gender, as well as racial/ethnic background. While many scholars argue that younger people and women tend to express less social distance toward immigrants, empirical studies have produced mixed results with respect to the impacts of age and gender on immigration attitudes (Chandler and Tsai 2001; Tsai 2011; Yi and Chang 2006). The lack of consistency implies that, with reference to a particular social occasion, the degree of intimacy can be interpreted differently depending on the cultural background of respondents (Sherif 1973) and their perception of threat aroused by the size of particular immigrants (Meuleman et al. 2009). Taiwan, as a society with a relatively long history of immigration, provides a fascinating case study for further exploration of the variation in attitudes toward foreigners.

A Brief Note on the Taiwanese Immigration-Related Background

Both anthropologists and sociologists have long been interested in the boundaries and relations within and between the Han population and aborigines. Aborigines have inhabited the island for a long time but constitute approximately 2% of the total population. The majority of Taiwanese are the descendants of immigrants who arrived in two main waves—the first wave in the 17th century consisted of people of Fujian and Hakka origins, and the other in 1949, when the nationalist government relocated to the island. As they occupied different social positions and resources, the possibility of intermarriage across ethnic boundaries was often used to reflect the degree of closeness of ethnic relationship in these studies (Chen et al. 1994; Chuang 1994; Tsai 1996; Wang 1993). It is worth noting that recent studies have demonstrated the effects of frequent social contacts (within family, at school, and at workplace) in contributing to boundary-crossing marriages among Han ethnic groups (Hsieh and Chen 2009; Tsay and Wu 2006; Wang 2001).

Since the 1990s, an increasing number of marriages between Taiwanese and foreign nationals, including many from Southeast Asia and Mainland China, has added to the diversity of Taiwan's ethnic makeup. Nevertheless, locals have explicitly expressed anxiety in response to a changing social context and less restrictive immigration policy. Concerning human capital, marriage immigrants from less developed countries were generally disfavored by the Taiwanese. Referring to Mainland Chinese brides, scholars have emphasized the significance of "ethnic politics" in explaining the differential attitudes between Han ethnic groups (Tsai 2011). Given pre-existing family and kinship relations, Mainlanders who moved to Taiwan after the Civil War are more likely to accept marriage immigrants from China than are their Fujian and Hakka counterparts (Chen and Yu 2005; Yi and Chang 2006). However, anxiety is also raised by the importation of less-skilled workers from the same regions. Several empirical studies have attempted to explore whether occupation-based competition exists in the local labor market and did find some evidence of a heightened unemployment rate among less-skilled Taiwanese workers, but not professional and managerial workers (Tsay and Lin 2001). The potential economic competition might not only lead to negative attitudes toward guest workers, but worsen the ethnic politics mentioned above (Tsai and Chang 2010).

The Economic Explanation

As a society becomes ethnically diverse, the political, economic, and social powers of locals might be threatened by foreign migrants. Many scholars have concluded that education is the most consistent characteristic in explaining individual attitudes toward immigrants under such circumstances (Rustenbach 2010). Two major arguments attempt to take account of this relationship. The first—based on the split labor market theory, or economic competition perspective—argues that less educated natives are more likely to feel antagonistic because they have lost, or fear to lose, their jobs at the bottom of labor hierarchy—a position in which immigrants are generally overrepresented (Bonacich 1972; Chandler and Tsai 2001; Fetzer 2000; Mayda, 2006; O'Rourke and Sinnott 2006; Schissel et al. 1989). Whether foreign migrants contribute to lowering wages and employment is still inconclusive, but a general feeling that migrants are to blame for economic hardship is prevalent in Taiwanese society (Tsai 2011). Since the concentration of foreign migrants in particular occupations also depends on their countries of origin, respondents who are laborers or have lower social status may exhibit antagonism toward immigrants from Southeast Asia. In contrast, those in professional or technical jobs may express negative attitudes toward foreigners from the developed world.

The Cultural Explanation: Contact and Ideology

Despite the importance of economic motives, the cultural exposure and contacts explanation has received more attention in recent years. Proponents of this view posit that higher education creates a social environment in which individuals have more opportunities to contact people from different cultures and racial/ethnic groups. As a result, more educated people are more likely to have a cosmopolitanism view that contributes to greater tolerance of outsiders and immigrants (Hainmueller and Hiscox 2007; Haubert and Fussell 2006). While previous studies have taken holding a college degree as a measure of cosmopolitanism (Chandler and Tsai 2001; Haubert and Fussell 2006), we tend to use the years of education to build a more parsimonious model, for two reasons. First, colleges in Taiwan are relatively diverse, and vocational colleges are hardly expected to offer students a multicultural education. Second, based on the descriptive statistics, a linear positive relationship exists between years of education and acceptance of foreigners.

In addition to education, the empirical evidence suggests that social distance can be conceptualized on the basis of other parameters, such as the frequency of interaction between different groups or normative social distinctions about who should be considered as an *insider* or *outsider* (Karakayali 2009). Drawn from Allport's (1954) contact hypothesis, also known as intergroup contact theory, interpersonal contact is one of the most effective ways of reducing prejudice and conflicts between groups. Allport distinguishes between several kinds of social contact, such as casual contact, acquaintance, and contact in pursuit of common objectives. He concludes that mutual prejudice could be reduced through true or sustained acquaintance (i.e., friends, colleagues, and co-workers), but he posited that superficial casual contact cannot decrease prejudice toward other groups. The empirical evidence following the contact hypothesis shows that the level of perceived threat is likely to decrease or even diminish as groups have more opportunities to interact and become familiar with an unknown culture. Studies have found that, in some cases, the positive effect of intergroup contact extends to other groups not involved in the particular two-group contact (Pettigrew 2009; Pettigrew and Tropp 2006). In this study, using "travel experience" and "have acquaintances" in each specified country or region, we test the effects of two types of intergroup contact on acceptance of six particular nationalities.

A variety of ideas, values, and courses of action are spreading from society to society through the process of cultural diffusion. Globalization generally promotes indirect diffusion, which results in cultural changes that are embedded in societies even when the two cultures do not have direct geographical contact. Thus, it is reasonable to propose that an individual who is interested in discussing, exploring, and sharing one's understanding and knowledge of global issues would be more likely to have a positive attitude toward immigrants.

Unlike the socio-demographic characteristics and intergroup contact hypothesis, for which more empirical evidence has been accumulated, the normative and structural aspects of social distance were less well explored in previous studies. While researchers are optimistic about cosmopolitanism emerging from global civil society, the existence of xenophobia remains evident in some opinion polls and news headlines. In Europe, public polls have found that prejudice may be more about society than individuals. The anxieties expressed by respondents seemed to result not so much from the actual presence of minority groups but from the perception as to the ability of the host country to accommodate these newcomers (European Commission 1997). Concerning both the size and density of the Taiwan population, some people tend to feel that the increase in foreign immigrants, regardless of nationality, would worsen employment opportunities in the local labor market and the progress of industrial restructuring. In addition to xenophobia and prejudice toward foreigners in general, the in-group bias is the other social phenomenon used to explain an overall negative attitudes toward acceptance of outsiders in the society. It is understandable that people tend to hold positive attitudes toward members of their own groups. However, in-group bias is the tendency for people to give preferential treatment to others when they are perceived as belonging to similar groups. In particular, in- and out-groups are often divided by cultures, genders, and languages. Studies have shown that out-group members are more likely to be discriminated against than in-group members due to favoritism displayed toward those most like oneself (Ahmed

2007). Additional research has shown that in-group bias is stronger when social identity is salient (Giannakakis and Fritsche 2011).

In short, applying the concept of Borgadus' social distance, we first estimate the perceived social distance of Taiwanese toward immigrants from six countries/regions with regard to being co-workers, neighbors, or close kin. Next, the multinomial logistic regression is used to examine the effectiveness of determinants discussed above. To explore the effects of higher education and social status on the attitudes of Taiwanese toward immigrants, we include only the socio-demographic characteristics in the baseline model. Then, we consider the predictive power of cultural contact hypothesis and cultural ideology within the model, and we examine whether these determinants significantly mediate the impacts of education and social status on attitudes toward foreigners.

DATA, MEASUREMENT, AND METHOD

Data

This study used data from the culture and globalization module of the 2008 Taiwan Social Change Survey (TSCS). In the mid-1980s, the TSCS was launched to collect data on public attitudes on social, economic, political, and moral issues for tracking long-term trends of social changes in Taiwan. To investigate cultural homogeneity and heterogeneity in East Asian, the 2008 survey was a collaborative project of four national surveys in the region: Chinese General Social Survey (CGSS), Japanese General Social Survey (JGSS), Korean General Social Survey (KGSS), and TSCS.

The 2008 TSCS survey included a variety of measures on values, attitudes, and behaviors with regard to migration and citizenship. Based on the three-stage stratified random sampling scheme, 4,604 Taiwanese aged 18 years and older were selected, and face-to-face interviews were conducted in the summer. The final sample consisted of 2,067 respondents, with a response rate of 53%.

Dependent Variable

To estimate the perceived social distance between Taiwanese and foreigners, six major regions were pre-selected, and respondents were asked to answer a series of questions: "Do you accept having foreigners from the following six countries or regions, Japan, South Korea, China, Southeast Asia, Europe, and North America: (1) working alongside with you, (2) living in your neighborhood, and (3) being your close kin by marriage?" Participants were required to indicate that they "approve" or "disapprove" of each specified relationship with foreigners from each country or region. Figure 9.1 shows the distribution of attitudes toward acceptance of immigrants from six different countries/regions in the specified circumstances.

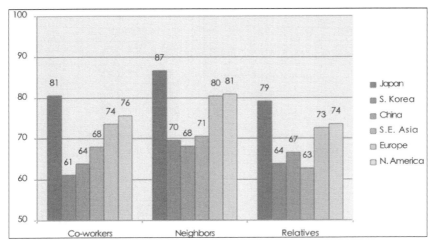

Figure 9.1 Acceptance of immigrants from six countries or regions.

In this study, 132 cases were excluded due to incomplete data on attitudes toward immigrants from different countries and regions. The relatively small number of aboriginals (33 respondents) and recent immigrants (11 respondents) was also eliminated. This is because the anti-immigrant attitude prevails among socioeconomically disadvantaged aboriginals, who tend to treat immigrants as a threat in the labor market competition (Fetzer 2000). As shown in Table 9.1, on the next page, those reporting the most positive attitudes toward immigrants from different countries and regions are themselves recent immigrants. Excluding missing data, the final sample size available for analysis was 1,867.

Each statement presents a situation indicating a certain level of acceptance of the specified relationship as well as the country/region. Answers gathered are regarded as indicative of the degree of social distance expressed by respondents. Unlike the original ordered items proposed by Borgardus (1954), regardless of the nationality of immigrants, "being neighbors on the same street" are most likely to be accepted by Taiwanese. For example, 87% of Taiwanese feel positive toward Japanese as neighbors, followed by North Americans and Europeans. For South Koreans, Chinese, and Southeast Asians, the corresponding positive figures are 70%, 68%, and 71%, respectively. In terms of "being co-workers," Japanese, Europeans, and North Americans were, again, more accepted than others. Surprisingly, the lowest acceptance goes to South Koreans (61%), which may reflect the potential competition between South Korea and Taiwan in high-tech and other industries. The situation least likely to be accepted is "being close kin by marriage." Owing to similarities in culture and language, more respondents expressed approval of Chinese individuals (67%). The above pattern suggests that Taiwanese tend to differentiate between foreigners not only according to the level of economic development, as social or cultural concerns also matter.

Table 9.1 Attitudes toward Acceptance of Migrants from Six Countries and Regions: Differences among Three Ethnic Groups

	Japan	S. Korea	China	S. E. Asia	Europe	N. America
	% of approval to "working alongside me in my job"					
Han	80.6	61.2	63.8	68.0	73.6	75.6
Aborigine	60.6	51.5	54.6	51.5	51.5	54.6
Immigrant	72.7	72.7	63.6	81.8	90.9	100.0
	% of approval to "on my street as neighbors"					
Han	86.7	69.6	68.2	70.5	80.4	80.9
Aborigine	66.7	54.6	57.6	57.6	54.6	57.6
Immigrant	72.7	81.8	63.6	100.0	81.8	100.0
	% of approval to "as close kin by marriage"					
Han	79.2	63.9	66.6	62.7	72.6	73.6
Aborigine	50.6	48.5	51.5	45.5	48.5	51.5
Immigrant	72.7	72.7	81.8	90.9	81.8	90.9

Note: The sample consists of 1,891 Han people (97.7%), 33 aboriginal people (1.7%), and 11 non-Taiwanese respondents (0.6%). Referring to The Republic of China Yearbook 2010, more than 95% of Taiwanese are of Han Chinese ancestry, and the remainder are composed of indigenous Austronesian people and recent immigrants (Government Information Office 2011).

As the social distance between Taiwanese and foreigners differs considerably depending on the specified relationship and from the country origin, multivariate analyses are performed for each country or region separately. Based on answers given to these three situations, the dependent variable was reconstructed as an integrated measure, and four typological attitudes toward acceptance of immigrants from a specified country or region were generated. The four types used for analyses are "willing to accept immigrants in all situations," "willing to accept immigrants as co-workers and either as neighbors or as relatives," "willing to accept immigrants either as neighbors or as relatives, but not as co-workers," and "rejecting immigrants in any situation." As shown in Table 9.2, 70% of Taiwanese expressed a willingness to accept Japanese as co-workers, neighbors, and relatives. In comparison with other countries or regions, it is obvious that Taiwanese feel the least social distance with Japanese. Only 9% of Taiwanese reject any Japanese immigrants, the lowest figure across six countries or regions. Immigrants from Europe and North America are accepted moderately by Taiwanese. In contrast, South Koreans, Mainland Chinese, and Southeast Asians are less approved of, with nearly one-fifth of Taiwanese report strongly negative feelings. Given the discrete nature of the dependent variable, multinomial logistic regression is performed to analyze the effects of determinants of four typological attitudes toward immigrants from each country and region separately. Those "willing to accept immigrants in all situations" are used as the reference category.

Table 9.2 Distribution of Typological Attitudes toward Acceptance of Migrants from Six Countries or Regions

	Japan	South Korea	China	S.E. Asia	Europe	North America
Accept immigrants in all situations*	70.2	49.6	52.6	52.2	63.1	65.1
Accept immigrants as co-workers, and as neighbors or relatives	10.4	11.4	11.1	15.7	10.4	10.5
Accept immigrants as neighbors and/or relatives, but not co-workers	10.5	17.3	14.3	12.2	11.3	10.0
Reject immigrants in any situations	8.9	21.7	22.0	19.9	15.2	14.4

* Reference category in the multinomial logistic regression analysis.

Independent Variables

Three sets of independent variables were used in the multivariate analysis to examine their effects on social distance or attitudes toward migrants. As previous studies have identified the effects of personal attributes such as age, gender, marital status, ethnicity, place of residence, education, and employment pattern on public attitudes toward immigrants, we include these standard socioeconomic and demographic control variables in the baseline model. Respondent's age was coded in years, and gender was recoded as a dichotomous variable, with female taken as the reference group. Marital status was divided into single and other (reference group). With respect to the multi-ethnic nature of Taiwan's society, we include the ethnic background of respondents, broken down into three categories: Fujian, Hakka, and Mainlanders. Two dummy variables were generated with Mainlanders as the reference group. Place of residence was divided into rural and urban areas, with the latter taken as the reference group.

Levels and years of education are two popular measures for reflecting people's human capital. Recent migration studies have shown a linear effect of education on the attitude toward immigrants (Rustenbach 2010; Tsai 2011). To make the multivariate analysis more parsimonious, years of education was used to represent respondents' educational attainment. While employment status and income per capita are better indicators for the economic situation of individuals, the lack of data (i.e., currently unemployed and non-workers) to some extent produces less powerful or biased prediction. Therefore, the economic security was measured by a subjective evaluation, social status. Respondents were asked, "In our society, some

180   Yu-Hua Chen and Chin-Chun Yi

may occupy higher social positions and others may be at lower positions. Given 10 points as the highest status and 1 point as the lowest status, would you say which score is more likely to represent your current social status?" Twenty-four respondents were excluded from the analysis due to data missing. The descriptive statistics of independent variables are presented in Table 9.3.

Table 9.3 Descriptive Statistics of Independent Variables (N = 1867)

Variables	Percent	Mean	S.D	Range
Sociodemographic Attributes				
Age		44.2	16.5	19~95
Gender				
Male	49.9			
Female	50.1			
Ethnic background				
Fujian	75.5			
Hakka	12.7			
Mainlander	11.8			
Marital status				
Single	29.5			
Married, divorced, widowed	70.5			
Place of residence				
Urban area	54.3			
Rural area	45.7			
Year of education		11.6	4.6	0~25
Social status		5.1	1.7	1~10
Cultural Contact				
Ever travel in Japan (%)	34.9	Having acquaintance in Japan (%)		16.7
China	36.3	China		31.3
S. Korea	15.2	S. Korea		7.2
S.E. Asia	43.1	S.E. Asia		19.8
Europe	13.2	Europe		7.2
N. America	17.3	N. America		15.1
Global knowledge		3.8	2.2	1~7
Cultural Ideology				
Xenophobia		3.2	1.4	1~7
In-group orientation		3.2	1.8	1~7

The concept of cultural contact includes three measures. Respondents were asked, "Have you ever been to this country or region?" and "Do you have acquaintances from this country or region?" Travel experience is used to represent the casual contact with foreigners, with the latter offering information on real contact with foreigners. Referring to six targeted countries and regions, all that applied to respondents' experience were recoded. Table 9.3 shows that Taiwanese are more likely to travel to Japan, China, and Southeast Asia, and 31.3% of respondents have acquaintances in China, followed by 19.8% in Southeast Asia. Fewer respondents have acquaintances in Japan or North America. The 2008 survey shows that Taiwanese are least likely to have substantial contact with people in South Koreans and Europeans. The third measure of global knowledge was generated from answers to the question: "How often do you talk about international issues with your family members, friends, or other people?" Seven categories ranging from *never* (one point) to *almost every day* (seven points) were recoded.

The third group of explanatory variables, cultural ideology, includes two measures to denote one's conservative ideology and preference. Xenophobia measures an overall evaluation by respondents with regard to economic and environmental threats resulting from immigration. Three questions were asked: "Mobility of people, goods, and capital etc. has been increasing among countries and regions; do you think it's good or bad for the economy, opportunities in the local labor market, and the environment in general?" Respondents were required to indicate, on a seven-point Likert-like scale, their level of approval of or disapproval of the three statements. The mean scores range from one to seven points. Xenophobia is represented by the higher score. The other variable, the in-group orientation, was recoded from the question: "When hiring someone at a private company, even if a person with whom you are unacquainted is the more qualified, it will be better to give the opportunity to relatives or friends." A seven-point Likert-like scale was also used to reflect the level of agreement, ranging from *strongly disagree* (one point) to *strongly agree* (seven points). A higher score indicates a stronger in-group orientation held by the respondent.

Analysis

In the next section, we use multinomial logistic regression method to assess separately the proposed independent variables on four typological attitudes toward migrants from six countries and regions. Since four attitudes toward migrants are not ordered measures, it is inappropriate to use ordered logistic regression. Two models are provided for evaluating whether the influence of education and economic condition on attitudes toward migration could be mediated by cultural contact, values, and preferences. The first baseline model includes only socio-demographic attributes, and the other model adds all explanatory variables for predicting attitudes toward migrants from different countries and regions.

DETERMINANTS OF ATTITUDES TOWARD ACCEPTANCE OF MIGRANTS

Applying the multinomial logistic regression model, the effects of explanatory determinants on four types of attitudes toward migrants from six targeting countries or regions were examined separately. To explore the most critical characteristics associated with anti-immigrant attitudes held by Taiwanese, the category of "willing to accept migrants in all situations" was chosen as the reference group. As a result, three equations including "reject migrants in all situations," "willing to accept migrants as neighbors or relatives, but not co-workers," and "willing to accept migrants as co-workers, and as neighbors or relatives" versus "willing to accept migrants in all situations" were compared.

Japan

The log odds of typological attitudes toward Japanese are regressed on age, gender, ethnicity, marital status, years of education, social status, and place of residence, and the results are shown in Model A in Table 9.4. Overall, Taiwanese hold a relatively positive attitude toward Japanese migrants as co-workers, neighbors, and relatives. The increase in years of education leads to significantly lower log odds of disapproving of Japanese, net of the effects of other socio-demographic attributes. A higher subjectively reported social status is also associated with positive attitudes toward Japanese. In comparison with Mainlanders, both Fujian and Hakka people are more likely to accept Japanese migrants. For other control variables, rural residents are less likely to welcome migrants from Japan than their urban counterparts. In terms of the effect of marital status, we find that single Taiwanese are less likely to entirely disapprove of Japanese migrants. The effects of age and gender on attitudes toward Japanese are not significant in the baseline model.

Next, we add other predicting variables into Model B, examining whether the effects of education and socioeconomic condition on Taiwanese attitudes toward Japanese immigrants are mediated by cultural contact and/or less conservative values and preferences. While ethnicity and marital status show a similar pattern in shaping Taiwanese attitudes toward Japanese migrants in the full model, the effects of education and social status become

The Perception of Social Distance in a Multi-ethnic Society 183

Table 9.4 Results of Multinomial Logistic Regression Predicting Taiwanese's Acceptance of Migrants from Japan

Independent variable	Model A Rejection All b (s.e.)	Model A No Co-worker b (s.e.)	Model A Co-worker b (s.e.)	Model B Rejection All b (s.e.)	Model B No Co-worker b (s.e.)	Model B Co-worker b (s.e.)
Socio-demographic						
Age	.01 (.01)	.003 (.01)	.0003 (.01)	.01 (.01)	.001 (.01)	-.002 (.01)
Male	.28 (.18)	-.15 (.16)	-.21 (.16)	.26 (.18)	-.13 (.16)	-.15 (.16)
Ethnic background						
Fujian	-1.14 (.24)***	-.58 (.23)*	-.49 (.23)*	-1.27 (.26)***	-.65 (.23)**	-.56 (.24)*
Hakka	-.75 (.32)*	-.46 (.30)	-.29 (.30)	-.99 (.33)**	-.60 (.31)*	-.33 (.30)
Mainlander (r.)						
Single	-.58 (.28)*	-.32 (.23)	.12 (.21)	-.66 (.29)*	-.38 (.23)	.15 (.22)
Rural residence	.52 (.18)**	-.03 (.16)	.31 (.16)*	.35 (.18)*	-.12 (.16)	.30 (.16)*
Year of education	-.11 (.03)***	-.04 (.02)*	-.02 (.02)	-.04 (.03)	-.01 (.03)	-.02 (.03)
Social status	-.12 (.05)*	-.10 (.05)*	.02 (.05)	-.06 (.05)	-.08 (.05)	.03 (.05)
Cultural Contact						
Travel				-.40 (.22)	-.16 (.18)	.07 (.18)
Acquaintance				-1.05 (.41)*	-.58 (.26)*	.36 (.20)
Global knowledge				-.22 (.05)***	-.14 (.04)**	-.02 (.04)
Cultural Ideology						
Xenophobia				.22 (.06)***	.09 (.06)	.25 (.06)***
In-group orientation				.03 (.05)	.06 (.04)	-.11 (.05)*
Intercept	-.12 (.69)	-.36 (.63)	-1.46 (.64)*	-.88 (.79)	-.65 (.70)	-1.94 (.71)**

Notes: The reference category for the equations is "willing to accept migrants in all situations."
*** p< .001, ** p< .01, * p< .05

statistically insignificant, as predicted. Cultural contact and value variables are significantly associated with attitudes toward Japanese immigrants in the anticipated direction, except the effect of general contact through travel. Having acquaintances in Japan and being interested in global issues are positively associated with acceptance of Japanese migrants. Concerns that immigration might worsen the local labor market or the environment are associated with opposition to migrants from Japan. Nevertheless, there is an unexpected effect that results from the sense of in-group preference reported by respondents. We assume that those who have a stronger perception of group differences are more likely to favor their own group and to penalize outsiders. The result shows in-group-oriented respondents are actually more willing to accept people from Japan, regardless of the situation. Do Taiwanese view Japanese migrants as in-group members due to the past colonial experience or cultural diffusion? It is worth exploring this social phenomenon in greater detail.

South Korea

Table 9.5 presents the results regarding the determinants of Taiwanese attitudes toward the acceptance of migrants from South Korea. The baseline model (Model A) shows that older people and men are more likely to oppose Korean migrants than are their younger counterparts and women, but ethnic background, marital status, social status, and place of residence do not have significant impacts on attitudes toward Korean migrants. Examining the effect of human capital, the increase in years of education does not reduce negative attitudes toward Korean people. In particular, more educated Taiwanese are less likely to welcome Koreans as co-workers.

Examining Model B in Table 9.5, higher education is still associated with an anti-immigrant sentiment toward Koreans, holding other independent variables constant. Although real cultural contact (having acquaintances in South Korea) and global knowledge might decrease the level of antagonism, Taiwanese remain least likely to accept any type of migrant from South Korea. Again, in-group orientation and economic and environmental threats negatively impact the likelihood of acceptance of Korean migrants. Unlike attitudes toward Japanese, in which the variation is effectively explained by independent variables, Taiwanese attitudes toward Korean migrants remain puzzling and a fit subject for further research.

China

Due to the controversial relationship across the Taiwan Strait, it is important to investigate how Taiwanese express their feelings and report their attitudes toward acceptance of Mainland Chinese with regard to being co-workers, neighbors, or close relatives by marriage. According to Model A in Table 9.6, more educated Taiwanese are less likely to accept a variety of

Table 9.5 Results of Multinomial Logistic Regression Predicting Taiwanese's Acceptance of Migrants from South Korea

Independent variable	Model A			Model B		
	Rejection All	No Co-worker	Co-worker	Rejection All	No Co-worker	Co-worker
	b (s.e.)	b (s.e.)	b (s.e.)	b (s.e.)	b (s.e.)	b (s.e.)
Socio-demographic						
Age	.03 (.01)***	.01 (.01)*	-.004 (.01)	.02 (.01)***	.01 (.01)	-.01 (.01)
Male	.35 (.12)**	.08 (.13)	-.27 (.16)	.37 (.13)**	.08 (.13)	-.22 (.16)
Ethnic background						
Fujian	.03 (.20)	.11 (.21)	-.48 (.22)	-.03 (.20)	.10 (.21)	-.54 (.23)
Hakka	.23 (.25)	.02 (.28)	-.19 (.28)	.14 (.25)	-.01 (.28)	-.21 (.29)
Mainlander (r.)						
Single	.04 (.17)	-.13 (.18)	.17 (.21)	.01 (.18)	-.14 (.18)	.19 (.21)
Rural residence	-.20 (.13)	-.25 (.13)	.08 (.16)	-.26 (.13)	-.26 (.14)	.05 (.16)
Year of education	.03 (.02)	.04 (.02)*	.04 (.02)	.06 (.02)**	.05 (.02)*	.03 (.03)
Social status	-.03 (.04)	-.02 (.04)	.04 (.05)	-.02 (.04)	-.01 (.04)	.05 (.05)
Cultural Contact						
Travel				.16 (.17)	.06 (.19)	.25 (.22)
Acquaintance				-.58 (.30)*	-.02 (.26)	.56 (.25)*
Global knowledge				-.09 (.03)**	-.05 (.04)	.03 (.04)
Cultural Ideology						
Xenophobia				.08 (.05)	.04 (.05)	.19 (.06)**
In-group orientation				.08 (.04)*	.005 (.04)	-.08 (.05)
Intercept	-2.34 (.50)***	-1.86 (.54)***	-1.61 (.64)**	-2.80 (.56)***	-1.90 (.60)***	-1.96 (.72)**

Notes: The reference category for the equations is "willing to accept migrants in all situations."
*** p< .001, ** p< .01, * p< .05

Table 9.6 Results of Multinomial Logistic Regression Predicting Taiwanese Acceptance of Migrants from China

Independent variable	Model A			Model B		
	Rejection All	No Co-worker	Co-worker	Rejection All	No Co-worker	Co-worker
	b (s.e.)	b (s.e.)	b (s.e.)	b (s.e.)	b (s.e.)	b (s.e.)
Socio-demographic						
Age	.002 (.01)	.004 (.01)	-.01 (.01)	-.001 (.01)	.0002 (.01)	-.01 (.01)
Male	-.06 (.12)	-.28 (.14)*	-.33 (.16)*	-.04 (.12)	-.29 (.14)*	-.30 (.16)*
Ethnic background						
Fujian	.90 (.22)***	.61 (.24)**	.05 (.24)	.83 (.23)***	.65 (.25)**	.001 (.24)
Hakka	.98 (.27)***	.58 (.30)*	.20 (.30)	.89 (.28)***	.61 (.30)*	.15 (.31)
Mainlander (r.)						
Single	-.18 (.17)	.08 (.19)	.07 (.21)	-.18 (.17)	.10 (.20)	.14 (.21)
Rural residence	-.18 (.12)	.05 (.14)	.32 (.16)*	-.24 (.13)	-.04 (.15)	.29 (.16)
Year of education	.01 (.02)	.04 (.02)*	.03 (.02)	.03 (.02)	.05 (.02)*	.03 (.03)
Social status	-.12 (.04)***	-.10 (.04)*	-.06 (.05)	-.11 (.04)**	-.10 (.04)**	-.06 (.05)
Cultural Contact						
Travel				.13 (.14)	.32 (.16)	.24 (.18)
Acquaintance				-.13 (.15)	.03 (.16)	-.09 (.18)
Global knowledge				-.06 (.03)	-.04 (.04)	.06 (.04)
Cultural Ideology						
Xenophobia				.17 (.05)***	.10 (.06)	.22 (.06)***
In-group orientation				.02 (.04)	.02 (.04)	.02 (.05)
Intercept	-1.12 (.50)*	-1.90 (.58)***	-1.18 (.64)	-1.70 (.56)**	-2.21 (.65)***	-2.17 (.73)**

Notes: The reference category for the equations is "willing to accept migrants in all situations."
*** p< .001, ** p< .01, * p< .05

Chinese migrants. In contrast, respondents of higher social status are more willing to accept people from China. For other control variables, women and rural residents are less likely to accept Chinese migrants than are their counterparts. Respondents' age is not associated with attitudes toward Chinese migrants. It is worth noting that, compared with Mainlanders, who themselves, or whose parents, moved to Taiwan after the Civil War, Fujian and Hakka people are more likely to disapprove of Chinese migrants.

After adding other predicting variables, respondents' socio-demographic attributes—including gender, ethnicity, years of education, and social status—are still significantly related to attitudes and show similar patterns of influence derived from the baseline model. In terms of type and frequency of cultural contact, however, no significant effect is found in Model B for predicting Taiwanese attitudes toward Chinese migrants. On the contrary, people who negatively associate economic or environmental threats with immigration are more likely to disapprove of Chinese migrants. Despite sharing the same cultural origins, the effects of an in-group orientation on attitudes toward Chinese migrants remain statistically significant.

Southeast Asia

Examining the regression coefficients in Model A of Table 9.7, only the age, years of education, and marital status of respondents are associated with acceptance of migrants from Southeast Asian countries. Older and married Taiwanese are less likely to support migrants from this region than are their younger and single counterparts. The results also indicate that more educated Taiwanese only partially approve of migrants in general and guest workers in particular. Other control variables do not show a significant impact on the attitudes of respondents.

In the full model, regardless of the status of the migrant, an increase in years of education does not reduce the likelihood of disapproving of migrants from Southeast Asia. The effect of age becomes insignificant in Model B, but single Taiwanese are still less likely to reject all migrants from this region. Concerning the impact of cultural contact, Taiwanese who have acquaintances in Southeast Asian countries, or who have more global knowledge, are less likely to reject people from this region. Consistent with our prediction, xenophobia and an in-group orientation are negatively association with acceptance of Southeast Asian migrants.

Europe and North America

According to our descriptive statistics, shown in Figure 9.1, in comparison with other countries or regions, fewer Taiwanese disapprove of migrants from Europe and North America. Since determinants of respondents' attitudes toward migrants from these two regions show similar patterns of influence, we decided to jointly present and evaluate both sets of major findings (Table 9.8 and Table 9.9). Several of the socio-demographic attributes

Table 9.7 Results of Multinomial Logistic Regression Predicting Taiwanese Acceptance of Migrants from South East Asia

Independent variable	Model A Rejection All b (s.e.)	Model A No Co-worker b (s.e.)	Model A Co-worker b (s.e.)	Model B Rejection All b (s.e.)	Model B No Co-worker b (s.e.)	Model B Co-worker b (s.e.)
Socio-demographic						
Age	.01 (.01)*	.005 (.01)	.01 (.01)	.01 (.01)	.01 (.01)	.005 (.01)
Male	.12 (.13)	-.10 (.15)	-.16 (.14)	.13 (.13)	-.11 (.15)	-.13 (.14)
Ethnic background						
Fujian	.16 (.20)	.37 (.25)	-.02 (.21)	.04 (.21)	.36 (.25)	-.06 (.21)
Hakka	.43 (.25)	.33 (.32)	.28 (.26)	.30 (.26)	.30 (.32)	.25 (.26)
Mainlander (r.)						
Single	-.35 (.18)*	-.18 (.21)	-.02 (.18)	-.41 (.19)*	-.24 (.21)	.02 (.19)
Rural residence	-.05 (.13)	-.09 (.15)	.10 (.14)	-.12 (.13)	-.13 (.16)	.07 (.14)
Year of education	-.02 (.02)	.03 (.02)	.07 (.02)***	.003 (.02)	.05 (.02)*	.06 (.02)**
Social status	-.03 (.04)	-.05 (.04)	.01 (.04)	-.02 (.04)	-.04 (.05)	.01 (.04)
Cultural Contact						
Travel				-.02 (.14)	-.15 (.16)	.01 (.15)
Acquaintance				-.96 (.20)***	-.23 (.20)	.12 (.16)
Global knowledge				-.02 (.04)	-.09 (.04)*	.06 (.04)
Cultural Ideology						
Xenophobia				.11 (.05)*	.02 (.06)	.14 (.05)**
In-group orientation				.12 (.04)***	-.02 (.05)	.01 (.04)
Intercept	-1.16 (.51)*	-2.19 (.61)***	-2.25 (.55)***	-1.79 (.58)**	-2.03 (.68)***	-2.98 (.62)***

Notes: The reference category for the equations is "willing to accept migrants in all situations."
*** p<.001, ** p<.01, * p<.05

Table 9.8 Results of Multinomial Logistic Regression Predicting Taiwanese Acceptance of Migrants from Europe

Independent variable	Model A Rejection All b (s.e.)	Model A No Co-worker b (s.e.)	Model A Co-worker b (s.e.)	Model B Rejection All b (s.e.)	Model B No Co-worker b (s.e.)	Model B Co-worker b (s.e.)
Socio-demographic						
Age	.02 (.01)***	.01 (.01)*	.02 (.01)*	.02 (.01)**	.01 (.01)*	.01 (.01)*
Male	.40 (.15)**	.25 (.16)	.27 (.16)	.44 (.15)**	.24 (.16)	.30 (.16)*
Ethnic background						
Fujian	.36 (.25)	.15 (.25)	.13 (.24)	.24 (.26)	.14 (.25)	.10 (.24)
Hakka	.62 (.31)	.26 (.31)	.45 (.31)	.45 (.32)	.19 (.32)	-.04 (.32)
Mainlander (r.)						
Single	-.62 (.24)**	-.29 (.22)	.18 (.21)	-.68 (.24)**	-.33 (.22)	.19 (.21)
Rural residence	.32 (.15)*	-.06 (.16)	.16 (.16)	.22 (.15)	-.10 (.16)	.13 (.16)
Year of education	-.11 (.02)***	-.06 (.02)**	.03 (.02)	-.06 (.02)**	-.03 (.02)	.04 (.03)
Social status	-.12 (.04)**	-.07 (.04)	.004 (.05)	-.09 (.04)	-.05 (.04)	.01 (.05)
Cultural Contact						
Travel				.18 (.25)	-.44 (.29)	.08 (.24)
Acquaintance				-.81 (.49)	-.38 (.40)	.23 (.28)
Global knowledge				-.16 (.04)***	-.06 (.04)	-.03 (.04)
Cultural Ideology						
Xenophobia				.15 (.05)**	.03 (.06)	.16 (.06)**
In-group orientation				.12 (.04)**	.01 (.04)	.03 (.05)
Intercept	-1.33 (.60)*	-1.43 (.62)*	-3.21 (.63)***	-1.91 (.66)**	-1.69 (.70)*	-3.79 (.72)***

Notes: The reference category for the equations is "willing to accept migrants in all situations."
*** p< .001, ** p< .01, * p< .05

Table 9.9 Results of Multinomial Logistic Regression Predicting Taiwanese Acceptance of Migrants from North America

Independent variable	Model A Rejection All b (s.e.)	Model A No Co-worker b (s.e.)	Model A Co-worker b (s.e.)	Model B Rejection All b (s.e.)	Model B No Co-worker b (s.e.)	Model B Co-worker b (s.e.)
Socio-demographic						
Age	.01 (.01)*	.01 (.01)	.01 (.01)	.01 (.01)*	.01 (.01)	.01 (.01)
Male	.39 (.15)**	.25 (.16)	.41 (.16)**	.40 (.15)**	.26 (.16)	.43 (.16)**
Ethnic background						
Fujian	.15 (.25)	.19 (.27)	.23 (.25)	.01 (.26)	.12 (.27)	.17 (.25)
Hakka	.46 (.30)	.20 (.34)	-.06 (.33)	.25 (.31)	.09 (.34)	-.14 (.34)
Mainlander (r.)						
Single	-.52 (.23)*	.02 (.23)	.02 (.21)	-.57 (.24)*	.02 (.23)	.02 (.22)
Rural residence	.47 (.15)**	-.11 (.16)	.26 (.16)	.34 (.15)	-.18 (.17)	.20 (.16)
Year of education	-.13 (.02)***	-.08 (.02)***	.02 (.02)	-.06 (.02)*	-.05 (.03)*	.05 (.03)*
Social status	-.13 (.04)**	-.09 (.05)*	.05 (.05)	-.10 (.04)*	-.08 (.05)	.06 (.05)
Cultural Contact						
Travel				-.38 (.28)	.18 (.25)	.08 (.23)
Acquaintance				-.68 (.37)*	-.67 (.32)*	-.25 (.25)
Global knowledge				-.20 (.04)***	-.06 (.04)	-.05 (.04)
Cultural Ideology						
Xenophobia				.19 (.05)***	.11 (.06)*	.18 (.06)**
In-group orientation				.09 (.04)*	.04 (.05)	-.01 (.05)
Intercept	-.64 (.61)	-1.24 (.67)	-3.38 (.63)***	-1.54 (.68)*	-1.76 (.75)*	-3.99 (.72)***

Notes: The reference category for the equations is "willing to accept migrants in all situations."
*** p< .001, ** p< .01, * p< .05

of respondents are predictive of a tendency to be accepting of migrants. For instance, Taiwanese who are younger, female, and single are more willing to approve of people from Western societies than are their older, male, and married counterparts, but regionally significant determinants (ethnic background in particular) have failed to show any significant influence on attitudes toward migrants. Our study suggests that Taiwanese with more education and higher social status are least likely to absolutely disapprove of migrants from Europe and North America.

Similar to results discussed above, the xenophobia and in-group orientation expressed by respondents are again associated with negative attitudes toward migrants from Western societies, regardless of the reasons for migration. In terms of the effects of various types and frequencies of cultural contact, it is important to note that Taiwanese who have acquaintances in North America are less likely to disapprove of people from this region, but this relationship has no significant impact on attitudes toward Europeans. Respondents who are more interested in global issues also reveal more positive attitudes toward people from these two regions.

CONCLUSION AND DISCUSSION

Against the background of rising numbers of foreign workers and cross-border marriages over the last two decades, this study explores general attitudes toward migrants in Taiwan. Based on historical, cultural, economic, and geographic similarities and differences, migrants are categorized as belonging to one of six sources of migrants: Japan, South Korea, China, Southeast Asia, Europe, and North America. Using data from the 2008 TSCS, we investigate how Taiwanese perceive different types of social distance between themselves and migrants, and we indicate the crucial determinants of their attitudes toward acceptance of migrants from a specified country or region, whether they are co-workers, neighbors, or close kin.

Unlike the original order of Borgadus' social distance scale, our results indicate that residential segregation between groups is not significant in Taiwan; however, Taiwanese pay much attention to who is allowed to work in the local labor market and who will marry Taiwanese. Regardless of the situation, Japanese, Europeans, and North Americans are most likely to be accepted by Taiwanese, as expected. In terms of the kinship relationship by marriage, Mainland Chinese are more approved of than are immigrants from South Korea or Southeast Asia. We suspect that while economic development may explain the positive attitudes toward migrants from Japan, Europe, and North America, and negative attitudes toward China and Southeast Asia, the perception of economic competition likely results in the expression of greater social distance with Korean immigrants.

Examining three social situations separately, like previous studies, we find the social distance toward foreign co-workers is somewhat greater than that toward neighbors or close kin. However, it is by no means easy to identify how an individual distinguishes his or her attitudes pertaining to the public versus private spheres. To create an integrative measure of social distance for the purpose of comparative study, four attitudinal types following a sequential order from pro-immigrants to anti-immigrants are re-constructed. They are "willing to accept migrants in all situations," "willing to accept migrants as co-workers and either as neighbors or as relatives," "willing to accept migrants either as neighbors or as relatives, but not as co-workers," and "reject migrants in all situations." With this constructed social distance, the majority of Taiwanese (49.6%–70.2%) fall into the total acceptance category, at some point, depending on the nationality and origin of the migrants in question.

Our research not only shows that a majority of Taiwanese hold positive attitudes toward migrants, it also contributes to the existing literature on the perception of migrants by demonstrating that socio-demographic attributes, cultural contact, as well as cultural ideology are empirically relevant to what attitudes are expressed by Taiwanese. To evaluate the predictive power of competing theoretical explanations, Table 9.10 presents a summary of major results from the multinomial logistic regression analyses conducted for each specified country and region.

Table 9.10 Summary of Predicted Effects of Independent Variables on Attitude toward Acceptance of Migrants from Six Countries or Regions

	Japan	S. Korea	China	S.E. Asia	Europe	N. America
Socio-demographic Attributes						
Older age		-			-	
Male			-	+		-	-
Mainlander	-		+			
Single	+			+	+	+
Rural residence	-					
Year of education			-		-	+	+
Social status			+			+
Cultural Contact						
Casual contact: travel						
Real contact: acquaintance	+	+		+		+
Global knowledge	+	+		+	+	+
Cultural Ideology						
Xenophobia	-	-	-	-	-	-
In-group orientation	+	-		-	-	
Intercept	+	+	+	+	+	+

It is obvious that positive attitudes toward migrants are generally associated with socio-demographic attributes of respondents: age, gender, marital status, and place of residence. The only exception is found in the survey of opinions concerning Mainland Chinese, with more men expressing acceptance of migrants from the Mainland regardless of the social situation. The decisive influence of ethnic background shows sharply different attitudes toward migrants from Japan and China. Compared with Fujian and Hakka, who have settled in Taiwan for several generations, Mainlanders are more likely to endorse Chinese immigrants the rights to work with or marry Taiwanese, but not Japanese immigrants. The anti-Japanese sentiment of Mainlanders is related to Japan's long history of invasions and war crimes in China between 1894 and 1945. The effect of education is apparent in two patterns, with a positive relationship found with regard to migrants from the more advanced regions and a negative relationship with regard to migrants from South Korea and Southeast Asia. In terms of economic competition theory, it is evident that higher status Taiwanese are less likely to reject migrants regardless of their origins.

For those behaviors related to cultural contact, casual cultural contact (i.e., travel experience) does not change or affect the social distance reported. In contrast, Taiwanese who have real cultural contact, or who have acquaintances in other countries, are more likely to accept migrants, except for those from China or Europe. The complicated relationship between China and Taiwan makes it more difficult to predict Taiwanese feeling toward Mainland Chinese. The cultural differences and geographic segregation between Taiwan and European countries also create a greater social distance. Hence, the cultural explanation fails to exhibit predictive effects.

Overall, both attitude and behavior related to the globalization are found to be significant predictors. As expected, a weak in-group orientation is positively associated with Taiwanese's acceptance of people from other countries. The only exception is that Taiwanese who are more in-group oriented seem to be more willing to accept Japanese. Perhaps this is a historical consequence of Japanese colonialization in Taiwan, which has resulted in greater cultural familiarity. In other words, the cultural contact and cultural ideology in a multi-ethnicity society are important in explaining reported social distance toward various groups of foreign migrants.

Our empirical findings suggest that hostility toward foreign migrants is more likely to be associated with economic rather than with racial motives. Given economic insecurity, a worsening of the economy and environment, some Taiwanese may have developed negative attitudes toward immigrants whom they consider potential competitors in the global market, for instance, South Koreans, or toward those they consider likely to compete for low-skill employment, for instance, people from Southeast Asian countries.

In brief, our study is able to document social distance as a valid indicator of attitudes reflecting the acceptance of foreign migrants in various spheres of one's life. Among six countries or regions from which migrants originate, more than half of Taiwanese respondents report a positive impression, with

Japanese being the most favored group. In the comparison between having migrants as co-workers, neighbors, or kin, our analyses point out that, in addition to expected demographic effects, cultural aspects also need to be taken into account. In particular, the experience of real contact with migrants, frequent discussions of global affairs, as well as generally favorable attitudes toward globalization contribute to a positive perception of foreign migrants in Taiwan.

REFERENCES

Ahmed, Ali M. 2007. "Group Identity, Social Distance and Intergroup Bias." *Journal of Economic Psychology* 28(3):324–37.
Allport, Gordon W. 1954. *The Nature of Prejudice*. Boston, MA: Addison Wesley.
Bogardus, Emory S. 1959. *Social Distance*. Yellow Springs, OH: The Antioch Press.
Bonacich, Edna. 1972. "A Theory of Ethnic Antagonism: The Split Labor Market." *American Sociological Review* 37(5):547–59.
Chandler, Charles R., and Yung-mei Tsai. 2001. "Social Factors Influencing Immigration Attitudes: An Analysis of Data from the General Social Survey." *The Social Sciences Journal* 38: 177–88.
Chen, Chung-min, Ying-chang Chuang, and Shu-min Huang, eds. 1994. *Ethnicity in Taiwan: Social, Historical and Cultural Perspectives*. Taipei: Institute of Ethnology, Academia Sinica.
Chen, Chih-jou Jay, and Te-lin Yu. 2005. "Public Attitudes toward Taiwan's Immigration Policies." *Taiwanese Sociology* 10:95–148. (in Chinese)
Chen, Yu-Hua. 2008. "The Significance of Cross-Border Marriage in a Low Fertility Society: Evidence from Taiwan." *Journal of Comparative Family Studies* 39(3):331–52.
Chuang, Ying-Chang. 1994. *Family and Marriage: A Comparison of Hokkien and Hakka in North Taiwan*. Taipei: Institute of Ethnology, Academia Sinica. (in Chinese)
European Commission. 1997. *Racism and Xenophobia in Europe*. Eurobarometer Opinion Poll No. 47.1. Retrived from http://ec.europa.eu/public_opinion/archives/ebs/ebs_113_en.pdf (01/11/2011)
Fetzer, Joel S. 2000. *Public Attitudes toward Immigration in the United States, France, and Germany*. New York: Cambridge University Press.
Giannakakis, Andrew E., and Immo Fritsche. 2011. "Social Identities, Group Norms, and Threat: On the Malleability of Ingroup Bias." *Personality and Social Psychology Bulletin* 37(1):82–93.
Government Information Office. 2011. *The Republic of China Yearbook 2010*. Taipei, Taiwan: Executive Yuan, Republic of China.
Hainmueller, Jens, and Michael J. Hiscox. 2007. "Educated Preferences: Explaining Attitudes toward Immigration in Europe." *International Organization* 61:399–442.
Haubert, Jeannie, and Elizabeth Fussell. 2006. "Explaining Pro-Immigrant Sentiment in the U.S.: Social Class, Cosmopolitanism, and Perceptions of Immigrants." *International Migration Review* 40(3):489–507.
Hsieh, Yeu-Sheng, and I-Chien Chen. 2009. "Changes in Intergenerational Influences on Cross-Ethnic Marriage in Taiwan." *Taiwanese Journal of Sociology* 42:1–53. (in Chinese)
Karakayali, Nedim. 2009. "Social Distance and Affective Orientations." *Sociological Forum* 23(3):538–62.

Kleg, Milton, and Kaoru Yamamoto. 1998. "As the World Turns: Ethno-Racial Distances after 70 Years." *Social Science Journal* 35:183–90.
Lee, Joseph. 2002. "The Role of Low-Skilled Foreign Workers in Taiwan's Economic Development." *Asia Pacific Business Review* 8(4):41–66.
Mayda, Anna M. 2006. "Who Is Against Immigration? A Cross-Country Investigation of Individual Attitudes toward Immigrants." *Review of Economics and Statistics* 88(3):510–30.
Meuleman, Bart, Eldad Davidov, and Jaak Billiet. 2009. "Changing Attitudes toward Immigration in Europe, 2002–2007: A Dynamic Group Conflict Theory Approach." *Social Science Research* 38(2):352–65.
O'Rourke, Kevin H., and Richard Sinnott. 2006. "The Determinants of Individual Attitudes toward Immigration." *European Journal of Political Economy* 22:838–61.
Ouellette-Kuntz, Hélène, Philip Burge, Hilary K. Brown, and Elizabeth Arsenault. 2010. "Public Attitudes towards Individuals with Intellectual Disabilities as Measured by the Concept of Social Distance." *Journal of Applied Research in Intellectual Disabilities* 23:132–42.
Owen, Carolyn, Howard C. Eisner, and Thomas McFaul. 1981. "A Half-Century of Social Distance Research: National Replication of the Bogardus' Studies." *Sociology and Social Research* 66(1):80–98.
Parrillo, Vincent N., and Christopher Donoghue. 2005. "Updating the Bogardus Social Distance Studies: A New National Survey." *The Social Science Journal* 42(2):257–71.
Pettigrew, Thomas F. 2009. "Secondary Transfer Effect of Contact: Do Intergroup Contact Effects Spread to Noncontacted Outgroups?" *Social Psychology* 40(2):55–65.
Pettigrew, Thomas F., and Linda R. Tropp. 2006. "A Meta-Analytic Test of Intergroup Contact Theory." *Journal of Personality and Social Psychology* 90(5):751–83.
Rustenbach, Elisa. 2010. "Sources of Negative Attitudes toward Immigrants in Europe: A Multi-Level Analysis." *International Migration Review* 44(1):53–77.
Schissel, Bernard, Richard Wanner, and James S. Frideres. 1989. "Social and Economic Context and Attitudes toward Immigrants in Canadian Cities." *International Migration Review* 23(2):289–308.
Sherif, Carolyn W. 1973. "Social Distance as Categorization of Intergroup Interaction." *Journal of Personality and Social Psychology* 25(3):327–34.
Triandis, Harry C., Earl E. Davis, and Shinichi Takezawa. 1965. "Some Determinants of Social Distance among American, German and Japanese Students." *Journal of Personality and Social Psychology* 2:540–51.
Tsai, Ming-Chang. 2011. " 'Foreign Brides' Meet Ethnic Politics in Taiwan." *International Migration Review* 45(2):243–68.
Tsai, Ming-Chang, and Chin-fen Chang. 2010. "China-Bound for Jobs? The Influences of Social Connections and Ethnic Politics in Taiwan." *The China Quarterly* 203:639–55.
Tsai, Shu-Ling. 1996. "The Relative Importance of Ethnicity and Education in Taiwan's Changing Marriage Market." *Proceedings of Humanities and Social Sciences* 6(2):301–15.
Tsay, Ching-lung, and Ji-ping Lin. 2001. "Labor Importation and Unemployment of Local Workers in Taiwan." *Asian Pacific Migration Journal* 10(3–4):505–34.
Tsay, Ruey-Ming, and Li-Hsueh Wu. 2006. "Marrying Someone from an Outside Group: An Analysis of Boundary-Crossing Marriages in Taiwan." *Current Sociology* 54(2):165–86.

Wang, Fu-Chang. 1993. "Causes and Patterns of Ethnic Intermarriage among the Hokkien, Hakka, and Mainlanders in Postwar Taiwan: A Preliminary Examination." *Bulletin of the Institute of Ethnology* 76:43–96. (in Chinese)

Wang, Fu-Chang. 2001. "Ethnic Intermarriage and Ethnic Relationship in Taiwan: A Revisit." In *Social Transformation and Cultural Outlook*, edited by S. Lau, P. Wan, M. Lee, and S. Wong, 393–430. Hong Kong: Chinese University of Hong Kong. (in Chinese)

Yi, Chin-Chun, and Ying-Hwa Chang. 2006. "Attitudes toward Having a Foreign Daughter-in-Law: The Importance of Social Contact." *Taiwanese Sociology* 12:191–232. (in Chinese)

Immigrant Adaptation in Multi-ethnic Cities

10 Diversity of Asian Immigrants and Their Roles in the Making of Multicultural Cities in Canada

Shuguang Wang and Paul Du

INTRODUCTION

Over the last two decades, the number of Asian immigrants in Canada more than doubled, from 1.1 million in 1991 to 2.5 million in 2006. In 1991, Asian immigrants accounted for only 25% of the total immigrants in Canada; by 2006, their share increased to 41%. According to a new population projection by Statistics Canada (2010), by 2031, the number of Chinese in Canada could double again from 1.3 million in 2006 to 2.4 million (by low growth projection) or to 3 million (by high growth projection). Similarly, South Asians[1] could increase from 1.3 million in 2006 to 3.2 million (by low growth projection) or to 4.1 million (by high growth projection).

Despite the challenges they face in their settlement, the Asian immigrants make important contributions to Canada in a variety of ways, and they play significant roles in the making of multicultural cities in Canada. Yet, their contributions and settlement difficulties are not always understood and appreciated, and their presence in Canada has unfortunately caused discomfort among some concerned Canadians.

In its 2010 November issue, the *Maclean's* magazine featured an article with such a provocative title as "Too Asian?"[2] Following up the widely held concern in the United States that many elite colleges and universities may have moved toward race-based admission policies, and some of them may even be redlining Asian students simply because there are too many of them on their campuses (Miller 2010), the two authors of the *Maclean's* article set out to speak to students, professors, and administrators in a number of Canadian universities to find out whether they feel their campuses are also "too Asian." The article starts with an interview of two (presumably white) students, who told the authors that when some of their high school classmates "were deciding which university to go, they didn't even bother considering the University of Toronto" because "the only people from [their] school who went to University of Toronto were Asian." As to why some white students turn away from the University of Toronto, the University of British Columbia, and the University of Waterloo, the article cites some high school guidance counselors as saying that these top-tier universities enjoy international profiles in such disciplines as math, science, and business, to which Asian students flock and in which they do well; whereas white students are more likely to choose universities and build their school lives around social interaction, athletics, and self-actualization (even including alcohol). When the two lifestyles collide, the result is separation rather than integration (Findlay and Köhler 2010).

Discomfort with the increased presence of Asians in Canada is not limited to university campuses, as is evidenced in a web posting by a deeply concerned Canadian: "I just went to the Superstore, and out of the hundred or so people I saw, most of them were Asian. I only saw a small handful of whites, what's the deal? Are we destined to be a minority in our country? When was this decided? When did Canadians vote that they wanted their country to become multicultural and to evidently become a minority?"[3] Another grumbling Canadian citizen is even more blunt: "[in the past 20 years,] Asian immigrants have moved from a small fraction of Canada's population to a group that wants to claim power." He or she continues, "All Canadians should take note of the following: Any country which does not protect its majority population through limitations on immigration invites the contempt of the immigrants who have entered its territory and who have become a majority in a part or whole of its territory" ("CBC Manager of Diversity: Vancouver Is Part of Asia" 2010).

There is no question that immigration has impacts on the receiving society, but the social tension and even animosity expressed in the above nativist sentiments are destructive to building a harmonious multicultural society. This chapter is devoted to a discussion of the Asian immigrants in Canada. We first examine the diversity of Asian immigrants as a valuable source of human capital. We then describe their settlement patterns and their impacts on the makeup of multicultural cities in Canada. The chapter concludes that as the population becomes more diverse and immigrants constitute a large proportion of the total population, the traditional expectation of a "one-way absorption" mode of settlement needs to be abandoned, and a "two-way (or even multi-way) acculturation" is necessary.

The Diversity of Asian Immigrants as a Valuable Source of Human Capital

Historically, Asian immigration to Canada has been closely linked to the economic and geopolitical conditions in the countries of origin, but it has also been attributed to the changes in the immigration policies of the receiving country. On the one hand, the lack of opportunities and freedom, frequent occurrence of natural disasters, and prolonged wars in many Asian countries have led to personal dissatisfaction among many Asians, which motivated them to leave their homelands for a better life elsewhere. On the other hand, the much higher standard of living together with better economic opportunities (or prospects), and the much appreciated political freedom, have made Canada a "dream land" for many Asian emigrants. In addition, the more open and favorable immigration policies have made Canada a much more attractive destination than Western Europe.

The contemporary Asian immigrants are far from homogenous. They consist of many groups that differ in place of origin, language, culture, religion, and also content of human capital. Table 10.1 shows the major groups of Asian immigrants in Canada. The top ten groups came from Mainland China, India, the Philippines, Hong Kong, Vietnam, Pakistan, Sri Lanka, South Korea, Iran, and Lebanon. Together, the immigrants from these ten places of origin account for 81% of all the Asian immigrants in Canada.

Table 10.1 Asian Immigrants in Canada by Country of Birth, 1996 and 2006

	1996		2006		% change 1996–2006
	No.	%	No.	%	
China	227,010	16.3	457,000	18.1	101.3
India	231,905	16.7	436,640	17.3	88.3
Philippines	181,245	13.0	297,240	11.8	64
Hong Kong	238,585	17.2	210,495	8.3	-11.8
Vietnam	136,355	9.8	154,975	6.1	13.7
Pakistan	38,195	2.7	130,540	5.2	241.8
Sri Lanka	66,280	4.8	104,065	4.1	57
South Korea	44,675	3.2	95,965	3.8	114.8
Iran	46,175	3.3	88,885	3.5	92.5
Lebanon	61,395	4.4	72,995	2.9	18.9
Taiwan	48,425	3.5	63,540	2.5	31.2
Afghanistan	n/a	n/a	35,545	1.4	63.2*
Iraq	16,550	1.2	32,540	1.3	96.6
Bangladesh	n/a	n/a	32,180	1.3	49.7*
Malaysia	18,855	1.4	20,865	0.8	10.7
Israel	14,930	1.1	20,240	0.8	35.6
Japan	n/a	n/a	20,155	0.8	n/a
Cambodia	18,575	1.3	19,520	0.8	5.1
Other Asian	n/a	n/a	231,770	9.2	n/a
Total Asian	1,389,155	99.9	2,525,155	100.0	81.8

*percent change between 2001-2006
Source: Statistics Canada, 1996 and 2006 census

The surge of contemporary Chinese immigrants to Canada in the 1990s was first prompted by the suppression of the student protest in Beijing's Tian-an-men Square by the Chinese government in 1989. It was later facilitated by the relaxation of the exit policies governing the emigration of the Chinese nationals. The uncertainty of Hong Kong's return from a British colony to the Chinese rule in 1997 served as a strong push factor for the large exodus of Hong Kong citizens in the late 1980s and early 1990s, who viewed Canada as a preferred destination. The Canadian landing data show that 89% of the Hong Kong immigrants who were admitted to Canada in the 26 years from 1980 to 2005 arrived between 1984 (when China and the UK signed the agreement) and 1997 (when Hong Kong was officially returned to China's sovereignty), though its number dwindled after the mid-1990s.

Immigrants from South Asia's India, Pakistan, and Sri Lanka also increased substantially. Many Indian immigrants came to Canada to pursue higher education or employment opportunities. In addition, as Singh and Thomas (2004) have noted, "with limited opportunities for permanent residence coupled with political instability and insecurity in the Middle East, many South Asians are immigrating to Canada [from the Middle East]. Canada has become the country of choice . . . [also] because of a shorter immigration-processing period" (p2).

Relative to the other major groups, immigration from Vietnam has increased very little since the mid-1990s, reflecting the restoration of political stability there and the resultant decrease in the outflow of refugees. In contrast, immigrants from the Middle East (particularly Iran and Iraq) have increased due to the destructive wars in the region.

Many studies of the composition of immigrants use "immigration class"[4] as an analytical framework. While a useful framework, it does not reveal the whole picture. For example, according to the landing records, only 46% of the 1.15 million economic immigrants who came to Canada from Asia between 1980 and 2005 were principal applicants; the rest were their spouses and dependent children, who accompanied the principal applicants in their immigration application but were not assessed with the Point System. Despite this, many of the spouses were highly educated individuals.

Using a combination of "age," "Canadian official language ability," and "education qualification" as an analytical framework, this study reveals that the Asian immigrants brought with them considerable human capital needed for Canada's economic development. Of the 2.65 million Asian immigrants who landed in Canada between 1980 and 2005, 54% were in their prime working age (23–50), and another 9% were in their later working age (51–65). Both groups were ready to participate in the labor force upon immigration (see Table 10.2). Thirty-three percent of those between 1 and 22 years of age were expected to acquire all or part of their education in Canada, but they would become more productive citizens than the adult immigrants, after they graduate from the Canadian institutions. Indeed, Asian immigrant youths tend to

Table 10.2 Asian Immigrants in Canada by Age Group, Canadian Official Language Ability, and Period of Landing

Age group	Asian immigrants #	%	English 1980–1995 (%)	English 1996–2005 (%)	French 1980–1995 (%)	French 1996–2005 (%)	Bilingual 1980–1995 (%)	Bilingual 1996–2005 (%)	None 1980–1995 (%)	None 1996–2005 (%)
0–5 (pre-school age)	177417	6.7	9.9	8.7	1.2	0.1	0.2	0.2	88.7	91.0
6–12 (elementary school age)	271457	10.2	22.7	25.1	1.8	0.4	0.7	0.6	74.8	73.9
13–15 (junior high school age)	118429	4.5	26.7	31.5	1.6	0.4	1.1	0.9	70.7	67.2
16–18 (senior high school age)	120091	4.5	31.6	33.7	1.6	0.4	1.6	1.1	65.2	64.8
19–22 (college/university age)	196039	7.4	37.0	39.7	1.7	0.6	2.1	1.1	59.2	58.6
23–50 (prime working age)	1433766	54.0	57.4	62.3	1.6	0.4	2.8	1.9	38.3	35.3
51–65 (later working age)	244813	9.2	26.2	29.9	1.1	0.4	1.2	0.9	71.4	68.8
>65 (seniors)	93786	3.5	23.0	25.9	1.1	0.6	0.6	0.5	75.3	73.0
Total (number)	2655812	100.0	551373	629141	19991	5278	26036	18925	731264	673804

Source: Citizenship and Immigration Canada, *Landed Immigrant Data System, 1980–2005*

be highly motivated and bright. Many of them are high achievers in Canadian schools. In 2007, three Asian immigrant students were among the top high school graduates (i.e., with the highest grade point average) in their respective school boards in the Toronto CMA (Rushowy 2007).[5] In 2008, six Asian students were ranked the top high school graduates in their respective school boards and were accepted by top universities (Rushowy 2008).[6] In a landmark survey of 105,000 students from Grades 7 to 12 by the Toronto District School Board in 2006–2007, it was found that Asian students, along with the white students, were ranked among the top groups in reading and writing (Brown 2008), and they outperformed the Canadian-born in general. Those who were not likely to participate in the labor force after immigration were the seniors, but the seniors constituted less than 4% of the total Asian immigrant intake. After all, enabling family reunification has always been a main theme in Canadian immigration policy, and the elderly Asian immigrants, like all other Canadians, are entitled to live with, or close to, their children in Canada (particularly if their only child has immigrated to Canada).

The more recent Asian immigrants possess higher levels of Canadian official language ability than the earlier arrivals. As the landing data show, the proportion of the 1996–2005 arrivals who had knowledge of English is higher than the 1980–1995 arrivals in all age groups except the 0–5 age group (see Table 10.2). In particular, 62% of the 23–50 age group in the cohort of the 1996–2005 arrivals had knowledge of English, compared with 57% of the same age group in the 1980–1995 cohort—a 5% improvement. The 51–65 age group showed an improvement of nearly 4%. Accordingly, the proportions of those with no Canadian official language ability declined across the board. This is not to say that the Asian immigrants who were recorded in the landing data as possessing Canadian official language ability had all achieved high levels of fluency in English or French, as their language ability was not assessed with formal testing until very recently; however, the improvement does mean less need for intensive language training after immigration and before they become productive citizens.

The Asian immigrants also came with considerable education credentials. Specifically, 31% of those in their prime working age possessed a bachelor's degree (see Table 10.3), 9% had a master's degree, and 1.3% had a doctoral degree. Another 22% of the same age group already had other forms of postsecondary education or training (certificate, diploma, or apprenticeship). In addition, the recent arrivals had much higher education qualifications than the earlier arrivals. According to the landing data, 40% of the prime working age group who arrived between 1996 and 2005 had a bachelor's degree, 13% had a master's degree, and 1.7% had a doctoral degree, compared, respectively, with 20%, 4%, and 1% for the cohort of the 1980–1995 arrivals. The 51–65 age group had similar improvement: 20% of the 1996–2005 arrivals came with at least a bachelor's degree, compared with 8.5% for the earlier arrivals.

Table 10.3 Education Qualifications of Asian Immigrants in Canada by Country/Region of Last Permanent Residence, 1980–2005 (in percentage)

Origin	Age Group	No Education	Secondary or Less	Postsecondary Certificate or Diploma (No Degree)	Bachelors	Master's	Doctorate	Total
Asia	23–50	1.7	34.9	22.2	31.0	8.8	1.3	41.2
	51–65	16.7	58.7	12.0	10.0	2.0	0.6	12.6
China	23–50	0.7	22.1	23.0	37.8	13.7	2.7	54.3
	51–65	7.2	60.9	20.2	10.7	0.8	0.4	11.8
India	23–50	4.6	30.2	13.1	36.0	14.7	1.5	52.2
	51–65	38.1	47.1	4.4	7.4	2.5	0.4	10.3
HK	23–50	0.6	46.0	32.4	17.1	3.5	0.3	21.0
	51–65	11.4	65.3	17.6	4.8	0.7	0.2	5.7
Philippines	23–50	0.8	22.8	29.1	45.4	1.6	0.3	47.3
	51–65	4.7	63.3	13.9	16.9	1.0	0.2	18.0
Pakistan	23–50	2.8	24.4	13.0	40.5	18.5	0.9	59.9
	51–65	19.8	49.1	7.4	16.3	6.8	0.6	23.7
Vietnam	23–50	1.6	83.4	10.7	3.9	0.4	0.2	4.4
	51–65	14.6	80.6	3.4	1.2	0.1	0.1	1.4
Iran	23–50	0.9	36.6	20.9	31.4	7.6	2.6	41.6
	51–65	4.5	51.7	13.0	20.4	7.0	3.4	30.8
Sri Lanka	23–50	1.6	68.3	20.2	8.0	1.4	0.4	9.9
	51–65	3.4	80.5	10.6	4.8	0.5	0.2	5.5
Taiwan	23–50	0.6	26.3	31.9	28.9	10.7	1.6	41.2
	51–65	2.5	51.3	24.0	18.1	3.2	1.0	22.2
Korea	23–50	0.8	25.0	18.7	44.0	9.4	2.0	55.5
	51–65	7.5	51.2	11.1	24.6	4.0	1.5	30.1

Source: Citizenship and Immigration Canada, Landed Immigrant Data System, 1980–2005.

The immigrants from Mainland China, India, the Philippines, Pakistan, and Korea had higher than average proportions in the prime-working age groups with universities degrees. These are 54%, 52%, 47%, 60%, and 56%, respectively, compared with the average of 41% for all Asian immigrants (see Table 10.3). Those from the Philippines, Pakistan, Iran, Taiwan, and Korea had higher than average proportions in the 51–66 age group with universities degrees. These are 18%, 24%, 31%, 22%, and 30%, respectively, compared with the average of 13%. The immigrants from Vietnam and Sri Lanka had the least higher education credentials because very high proportions of them were admitted to Canada as humanitarian immigrants and for family unification (50% and 49% for the Vietnamese; 49% and 40% for the Sri Lankans). It should be pointed out that 88% of the Vietnam immigrants came in the period of 1980–1995, and their number has declined significantly since the mid-1990s. While 44% of the Sri Lankan immigrants were recent arrivals, they were admitted largely as a Canadian response to the political turmoil and destructive civil war in that country—a commitment that Canada made to the international community.

Likely due to their good education credentials, the Asian immigrants have higher proportions of them working in the fields of professional/technical services and finance/insurance/real estate than do the general immigrant population (Wang and Wang 2012). There is no lack of success stories about Asian immigrants in Canada. For example, among the Top 25 Canadian Immigrant Award winners in 2010, who made significant contributions to Canada and their local communities, 12 were from the Greater Toronto Area; except for Donnovan Bailey—the Olympian sprinter originally from Jamaica—all the GTA winners are immigrants from Asia (Keung 2010; Wong 2010).

It should also be noted that the quality of education in many Asian countries has improved considerably in the last two decades due to the "globalization of curricula." Nowadays, most universities in the Western English-speaking countries (Canada included) admit international students from Asian countries to various degree programs (including graduate programs) based on their education received from the colleges and universities in their home countries. This is a welcome recognition of the improvement in the Asian education systems on the part of the Canadian institutions. Unfortunately, the Asian immigrants in general still face high barriers in the Canadian labor market, and their employment income is much lower than that of the non-immigrant Canadians (Wang and Lo, 2005). According to the 2006 Canadian census, Asian immigrants on average earned $31,500 from employment, while the non-immigrant Canadians earned an average of $36,600 (Wang and Wang 2012).

Settlement Patterns and Impacts on the Makeup of Multicultural Cities

Within Canada, the Asian immigrants are heavily concentrated in two provinces: Ontario (55%) and British Columbia (24%). Together, these two provinces receive nearly 80% of all Asian immigrants in the country. The other two provinces where a relatively large proportion of Asian immigrants have settled are Quebec (9.2%) and Alberta (8.9%). A much smaller number of Asian immigrants chose to live in the Prairies, Atlantic Canada, and the Territories.[7]

Eighty-four percent of the Asian immigrants concentrate in ten Census Metropolitan Areas (CMAs), as listed in Table 10.4. In addition to the three gateway cities of Toronto, Vancouver, and Montreal, five other CMAs—namely, Calgary, Edmonton, Ottawa, Hamilton, and Winnipeg—began to attract Asian immigrants in large numbers. The trend of concentration in the top ten CMAs has intensified: only four CMAs—Vancouver, Calgary, Toronto, and Edmonton—have more than 40% of their *total immigrants* coming from Asia, but seven CMAs have more than 40% of their *recent immigrants*[8] coming from Asia.

Within metropolitan areas, Asian immigrants clearly suburbanized, as exemplified by the Chinese and South Asians in the Toronto CMA (see Table 10.5). In 1996, 60% of the South Asian immigrants lived in the Central City (i.e., the City of Toronto), and only 40% lived in the suburbs. A decade later, in 2006, 55% of the South Asians live in the suburbs. The Chinese also suburbanized, albeit to a lesser extent. Interestingly, the largest two groups of Asian immigrants—the South Asians and the Chinese—exhibit

Table 10.4 Distribution of Asian Immigrants in the Top Ten CMAs in Canada, 2006

CMA	Province	Total Asian Immigrants No.	% of Total Immigrants	Recent Asian Immigrants* No.	% of Total Recent Immigrants
Toronto	ON	1,048,680	45.5	286,790	64.7
Vancouver	BC	508,760	62.0	109,625	73.8
Montreal	Quebec	179,705	24.4	43,220	26.5
Calgary	Alta	116,345	46.2	33,230	57.9
Ottawa-Hull	ON	66,915	33.3	13,650	39.5
Edmonton	Alta	75,760	40.2	17,510	56.3
Hamilton	ON	32,190	19.4	8,780	43.4
Winnipeg	Man	45,155	37.7	13,270	56.5
Kitchener	ON	22,070	21.6	7,655	46.4
London	ON	16,000	18.5	4,685	36.3

*Recent immigrants are those who immigrated to Canada within the last five years of the most recent census.
Source: Statistics Canada (2006) census.

distinctive settlement patterns in the metropolitan regions where they concentrate. According to the 2006 census, 41% of Toronto CMA's South Asians live in Brampton and Mississauga, and more than 50% of the Chinese live in the area consisting of Markham, Richmond Hill, Northwest Scarborough, and northeast North York. Of the South Asians, the Punjabi Sikhs congregate in Brampton, while the Sri Lankan Tamils concentrate in Scarborough. Similar spatial distinctions can be observed in the Vancouver CMA, where the Chinese concentrate in the municipalities of Richmond, Vancouver, and Burnaby, while the South Asians heavily concentrate in Surrey (Figure 10.1). As Quadeer and Kumar (2003) explain, people of the same ethnic origin concentrate in the same geographic areas as a defense against discrimination, to support each other, to preserve cultural heritage, and to join forces for political actions and lobbying. Often, it is in these areas of concentration where the impacts of immigration are felt the most and social tensions arise.

Asian immigrants contribute to the economic and cultural well-being of Canada and enrich the meanings and contents of the multicultural cities in no small ways. They not only changed the population composition in the receiving cities, but also altered the local economic and cultural structure. Their settlement in the Canadian cities has often resulted in booming local economies. In addition, they began to exert influences on the local political landscape.

Table 10.5 Distribution of South Asian and Chinese Immigrants in the Toronto CMA, 1996 and 2006

	South Asian*				Chinese			
	1996		2006		1996		2006	
	No.	%	No.	%	No.	%	No.	%
Central city (City of Toronto)	104,260	59.8	180,355	44.5	135,110	64.9	181,780	59.7
Suburbs	69,960	40.2	225,000	55.5	73,115	35.1	122,645	40.3
Mississauga	33,960	19.5	84,205	20.8	18,025	8.7	26,525	8.7
Brampton	18,110	10.4	81,455	20.1	1,735	0.8	2,860	0.9
Markham	7,465	4.3	26,235	6.5	30,595	14.7	58,760	19.3
Vaughan	2,975	1.7	11,195	2.8	3,500	1.7	4,180	1.4
Richmond Hill	1,595	0.9	5,050	1.2	15,285	7.3	23,100	7.6
others	5,855	3.4	16,860	4.2	3,975	1.9	7,220	2.4
CMA Total	174,220	100.0	405,355	100.0	208,225	100.0	304,425	100.0

*South Asians include immigrants from India, Pakistan, Sri Lanka, and Bangladesh.
Source: Statistics Canada (1996, 2006) census.

Diversity of Asian Immigrants 209

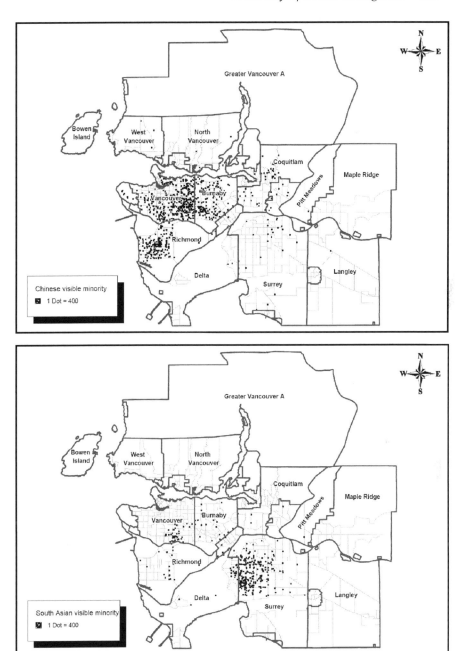

Figure 10.1 Distribution of the Chinese and South Asians in Vancouver CMA.
Source: Statistics Canada (2006) census.

The health of the housing market is often regarded as a barometer for economic vitality, and it has been widely acknowledged that immigrants are a driving force of the housing market (Dupuis, 2009). In a study based on Statistics Canada's Longitudinal Survey of Immigrants to Canada[9] (Hiebert and Mendez 2009), the authors found that home ownership rates of immigrants in the three gateway cities of Toronto, Vancouver, and Montreal rose rapidly within a few years of landing in Canada, from less than 20% six months after arrival to more than 50% four years after arrival. Further, the same study reveals that the South and Southeast Asian immigrants exhibit "extraordinary degrees of home ownership" (p3). Not only do Asian immigrants have a high propensity to own a home (they often cut consumption in other areas in order to own a home), many of them bring large sums of money to Canada and invest it in a residential property (Starr 2010). The positive impacts of the South Asian immigrants on the booming Canadian housing market is also confirmed by Agrawal and Lovell's (2010) study.

In the late 1980s and the early 1990s, the affluent Hong Kong immigrants were "scooping up properties in specific areas" of metropolitan Vancouver, such as Shaughnessy and Richmond (Ley 2009; Ray et al. 1997). More recently, those from Mainland China comprise a major army of real estate buyers in Vancouver, who immigrated to Canada with considerable wealth. Tom Gradecak, a Vancouver realtor, told news reporters that "our office has done 50 sales this year [January 1– May 16, 2011], which is pretty incredible; half of those sales are [made to immigrants] from Mainland China" (Wasserman 2011). According to Cam Good, president of a leading sales and marketing firm in Vancouver, as many as 500 houses have already been bought by Chinese immigrants (and investors) in Toronto and Vancouver in the first two months of 2011 alone (Kaur 2011). The affluent Chinese immigrants reportedly dominate the high end of the housing market (Freeman 2011; Sutherland 2010). More wealthy Chinese immigrants are expected to arrive in the near future. Now that the Chinese government has introduced new regulations to curb real estate speculations and restrict home ownership to two apartments per family, more "surplus money" is expected to be invested in residential properties in Canada.

The increase (and anticipated increase) in Asian immigrants in the major Canadian cities also attracted large sums of investment from investors based in their places of origin. In 1988, the site of Expo 86 in Vancouver was acquired by Concord Pacific Developments with investors led by Hong Kong billionaire Li Ka-Shing (whose son Victor Li became a Canadian immigrant in 1983) and was subsequently developed into the Concord Pacific Place—Canada's largest master-planned urban community, comprising about 50 buildings with 10,000 homes (Ley 2009; Wasserman 2011). In the City of Toronto, the same developer has been building two new master-planned communities: one is Concord City

Place in downtown Toronto (West of Sky Dome), and the other is Concord Park Place in North York (with 4,000 homes being planned). In addition, Concord Pacific Development is planning to build a similar but smaller community in Calgary.

The Asian immigrants have not only created a large pool of labor that the Canadian employers can utilize, they have also formed a critical mass of consumers, stimulating development of ethnic businesses. In the major immigrant-receiving cities, they are pivotal to the growth of local economies.

Until the mid-1980s, Chinese grocery stores and supermarkets were small in size and concentrated in the inner-city Chinatowns (Wang 1999). Since the mid-1980s, many larger stores have opened in the suburbs. As of April 2010, 53 Chinese supermarkets of various sizes (excluding small, convenience-style grocery stores) exist in the Toronto CMA to serve the half million ethnic Chinese (Figure 10.2). Most of the modern and large-scale supermarkets were newly developed after 2000. Two important characteristics are noted. First, many of the new Chinese supermarkets have opened in succession to mainstream supermarkets or other types of retail outlets (such as junior department stores and hardware stores). This pattern of succession has resulted in some very large Chinese supermarkets. Second, and related to the first, a number of them have taken the position of anchors in mainstream community shopping plazas, serving none-Chinese, as well as Chinese, consumers living in the nearby neighborhoods (Wang et al. 2012).

During the last two decades, more than 60 Chinese shopping centers were also developed in the Toronto CMA. Most of them are located in the areas of Chinese concentration (Figure 10.2). In the Vancouver CMA, more than a dozen large ethnic Chinese shopping centers are in operation. The largest cluster, anchored by Yaohan Centre, Aberdeen Center, and President Plaza, is situated in Richmond. Many of the Chinese malls are condominium shopping centers, where the merchants own their store space.

The commercial activity engaged by the South Asian immigrants is much less significant in both number and scale than that of the Chinese. Still, the South Asians are running fruitful businesses in the Toronto and Vancouver CMAs, and a trend of suburbanization can also be observed. The traditional Punjabi Market established in the central city of Vancouver in the 1970s has witnessed a decline in business, and merchants started moving to Surrey to reach the growing number of South Asian consumers there (Aryal 2011). Similarly, Little India (also known as the India Bazaar) in the City of Toronto is losing customers to suburban competitions (Vukets 2011). In response to the flood of immigrants into Scarborough, Brampton, and Mississauga, South Asian malls are being built or planned (Hertz 2007; Radhika 2008).The first indoor South Asian-oriented shopping mall—the GTA Square—opened in Scarborough in 2008 in a two-story structure

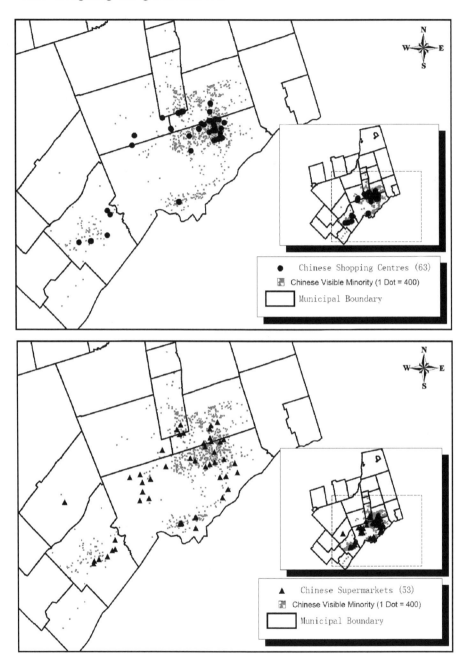

Figure 10.2 Distribution of ethnic Chinese supermarkets and shopping centers in the Toronto CMA.

with 40,000 square feet of floor space. Soon after, two more shopping centers dedicated to a South Asian clientele were opened: Greater Punjab in Mississauga (160,000 square feet) and T. Junction in Scarborough (80,000 square feet). Two much larger ones are planned: Tah Center in Brampton (220,000 square feet) and Sitara in Scarborough (240,000 square feet). These malls/plazas serve (or are planned to serve) as cultural hubs as well as business centers, combining retail, professional services, and, in some cases, religious institutions.

Asian immigrants also contribute to their local communities through generous donations. A recent study reveals that a new high-income class of Indo-Canadians has been created who are giving back significantly to their communities (Agrawal and Lovell 2010). In 2007, a new hospital was developed and opened in the City of Brampton in the Toronto CMA for $790 million. The hospital aimed to raise $10 million in donations from private donors. The South Asian community responded enthusiastically and raised $7 million (Yelaja 2007). For their significant contributions, the new emergency department was named Guru Nanak Dev, the founder of Sikhism. In return, the community made it clear that they wanted to be involved, ensuring that the new hospital is sensitive to their cultural and religious needs. They recommended that the new hospital offer Indian vegetarian meals, Punjabi and Hindi language translations and signage, large family waiting rooms, as well as expanded treatment areas for cardiac care, nephrology, and diabetes, as these diseases are more prevalent among South Asians.

The large groups of Asian immigrants, particularly the Chinese and South Asians, have achieved high degrees of institutional completeness. Within the Toronto CMA, the South Asians developed 57 Indo temples (Figure 10.3). These temples are not just places of worship for the South Asian immigrants, but are symbols of their new home in Canada (Porter 2007). The Chinese have formed more than 100 associations of various types (Figure 10.4). These modern associations are fundamentally different from the old-day clansmen organizations, and they consist of broad memberships. The largest is Chinese Professionals Association of Canada (CPAC) with 26,000 members. Its objectives are defined as:

- to provide opportunities for interaction and networking among Chinese Canadian professionals;
- to help members integrate and contribute to Canadian society;
- to facilitate members' careers and professional development;
- to provide training, employment, settlement, education, cultural, and recreational services to internationally trained professionals and families;
- to be a national voice and representative of the Chinese Canadian community (CPAC, http://www.chineseprofessionals.ca/mission.php)

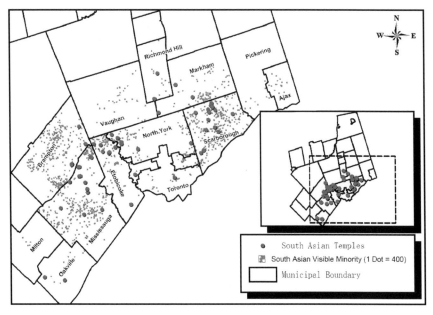

Figure 10.3 South Asian temples in the Toronto CMA.

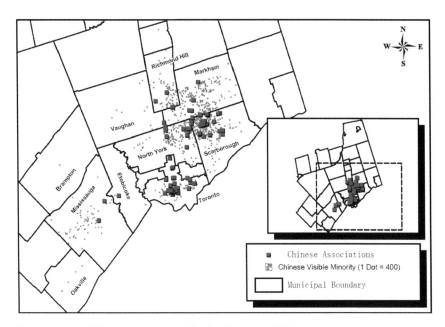

Figure 10.4 Chinese associations in the Toronto CMA.

Increased political participation and representation has also been observed in the cities and areas of Asian concentration, where the usually silent minorities become more vocal and ethnic votes are growing in size. More Asian immigrant candidates are running for elections to change the political landscape. In the 2008 federal election, three South Asians won seats in the Brampton-Mississauga area, and two Chinese ran in the Markham-Richmond Hill-Scarborough ethnoburb, though they both lost. In the 2006 provincial election, Michael Chan (a Chinese immigrant) won in Markham-Unionville, and Amrita Mangat (a South Asian) won in Mississauga-Brampton South. Alex Yuan (a Chinese) ran in Richmond Hill, and Max Wang (also a Chinese) ran in Scarborough-Agincourt, but both lost. In the 2010 municipal elections in the Province of Ontario, nearly 40 ethnic Chinese candidates were running for councilors (*The Chinese Canadian Post* 2010; *Today Daily News* 2010). Politicians now see the areas of Asian concentration as important sources of political capital, and party leaders often take time to attend ethnic festivals to solicit ethnic votes. Shelley Carroll, a Toronto City councilor representing Ward 3, distributes her annual newsletter to her constituents consistently in two languages: English and Chinese. She even gave herself a Chinese name: 高雪莉.

In the City of Vancouver, the Chinese and South Asian Canadians have become a political force for the city's mayor. It is reported that former Mayor Sam Sullivan learned to speak Cantonese and Panjabi in order to develop a close relationship with the large ethnic communities in the city; he later was picking up Tagalog—the language of most Filipinos—in preparation to run for re-election in 2001. As Charlie Smith, one of Vancouver's most respected political commentators, predicted, any "Neighborhood. People. Accountability" (NPA)[10] candidate who runs for the 2011 election probably has to win a huge share of the first-generation Chinese Canadian votes in order to become mayor (Smith 2008).

Along with their various forms of contribution and participation were the impacts on the receiving communities. On the one hand, Asian immigrants are hailed for driving the housing market growth in Canadian cities (Lebour 2011; Wong 2007); on the other hand, they are blamed for driving up the housing prices beyond what native-born Canadians can afford. In the early 1990s in Vancouver, many homes were bought by immigrants from Hong Kong in middle-class neighborhoods. The homes were torn down, sometimes along with large trees, and replaced with homes that were much larger than the others in the immediate neighborhood, called "monster homes" by the locals. As one Letter to the Editor of *The Richmond Review* reads, "We cannot allow this way of life to disappear for the short term benefit of sudden money from Hong Kong" (*The Richmond Review* 1991). As well, the contention was frequently raised in local Richmond newspapers that Chinese settlement has promoted "white flight," accompanied with stories of long-time residents "[fleeing] to deep suburbia" (Ray et al. 1997, 94).

Similar conflicts happened in the Toronto CMA. When the first suburban concentration of commercial activity began to form in Scarborough's Agincourt community in 1984, hundreds of non-Chinese residents and business owners in the surrounding area lodged complaints and protests. At a residents' meeting, when a suggestion was made that street signs in both English and Chinese be put up, the nearly all-white audience shouted: "never," "let'em learn English" (*The Scarborough Mirror*, May 30, 1984). In the mid-1990s, when many ethnic Chinese shopping centers were built in suburban municipalities, the deputy mayor of Markham remarked, at a regional council retreat in July 1995, that a growing concentration of ethnics is causing conflict in some communities in Markham, and large Asian commercial developments that are being exclusively marketed to the Chinese community with signs written in Chinese only are chasing residents of other races away from the city (Wang 1999). Many Chinese were offended by the deputy mayor's remark and accused her of racism.

Because the new development of ethnic businesses has posed challenges to the long-established municipal planning systems, some cities responded with changes to their municipal zoning bylaws. For example, Richmond Hill in the Toronto CMA made changes to its existing bylaws, which imposed a maximum size on restaurants in the city (with the effect of disallowing large Chinese restaurants from being built), introduced a cap on the number of stores in one mall and a minimum size for stores (to reduce the number of stores and increase store size), and required a larger number of parking spaces against the square footage used for stores (encouraging vertical intensification) (Preston and Lo 2000; Wang 1999). In the City of Vancouver, after a series of emotional hearings in 1993 about the "monster houses," a compromise was reached. In exchange for permission to build large houses, the city's planning authority insisted that builders of new homes take into consideration the style of the surrounding dwellings (Ley 2009).

CONCLUDING DISCUSSIONS

Canada needs to accept 250,000 or more immigrants each year to maintain its population growth and sustain its economic development due to the country's low birth rate and low fertility rate.[11] At the core of Canada's immigration program is the Points System, designed to screen applicants with the most potential to make positive contributions to Canada. The landing data show that in the past two decades, Canada has been getting better and better immigrants in terms of human capital through the Points System.

The large in-flow of Asian immigrants is largely the result of the Points System, which has been followed to select immigrants on the basis of merits and been applied to all immigrants on a equal basis. It also reflects the fact that China and India have the largest pools of potential immigrants to select from. It is legitimate to debate how many immigrants Canada should accept and can accommodate each year, but it is prejudicial and discriminatory to suggest limiting Asian immigration to Canada. If Asians were to be disproportionately reduced, who should be admitted to make up the gaps in the immigration quota? Canada cannot go back to its old "ethnocentric" immigration policy. Even if it did, the immigrants from the traditional source countries (namely, Western Europe, the United States, Australia, and New Zealand) could not meet Canada's population and labor needs. Therefore, the concern about too many Asians in Canada is unnecessary and unrealistic. After all, the Asian immigrants make significant contributions to Canada, as this chapter demonstrates.

Central to the societal concern about immigration in Canada is, "Whose values will prevail: those of the longer standing citizens, or those of the newcomers?" As the population becomes more diverse and immigrants constitute a large proportion of the total population, the traditional expectation of the "one-way absorption" mode of settlement must be abandoned, and a "two-way (or even multi-way) acculturation" is necessary, meaning that the "majority" of the receiving society needs to learn and adapt to the cultural values and business practices transplanted to Canada by the ethnic minorities (Figure 10.5). Knox and Pinch (2000) advocate the same process of acculturation with a new form of assimilation: assimilation is not simply the process of one culture being absorbed into another; instead, both mainstream and minority cultures are changed by assimilation through the

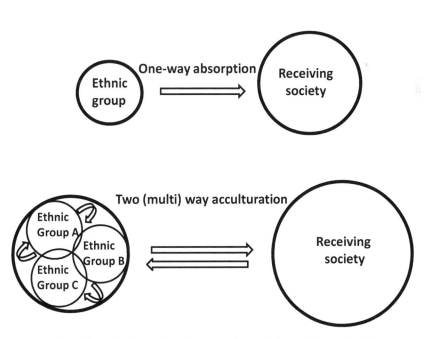

Figure 10.5 Changing interactions between the receiving society and ethnic groups.

creation of new hybrid forms of identity. In this course of transition in attitude toward immigrants, the use of such terms as "mainstream," "host society," and "visible minority" has been questioned for their appropriateness and political correctness (Canwest News Services 2007). Building social harmony calls for equal partnerships, and the "us-vs.-them" and "majority-vs.-minority" references are discouraged. Both public institutions and private organizations in Canada should mirror the country's population composition. More efforts are needed to increase the representation of the various ethnic groups at the leadership levels (Ryerson University 2011).

Asian immigrants, like all others, tend to concentrate in the urban areas with good job opportunities and already established co-ethnic communities, especially the Toronto and Vancouver CMAs, where most social tensions are reported. One way to encourage dispersion of immigrants, to the benefit of both the immigrants themselves and the country's regional development, is to create job opportunities in other cities. Canadian employers are strongly encouraged to capitalize on the talents of the highly educated Asian immigrants and their multilingual and multicultural children, and follow the Canadian universities to recognize their foreign education credentials.

On the part of immigrants, they need to consciously develop intercultural skills. Asian immigrants should avoid making such provocative claims as "Vancouver is part of Asia."[12] Such claims may invoke a feeling of Canada being "colonized," among the longer-standing Canadians who already resentfully call Vancouver "Hongcouver" (de Beer 1994). Immigrant entrepreneurs should consciously learn the broad knowledge of the Canadian business environment that entails a balance between economic development and community life, and they should be sensitive to the different needs of communities composed of ethnically diverse people. Asian candidates running for public offices should not promote themselves as the "best candidate" to represent their co-ethnics. Such promotions may give an impression to the other constituents that such a candidate would only represent the members of his or her own ethnic group.

On a Sunday in May 2009, a protest by thousands of members of Toronto's Tamil community, including women and children, blocked and shut down the Gardiner Expressway in downtown Toronto for more than five hours, demanding that the federal government of Canada impose sanctions on Sri Lanka until the Sri Lankan government signs a ceasefire with Tamil rebels.[13] This prompted Toronto Mayor David Miller to issue a statement saying that while he understood the protesters' deep concern over what is happening in Sri Lanka, "endangering public safety by occupying the Gardiner or other public highways is not the right way to make that statement." Similarly, Ontario Premier Dalton McGuinty criticized the protesters' tactics, saying the bloodshed in Sri Lanka does not justify blocking streets in Toronto and Canada (CBC News 2009). Indeed, there are other and better ways to express their demand. As Premier McGuinty offered, "the demonstrators were welcome to protest on the front lawn of the legislature or Parliament Hill."

Neither is it conducive for the newcomers, who are frustrated for not being able to find suitable jobs, to complain that they are "cheated" (by the Canadian government). Although Canada welcomes immigrants, application for immigrating to Canada is a voluntary process and a personal choice. Newcomers need patience in finding jobs that match their professional backgrounds. When one moves within his or her home country from one city to another, he or she would still encounter challenges and barriers, not to mention the difficulties one has to face when moving to a different country.

Investor and business immigrants should focus on creating jobs in Canada to fulfill their immigration obligations. The "astronauts" who need to spend extended time out of Canada to attend their overseas businesses need to abide by the Canadian tax laws and the overseas assets declaration law. Ethnic businesses operated within Canada are encouraged to widen their business scope, reaching out to serve beyond their co-ethnics and cater to different communities. T&T Supermarket, Canada's largest Chinese supermarket chain recently purchased by Loblaw Cos Ltd., has been moving in this direction. Within the Toronto CMA, T&T locates most of its stores in shopping malls and plazas, where they mix with non-ethnic Chinese businesses (Wang et al. 2011).

Canada is proud of its multicultural policy. As former Multiculturalism Minister Sheila Finestone told a news conference in 1995, multiculturalism is a policy that "the whole world is looking at to solve social and cultural frictions," and "Canada proved to the world that people of different credos, races, and cultures can live together in peace and harmony" (Persichilli 2010). For an immigrant-dependent country like Canada, "when newcomers thrive, we all do" (Fiorito 2010).

NOTES

1. South Asians consist of immigrants from India, Pakistan, Bangladesh, and Sri Lanka
2. The article was condemned by various groups of concerned citizens, students, and university faculty members after its publication. In response to the reactions, *Maclean's* later changed the title of the web edition of the article to "The Enrolment Controversy."
3. See this web page: http://ca.answers.yahoo.com/question/index?qid=20080126181309AA5bzXM
4. Immigration class is one of many variables in the Canadian Landed Immigrant Data System (LIDS). This variable distinguishes immigrants as independents (i.e., skilled workers/professionals), investors, entrepreneurs, family members, refugees, etc.
5. These were: Sophie Chen of Pickering graduating from Pine Ridge SS with 97.6% average (immigrated from China in 2001); Amy Wang of Toronto graduating from Northern SS with 99.7% (immigrated from China in 2002); Manan Arya of Brampton graduating from Turner Fenton SS with 99.7% (immigrated from India in 2003) (Rushowy, 2007).
6. In 2008, Jaymin Kim of Burlington graduated from Robert Bateman SS with 99% average (accepted by Harvard University); Anna Yue Shen of Mississauga

graduated from Glenforest SS with 100% average (accepted by the University of Waterloo); Keith Ng of Mississauga graduated from St. Francis Catholic SS with 98.8% average (accepted by the University of Toronto); Griselda Lam of Thornhill graduated from St. Robert Catholic SS with 99.1% average (accepted by McMaster University); Jennifer Chung of Pickering graduated from St. Mary Catholic SS with 95.8% average (accepted by McMaster University) (Rushowy 2008).

7. The Prairies refer to Manitoba and Saskatchewan. Atlantic Canada consists of Nova Scotia, New Brunswick, Newfoundland, and Prince Edward Island. The Territories refer to Yukon, Northwest Territories, and Nunavut.
8. Recent immigrants are those who immigrated to Canada within the last five years of the most recent census. In the 2006 census, recent immigrants refer to those who arrived in Canada between 2001 and 2005.
9. The Longitudinal Survey of Immigrants to Canada was taken with three waves of questionnaires approximately 6, 24, and 48 months after landing in Canada. It covered the period from 2001 to 2005.
10. NPA is a political organization in Vancouver.
11. The fertility rate in Canada declined significantly between 1971 and 2001, dropping from slightly over 2.1 in 1971 to approximately 1.5 in 2000. In fact, 1971 was the last year when Canada's fertility rate exceeded the replacement level.
12. Alden E. Habacon, Manager of Diversity Initiatives at CBC Television and Director of Intercultural Understanding Strategy Development at the University of British Columbia, posted a commentary on Blogra on February 13, 2010, titled, "Vancouver 2010 Olympic Winter Games: Whitest Opening Ceremony Ever?" In that piece, Habacon complained about the lack of diversity in the Canadian delegation at the opening ceremony; he also referred to Vancouver "as a city that is considered by many (including myself) as part of Asia." http://www.straight.com/article-289674/vancouver/vancouver-2010-olympic-winter-games-whitest-opening-ceremonies-ever?page=1
13. In 2006, Canada added the Tamil Tigers to its official list of terrorist organizations.

REFERENCES

Agrawal, S. K., and A. Lovell. 2010. "High-Income Indian Immigrants in Canada." *South Asian Diaspora* 2(2):143–63.

Aryal, A. R. 2011. "Vancouver's Punjabi Market Looks to Better Times." *UBC Journalism News Services.* http://thethunderbird.ca/2010/10/28/vancouvers-punjabi-market-falls-on-hard-times/ (Retrieved on June 2, 2012)

Brown, L. 2008. "Exclusive Snapshot of Student Achievement." *Toronto Star* June 13:A1.

Canwest News Service. 2007. "UN Calls Canada Racist for 'Visible Minorities' Tag." http://www.canada.com/topics/news/national/story.html?id=f469b36e-c587–40e7–98e5–3aa50a371318&k=23802 (Retrieved on June 2, 2012)

"CBC Manager of Diversity: Vancouver Is Part of Asia." 2010. *Immigration Watch Canada.* http://www.immigrationwatchcanada.org/2010/02/13/cbc-manager-of-diversity-vancouver-is-part-of-asia/ (Retrieved on June 2, 2012)

CBC News. 2009. "Tamils' Highway Closure Was 'Wrong Way to Protest'": Ont. Premier." May 11. http://www.cbc.ca/news/canada/toronto/story/2009/05/11/tamil-protest-toront051109.html (Retrieved on June 2, 2012)

de Beer, P. 1994. "Sweet and Sour for 'Hongcouver' Asians." *Guardian Weekly* January 20:P15.

Dupuis, S. 2009. "Immigration a Boon to Housing Market." *Toronto Star* September 19. http://www.thestar.com/article/696854. (Retrieved on June 2, 2012)
Findlay, S., and N. Köhler. 2010. "The Enrolment Controversy" (originally Too Asian?). *Maclean's* November. http://www.straight.com/article-133771/why-peter-ladner-will-likely-never-become-mayor-vancouver (Retrieved on June 2, 2012)
Fiorito, J. 2010. "When Newcomers Thrive, We All Do." *Toronto Star* March 8:GT1.
Freeman, S. 2011. "Vancouver: Wealthy Chinese Immigrants Cause House Prices to Soar." *Canadian Immigration Report.* http://www.cireport.ca/2011/05/vancouver-wealthy-chinese-immigrants.html (Retrieved on June 2, 2012)
Hertz, B. 2007. "$60M South Asian-Themed Mall to Be Built in Markham." *The National Post* November 2. http://network.nationalpost.com/np/blogs/toronto/archive/2007/11/02/60m-south-asian-themed-mall-to-be-built-in-markham.aspx (Retrieved on June 2, 2012)
Hiebert, D., and P. Mendez. 2009. "Settling in: Newcomers in the Canadian Housing Market, 2001–2005." *Research Highlight*, CMHC, February issue.
Kaur H. 2011. "Vancouver Housing Market Allures Investment from Chinese." *Canadaupdates.* http://www.canadaupdates.com/content/vancouver-housing-market-allures-investment-chinese-16234.html (Retrieved on June 2, 2012)
Keung, N. 2010. "Newcomers Who Make Canada Better." *Toronto Star* June 14:GT3.
Knox, P. and S. Pinch. 2010. *Urban Social Geography*: An Introduction. Prentice Hall.
Lebour, T. 2011. "Immigration Helps Drive Housing Market." *Toronto Star* January 1. (a special Real Estate News page with no page number)
Ley, D. 2009. *Millionaire Migrants: Tran-Pacific Life Lines.* West Sussex, UK: Wiley-Blackwell.
Miller, K. 2010. "Do Colleges Redline Asian Americans?" *The Boston Globe* February 8. http://www.boston.com/bostonglobe/editorial_opinion/oped/articles/2010/02/08/do_colleges_redline_asian_americans/ (Retrieved on June 2, 2012)
Persichilli, A. 2010. "Patronizing Policy Keeps Immigrants in Ethnic Ghettos While Deceiving Them That They Have Been Fully Accepted." *Toronto Star* April 25:A15.
Porter, Catherine. 2007. "Thousands Drawn to Temple's Dazzle." *Toronto Star* July 23:A3.
Preston, V., and L. Lo. 2000. "Asian Theme Malls in Suburban Toronto: Land Use Conflict in Richmond Hill." *The Canadian Geographer* 44:182–91.
Quadeer, M., and S. Kumar. 2003. "Toronto's Residential Mosaic." *The Ontario Planning Journal* 18(5):7–9.
Radhika, V. 2008. "Step Aside, Pacific Mall, There's a New Haj in Town." *The Globe and Mail* November 1. http://www.vradhika.com/articles/TAJ.htm
Ray, B. K., G. Halseth, and B. Johnson. 1997. "The Changing Face of the Suburbs: Issues of Ethnicity and Residential Change in Suburban Vancouver." *International Journal of Urban and Regional Research* 21(1):75–99.
Rushowy, K. 2007. "Newcomers Reach for the Top." *Toronto Star* August 30:A10.
Rushowy, K. 2008. "The Top Grads in the GTA." *Toronto Star* August 25. http://www.thestar.com/article/484849 (Retrieved on June 2, 2012)
Ryerson University. 2011. "Few Visible Minorities among GTA Legal Leaders, Diversity Institute Reports." *Ryerson Today* (news release) June 8.
Singh, P., and T. V. Thomas. 2004. "Ministering to South Asians in Canada and Beyond." *Global Missiology.* ojs.globalmissiology.org/index.php/english/article/viewFile/125/362. (Retrieved on June 2, 2012)

Smith, C. 2008. "Why Peter Ladner Will Likely Never Become Mayor of Vancouver?" February 23. *Blogra*. http://www.straight.com/article-133771/why-peter-ladner-will-likely-never-become-mayor-vancouver (Retrieved on June 2, 2012)

Starr, R. 2010. "Developers, Brokers Court Real Estate-Hungry South Asian Market." *Toronto Star* September 29. http://www.yourhome.ca/homes/realestate/article/867861—developers-brokers-court-real-estate-hungry-south-asian-market (Retrieved on June 2, 2012)

Statistics Canada. 2010. *Projection of the Diversity of the Canadian Population 2006–2031*. (Catalogue NO. 91–551-x). Ottawa: Author.

Sutherland, J. 2010. "Is Vancouver in a Real Estate Bubble?" *The Globe and Mail* November 24. http://www.theglobeandmail.com/report-on-business/rob-magazine/is-vancouver-in-a-real-estate-bubble/article1808967/ (Retrieved on June 2, 2012)

The Chinese Canadian Post. 2010. "Forty Chinese Candidates Run in Ontario's Municipal Elections." October 23:4.

The Richmond Review. 1991. "Housing Explosion Needs Brake" (Letter to the Editor). March 1.

The Scarborough Mirror, May 30, 1984.

Today Daily News. 2010. "List of Chinese Candidates in the GTA Municipal Elections," October 24:P3.

Vukets, C. 2011. "The Changing Face of Little India." *Toronto Star* February 22:GT5.

Wang, S. 1999. "Chinese Commercial Activity in the Toronto CMA: New Development Patterns and Impacts." *The Canadian Geographer* 43(1):19–35.

Wang, S. and L. Lo. 2005. "Chinese Immigrants in Canada: Their Changing Composition and Economic Performance." *International Migration* 43(3):35–71.

Wang, S., R. Hii, J. Zhong, and P. Du. 2012. "Recent Trends in Ethnic Chinese Retailing in Metropolitan Toronto." *International Journal of Applied Geospatial Research* 4 (4) (forthcoming)

Wang, S., and Q. Wang. 2012. "Contemporary Asian Immigrants in the United States and Canada." In *Immigrant Geographies of North American Cities*, edited by Carlos Teixeira, Wei Li, and Audrey Kobayashi, 208–30. Toronto: Oxford University Press.

Wasserman, J. 2011. "Vancouver Housing Market Surges Thanks to Chinese Buyers." *Financial Post* May 17. http://www.financialpost.com/personal-finance/mortgages/Vancouver+housing+market+surges+thanks+Chinese+buyers/4796258/story.html (Retrieved on June 2, 2012)

Wong, T. 2007. "Immigrants Drive House Market." *Toronto Star* December 6:B5.

Wong, T. 2010. "Recipe for Success: Indo-Canadian Entrepreneurs Who've Made Their Mark Are Giving Back Significantly to the Mainstream Community." *Toronto Star* January 18:B1.

Yelaja, P. 2007. "South Asians Raise Millions for Hospital." *Toronto Star* February 3:B5.

11 Family Forms Among First- and Second-Generation Immigrants in Metropolitan America, 1960–2009

Tim F. Liao and Berkay Özcan

INTRODUCTION

It is common demographic knowledge that metropolitan areas in America have been the major destinations for immigrants to the United States (Portes and Rumbaut 2006). The degree to which an immigrant integrates in a host multi-ethnic city can be understood in the social distance between the immigrant and local residents. The classical measure of social distance of Borgardus (1947) deals with an individual's acceptance of people from other racial or ethnic groups into one's country, society, profession, neighborhood, friendship network, and marriage. Such type of social distance indeed describes at least two of Gordon's (1964) seven stages of assimilation—marital and structural assimilation.

To understand immigrant integration, researchers often examine immigrants' socioeconomic status such as education, income, and occupation. It is commonly assumed that immigrants' holding the same kind of jobs with similar income levels certainly suggests integration. In this chapter, we examine immigrants' integration in America's metropolitan areas by their residential patterns or family structures, an unconventional indicator of integration.

Recent years have seen the increase of both the horizontally and vertically extended-family households among recent immigrants (Glick, Bean, and Van Hook 1997; Glick and Van Hook 2002; Van Hook and Glick 2007). The recent uptick in the new century interrupted the long-run secular decline of extended-family households, bringing intergenerational co-residence of persons aged 65 or older with their adult children from a high of 70% in the mid-19th century to lower than 15% by the end of 20th century in the United States (Ruggles 2007; Ruggles and Bower 2003). Actually, the downward trend in the percentage of extended-family households had already come to a stop in the 1980s (Glick, Bean, and Van Hook 1997).

The purpose of this chapter is to study the trends of family forms—the prevalence of vertically and horizontally extended-family households versus single-unit nuclear-family households—among first- and second-generation immigrants compared with non-immigrants in metropolitan areas in the United States. Two prominent explanations of the changing trends in extended-family households include the affluence hypothesis, that people living in extended-family households out of necessity, and the economic development hypothesis, that the rise in wage labor and education would lead to the decline in extended-family households (Ruggles 2007). In this chapter, we entertain an alternative explanation, an explanation of immigrant assimilation. Some immigrants may have come from countries of origin where extended-families are more the norm than the exception. An interesting question, then, is whether the same immigrants would assimilate and adopt the cultural values of the nuclear family that has long been the norm of the majority residential population in the United States.

There has been a long research tradition on assimilation, studying how immigrants assimilate into American life, from Gordon's (1964) ideal-typical conceptualization of assimilation to the more recent literature on segmented assimilation (e.g., Portes and Rumbaut 2006; Portes and Zhou 1993). However, the past literature has primarily focused on various dimensions of racial, ethnic, or immigrant assimilation, related to Gordon's conceptualization: spatial or residential, economic, educational, occupational, linguistic, and marital (e.g., Massey and Mullan 1984; Reitz and Sklar 1997; Rosenfeld 2002; Schultz 1998). In the chapter, we study how immigrants may have assimilated the family form of the host society. We seek to answer the following questions: If immigrants come from a background where extended households are prevalent, do they assimilate the predominant family form in the country of destination over immigration generations? What socioeconomic factors also assist family form assimilation?

Following the introduction, we review the relevant literature on the topic, starting from that on family forms in some popular immigrant regions of origin. We analyze data from the 1960 and 1970 U.S. censuses as well as the 1994, 1999, 2004, and 2009 March Current Population Surveys, via a version of the hierarchical age-period-cohort model that properly estimates age, period, and cohort effects because these are repeated cross-sectional data. We aim to answer the research questions by separately analyzing both vertical and horizontal household extensions among immigrants of the four major origin groups from Asia, Canada, Europe, and Mexico and Latin America. After a description of the data and our analytic method, we present the results from our analysis. We then offer some discussions of the results as well as some tentative conclusions.

LITERATURE REVIEW

Our theoretical premise is a high level of extended-family households in the country of origin of those first-generation immigrants who exhibit a higher prevalence of such living arrangements in the United States if not among

Family Forms Among First- and Second-Generation Immigrants 225

second-generation immigrants as well. If assimilation occurs, second-generation immigrants should show a lower level of living in extended-family households. In this review section, we begin by examining extended-family living among some of the popular societies sending immigrants to the United States. Next, we review some extant literature on assimilation. We conclude our literature review with the research on trends and patterns in extended households in the United States.

Extended-Family Living in Popular Countries of Origin

Although the English-language literature is a bit sparse on family forms in immigrant-sending countries, we found some evidence for a high level of extended-family households in a number of immigrant countries of origin. For example, using household samples of the World Fertility Survey, De Vos (1990) found that a majority of the elderly population aged 60 and over lived in extended-family households in the six Latin American countries of the Dominican Republic, Colombia, Costa Rica, Mexico, Panama, and Peru, with the Dominican Republic having the highest level among the six countries and Mexico the lowest. The percentage of such living arrangements among the elderly population was at 64% in the Dominican Republic and 52% in Mexico in the mid-1970s. Despite the relative differences among these countries, the similarities among them compared with most other parts of the world were worth noting (De Vos 1990). The focus on the elderly population notwithstanding, the implication is that these people aged 60 and over lived with their offspring who were the younger generation in an extended-family household. The percentage of elderly living in extended-family residence in Mexico, the most popular sending country of immigrants to the United States, remained at the same level in the mid-1990s (De Vos, Solís, and Montes de Oca 2004; Solís 1999).

Like Latin America, Asia is another region of the world where a large number of immigrants have originated from in recent decades. The most developed country of the region, Japan, had more than 20% multiperson households including a married couple and the parents of at least one spouse, and more than 30% of households with children under age six were also so extended, according to its 1980 census (Morgan and Hirosima 1983). Taiwan, a society not far from Japan that was fast developing at the time, had extended residence found to be persistent as well (Freedman et al. 1978). In 1980, at least 48% of Taiwanese with parents alive lived in extended arrangements (Freedman, Chang, and Sun 1983). In China, the one-child population policy has greatly reduced the popularity of extended-family residence, with only 5% three-generation households in Beijing around 1980 (Chen 1985). Still, if we include rural areas where the majority of the Chinese population resided, likely in extended households as well, the prevalence must have been higher in the recent decades. In another popular Asian immigrant-sending country, South Korea, the prevalence has been much higher. Despite the declining popularity of extended-family living, the percentage of people 60 and over living in extended households in South Korea was 71 in 1970 and 64 in 1980, according to the country's censuses (De Vos and Lee 1993). This level was unmatched by any of the Western societies.

Immigration and Assimilation

In spite of the early 20th-century melting pot analogy in the popular media suggesting America reached out its welcoming arms to immigrants from around the world who assimilated into American life, scholarly work later showed that America was anything but a huge melting pot. Relying on empirical data, sociologist Ruby Jo Reeves Kennedy (1944) propounded the triple melting pot thesis and demonstrated that intermarriages occurred mainly *within*, rather than *between*, the three dominant religious groups of Protestants, Catholics, and Jews. Kennedy's (1944) historical data of more than 9,000 marriage records from New Haven, Connecticut, showed that the United States was a religiously divided society in terms of intermarriages. Her analysis excluded the small number of racial intermarriages, a much more important issue in later decades.

In the post-triple melting thesis era, numerous influential social scientists have conducted significant scholarship on the issues of assimilation and integration, including important sociological works by Gans (1997), Park (1950), Gordon (1964), Glazer and Moynihan (1963), Portes and Rumbaut (2006), Portes and Zhou (1993), and Rumbaut (1997). In this chapter, we focus on the concepts of assimilation by Gordon (1964), Portes and Rumbaut (2006), and Portes and Zhou (1993).

Studying how the early 20th-century immigrants, especially those of southern and eastern European origins, managed to assimilate into mainstream American society, Gordon (1964) found that the Poles, Italians, and Greeks (among others) had originally faced a lot of discrimination in the United States upon arrival; however, over the course of three generations, these immigrants managed to become integral parts of the dominant white ethnic group. He proposed a seven-stage theory of assimilation in acculturation, structural assimilation, marital assimilation, identificational assimilation, attitude receptional assimilation, behavioral receptional assimilation, and civic assimilation.

Gordon (1964) concluded that common intermarriages between the early 20th-century immigrant groups (such as Italians, Poles, and Greeks) and the established white ethnic groups (English, Germans, and Irish) were a clear indication that southern and eastern European national groups had assimilated into mainstream America.

Gans (1992) described several paths that children of the new immigrants might take, including possible downward and upward mobility. Recognizing the more recent diverse social reality in the United States, especially the social phenomenon of urban underclass, Portes and Zhou (1993; see also Portes and Rumbaut 2006) proposed segmented assimilation theory. The theory acknowledges the divergent paths of assimilation; that is, all immigrants may not take the "straight-line," upward assimilation. In addition to upward assimilation, there can be downward assimilation and selective assimilation. Thus, the processes of adaptation and assimilation among recent or new immigrants may be different from those experienced by earlier European immigrants, including the groups studied by Gordon (1964). In summary, there are three possible paths (Portes and Zhou 1993). The first is the upward assimilation as predicted by the classical assimilation literature, that is, acculturation and integration into the mainstream, middle-class American life; the second path, or downward assimilation, leads to assimilation into the underclass in American cities and to poverty; the third path leads to the so-called "selective assimilation" that encourages the preservation of the immigrant group's ethnic culture and values while getting economically integrated. This theory makes more sense in contemporary American reality, allowing for different ways of becoming an American, and reconciling with the presence of a wider range of socioeconomic backgrounds than in previous waves of immigration as recognized by various scholars (e.g., Alba and Nee 1997, 2003; Portes and Rumbaut 2006). Note that social scientists have viewed assimilation as primarily a matter of socioeconomics instead of family culture.

Household Composition of Immigrants

Recent scholarship on family composition all recognized the contributions by immigrants to the trends of extended-family forms (e.g., Glick, Bean, and Van Hook 1997; Glick and Van Hook 2002; Van Hook and Glick 2007). The explanations offered and tested by researchers like Ruggles (2007) include the affluence hypothesis, the economic and development-based theory, and explanations based on social mobility, urbanization, demographic changes (as in age structure), and attitudinal changes (in family values) over historical time. What is missing from the literature is an understanding of the interplay between assimilation and family structure. The only research focused on family structure and assimilation was done by Gratton, Gutmann, and Skop (2007), who analyzed the U.S. census data from 1880 to 1970 to assess the influence of ethnicity and generation on family structure of some major immigration groups. They found few consistent ethnic effects and argued that the results disconfirmed segmented assimilation theory.

One important aspect of the immigrant life neglected thus far in research on household composition is immigrant neighborhood residential patterns. Hispanic residential segregation, for example, has increased in recent decades, possibly reflecting an increase in Hispanic immigration to metropolitan areas (Iceland 2004). Asian segregation, too, has increased, where overall minority population has increased (Iceland 2004; Logan et al. 2004). Both Asians and Hispanics prefer to reside in integrated neighborhoods with whites than with blacks (Fong and Shibuya 2005). Assimilation involves intergroup interaction. If members of an ethnic group reside in a segregated community, intergroup interaction is going to diminish. When intergroup interaction diminishes, assimilation is going to be affected as well.

Another dimension of intergroup interaction is gauged through ethnic businesses. Ethnically owned businesses tend to be located in ethnic neighborhoods. Perhaps more importantly, ethnic business networks tend to concentrate within their own sub-ethnic groups. For example, Chiu's (2001) study showed that Chinese from Hong Kong, Taiwan, and Mainland China tend to have their own subethnic business networks catering to their own sub-ethnic groups. When intra-ethnic group interaction increases, intergroup interaction is likely to decline, thus affecting assimilation.

We propose to study family composition of major immigrant regions of origin groups in the United States especially in the post-1965 immigration act era. Living in an extended family can be considered as a cultural value, and acculturation of the host society's customs, values, and norms is indeed a primary dimension of Gordon's (1964) theory of assimilation. The process of assimilation takes much longer than a single generation, and if it happens, it takes three generations, as Gordon (1964) found. Recognizing the fact that immigrants came from places where extended-family living varies a great deal in its popularity and prevalence, we consider the difference between places of immigrant origins as important. Some prior research also questioned whether extended-family forms were solely a result of immigration or they are inherent in the culture of certain country of origins (Van Hook and Glick 2007). In the chapter, we set out to answer these research questions: Do immigrants coming from a society where extended-family living is prevalent assimilate the predominant family form in the country of destination over immigration generations? What socioeconomic factors including ethnic business ownership assist family form assimilation?

DATA

The data source for our analysis must have three major characteristics. First, it should contain detailed information about nativity (e.g., ideally generation status of higher than three). Second, it should have a large enough sample size to capture variations in each immigrant group by demographic characteristics and cohorts. Third, it should provide fine-grained information about the household structure to correctly classify them into either vertically or horizontally extended households. In addition to these characteristics, we would like to keep the analysis as updated as possible. To this end, we combined data from the 1960 and the 1970 censuses where we have all of the information above with the Current Population Survey's (CPS) last four waves for every five years (i.e., 1994, 1999, 2004, and 2009).[1] For this chapter, we select only those people residing in a metropolitan area.

In order to make sample sizes comparable between CPS and Census data, we drew a random sample of 0.1% U.S. population out of each of the 1960 and 1970 censuses. As a result, we obtained samples with comparable sizes that vary between 130,000 and 220,000 observations per wave. With such data, we are able to see whether the extended-family household tends to be popular among only first-generation immigrants and whether it declines (indicating assimilation) for the second-generation immigrants, and by how much. We also examine the differences of family form prevalence between regions of origin and the effects of socioeconomic status on residential patterns.

Another advantage of using the CPS data in combination with the census data over the previous studies that used only census data is that we are able to take a closer look at more recent trends with the additional waves from the CPS data between early 1990s up to 2009. This was not possible in the previous research that used only the decennial census data and allowed only additional two data points after 1970. This would be regrettable because in the last two decades but especially after 2000, a century-long declining trend may have been reversed. Thus, it is necessary to look at these years more closely. We provide the descriptive evidence for the reversed trends in a later section.

We have two dichotomous dependent variables, each of which indicates whether the household is vertically or horizontally extended, respectively. We define vertically extended households as those that include adult children and grandchildren of the head or those households where head lives with at least one of his or her parents and his or her children. In other words, the household must contain members of three generations. Therefore, we exclude households that include only two generations even if they are the first and the third (i.e., head lives with grandchildren, but the parents of the grandchildren are absent) according to our definition of vertically extended households. On the other hand, horizontally extended households are those that contain at least either one adult sibling of the head or one other adult relative (e.g., cousin, nephew). In these cases, either head or the co-residing sibling (or other relative) or both should be married in order to define the household to be horizontally extended. Put differently, the household must contain another family unit apart from head's own.

Our unit of analyses is household head, and we use their relational attributes to estimate the household structure information for the dependent variables. To understand the mechanisms of immigrants' assimilation regarding residential patterns, our analysis focuses on the possible determinants of residing in a vertically or horizontally extended household for a household head. The set of potential explanatory factors are taken from the previous literature (e.g., Glick, Bean, and Van Hook 1997; Glick and Van Hook 2002; Ruggles 2007; Van Hook and Glick 2007). These factors include sociodemographic variables such as age, race, sex, education, and income. One of our key variables is immigration generation status of household head (i.e., first- or second-generation immigrant versus non-immigrant, which is defined as third-generation or higher). This is determined by their or their fathers' birth places. Another key variable is (ethnic) business ownership. This is constructed by the question about the head of household reporting to have any amount of positive or negative income from business (to be more precise, more than $1 per year or less than $–1 per year) because business income can take a large amount of negative values resulting from business losses.[2]

We define first- and second-generation immigrant groups from four major regions of origin: Asia, Europe, Canada and U.S. territories, and Latin America. We restrict our analysis to these four groups plus the group of non-immigrants in metropolitan areas in the United States. The group of Canada and U.S. territories includes American Samoa, Guam, Puerto Rico, U.S. Virgin Islands, other U.S. Possessed Territories and Outlying Areas, Canada, and Atlantic Islands, but Canadians and Puerto Ricans make up 80% of this group, with Canadians comprising of about half of this group. Mexicans are the largest sized place of origin in the Latin American group. The European group consists of Western and Eastern Europe, including Russia. We exclude immigrants from Africa and the Middle East because they have a much smaller size for conducting a meaningful analysis.

METHODS

A major methodological challenge arises in analyzing repeated cross-sectional surveys due to the "identification problem" because of the exact linear dependency among age, period, and cohort (Period = Age + Cohort) existing in the age, period, and cohort data. Conventional solutions to the problem include non-linear function of at least one of the age, period, and cohort variables, proxy variables for them, and applications of constraints between their effects. We use a variation of the Hierarchical Age-Period Cohort (HAPC) model proposed by Yang and Land (2006, 2008) to address this problem. This model is useful because it (1) does not assume additive fixed age, period, and cohort effects, thus avoiding the identification problem; (2) can capture contextual effects of historical time and cohort membership; and (3) can accommodate covariates necessary for representing social processes and mechanisms (Yang forthcoming).

To apply the HAPC model, we first define cohorts in five-year groups,[3] a common practice in demographic and sociological research. A non-linear transformation can also be applied to the age variable, depending on the substantive meaning of age effects. In our case, we include a quadratic age term that is in line with theoretical considerations regarding an individual's choice of household structure (i.e., middle-aged heads of household have a higher likelihood of residing in an extended family than very young or very old heads of household). Above all, instead of estimating a standard fixed-effects model by including control variables for age, period, or cohort, the HAPC model takes into account the multilevel structure of the data. In this case, the respondents are cross-classified in different socio-temporal contexts defined by birth cohorts and time periods. Because respondents might have a common random error component due to their joint membership to the same period and cohort, for valid statistical inference, such contextual effects are typically estimated as random effects in hierarchical (or mixed-effects) models (Yang 2008; Yang and Land 2006). Such models are also known as cross-classified mixed-effects model. Imagine a multilevel model of individuals with two higher levels, one representing cohort and the other representing period. Instead of one level embedded in the other, these two levels are cross-classified because individuals of one particular cohort can belong to multiple time periods, and vice versa. When at least one of these two effects is regarded as random, the APC linear dependency is broken.

In other words, the typical HAPC model estimates fixed effects of age and other individual-level characteristics on the first level and random cohort and period effects on the second level. We adopt a generalized linear version of the HAPC model via a logit link, also known as the cross-classified mixed-effects (random and fixed-effects) logistic regression model or cross-classified multilevel logit model.

$$\ln\left[\frac{p(y_{ijk}=1)}{1-p(y_{ijk}=1)}\right] = X\beta + u_j + v_k + e_{ijk} \qquad (1)$$

where $p(y = 1)$ stands for the observed proportion of $y = 1$ (as opposed to the expected probability), in this case either the vertically or horizontally extended household type, X is a matrix containing all fixed-effects variables including age, immigrant generational status, education, country of origin, and others, β is the vector of parameter estimates for the fixed-effects variables, u_j stands for the random period effects, v_k represents the random cohort effects, and e_{ijk} is the random error term.[4] The cross-classification of u_j and v_j enables us to (1) take into account influences coming from both contexts of cohort and period, and (2) estimate and evaluate the importance of the two contexts vis-à-vis the fixed effects in analyzing the process of acculturation of family form.

Because we have only six time periods (two censuses and four CPS surveys), it is rather difficult to argue for modeling such effects as random as in the applications of Yang (2008) and Yang and Land (2006). This is especially true when our periods have important substantive meanings. That is, the first two periods sandwiched the 1965 Immigration Act, and the later surveys were conducted with a rise in the number of immigrants. To better capture and understand such period effects, we estimate a different version of (1) by treating the period effects u_j as fixed instead of random.[5]

To our knowledge, this extension to the typical HAPC model has not been applied in the empirical literature. The model specification of (1) remains unchanged for this variation other than the modification above. In the section to follow, we report only results from this variation of the HAPC model with fixed age, fixed period, and random cohort effects.

To facilitate interpretation and to compare the effect of immigration generations of various places of origin on household structure, we compute predicted probabilities from the logistic estimates and sample data. This gives us a better sense of cultural assimilation of family form over immigration generations for various immigrant groups when the key determinants are taken into account.

RESULTS

Sample Description

We begin with a description of the sample for our analysis. Table 11.1 reports summary statistics by immigrants' region of origin versus non-immigrants. First- and second-generation immigrants from Europe represent the largest group of all immigrants, totaling more than 23,000. Next is the first- and second-generation immigrant group from Mexico and other parts of Latin America, with more than 20,000. Asian immigrants and those from Canada are smaller groups. The largest group is of course the non-immigrant, meaning anyone who is a third generation or beyond, totaling more than 205,000 in our sample. The country saw a sharp rise in the number of first- and second-generation immigrants from Asian and Hispanic origins, from a low of 2% to 3% of their individual samples in 1960 to a high of 31% to 32% in 2009. An overwhelming majority of these were first-generation immigrants, constituting 86% of Hispanic immigrants and 88% of Asian immigrants.

Both Hispanic and Asian first- and second-generation immigrants had a younger mean age than non-immigrants at the time of the survey, at 43% and 46%, respectively, and European immigrants had the oldest mean age at 57 years. In terms of education attainment, the two generations of Asian immigrants had an average of above high school education while their Hispanic counterpart had an education level about two years shy of high school graduation on the average. Some of the differences can be accounted for by their age difference. We observe the same pattern in family income, with the two generations of Asian immigrants earning on average $34.6 thousands while the two generations of Hispanic immigrants earn $21.9 thousands.[6]

Of the first- and second-generation immigrants from Europe, their ethnic business ownership rate is at 10%, with all the other origin groups varying between 5% and 7%. We kept the race variable in the

Table 11.1 Summary Statistics by Subsamples of Immigrants' Regions of Origin

Variables	Hispanics Mean	Hispanics Std. Dev.	Asians Mean	Asians Std. Dev.	Europeans Mean	Europeans Std. Dev	Canadians & U.S. Territories Mean	Canadians & U.S. Territories Std. Dev.	Natives: Third Generation Mean	Natives: Third Generation Std. Dev.
Vertical	0.07	0.25	0.05	0.23	0.04	0.19	0.04	0.21	0.03	0.18
Horizontal	0.06	0.23	0.05	0.22	0.02	0.14	0.02	0.14	0.01	0.12
Age	42.75	14.89	45.68	15.79	56.80	16.35	47.88	16.61	47.32	16.10
Age^2	2,049.19	1,462.90	2,336.15	1,619.70	3,493.90	1,862.07	2,568.67	1,728.89	2,498.17	1,657.14
Female	0.42	0.49	0.38	0.49	0.31	0.46	0.46	0.50	0.39	0.49
White	0.86	0.35	0.18	0.39	0.99	0.10	0.89	0.31	0.83	0.37
Black	0.10	0.30	0.03	0.18	0.01	0.07	0.06	0.23	0.14	0.35
Other	0.04	0.20	0.78	0.41	0.00	0.07	0.05	0.22	0.02	0.15
Education	10.21	3.75	12.80	3.05	10.51	3.65	10.99	3.32	12.29	2.56
Family Income	$21,920	$23,313	$34,614	$33,495	$27,900	$27,409	$23,972	$25,714	$30,767	$29,711
First Generation	0.86	0.35	0.88	0.33	0.44	0.50	0.72	0.45		
Second Generation	0.14	0.35	0.12	0.33	0.56	0.50	0.28	0.45		
1960	0.02	0.15	0.03	0.16	0.31	0.46	0.11	0.32	0.11	0.31
1970	0.04	0.19	0.06	0.23	0.28	0.45	0.14	0.34	0.15	0.36
1994	0.16	0.37	0.20	0.40	0.11	0.31	0.19	0.39	0.15	0.36
1999	0.19	0.39	0.12	0.33	0.10	0.30	0.16	0.37	0.15	0.35
2004	0.27	0.45	0.28	0.45	0.11	0.31	0.20	0.40	0.22	0.41
2009	0.32	0.47	0.31	0.46	0.10	0.29	0.20	0.40	0.22	0.42
Own a business?	0.05	0.23	0.07	0.25	0.10	0.30	0.05	0.21	0.07	0.26
N	20,135		9,460		23,083		5,769		205,801	

analysis because there were immigrants from many parts of the world who belong to a non-dominant race of that region. Likewise, we used the gender variable as a control even though it may not represent the true headship of household, which is likely to be lower than these statistics show.

As expected, non-immigrants exhibited the lowest level of vertically and horizontally extended households, at 3% and 1%, respectively. First- and second-generation immigrants from Mexico and other parts of Latin America had the highest rates, with 7% of them residing in vertically extended arrangements and 6% of them living in horizontally extended families. The other origin groups fall between the two extremes, with the Asian immigrant group having the second highest combined rate of extended living.

Descriptive Analysis

In this subsection, we examine the trends of both vertically extended and horizontally extended households over time and over immigration generation status. Immigration generation status is defined by an immigrant's nativity status and his or her parents' immigration status. One is a first-generation immigrant if he or she was foreign-born, a second-generation immigrant if at least one parent was foreign-born (we separate inter-immigration status parent groups), and a third or older immigration generation (or native) if neither parent was foreign-born. For the descriptive analysis below, we separate immigrants by their first- versus second-generation statuses.

As a support to the earlier point about the reversal of the century-long declining trend, we can clearly see in Panel a of Figure 11.1 an overall declining trend in the percentage of vertically extended households almost in all first-generation immigrant groups as well as the non-immigrant group, followed by a rise after the mid-1990s. This upward trend among the first-generation immigrants shows a result consistent with the implications of previous research (Glick, Bean, and Van Hook, 1997; Glick and Van Hook, 2002). First-generation Hispanic immigrants had a higher percentage than all the other groups in five out of the six periods. In the post-2000 period, first-generation Asian immigrants exhibited a level lower than only Hispanic immigrants. The trends for second-generation immigrants in Panel b are less clear, except that Asian and Hispanic immigrants showed a higher rate of extended-family living than the other groups.

Horizontally extended household arrangements appeared to be more popular among first-generation Asian and Hispanic immigrants in the 1990s and 2000s (Figure 11.2, Panel a). This pattern is followed by first-generation immigrants from Canada. European immigrants had a similar rate to non-immigrants. There seems to be a slight decline and then a small rise for the four immigrant groups. But any change is rather moderate.

Family Forms Among First- and Second-Generation Immigrants   235

a) First-generation immigrants versus natives.

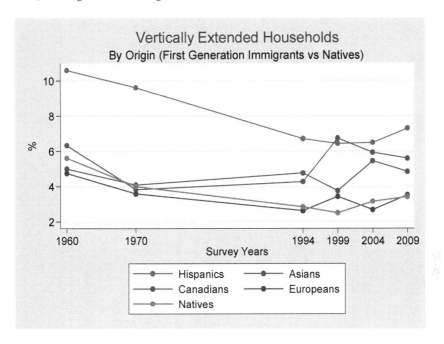

b) Second-generation immigrants versus natives.

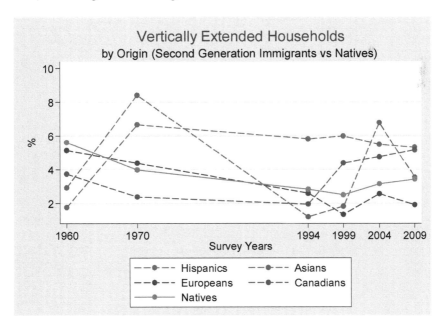

Figure 11.1 Percentages of vertically extended households by year and region of origin.
Note: Households with an unknown nativity status are excluded.

a) First-generation immigrants versus natives.

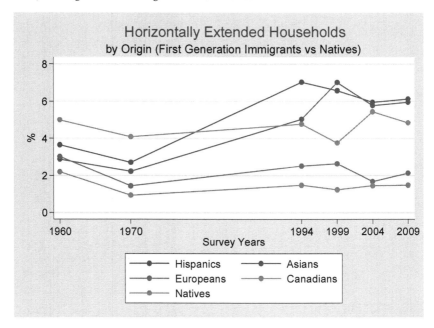

b) Second-generation immigrants versus natives.

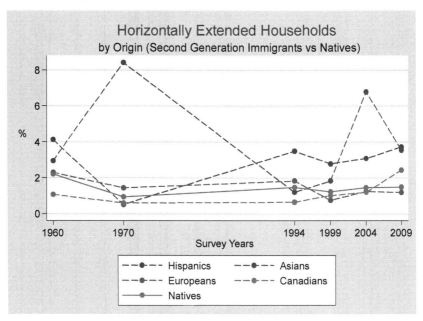

Figure 11.2 Percentages of horizontally extended households by year and region of origin.

Note: Households with an unknown nativity status are excluded.

Panel b of Figure 11.2 shows convergence in percentage of horizontally extended-family living between the second-generation immigrant groups and the non-immigrant group. However, second-generation Asian immigrants had two outlying observations in 1970 and 2004 (possibly due to the smaller number of data points in those two subgroups), and second-generation immigrants from Latin America also showed a higher rate than the other groups in five out of six periods. Overall, however, the information conveyed in Figures 11.1 and 11.2 suggests that immigrants to the United States did assimilate the cultural trait of simple household structure from the first to the second generation. It is important to note that these two figures are rather preliminary, based on raw data, before controlling for the potentially confounding effects of age, cohort, and demographic and socioeconomic factors that may influence family structure.

Results from the HAPC Analysis

In this section, we present results from mixed-effects logistic regression with fixed age and period effects and random cohort effects (although for a few models, fixed cohort effects must be included as footnoted earlier). The following tables present the estimates from the four models with whether one lived in a horizontally extended-family household as the dependent variable in the first four columns and the estimates from the four models with whether one lived in vertically extended-family household as the dependent variable in the next four columns, for the first- and second-generation immigrants from Mexico and other parts of Latin America (Table 11.2), Asia (Table 11.3), Europe (Table 11.4), Canada and American Territories (Table 11.5), and non-immigrants (Table 11.6). There are four models for each type of family form for each (immigrant) group because we first estimated a baseline model with only age, period, and cohort effects. We then added demographic variables in a second model, socioeconomic variables in a third model, before bringing in immigration generation status and ethnic business variable in the final model.

Despite the clear trend of vertically extended households in Figure 11.1, there is virtually no period effect for Hispanic immigrants. There are, however, clear period effects for the horizontal extension, especially for the models with more independent variables. Compared with 1960, 1970 had a lower level of horizontal extension, with 1994 and later years all showing a significantly higher level. For first- and second-generation Asian immigrants, there appears to be significant increasing effects of period over time on horizontal extension in the 1990s and afterward, but the same effects are not found on the vertical extension either. For European immigrants, however, the results are the opposite. There are no period effects on living in horizontally extended households, but some vertical extension appears to be on the decline over the first three time

Table 11.2 Estimates from Mixed-Effects Logit Models, First- and Second-Generation Hispanic Immigrants

Fixed Effects	Horizontally Extended Households				Vertically Extended Households			
	Model 1	Model 2	Model 3	Model 4	Model 1	Model 2	Model 3	Model 4
Age	0.040***	0.038***	0.026**	0.017	0.107***	0.110***	0.109***	0.108***
	(0.013)	(0.013)	(0.013)	(0.013)	(0.014)	(0.015)	(0.015)	(0.015)
Age^2	−0.000***	−0.000**	−0.000***	−0.000*	−0.001***	−0.001***	−0.001***	−0.001***
	(0.000)	(0.000)	(0.000)	(0.000)	(0.000)	(0.000)	(0.000)	(0.000)
Year 1970	−0.597*	−0.608*	−0.581*	−0.681*	0.204	0.188	0.236	0.221
	(0.349)	(0.349)	(0.350)	(0.350)	(0.224)	(0.225)	(0.226)	(0.226)
Year 1994	0.576**	0.610**	0.784***	0.620**	−0.091	−0.226	−0.116	−0.141
	(0.259)	(0.260)	(0.261)	(0.263)	(0.204)	(0.206)	(0.208)	(0.209)
Year 1999	0.496*	0.574**	0.734***	0.560**	−0.087	−0.243	−0.119	−0.145
	(0.258)	(0.259)	(0.260)	(0.262)	(0.204)	(0.206)	(0.208)	(0.209)
Year 2004	0.402	0.512**	0.680***	0.497*	−0.063	−0.242	−0.102	−0.131
	(0.256)	(0.257)	(0.258)	(0.260)	(0.201)	(0.204)	(0.206)	(0.207)
Year 2009	0.433*	0.537**	0.728***	0.561**	0.002	−0.184	−0.029	−0.055
	(0.254)	(0.256)	(0.258)	(0.259)	(0.200)	(0.203)	(0.205)	(0.206)
Female Head		−0.518***	−0.447***	−0.442***		0.589***	0.597***	0.596***
		(0.066)	(0.067)	(0.067)		(0.058)	(0.059)	(0.059)

Race (Ref. Cat: Other)						
White		−0.231*	−0.262*	−0.269*		−0.086	−0.087
		(0.138)	(0.139)	(0.139)		(0.146)	(0.146)
Black		−0.762***	−0.689***	−0.737***	−0.057	−0.248	−0.260
		(0.184)	(0.185)	(0.185)	(0.145)	(0.170)	(0.170)
Education in Years		−0.087***	−0.081***		−0.298*		
		(0.008)	(0.008)		(0.169)		
					−0.045***	−0.044***	
					(0.008)	(0.008)	
Log Family Income		0.284***	0.303***		0.019	0.021	
		(0.041)	(0.041)			(0.033)	(0.033)
First Generation			0.575***			0.109	
			(0.116)			(0.093)	
Own a Business			−0.307**			−0.108	
			(0.148)			(0.134)	
Constant	−4.025***	−3.637***	−5.135***	−5.496***	−5.524***	−5.272***	−5.341***
	(0.383)	(0.408)	(0.512)	(0.519)	(0.436)	(0.501)	(0.504)
Random Effects							
	−2.843***	−2.785***	−2.772***	−2.782***	−1.873***	−1.858***	−1.856***
Cohort Effects	(0.898)	(0.839)	(0.823)	(0.829)	(0.339)	(0.335)	(0.336)
Log-Likelihood	−4395.055	−4348.031	−4289.504	−4273.249	−4792.01	−4774.268	−4773.226
Chi2	37.2773***	123.4089***	237.3648***	262.9589***	195.5253***	230.522***	232.3991***
BIC	8,879.302	8,814.984	8,717.751	8,705.061	9,702.942	9,687.279	9,705.015
N	20,135	20,135	20,135	20,135	20,135	20,135	20,135

Table 11.3 Estimates from Mixed-Effects Logit Models, First- and Second-Generation Asian Immigrants

	Horizontally Extended Households				Vertically Extended Households			
	Model 1	Model 2	Model 3	Model 4	Model 1	Model 2	Model 3	Model 4
Age	0.013	0.014	0.006	−0.001	0.163***	0.167***	0.170***	0.171***
	(0.040)	(0.040)	(0.040)	(0.040)	(0.041)	(0.041)	(0.041)	(0.041)
Age^2	−0.001**	−0.001**	−0.001**	−0.001*	−0.001***	−0.001***	−0.001***	−0.001***
	(0.000)	(0.000)	(0.000)	(0.000)	(0.000)	(0.000)	(0.000)	(0.000)
Year 1970	−0.170	−0.092	−0.031	0.027	−0.190	−0.182	−0.155	−0.169
	(0.592)	(0.594)	(0.593)	(0.596)	(0.468)	(0.470)	(0.473)	(0.472)
Year 1994	2.395**	2.435**	2.617**	2.582**	−1.137	−1.185	−1.025	−1.033
	(1.128)	(1.143)	(1.143)	(1.141)	(1.132)	(1.138)	(1.150)	(1.151)
Year 1999	2.968**	2.875**	3.052**	3.034**	−0.811	−0.942	−0.763	−0.772
	(1.269)	(1.285)	(1.287)	(1.285)	(1.282)	(1.291)	(1.305)	(1.304)
Year 2004	3.066**	2.985**	3.178**	3.173**	−1.009	−1.148	−0.949	−0.961
	(1.420)	(1.436)	(1.436)	(1.435)	(1.432)	(1.441)	(1.455)	(1.455)
Year 2009	3.376**	3.257**	3.475**	3.472**	−1.276	−1.438	−1.208	−1.220
	(1.561)	(1.578)	(1.578)	(1.577)	(1.575)	(1.584)	(1.601)	(1.600)
Female Head	−0.375***	−0.398***	−0.390***		0.102	0.061	0.057	
	(0.101)	(0.101)	(0.102)	(0.102)		(0.097)	(0.098)	(0.098)

Family Forms Among First- and Second-Generation Immigrants

Race (Ref. Cat: Other Races)							
White		−0.526***	−0.557***	−0.573***		−0.277**	−0.277**
		(0.157)	(0.157)	(0.157)		(0.140)	(0.140)
Black		−0.407	−0.413	−0.428		−0.221	−0.220
		(0.303)	(0.305)	(0.305)		(0.281)	(0.281)
Education in Years		−0.085***	−0.083***		−0.265*	−0.076***	
		(0.014)	(0.014)	(0.014)	(0.141)	(0.014)	(0.014)
					−0.188		
					(0.281)		
					−0.076***		
Log Family Income	0.145***	0.156***		0.015	0.013		
			(0.042)	(0.042)		(0.038)	(0.039)
First Generation			0.477**	−1.984		−0.030	
				(0.188)		(0.155)	
Own a Business			0.048			−0.085	
				(0.180)		(0.187)	
Constant	−1.558	−1.347	−1.637	−8.184***	−8.144***	−7.531***	−7.511***
	(2.193)	(2.186)	(2.222)	(2.161)	(2.153)	(2.187)	(2.194)
Cohort	−3.312	−3.317	−3.227	−3.235	1.783	1.761	1.841	1.847
Log-Likelihood	−1,929.212	−1,915.217	−1,901.077	−1,897.605	−1,955.524	−1,953.025	−1,939.944	−1,939.821
Chi2	51.2369***	80.4989***	128.337***	134.469***	79.2002***	83.9862***	127.810***	128.268***
BIC	4,096.45	4,095.925	4,085.953	4,097.319	4,149.073	4,171.54	4,163.687	4,181.751
N	9,460	9,460	9,460	9,460	9,460	9,460	9,460	9,460

Table 11.4 Estimates from Mixed-Effects Logit Models, First- and Second-Generation European Immigrants

Fixed Effects	Horizontally Extended Households				Vertically Extended Households			
	Model 1	Model 2	Model 3	Model 4	Model 1	Model 2	Model 3	Model 4
Age	0.100***	0.091***	0.082***	0.081***	0.165***	0.166***	0.168***	0.167***
	(0.024)	(0.025)	(0.024)	(0.024)	(0.021)	(0.021)	(0.021)	(0.021)
Age^2	−0.001***	−0.001***	−0.001***	−0.001***	−0.002***	−0.002***	−0.002***	−0.002***
	(0.000)	(0.000)	(0.000)	(0.000)	(0.000)	(0.000)	(0.000)	(0.000)
Year 1970	−0.595***	−0.574***	−0.520***	−0.529***	−0.237***	−0.240***	−0.170*	−0.165*
	(0.128)	(0.129)	(0.131)	(0.132)	(0.089)	(0.089)	(0.091)	(0.091)
Year 1994	−0.085	0.037	0.221	0.166	−0.554***	−0.563***	−0.383**	−0.386**
	(0.162)	(0.164)	(0.174)	(0.175)	(0.165)	(0.167)	(0.174)	(0.176)
Year 1999	−0.331*	−0.137	0.054	−0.023	−0.623***	−0.626***	−0.405**	−0.410**
	(0.187)	(0.189)	(0.202)	(0.203)	(0.181)	(0.183)	(0.192)	(0.194)
Year 2004	−0.440**	−0.190	0.023	−0.087	−0.486***	−0.496***	−0.248	−0.254
	(0.186)	(0.189)	(0.203)	(0.206)	(0.171)	(0.174)	(0.186)	(0.189)
Year 2009	−0.273	−0.017	0.194	0.072	−0.380**	−0.392**	−0.121	−0.129
	(0.179)	(0.183)	(0.199)	(0.203)	(0.173)	(0.177)	(0.191)	(0.194)
Female Head		−1.187***	−1.166***	−1.170***		−0.033	−0.061	−0.052
		(0.152)	(0.153)	(0.153)		(0.086)	(0.087)	(0.088)

Race (Ref. Cat: Other)						
White	−0.780	−0.727	−0.640		−0.546	−0.527	−0.517
	(0.600)	(0.599)	(0.600)		(0.522)	(0.523)	(0.523)
Black	−0.699	−0.664	−0.647		−0.115	−0.122	−0.126
	(0.929)	(0.928)	(0.929)		(0.690)	(0.691)	(0.691)
Education in Years	−0.058***	−0.048***			−0.050***	−0.050***	
	(0.016)	(0.016)			(0.012)	(0.012)	
Log Family Income	0.107*	0.113*			−0.058	−0.057	
		(0.064)				(0.040)	(0.040)
First Generation		0.269***					
		(0.065)					
Own a Business			−0.146				0.058
			(0.101)				(0.078)
			(0.159)				0.116
							(0.107)
Constant	−6.226***	−5.208***	−5.405***	−5.731***	−6.818***	−6.307***	−5.290***	−5.336***
	(0.647)	(0.871)	(0.976)	(0.983)	(0.550)	(0.734)	(0.800)	(0.805)
Random Effects							
Cohort Effects	−10.221	−3.465	−10.397	−20.245	−1.338***	−1.321***	−1.224***	−1.203***
	(6,330.105)	(6.789)	(5,072.761)	(6.33e+07)	(0.257)	(0.255)	(0.243)	(0.241)
Log-Likelihood	−2,165.349	−2,125.643	−2,118.657	−2,114.739	−3,588.152	−3,587.25	−3,575.357	−3,574.487
chi2	46.4392***	101.8034***	118.9235***	127.1358***	137.3916***	138.7447***	160.2029***	161.9516***
Bic	4,421.119	4,371.849	4,377.969	4,390.227	7,266.726	7,295.061	7,291.369	7,309.724
N	23,083	23,083	23,083	23,083	23,083	23,083	23,083	23,083

Table 11.5 Estimates from Mixed-Effects Logit Models, First- and Second-Generation Canadian and U.S. Territory Immigrants

Horizontally Extended Households

Fixed Effects	Model 1	Model 2	Model 3	Model 4
Age	0.107**	0.096**	0.082*	0.072*
	(0.042)	(0.043)	(0.043)	(0.043)
Age^2	−0.001**	−0.001**	−0.001*	−0.001
	(0.000)	(0.000)	(0.000)	(0.000)
Year 1970	−0.899**	−0.858*	−0.890**	−0.906**
	(0.438)	(0.438)	(0.439)	(0.440)
Year 1994	−0.188	0.038	0.050	0.087
	(0.345)	(0.350)	(0.358)	(0.358)
Year 1999	−0.492	−0.272	−0.289	−0.230
	(0.381)	(0.385)	(0.396)	(0.396)
Year 2004	−0.352	−0.101	−0.108	−0.078
	(0.349)	(0.355)	(0.368)	(0.368)
Year 2009	0.023	0.318	0.316	0.375
	(0.330)	(0.338)	(0.356)	(0.356)
Female Head		−0.930***	−0.847***	−0.826***
		(0.223)	(0.228)	(0.228)

Vertically Extended Households

Fixed Effects	Model 1	Model 2	Model 3	Model 4
Age	0.100***	0.110***	0.115***	0.116***
	(0.030)	(0.030)	(0.030)	(0.030)
Age^2	−0.001***	−0.001***	−0.001***	−0.001***
	(0.000)	(0.000)	(0.000)	(0.000)
Year 1970	−0.223	−0.272	−0.243	−0.249
	(0.270)	(0.270)	(0.271)	(0.271)
Year 1994	−0.149	−0.355	−0.239	−0.249
	(0.266)	(0.271)	(0.274)	(0.274)
Year 1999	−0.136	−0.310	−0.146	−0.158
	(0.277)	(0.279)	(0.283)	(0.284)
Year 2004	0.107	−0.098	0.083	0.071
	(0.259)	(0.263)	(0.269)	(0.269)
Year 2009	0.071	−0.155	0.055	0.042
	(0.265)	(0.269)	(0.276)	(0.277)
Female Head		0.553***	0.500***	0.495***
		(0.135)	(0.137)	(0.137)

Race (Ref. Cat: Other)							
White		-0.006	-0.047	-0.037		-0.375	-0.358	-0.353
		(0.432)	(0.433)	(0.434)		(0.259)	(0.260)	(0.260)
Black		-1.149	-1.155	-1.184		-0.167	-0.185	-0.181
		(0.824)	(0.824)	(0.825)		(0.348)	(0.348)	(0.348)
Education in Years			-0.024	-0.025		-0.055**	-0.053**	
			(0.035)	(0.035)		(0.021)	(0.021)	
Log Family Income		0.227*	0.225*			-0.084	-0.084	
			(0.126)			(0.064)	(0.065)	
First Generation			0.557**				0.032	
				(0.254)				(0.154)
Own a Business			0.752**				-0.205	
				(0.325)				(0.351)
Constant	-6.413***	-5.964***	-7.443***	-7.699***	-5.428***	-5.432***	-4.288***	-4.322***
	(1.093)	(1.161)	(1.447)	(1.445)	(0.753)	(0.794)	(0.902)	(0.910)
Random Effects								
Cohort Effects	-1.458**	-1.406**	-1.366**	-1.464**	-1.142***	-1.171***	-1.195***	-1.199***
	(0.684)	(0.639)	(0.604)	(0.709)	(0.309)	(0.314)	(0.323)	(0.325)
Log-Likelihood	-534.9491	-523.258	-521.4788	-516.4584	-1032.733	-1022.899	-1016.971	-1016.771
Chi2	14.804**	34.567***	37.34***	47.85198***	15.87783**	35.19612***	47.13992***	47.44527***
BIC	1,147.84	1,150.439	1,164.201	1,171.481	2,143.408	2,149.72	2,155.186	2,172.105
N	5,769	5,769	5,769	5,769	5,769	5,769	5,769	5,769

Table 11.6 Estimates from Mixed-Effects Logit Models, Non-Immigrants

Fixed Effects	Horizontally Extended Households				Vertically Extended Households			
	Model 1	Model 2	Model 3	Model 4	Model 1	Model 2	Model 3	Model 4
Age	0.118***	0.111***	0.102***	0.103***	0.181***	0.187***	0.193***	0.193***
	(0.009)	(0.009)	(0.009)	(0.009)	(0.007)	(0.007)	(0.007)	(0.007)
Age²	−0.001***	−0.001***	−0.001***	−0.001***	−0.002***	−0.002***	−0.002***	−0.002***
	(0.000)	(0.000)	(0.000)	(0.000)	(0.000)	(0.000)	(0.000)	(0.000)
Year 1970	−0.862***	−0.846***	−0.797***	−0.802***	−0.395***	−0.437***	−0.359***	−0.361***
	(0.076)	(0.076)	(0.076)	(0.076)	(0.046)	(0.046)	(0.047)	(0.047)
Year 1994	−0.437***	−0.363***	−0.106	−0.113	−0.650***	−0.777***	−0.521***	−0.523***
	(0.072)	(0.072)	(0.077)	(0.077)	(0.080)	(0.082)	(0.084)	(0.084)
Year 1999	−0.649***	−0.546***	−0.279***	−0.287***	−0.749***	−0.902***	−0.602***	−0.605***
	(0.077)	(0.077)	(0.083)	(0.083)	(0.089)	(0.091)	(0.094)	(0.094)
Year 2004	−0.494***	−0.389***	−0.097	−0.105	−0.467***	−0.695***	−0.364***	−0.367***
	(0.070)	(0.070)	(0.077)	(0.078)	(0.093)	(0.096)	(0.099)	(0.099)
Year 2009	−0.490***	−0.386***	−0.071	−0.080	−0.358***	−0.591***	−0.228**	−0.232**
	(0.070)	(0.071)	(0.079)	(0.079)	(0.101)	(0.104)	(0.107)	(0.107)
Female Head	−0.551***	−0.506***	−0.510***		0.503***	0.461***	0.458***	
		(0.043)	(0.044)	(0.044)		(0.026)	(0.026)	(0.026)

Race (Ref. Cat: Other)							
White		−0.701***	−0.677***	−0.677***		−0.798***	−0.731***	−0.731***
		(0.097)	(0.097)	(0.097)		(0.068)	(0.068)	(0.068)
Black		−0.445***	−0.487***	−0.490***		−0.087	−0.196***	−0.198***
		(0.105)	(0.106)	(0.106)		(0.070)	(0.071)	(0.071)
Education in Years		−0.110***	−0.110***	(0.008)		−0.081***	−0.081***	(0.005)
			(0.008)			(0.005)		
Log Family Income	0.177***	0.178***		−0.122***				(0.005)
Own a Business			−0.129*				−0.067	
			(0.073)				(0.050)	
Constant	−6.966***	−6.100***	−6.368***	−6.385***	−7.495***	−7.038***	−5.247***	−5.248***
	(0.232)	(0.250)	(0.310)	(0.311)	(0.186)	(0.200)	(0.221)	(0.221)
Random Effects								
Cohort Effects	−2.465***	−2.494***	−2.434***	−2.435***	−1.270***	−1.233***	−1.199***	−1.199***
	(0.319)	(0.338)	(0.311)	(0.312)	(0.177)	(0.173)	(0.167)	(0.167)
Log-Likelihood	−15,139.5	−15,027.24	−14,929.87	−14,928.26	−29,863.78	−29,296.14	−29,064.54	−29,063.62
Chi2	393.7727***	618.4477***	825.1812***	828.2275***	853.3841***	2,057.852***	2,531.088***	2,532.394***
BIC	30,389.11	30,201.3	30,031.03	30,040.04	59,837.68	58,739.1	58,300.36	58,310.76
N	205,801	205,801	205,801	205,801	205,801	205,801	205,801	205,801

periods. For the Canadian and U.S. territory group, there is no significant period effect of any kind except for the lone negative 1970 estimate. For the non-immigrant group—our reference baseline—the period effect estimates show an inconsistent decline in horizontal extension (in 1970 and 1999) but a consistently significant decline in vertical extension in later periods as compared with 1960. The decline appears to be leveled off after 1999, however. We are only interested in controlling for cohort effects, thus not going into any interpretation. Age exhibits a concave function, suggesting that middle-aged Hispanic immigrants tended to reside in (vertically and horizontally) extended living arrangements.

Having a female head tends to depress the likelihood of horizontal extension but heightens the chance of vertical extension. The same results are found for all the other groups except for Asians and Europeans where the gender of head of household is unimportant. Claiming a white or black race among Hispanic immigrants also could suppress the likelihood of living in a horizontally extended household. Compared with the other racial categories, being either white or black would be less likely to live in an extended household of either kind among non-immigrants, though race would not matter much for most other groups. A higher education attainment would decrease the probability of both types of extended-family living for non-immigrants and all first- and second-generation immigrants. Those Hispanic immigrants living in horizontally extended households were associated with a higher amount of family income, possibly due to more income earners in the family. Notice the same is not observable for vertically extension. The same pattern is observed for all the other immigrant groups. For non-immigrants, however, having a higher level of income is associated with a lower likelihood of living in a vertically extended household.

Does immigration generation status matter? Compared with their second-generation counterpart, first-generation immigrants showed a significantly higher likelihood of living in a horizontally extended household. The effects are particularly strong for Asian, Hispanic, and Canadian and U.S. territory immigrants. For example, first-generation Hispanic immigrants' probability of living in a horizontally extended household is higher by 77% than second-generation immigrants. Despite what the descriptive figure showed, there is little significant effect of immigration generation status on the chance of vertical extension. The effect of owning a business has some inconsistent effects across the groups. Owning a business would have no impact on the chance of living in a vertically extended-family household for any of the groups. We found opposite effects on horizontal extension for two of the immigrant groups. For the first- and second-generation Hispanic immigrant group, owning an ethnic business would decrease the probability of residing in a horizontally extended-family household by 64%. However, for the first- and second-generation immigrants from Canada and U.S. territories, owning a business would increase the same probability by 145%, more in line with the thinking of relating ethnic business with ethnic network and culture.

DISCUSSIONS AND CONCLUSION

The results from our mixed-effects logit analysis suggest some inconsistent answers to our initial research questions. First-generation immigrants from societies where extended-family forms have been relatively prevalent, such as Asia and Latin America, exhibited a much higher probability of horizontally extended-family living than their second-generation counterpart, implying an over-generation assimilation discussed by Gordon (1964). Such effect, however, is absent with regard to vertically extended-family arrangements. This finding suggests that, in spite of traditional values of filial piety, horizontal extension is easier than vertical extension to practice *and* to stop practicing.

Does owning an ethnic business imply living with one's own ethnic group and a reduced amount of intergroup interaction, and thus a lowered likelihood of assimilation? This seems to be the conclusion one can make about first-and second-generation immigrants from Canada and American territories. It is also possible that some Canadian immigrants into the United States had been themselves immigrants in Canada. The negative effect of owning a business for first- and second-generation Hispanic immigrants is counterintuitive upon the first glance. However, the result suggests that the locations of these businesses may not be in ethnic neighborhoods. Despite an increase in Hispanic residential segregation (Iceland 2004), Mexican towns are not as established as China towns or Korean towns in metropolitan America. If these businesses are located in an integrated or predominantly white area, then intergroup interaction will be enhanced, rather than dampened, thereby explaining a lowered chance for having a horizontally extended-family household. This finding also reveals an important limitation in our data. Ideally, we would want to have measurements of immigrants' communities, including their residential integration/segregation and the ethnic makeup of the locations of their ethnic businesses. Those measures would allow us to tease out what is exactly happening with regard to ethnic integration and assimilation.

Some of the control factors also produced interesting findings. When a household has a female head, the chance for the household to extend horizontally is decreased for all groups. Between 1970 and 1993, the percentage of families with children headed by a single mother increased from 11.5% to 25.9% (Lichter, McLaughlin, and Ribar 1997). Such female-headed families are unlikely to have a sibling, especially a brother, living in the same household. According to our analysis, it is possible, however, for female-headed families to have a third-generation relative living in the household among non-immigrants as well as immigrants from Latin America, Canada, and U.S. territories. For the Hispanic immigrants, for example, the likelihood of living in a vertically extended-family arrangement would be increased by 81%, compared with male-headed families.

What can we say about the recent upward turn in the trends of extended-family living that interrupted the long-run declined in the United States, as observed by Ruggles and Bower (2003) and Ruggles (2007)? Past research attributed the recent increasing trend of both the horizontally and vertically extended-family households to recent immigration (Glick, Bean, and Van Hook 1997; Glick and Van Hook 2002; Van Hook and Glick 2007). Our descriptive analysis in Figures 11.1 and 11.2 also supported such a claim, to a degree.

Applying the hierarchical age-period-cohort model, we were able to estimate period effects that have been cleansed of the influence of not only age and cohort but also demographic and socioeconomic factors. We present predicted probabilities from the Model 11.4s in Tables 11.2, 11.3, 11.4, 11.5, and 11.6 in Panel a of Figure 11.3 and from the Model 11.4s in the same tables in Panel b of Figure 11.3. These probabilities represent "pure" period effects on vertical and horizontal extensions.

The pattern of vertical extension goes against conventional wisdom. That is, despite minor fluctuations, most origin groups show a moderate decline in vertically extended-family living in recent years. This finding indicates that what was observed before applying the age-period-cohort model is likely to be compositional effects contributed by other factors instead of periods. Horizontal extension is a different story, however. Following on the recent scholarship on family composition, which recognized the contributions by immigrants to the trends of extended-family forms (Glick, Bean, and Van Hook 1997; Glick and Van Hook 2002; Van Hook and Glick 2007), we suggest that there appears to be an upward period trend in horizontal extension for the two major contributors to immigration in the past two decades—Asian and Hispanic immigrants. While we do not have the data to confirm the point, it is possible that the recent rise in the total number of immigrants in these two groups enabled relatives of those immigrants already in the country to follow in their footsteps. The later-coming immigrant relatives would tend to be siblings and relatives who are similar in age and likely in the same generation.

More generally, judged by immigrants' residential patterns, their integration into America's multi-ethnic cities has been incomplete. This integration, however, varies by place of origin and immigrant generation. First-generation immigrants from Asia and Latin America have been the least integrated among the immigrant origins we examined. On the other hand, horizontal family form integration has been significantly stronger among second-generation immigrants regardless of their place of origin.

Family Forms Among First- and Second-Generation Immigrants 251

a) Vertical extension-based Model 9 in Tables 11.2 to 11.6.

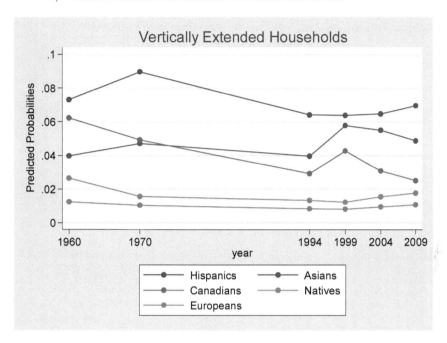

b) Horizontal extension-based Model 4 in Tables 11.2 to 11.6.

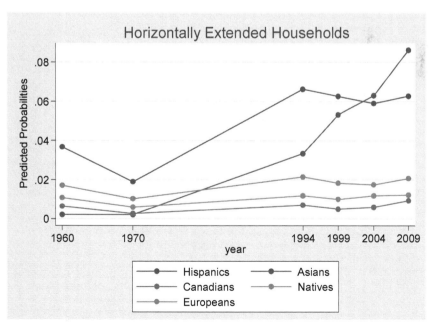

Figure 11.3 Predicted probabilities for the five origin groups.

NOTES

1. Nativity information in CPS is only available since early 1990s. Therefore, we could not use its previous waves.
2. In 1960, we included those who report any income from business or farm since we cannot distinguish these variables in that census.
3. We have 27 cohorts with varying sample sizes in each. In this respect, our data are unbalanced.
4. We use the xtmelogit command in Stata for the estimation of the model with fixed age and period effects and random cohort effects.
5. We estimated this model by using the dummy variable approach to modeling period effects of cross-section time series data using Stata's xtmelogit procedure. For a few model runs, however, we had to treat cohort effects as fixed as well because the combination of smaller sample size and low event counts affected random effect estimation.
6. The income variable is adjusted for family size using the OECD equivalized scale and with consumer price index for inflation.

REFERENCES

Alba, Richard, and Victor Nee. 1997. "Rethinking Assimilation Theory for a New Era of Immigration." *International Migration Review* 31(4):826–74.

Alba, Richard, and Victor Nee. 2003. *Remaking the American Mainstream: Assimilation and Contemporary Immigration.* Cambridge, MA: Harvard University Press.

Bogardus, Emory S. 1947. "Measurement of Personal-Group Relations." *Sociometry* 10:306–11.

Chen, Xiangming. 1985. "The One-Child Population Policy, Modernization, and the Extended Chinese Family." *Journal of Marriage and the Family* 47:193–202.

Chiu L. 2001. Subethnicity and identity: socio cultural interpretations of Chinese business titles in Toronto. *Asian Pacific Migration Journal* 10:145 67

De Vos, Susan. 1990. "Extended Family Living among Older People in Six Latin American Countries." *Journal of Gerontology: Social Science* 45:S87–S94.

De Vos, Susan, and Yean-Ju Lee. 1993. "Change in Extended Family Living among Elderly People in South Korea, 1970–1980." *Economic Development and Cultural Change* 41:377–93.

De Vos, Susan, Patrico Solís, and Verónica Montes de Oca. 2004. "Receipts of Assistance and Extended Family Residence among Elderly Men in Mexico." *International Journal of Aging and Human Development* 58:1–27.

Fong Eric, and Kumiko Shibuya. 2005. "Multiethnic Cities in North America." *Annual Review of Sociology* 31:285–304.

Freedman, Ronald, Ming-Cheng Chang, and Te-Hsiuing Sun. 1983. "Household Composition, Extended Kinship and Reproduction in Taiwan: 1973–1980." *Population Studies* 36:395–411.

Freedman, Ronald, Baron Moots, Te-Hsiung Sun, and Mary Beth Weinberger. 1978. "Household Composition and Extended Kinship in Taiwan." *Population Studies* 32:65–80.

Gans, Herbert J. 1992. "Second-Generation Decline: Scenarios for the Economic and Ethnic Futures of the post-1965 American Immigrants" *Ethnic and Racial Studies* 15(2):173–92.

Gans, Herbert J. 1997. "Toward a Reconciliation of 'Assimilation' and 'Pluralism': The Interplay of Acculturation and Ethnic Retention." *International Migration Review* 31:875–92.

Glazer, Nathan, and Daniel Patrick Moynihan. 1963. *Beyond the Melting Pot: The Negroes, Puerto Ricans, Jews, Italians, and Irish of New York City.* Cambridge, MA: MIT Press.
Glick, Jennifer E., Frank D. Bean, and Jennifer V. W. Van Hook. 1997. "Immigration and Changing Patterns of Extended Family Household Structure in the United States: 1970–1990." *Journal of Marriage and the Family* 59:177–91.
Glick, Jennifer E., and Jennifer V. W. Van Hook. 2002. "Parents Coresidence with Children: Can Immigration Explain Racial and Ethnic Variation?" *Journal of Marriage and the Family* 64:240–53.
Gordon, Milton. 1964. *Assimilation in American Life: The Role of Race, Religion, and National Origin.* New York: Oxford University Press.
Gratton, Brian, Myron P. Gutmann, and Emily Skop. 2007. "Immigrants, Their Children, and Theories of Assimilation: Family Structure in the United States, 1880–1970." *Historical Family* 12:203–22.
Iceland, John. 2004. "Beyond Black and White—Metropolitan Residential Segregation in Multiethnic America." *Social Science Research* 33:248–71.
Kennedy, Ruby Jo Reeves. 1944. "Single or Triple Melting Pot? Intermarriage Trends in New Haven, 1870–1940." *American Journal of Sociology* 49:331–39.
Lichter, Daniel T., Diane K. McLaughlin, and David C. Ribar. 1997. "Welfare and the Rise in Female-Headed Families." *American Journal of Sociology* 103:112–43.
Logan, John R., Brian J. Stults, and Reynolds Farley. 2004. "Segregation of Minorities in the Metropolis: Two Decades of Change." *Demography* 41:1–22.
Massey, Douglas, and Brendan Mullan. 1984. "Process of Hispanic and Black Assimilation." *American Journal of Sociology* 89:836–73.
Morgan, S. Philip, and Kiyosi Hirosima. 1983. "The Persistence of Extended Family Residence in Japan: Anachronism or Alternative Strategy?" *American Sociological Review* 48:269–81.
Park, Robert E. 1950. *Race and Culture.* New York: The Free Press.
Portes, Alejandro, and Rubén G. Rumbaut. 2006. *Immigrant America: A Portrait*, 3rd edition. Berkeley, CA: University of California Press.
Portes, Alejandro, and Min Zhou. 1993. "The New Second Generation: Segmented Assimilation and Its Variants." *Annals of the American Political and Social Sciences* 530:74–96.
Reitz, Jeffrey G., and Sherrilyn M. Sklar. 1997. "Culture, Race, and the Economic Assimilation of Immigrants." *Sociological Forum* 12:233–277.
Rosenfeld, Michael J. 2002. "Measures of Assimilation in the Marriage Market: Mexican Americans 1970–1990." *Journal of Marriage and the Family* 64:152–62.
Ruggles, Steven. 2007. "The Decline of Intergenerational Coresidence in the United States, 1850–2000." *American Sociological Review* 72:964–89.
Ruggles, Steven, and Susan Bower. 2003. "Measurement of Household and Family Composition in the United States, 1850–2000." *Population and Development Review* 29:73–101.
Rumbaut, Rubén G. 1997. "Assimilation and Its Discontents: Between Rhetoric and Reality." *International Migration Review* 31:923–60.
Schultz, T. Paul. 1998. "Immigrant Quality and Assimilation: A Review of the US Literature." *Journal of Population Economics* 11:239–252.
Solís, Patrico. 1999. "Living Arrangements of the Elderly in Mexico." Paper presented at the 1999 Population Association of America Conference.
Van Hook, Jennifer, and Jennifer E. Glick. 2007. "Immigration and Living Arrangements: Moving Beyond Economic Need versus Acculturation." *Demography* 44(2):225–49.
Yang, Yang. 2008. "Social Inequalities in Happiness in the United States, 1972 to 2004: An Age-Period-Cohort Analysis." *American Sociological Review* 73(2):204–26.

Yang, Yang. forthcoming. "Aging, Cohorts, and Methods." In *Handbook of Aging and the Social Sciences*, 7th edition, edited by Robert H. Binstock and Linda K. George. New York: Academic Press.

Yang, Yang, and Kenneth C. Land. 2006. "A Mixed Models Approach to Age-Period-Cohort Analysis of Repeated Cross-Section Surveys: Trends in Verbal Test Scores." In *Sociological Methodology*, Vol. 36, edited by Ross M. Stolzenberg. Boston: Blackwell Publishing.

Yang, Yang, and Kenneth C. Land. 2008. "Age-Period-Cohort Analysis of Repeated Cross-Section Surveys: Fixed or Random Effects?" *Sociological Methods and Research* 36(Special Issue):297–326.

12 Different Voices
Identity Formation of Early Taiwanese Migrants in Canada

Lan-hung Nora Chiang

INTRODUCTION

Canada ranks second as the most popular destination for Taiwanese immigrants. However, there is a research gap on Taiwanese immigrants residing in Canada, mainly because they are not as numerically significant as the Chinese who immigrated from Hong Kong and Mainland China, which forms the main source of immigrants among Chinese internationally. A few studies to date have not differentiated immigrants according to the time of migration or to generational gaps (Chiang 2009; Hsu and Chi 2005; Wong 2004). This research argues that Taiwanese migrants differ by time of arrival in Canada due to immigration policies and the socio-political history of Taiwan. Using a different perspective of inquiry from my previous studies of new immigrants who tend not to settle permanently, or leading *de facto* transnational lives (Chiang 2006, 2008), I try to use this study as an example to emphasize the significance of timing in migration toward settlement decisions and migrants' identity formation.[1]

Autobiographical interviews have been used to reconstruct the lives of these early Taiwanese immigrants to Canada to reflect their experiences [of hardship], social and political values, and attitudes of self-presentation. Attempts have been made to interpret immigrants' experiences within a broader historical context and by drawing attention to the structural (political) causes of mobility. Twenty-four in-depth interviews were conducted in Vancouver and Toronto in 2008, 2009, and 2011. This study is intended to give voice to those who emigrated from Taiwan due to their dissatisfaction with the political climate at the time that they left and have subsequently found ways of making a living in Canada. Arrival of these early migrants in Canada, often from another country, such as the United States, Japan, and Sweden, led on to establishing themselves in various occupations that differ from their education. They have nevertheless developed good language and social skills/local knowledge in Canada, and they have earned steady incomes and raised children who are well-educated and well-integrated into the Canadian society. Other than having a strong sense of commitment to Canadian citizenship, the main difference between the early and the new immigrants is that the former immigrated with their whole families and have made every effort to settle down. However, "*Guanxin* Taiwan" (關心台灣) depicts their commonly shared nostalgic sentiment, since their paths to return earlier have been strenuous and stories still haunt them over the decades after the period of "White Terror" in Taiwan ended in 1987. Due to their involvement with anti-Nationalist Party activities abroad, they could not return freely to Taiwan, before Taiwan's gradual democratization in the late 1980s.

Unanimously, they identity themselves as Taiwanese-Canadians and are proud of their cultural heritage as Taiwanese. With a strong sense of commitment to Canadian mainstream society, they work hard to get their culture represented in multicultural Canada. In the following sections, I will present the literature on Taiwanese immigrants and Taiwanese identity, discuss the methodology in detail, and present the findings.

REVIEW OF PERTINENT LITERATURE

Taiwanese Immigrants

Research on new Taiwanese immigrants has primarily been conducted in Australia, New Zealand, the United States, and Canada (Chiang 2004, 2008, 2009, 2011a; Chiang and Hsu 2006; Chiang and Yang 2008; Yu and Chiang 2009). Only recently has there been an interest in Taiwanese returnees (Chiang 2011b; Chiang and Liao 2008) focusing on the 1.5 generation. Prior to this research, a pilot study was carried out in Canada on nine early immigrants in Vancouver (Chiang and Huang 2009).

In the 1990s, the term "new Asian immigrant" was conceived to describe the middle-class professionals and entrepreneurs who were arriving in large numbers to the United States, in contrast to the older Asian migration of working-class laborers. Taiwanese participate in a global immigration marketplace where there is competition primarily among Australia, New Zealand, and Canada, and to a lesser extent, the United States and other countries. This is reflected in these countries' respective business migration policies, which are receptive and welcoming; the commodity offered by these countries is their respective "visa," which reflects the right of immigration to their country and perhaps an eventual citizenship (Wong 2003). However, citizenship is not analogous to permanent residence, as indicated by an internet survey conducted in 2002 of recent Chinese immigrants by the Toronto-based

North Chinese Community of Canada, which found only 20% of the 1,345 participants who indicated they would remain in Canada after obtaining Canadian citizenship (*World Journal* 2003; cited in Wang and Lo 2005). The migration outcome of new immigrants, which may result in a transnational family, is different from the early immigrant family, which made a linear movement pattern and settled permanently. Immigration agents play an important role in migration decisions regarding the selection of the country and the city where the new immigrant lives (Chiang 2011a). Subsequent to immigration, the "astronaut strategy" has been adopted by many Taiwanese immigrant families; typically, men return to work in their country of origin, but their wives remain abroad while the children complete their education (Chiang 2008). As children's education came foremost in the families' decision to emigrate from Taiwan, the completion of tertiary education is a critical time for parents who return to their base in Taiwan, although others choose to stay in the destination countries (Chiang 2011a). While parents re-unite and live in the same country, the younger generation disperses over more than one country (Chiang 2011b), as in the case of Hong Kong. Because of high levels of uncertainty and insecurity about future employment prospects among this generation of immigrants, many are prepared to leave the destination country and go back to their country of birth, or even re-immigrate to countries where they could find work (Ho and Bedford 2008). The so-called "astronaut strategy" results in transnational arrangements that sustain social fields in both the origin and destination countries, a phenomenon that is quite different from early immigration in the 1960s and 1970s.

One should also note that the background of immigration of Taiwanese differs from that of Hongkongers and Mainland Chinese. Taiwanese immigrants are engaged in three waves of immigration to Canada. Since 1979, a year before the United States severed diplomatic relations with Taiwan, Canada had implemented the business migration program to attract wealthy entrepreneurs and investors, a program that led to the first wave of migrants there. A second wave of increased migration from Taiwan to Canada culminated in 1997 at the time of the handover of Hong Kong to China. Before the turn of the century, a third wave of skilled migrants resulted from the political instability caused by Mainland China's stance toward Taiwan.

Approximately one-half of the Taiwanese immigrants to Canada in recent years came as business immigrants while the other half came via the independent skilled worker or family classes. The 2001 Census records 70,790 Taiwan-born immigrants living in Canada: Vancouver (64%), Greater Toronto (22%), and Calgary (2.2%). In 2006, this total has declined to 60,205. Table 12.1 shows number of Taiwanese entering Canada (Hsu and Chi 2005).

258 Lan-hung Nora Chiang

Table 12.1 Trend of Population Increase of Taiwan-born in Canada, 1961–2001

Period of Immigration	Total	Female	Male
Total Population (2001)	70,790	36,770	34,020
(2006)	65,205		
Before 1961	20	15	10
1961–1970	1,255	645	610
1971–1980	3,540	1,990	3,870
1981–1990	8,530	4,655	3,870
1991–2001	53,750	27,600	26,155
1991–1995	23,405	11,885	11,520
1996–2001	30,345	15,715	14,630
Immigrant population	67,095	34,905	32,190
Non-immigrant	170	110	60
Non-permanent residents	3,525	1,755	1,770

Source: Hsu and Chi (2005, 28). The tabulation was based on unpublished data from Statistics Canada

Previous research on Taiwanese immigrants in Canada has focused on new Taiwanese migrants who were in most cases transnationals, living in two social fields.

While the transnationalism paradigm seems to dominate the literature on Asian or Taiwan immigrants, there is a research gap in addressing the situation of the early migrants who were settled permanently, which forms a significant part of the migration history of the Taiwanese in Canada, despite a smaller number.

Often, it is hard for the host country population, or even researchers, to be sensitive enough to recognize the significant internal differences among the sub-ethnic groups of Chinese immigrants, as well as the generational differences. Political differences among the same ethnic group, as reflected by time-honored or new associations, cannot be taken for granted among old and new immigrants, apart from the economic, social, and cultural links that play an important part in their transnational lives. One therefore needs to step into the community to get an insider view to appreciate the uniqueness of their paths of migration and integration, which cannot be teased out from the statistics. The methodology I adopted for this study is based on such a stance.

Identity Politics in Taiwan and Its Manifestation Abroad

Recently, identity forms a critical part of studies of immigration, particularly with regard to the transnational nature of migration (Ghosh and Wang 2003; Kong 1999; Portes et al. 1999; Vertovec 2011). Identity has always been a very complex phenomenon, which often evokes strong emotion and fierce political reaction, especially among Taiwanese living on the island, as reflected in the mass media, particularly in local news and TV programs. Identity politics is related to the history of settlement and governance of Taiwan culminating in the last 60 years beginning with the KMT (Nationalist Party), which ruled Taiwan in 1949. A small population living on an island with the highest population density in the world, Taiwan's demographic composition[2] is situated in a complex political history.

The meaning of "Taiwanese," which originally referred to the indigenous population, and the "native Taiwanese" has changed over time, with regard to the rise of Taiwanese consciousness in Taiwan's recent political history (Wang 2005, Rigger 2010). While there is more and more intermarriage between the *waishenjen* (Mainlander Taiwanese) and *benshenjen* (native Taiwanese), ethnic boundaries can be blurred in theory. However, identity politics ran rampant, as political disputes intensify particularly during election campaigns between the Democratic Progressive Party (DPP) and the KMT. While the KMT promotes cross-Strait integration and eventual unification, the DPP encourages the maintenance of the status quo of separation and Taiwan's independence against China. Later on, anti-China ideology in vogue between 2000 and 2008, when the DPP was ruling Taiwan, intensified the tension between the discourses that were already polarizing in the eight-year regime. Although democratic values were held by both parties, the DPP's rise in power was symbolically a rebellion toward the un-democratic ruling Nationalist Party, which was in power since 1949 and ruled until 1996, when the first native Taiwanese president was elected (Gold 1993; Chu and Lin 2001). Regaining power in 2009 for the Nationalist government, the two parties again face a fierce competition in the coming election in January 2012.

Several events were significant in the liberalization of Taiwan, including formation of the DPP in 1986 and the lifting of the Martial Law in 1987, which marked the end of the period of "White Terror" in place since 1949. Political movements have always been supported by dissidents of KMT rule abroad, quite often headed by elites and academics who at one time have been actively engaged in professional associations such as the Formosa Association for Public Affairs (FAPA) and the *Tunghsianghui* (同鄉會). The Nationalist government took note of their activities abroad and prevented the dissidents residing abroad from coming back to Taiwan, thus making return migration impossible or difficult for some.

The focus of this research is on the political dissidents [of the KMT] who have stayed overseas even to this day. Rather than staying overseas by choice, they are "Reluctant Exiles," a term I borrowed from Skeldon (2004), who studied the Hongkongers who moved overseas before the handover to China before 1997. Four major questions are related to their experiences in this study: (1) What are the circumstances under which they decided to leave Taiwan and immigrate to Canada? (2) To what extent are they affected by the Canadian immigration policy and Taiwan's political history in their decision to stay? (3) What are their lived experiences like, and how do they fare economically or establish their niche? (4) What constitutes their self-identity and their sense of home toward Taiwan and Canada? These questions were raised to support the premise that their immigration experiences are intertwined with the political history of Taiwan, in addition to human agency.

Although scholars in both Taiwan and the United States have thoroughly studied the rising Taiwanese consciousness in Taiwan (Baum and Sherry 1999, Liu and Ho 1999, Wu 2001, Wang and Chang 2005), the identity formation of Taiwan-born immigrants is much less documented. Through statistical analysis, Yu and Chiang (2009) found that the older generation of Taiwanese immigrants and recent arrivals to the United States, as well as those who live in Los Angeles, are the most likely to regard themselves as Taiwanese rather than ethnic Chinese. In contrast, Taiwan-born immigrants who have greater English proficiency, who have less education, and who have [Mainland] Chinese as their neighbors are less likely to do so.

Based on ethnographic fieldwork conducted in Orange County, California, in 1997 and 1998, Avenarius (2007) wrote that the community organizations in which they participate have predominantly Taiwanese members who speak Hoklo when they are together. They are connected to similar groups because they have members in common and are therefore part of a cluster of Taiwanese organizations. Older immigrants emphasize sub-ethnic differences more than most people in Taiwan itself. In contrast, the interaction patterns of younger first-generation immigrants from Taiwan depend on their self-identification and degree of participation in the ethnic community. In Orange County, Mainlander immigrants may choose to mingle exclusively with Mainlanders, and Taiwanese immigrants may choose to interact mainly with other Taiwanese.

In a different context, Kong (1999) analyzed how Singaporean transmigrants working in China construct and negotiate their sense of "nation" and national identity. It is found from the perspective of individuals that transnational location enhances their sense of national identity rather than its demise, leading to assertions of "Singaporeaness" and rootedness. Using empirical evidence, she demonstrated that physical presence in a territory is not a necessary condition for a feeling of nationhood, but everyday actions count in maintaining a sense of national identity.

METHODOLOGY AND PROFILE OF INTERVIEWEES

My previous visits with Taiwanese immigrants in Canada for studying "astronaut families" (Chiang 2008, 2009) in a number of trips were useful as an experience for this qualitative study, which is more demanding in time and the intensity of interviews. It was in fact by accident that I discovered a particular group of early settlers who came to Canada in the 1960s and

1970s and have had quite a different experience from the new transnational immigrants whom I have written about (Chiang 2004, 2006). The Taiwan Cultural Festival, which I attended in Toronto and Vancouver in 2006, introduced me to early emigrants from Taiwan who are involved in an oral history project attached to the Taiwanese Canadian Cultural Society (TCCS), which has a history of 20 years since its formation in 1991.[3] Since I had not found any studies devoted to this group in the migration literature, my immediate response is that their experiences need to be recorded as soon as possible, particularly in relation to the postwar political history of Taiwan, as a significant part of her democratization movement in the last 50 years. Having been a graduate student in the United States in the late 1960s myself, I was aware of the differences in political ideology among the same cohort of graduate students from Taiwan. Once in a while I heard of political dissidents who did not come back to Taiwan with the first wave of returnee migrants mainly from the United States in the 1980s, but have not conceived this issue in terms of international migration. The relationship between identity politics and mobility is still an area to be explored in contemporary Taiwan, since internal politics and cross-strait tension have formed major reasons in the timing of emigration decisions.

My fieldwork depends a lot on local Taiwanese collaborators for looking up the self-identified Taiwanese-Canadians on whom I am focusing in this chapter. They are the key members of the Society of Taiwanese Canadian History in British Columbia (the Society). The first part of fieldwork covering nine case studies was carried out in Vancouver from April 8 to 14, 2008. The second round of eight interviews took place in Vancouver from April 3 to 11 in the following year. In addition, two short rounds of visits of altogether seven interviewees were made on February 19, 2011, and April 17–22, 2011, in Toronto and Vancouver, respectively, while carrying on other types of ongoing research work.[4] Of the 17 interviews that took place in Vancouver, 14 were carried out in the presence of the key persons of the Society who introduced me to the interviewees from their original roster of around 86 persons who share a similar identity and depending on their availability. Of utmost importance is the idea of trust being given to my research, as the respondents reveal their past history, which was highly sensitive at one time in Taiwan. The advantage of working with local collaborators includes division of work, such as making appointments, driving, recording, photography, and video taping. I did all the interviews, applying the method of ethnographic interpretation in order to understand the "emotions, experiences, and significance" of migration (Graham 1999). Following lines of inquiry designed in my semi-structured questionnaire, my interviewees provided me with their autobiographical reflections, newspaper cuttings, and documents of various kinds. I needed to be a sensitive interviewer, who listened attentively for three to five hours for each interview. In addition, both Hoklo and Mandarin dialects were used, tape recorded, and later transcribed in Taiwan. As mentioned in Gilmartin (2008), migration studies have recently turned to themes of identity and belonging, placing migrant stories at the root of much of this research, with interviews, focus groups, life histories, photographs, and documents to illuminate the experience of migrants and the patterns and processes of migration.

I greatly appreciate the cooperation and candor of the interviewees whose stories are included in my chapter. Having lived in Taiwan for close to 40 years, I have a sense of local politics and international migration, and I was able to conduct the interviews in a sensible manner. An introduction by key members of the Society would not be taken for granted to access the interviewees, who received me with friendliness, hospitality, and flexibility, given the short time of my stay in Canada. The interviews took place in the respondents' homes, in most cases, with both husband and wife present. The trust given to me as a university professor, and as a fellow Taiwanese (*xiangqin* 鄉親), made me feel almost like an insider in the oral history project.

All of the interviews were conducted in a friendly atmosphere, with snacks and tea prepared in Taiwanese style, and often included an additional tour of the interviewees' house or garden. This is quite different from my past experience of conducting surveys with larger samples, which took less time in face-to-face conversation, a major difference being the depth of the qualitative research that goes beyond the semi-structured questionnaire. As the fieldwork spans through four years, the questions being asked also developed to accommodate individual differences and change of circumstances. My empathy toward the community that I studied also deepened over the years, and my friendship with members of the Society grew as a result.

This study also took a methodological turn as I got immersed in the project by reading between the notes many times reflexively. Even with a small sample, I feel that I have grasped the meanings of common terms used by my informant. Having done the fieldwork at four different time periods in two different locations, I am confident that the 24 cases show a great diversity of backgrounds, experiences, and mobility patterns. Deep down I feel that their voices should be heard, and this chapter should be based on their stories. I took a careful and sensitive approach to carry out my micro-level study, with a trusting relationship built by members of the Taiwanese-Canadian Oral History Project, and even friendships forged with particular interviewees who visited me later in Taiwan. Unlike other qualitative research I have undertaken earlier, I believe that this research has special meanings and lasting values in methodology and context.

Originally, I was introduced to male informants mainly, as it is customary to recognize the man as the head of the household in Taiwan.[5] However, I found that it would be an oversight to interview the husbands only, as the wives also play very significant roles in their migration experiences, such as caring for family members before everyone migrated, participating in family business, earning an income to support the family, and educating the children. Wives quite often go through thick and thin of various kinds, keeping the family intact in the absence of husbands. To support their husbands in their political activities was also critical. The wives all tend to speak fluent English, drive, and some do volunteer work (Chiang 2009).

Apart from the time of arrival (1964 to 1987), their self-identity is the key in delineating the group. Earlier, I used the term "reluctant exiles" to describe this group of early timers (Chiang and Huang 2009). As sub-ethnic groups among the Taiwanese, they speak Hoklo or Hakka, instead of *"Beijinghua"* (北京話), which they refer to as Mandarin or *Putonghua* (普通話), which is the official dialects used in Taiwan and Mainland China, respectively. Some of them have participated in the Taiwan independence movement and raised funds for dissidents, and they protested to express their anti-KMT commitments. A common denominator is joining the *Tunghsianghui* (TCA) when they first went abroad to study to share common sentiments and friendships with other Taiwan immigrants. This factor is closely associated with their names being put on the "black list," and thus their inability to get visas to come back to Taiwan, and they have therefore stayed abroad reluctantly.

Table 12.2 shows the profile of interviewees. They included 16 males and 8 females. They were all born in Taiwan, in both urban and rural areas. The earliest arrival in Canada was in 1964, and the rest arrived before the second wave of Taiwanese immigrants in the late 1980s. Half of them have lived in another country before immigrating to Canada because of further studies after their tertiary education and work in Taiwan. These countries include Singapore, Brazil, Japan, Sweden, United States, Germany, and Vietnam. Twenty came to Canada as "independents" from another country, while four changed their Canadian student visa to permanent residency status.

They are highly educated and have varied working experiences before migration. All of them have completed their tertiary education in Taiwan (including three in vocational schools of nursing), one-third has obtained master's degrees, three had PhD degrees, two obtained ABD, and one obtained a postdoctorate as their highest degrees earned. Born between 1930 and 1949, most of them lived in the latter part of the Japanese period (1895–1945) and before the democratization of Taiwan that started in the late 1970s.

A diversity of occupations in Taiwan before moving abroad is represented, while five students who came to pursue further studies in Japan, the United States, and Canada are included. With the exception of three women in the nursing profession and a medical doctor, a majority have changed their professions after arrival in Canada. The details of how they look for work in Canada are discussed in the following section.

Table 12.2 Profile of Respondents

No. Name (pseudonym)	Year of Birth	Sex	Date of Arrival in Canada	Occupation in Taiwan/ Last Occupation in U.S./Canada	Education Level (Highest Degree Earned)	Self-Identity
#1_Ron	1935	M	1976	Export Business Manager/ Superstore Manager (retired)	B.A. Foreign Language (TW)	1, 2
#2_Peter	1935	M	1974	Electrical Engineer/ TV Engineer (retired)	B.Sc. Eng. (TW)	1,2
#3_Abraham	1930	M	1980s (from Singapore and Brazil)	Pastor/Pastor (retired)	B.A. Theological Seminary (TW)	1, 2
#4_Titan	1932	M	1964	Student/ Gynecologist (retired)	M.D., Post-doctorate (Canada)	1, 2, 3
#5_Karl	1937	M	1971 (from Japan)	School Teacher/ Head Gardener in Hospital (retired)	B.Sc. Horticulture (TW); M.Sc. Horticulture (Japan)	1, 3
#6_Sonia	1939	F	1975 (from Sweden)	Nurse/Nurse (retired)	[Vocational] School of Nursing (TW)	1, 2
#7_Susan	1942	F	1969	High School Teacher/Actuarial Assistant (retired)	B.A. Economics (TW); M.A. Statistics (Canada)	1, 3
#8_Sean	1941	M	1972 (from Japan)	Student/Real Estate	B.A. English (TW); Graduate studies in English (Japan)	1, 3
#9_Henry	1940	M	1979	High School Teacher/ Supplementary School Manager	B.Sc. Physics (TW); M.Sc. Geophysics (TW); A.B.D. Hydro Dynamics (U.S.)	1
#10_Jay	1937	M	1970 (from Japan)	High School Teacher/Technician, Pulp and Paper Industry (retired)	B.Sc. Forestry (TW); M.Sc. Chemistry of Forestry Products (Japan)	1, 2
#11_Pansy	1941	F	1974 (from U.S.)	Secretary in I/E Company/ Accountant (retired)	B.A. Industrial Management (TW); M.B.A. (U.S.)	1

(continued)

Different Voices 265

Table 12.2 (continued)

No. Name (pseudonym)	Year of Birth	Sex	Date of Arrival in Canada	Occupation in Taiwan/ Last Occupation in U.S./Canada	Education Level (Highest Degree Earned)	Self-Identity
#12_Jack	1940	M	1966	Hydraulic Engineer/ Hydraulic Engineer(retired)	B.Sc. Water Resources and Eng. (TW); M.Sc. Civil Engineering (Canada)	2, 3
#13_Kirsten	1942	F	1973 (from U.S. and Germany)	High School Teacher/Gift Shop Manager	B.Sc. Math (TW)	1
#14_Winnie	1950	F	1976	Civil Servant/Real Estate Agent	B.A. Public Administration (TW)	1, 2
#15_Duncan	1932	M	1970 (from Vietnam)	Salesman/Air Force Technician (retired)	[Vocational School] Civil Engineering (TW)	2, 3
#16_Rich	1944	M	1974 (from U.S.)	ESL Lecturer (retired)	B.A. Modern Language (TW); Ph.D. Candidate (U.S.)	1, 2, 3, 4
#17_Julita	1947	F	1975	Nurse/Housewife	[Vocational] School of Nursing (TW)	1, 2, 3
#18_Dennis	1945	M	1972 (from U.S.)	Student/Real Estate	[Vocational School] Mechanical Engineering (TW); M.Sc. in Mechanical Engineering (U.S.)	1, 2, 3
#19_Jacob	1945	M	1972 (from U.S.)	Student/Engineer	B.Sc. Chemical Engineering (TW); M.Sc. Chemical Engineering (U.S.); Ph.D. Chemical Engineering (Canada)	1, 2
#20_Jean	1947	F	1987 (from Germany and Sweden)	Nurse/Manager in Sales	[Vocational] School of Nursing (TW)	1, 2, 3
#21_Fiona	1949	F	1974 (from U.S.)	Librarian/Artist + Architect	B.A. in Library Science (TW); further studies in Art and Design (Canada)	1, 2, 3

(continued)

Table 12.2 (continued)

No. Name (pseudonym)	Year of Birth	Sex	Date of Arrival in Canada	Occupation in Taiwan/ Last Occupation in U.S./Canada	Education Level (Highest Degree Earned)	Self-Identity
#22_Peter	1944	M	1965	Teaching Assistant/ Actuary	B.Sc. Math (TW); Ph.D. Math (Canada)	1, 2, 3
#23_Joe	1944	M	1972	Accountant/ General Manager in Sales	B.A. Accountancy (TW); M.A. Business Management (Japan)	1, 2, 3
#24_Oscar	1944	M	1978	Entrepreneur/ Power Engineer	B.Sc. Water Resources and Engineering (TW)	1

Notes: Self-Identities: 1. Taiwanese-Canadian; 2. Taiwanese; 3. Canadian; 4. Chinese-Canadian. TW = Taiwan.

RESEARCH FINDINGS

This study focuses on Taiwanese-Canadians who arrived in Canada between 1964 and 1987 to investigate their lived experiences, social and political values that enter their decision to stay in Canada, identity-formation, and sense of belonging.

Several macro-events form the background for individual migrants to leave Taiwan for another country and come to Canada. Due to postwar economic recession and military control by the KMT that rule Taiwan, it was unusual for Taiwan citizens to go abroad freely as tourists, or for further studies, except for a few privileged individuals. Between 1966 and 1970, the number of students going abroad surged mainly with government scholarships and assistantships offered by North American universities. Starting in 1967, Canada adopted a universal points system for assessing potential immigrants enabling them to apply as "independents." It was also the time when quite a few students who finished their studies in Japan and the United States, but could not obtain residency status and were unable to return to Taiwan safely because of political reasons, considered Canada as an alternative destination. Withdrawal of Taiwan (R.O.C.) from the U.N. in 1971 was also a major event for those who completed their studies in the United States to consider moving to Canada, due to their anxiety over the uncertainty of Taiwan's future. The democratization movement in Taiwan and abroad exerted pressure on political reforms at home, at the time when Chiang Ching Kuo, Taiwan's president, passed away, followed by the lifting of the martial law in 1987[6] and permission of her citizens to go abroad in

1989, which were major events that opened up Taiwan to the outside world. All this was preceded by the era of "White Terror," when some of the early immigrants could not return to Taiwan without being interrogated officially by the KMT-ruled government at that time.

While Canada expanded the categories of immigrants, many Taiwanese were attracted and joined other immigrants from East Asia mainly in the business category (Wong 2004). The "astronaut strategy" was commonly adopted among the new immigrants by having transnational families, where the husband earned the family income in Taiwan while the wives and children stayed back in Canada (Chiang 2008). However, business immigrants were greatly reduced in the late 1990s, and a return flow started in 1996 when Lee Teng-hui, the first elected president, came to office. Even more Taiwanese emigrants returned when the Democratic Progressive Party ruled Taiwan in 2000. This background forms the conceptual framework for me to proceed in the discussion that follows.

Reasons/Process of Immigration

Among my 24 respondents, 10 studied in the United States (#5, #9, #11, #16, #18, #19, #21) and Japan (#8, #10 #23) before entering Canada, while quite a few lived in another country (#3, #6, #13, #15, #20) with different reasons before immigrating. Five studied in Canada and changed to immigrant status later on (#4, #7, #12, #19, #22). Some of them chose Canada because their friends were there earlier. The process of immigration did not sound difficult, as in the experience of Ron (#1):

> Immigration procedure was quick and easy in those days when I applied in 1976. After submitting a letter of credit, I was interviewed one month later. There were ten of us. Everyone else was a medical doctor who was asked to sign an agreement that they would not practice in Canada. My plan was to start a trading company, and was the only one who got the visa. The immigration office in Hong Kong was really quick in their approval of my application. . . . I went to have a medical check up on Tuesday, and got an immigration visa [as an independent] on Thursday.

A common reason given by my respondents to leave Taiwan for further studies was to leave the dictatorial government, when martial law was enforced by the one-party rule:

> I left as early as I can for freedom and democracy. There were no dignity for the individual, and even inhuman. . . . We sold electronic appliances in our shop . . . the better business we got, the more visits were paid by the police, to make sure that we were not listening to the FM radio, and to news from China. When I was studying in Japan, I saw the student

movement, and envied the students for their freedom. [Another reason for me to leave is because my parents wanted me to get married.]

The "white terror" rule of 40 years ago (1949–1987) was still vivid in their memories:

> I grew up at the time of the "White Terror," when my father was suspected by the KMT as a communist, and was sent to jail as a political prisoner for 12 years in Green Island when he was 37 years old. My mother had a hard life raising five children. Even when my father was released, we were under surveillance. For a long time I did not want to go back to Taiwan. After getting married and joining the *Tunghsianghui*, I changed from a pessimistic, quiet person with no confidence to an independent, talkative, open-minded and optimistic person. (#13_Kirsten)

> With a bachelor's degree in Horticulture, I could not find a job in Taipei because I could not pay NTD20,000 [to bribe the employer] to get it. When I went to Japan to study for a master's degree, I had to go through all kinds of red tapes, but I refused to pay any extra fees to the officials. (#5_Karl)

The difficulty of leaving Taiwan was well remembered by everyone, including Abraham (#3), who was hired as a pastor in Singapore:

> It was hard to go abroad in 1965, because of the KMT's national interest to retake China, with the exception of children whose parents are high-ranking government officials. Even Singapore has accepted my application to go there as a rector, Taiwan did not give permission, until after negotiation between the British embassy and the Taiwan government took place.

A taste of democracy in Japan or the United States deepened their dislike of the KMT back home. Nostalgic feelings while living abroad drew them to join the *Tunghsianghui* (same as Taiwan Canadian Association [TCA]), which provided them with warm friendship, helped with day-to-day needs, and offered a platform to express their common political beliefs and activities. But then, due to being actively engaged in political activities abroad, such as fund-raising for political dissidents in Taiwan and rallying, their names were added to the "blacklist" of the Taiwan (ROC) government, thus making it hard for them to return to Taiwan as freely as they wanted later on.

Tunghshianghui *and Reluctant Exiles*

"Reluctant Exiles," the name coined by Skeldon (1994) to describe the Hong Kong emigrants who left before the handover to China 1997, actually applies to this specific group of Taiwanese immigrants even better. The following stories tell us how they wanted to come back to Taiwan, but why they were prevented from doing so for one reason or another.

> The "black list" (compiled between 1971 and 1980) includes names of those who speak unfavorably of the Nationalist government. . . . Every time he went back to Taiwan, his brother stayed with him, because he did not want to be like Chen Wen-chen (陳文成), whose dead body was found in the NTU campus in 1981, after his visit with the Taiwan Garrison Command. (#7 Susan)

> I was on the "black list" for being the president of the *Tunghsianghui* in 1968 when I was studying in the United States. At K University where I did my graduate work, I organized a seminar for Peng Ming-min (leader of the Taiwanese Independent Movement). When I went back to Taiwan for the first time in 1987, I was told that the computer was down, and I was detained for hours at the airport. When I went home, someone was strolling in front of our house every week and watched. My mother was very worried. . . . The *Tunghsianghui* made a big contribution to Taiwan's movement for democracy. . . . The future of Taiwan should be decided by the Taiwanese. . . . We also count on our younger generation. The Formosa Cup in Toronto is a softball tournament that started in 1974. We are joined by a lot of Asians. (#18_Dennis)

> While staying in the U.S., we [my husband and I] joined the TCA (*Tunghsianghui*) because we hope that Taiwan would be more democratic. My family in Taiwan received warning because of my activities abroad. We never applied to go back. (#21_Fiona)

Jean (#20) participated in the activities of the *Tunghsianghui* in Europe where she first went as a nurse. Because of her husband's political activities, she could not get a visa to come back to attend her father's funeral. She protested in TECO in Los Angeles until she got the visa. Her good friends, Susan (#7) and Peter (#22), went to Canada after finishing their undergraduate education in Taiwan. Dreaming of democracy in Taiwan 40 years ago, Peter founded the TCA in Canada in 1968 and the Vancouver chapter in 1975. Following similar ideologies, he also co-founded the TCCS in 1991 and the Society of Taiwanese Canadian History in British Columbia in 2011. Due to his early political activities such as alliances of immigrant committee with home country political associations, fund-raising for home country electoral candidates, and related activities, his name was on the "black list," and he was prevented from going back to Taiwan for the first time in 1985. His father was in a coma, and when he went back with his sister, he was not allowed to enter Taiwan the first day, but was detained for one night at the airport hotel.

> It took me three hours to leave the airport after being interrogated by the police, and my sister was very scared. I was sent to the transit hotel in Taoyuan, with two policemen living next to my room, one on each side, to make sure that I did not leave my room. I was also asked to sign a document saying that I will abstain from participating in any political activities during my visit. I was also instructed to inform the police before I leave Taiwan. (#22_Peter)

The worst experiences occurred to those who wanted to visit family members at critical times but could not get visas, or who have taken strenuous routes to do so, even in the late 1980s, when martial law was lifted:

> I returned to Taiwan for the first time in 1981 with my wife and three children. I had to wait for my visa for a long time, probably because I was once the president of the TCA, even though the "black list" was removed [in President Lee's term]. (#10_Jay)

Rich (#16) can never forget being interrogated by the KMT police in 1984, upon return to Taiwan, and the strenuous path of getting a visa to come back home with his family for the first time. Ironically, he was given a free tour by a key government agency.

Joe (#23) recalled his experience with sadness when he was interviewed:

> I joined the *Tunghsianghui* in Tokyo 40 years ago, mainly to socialize with other Taiwanese immigrants. In Vancouver, I raised funds to support Taiwanese independent movement, joined rallies to protest against breaking up of Taiwan-Canada diplomatic relations, and participated in various protests in Seattle. In 1979 I went back with my wife, my sister and my son to Taiwan to visit my mother who was [very] ill. At the airport, my wife and me were prevented entry and were asked to return to Canada on the same plane. [Sadly], I never got a chance to see my mother before she died; and I was turned down the second time I applied for a visa to go back to Taiwan. [Since then] I became a strong supporter of the DPP. Although I did not fly back to vote, I called up my friends to ask them to vote for the DPP candidates. If I return to Taiwan, I will join the DPP.

Jack (#12), a well-established hydraulic engineer who graduated from a leading National university in Taiwan, came to Canada in 1966 to get his MSc degree, but he could not get a visa to come to Taiwan at two different times:

> The first time I applied for a visa to go back to Taiwan to present a paper at a conference, TECO in Seattle put the stamp "cancelled" on my Canadian passport, so that I cannot go anywhere. The second time was when my wife wanted to visit her mother who was very ill. We were interrogated at the airport upon entry and exit. One day, a policeman

came to our home and put his rifle on the table. We were very scared... [professor], do we look like bandits? I think it is because I was the head of the Vancouver TCA for two years. I wrote the article for the *Vancouver Sun* saying: "For years, Taiwanese have wanted independence and wanted to disassociate themselves from Chiang's self-proclaimed R.O.C.... Peking's claim to Taiwan is as ridiculous as Chiang's claim to the Mainland.... The real Taiwanese want nothing but self-respect and independence."

On his short CV, Jack wrote: "He has worked for freedom, democracy and human right in his native Taiwan, in Canada, and in other countries around the world.... He is a Past President of the Taiwanese Canadian Association, which works to assist new immigrants integrate into Canadian society and promotes cultural exchange and racial harmony."

These narratives by migrant agencies inform us why they want to be self-identified as Taiwanese-Canadian. Their collective memories would be written up for the records of the Society of Taiwanese Canadian History in British Columbia, which was registered with the Canadian government in 2010. We now turn to study how they make a living in Canada.

Lived Experiences/Ways of Integration

Working hard for a living is common in general among the early Taiwan immigrant. In order to raise his family, Jay (#10) gave up studying for a PhD during his first year of arrival from Japan.

> I earned a master's degree in Japan in Chemistry of Forestry Products, but it had not helped me to get a job in Canada. In fact, I did not tell my employer that I had such a [high] qualification, in order to be hired. I worked for six weeks in the masonry, and then a technician in the paper pulp company from 1971 to 2003. We took turns to drive to work between Vancouver and city S, two hours each way. It would mean going around the world eight times in 32 years.

Sonia (#6), who came to Canada in 1975, was a well-qualified nurse working in a leading university hospital in Taiwan before she went for training in Sweden. She recalls vividly how she tried hard to get accreditation as a nurse in Canada:

> Without knowing anyone at first, I started as an on-call graduate nurse. After preparing for four years, I passed the English examination and accreditation test for nursing.... I woke up at 4:00 a.m. to study until I went to work at 7:00 a.m. As a single parent, I took my daughter to the park so that I could study there. I took the examination three times before I finally passed to become a registered nurse in 1984.

Ron (#1), who left his export business in Taiwan in 1976, started a superstore in Vancouver:

> At 4:30 a.m., we woke up to go to the wholesale market to get our merchandise. Working from 7 a.m. to 11 p.m. each day, 7 days a week— For us, it was like carrying out thirteen years of work in six and a half years. . . . We lost money in the first year. Later on, our customers found that our flowers lasted for a longer time, and were cheaper than those sold in two neighboring stores. We started to make a profit; our best sales were during Valentine day, Easter, Mother's day, Thanksgiving, Christmas, and New Year. Our children all helped in the store as cashiers and trimming the flower at the back of the store, when they were not at school. (#1_Ron)

> My pay as a rector in Singapore was too low to pay for my children's school fees. In Singapore, church members saw us eating salted fish which was taken by the poor people, and they brought us food, and gave our children red packets. I never felt discouraged by hardship because of the support I get from my religious belief. I started the *Tungshianghui* in Singapore, so that we can do something for Taiwan immigrants there. In 1979, I re-migrated to Brazil for my children's education, since my application to renew my extension to stay as a Taiwan citizen was not approved. My wives' brother was in Brazil, so we went. I came back to Canada in the eighties as a pastor in the Presbyterian Church. (#3_Abraham)

Henry (#9) vividly described his struggles in looking for work:

> When I arrived in Canada, I was an ABD in hydro-dynamics at a State University in the U.S. I took up all kinds of work, including cleaning toilets and chopping vegetables in a Jewish restaurant [on the same day], selling encyclopedia, and washing dishes. I guess it is due to my poor English that I did not get a job teaching arithmetic, or physics [that I am good at]. I was laid off . . . and was very frustrated.

Finally, Henry started his supplementary school [as self-employment] in Richmond for immigrants' children who arrived in the late 1980s and early 1990s.

Getting re-training is a way to be employed, in the case of Sean (#8):

> I could only get part-time work in the beginning, and my wife got supplementary expenses by joining money loan club among the Taiwanese. I studied for certificates at the Vancouver Vocational Institute and British Columbia Institute of Technology. This enabled me to get

into steady full-time jobs, while my wife started her business in real estate. (#8_Sean)

As summarized by Julita (#17), whose husband came to Canada in the employee category:

> My husband who worked in the leading University hospital in Taipei in 1975 was the only one person among his classmates who got employment visa, and found work right away. Both of us quit our [good] jobs to come here. I was a professional nurse who managed 1,000 employees at one time. Many first generation immigrants struggled for a living here—either they could not find work, or they switched to other jobs.

At times, racial discrimination was felt by a few early migrants in various occasions:

> I did not tell them that I had a master's degree when I applied for a job in tropical horticulture in 1979. In the interview, another white man [from Europe] got the job, even though he was fired three years ago. Even though I earned a Master's Degree majoring in Orchids from Japan, I did not get the job from the British owned company. I finally got a job as a head gardener in a hospital, which hired a lot of Indians and Philippines. So, that was the reason why I got my job. (#5_Karl)

Rich (#16), who just retired from a community college where he has been teaching for the last 33 years, is highly regarded among the Taiwanese for teaching English and for his volunteer work in the TCCS. He is well-qualified in his career, after earning his BA in Modern Languages in Taiwan, but he did not complete his PhD in Linguistics in the United States. He does not recall any experiences of discrimination by local Canadians. He did, however, have one experience to tell:

> I was discriminated by the Cantonese. Even though I spoke Cantonese. I could not get an interview for a job. (#16_Rich)

> After working for 11 years, I was 1 of the 15 nurses selected by the professors of the university teaching hospital to work in Switzerland, from where I obtained a visa to come in Canada in a very short time. As we flew from Bangkok to the U.K. before coming to Switzerland, we were mistaken as refugees and were not given drinks like others. But when we were greeted by the director of the hospital, and reporters, they were surprised that we are nurses. The German nurses were arrogant and looked down on us. (#6_Sonia)

Sonia's struggles in raising her daughter as a single mother, studying to get a certificate, and finding work were all paid off:

> Even though I am retired, I still work on a casual basis in the "Nurse Next Door" program. For every hour I work in palliative care, I earn 36 Cdn, while the private agent gets 24 Cdn.

Fiona (#21), who came to Canada with her husband in 1974, felt rewarded after having a hard life raising their children for a good education:

> We had a hard life in Vancouver in the early days to support our children's education. They also applied for student loans and work part-time. My children are my greatest achievement. They are good citizens, and not becoming a burden to their parents and the society.... [as for myself] I built three new houses, remodeled eight houses, and built two commercials. It includes working with [white] men, completing the house on time, meeting the budget and working on the interior design. They are like products of art and sculpture combined.

Identity and Sense of Home

In all 24 cases, their self-identity is clear and strong, calling themselves Taiwanese-Canadians, Taiwanese, and Canadians, not Chinese or Chinese-Canadians:

> Racially, I am Chinese; culturally, I am Taiwanese-Canadian, or Chinese-Canadian, but I am NOT a Chinese. Politically, I am Canadian; nationally, I am both Taiwanese and Canadian. (#16_Rich)

The four organizations representing similar interests in Taiwanese-Canadian identity are: Taiwanese Canadian Cultural Society (Vancouver), Greater Vancouver Taiwanese-Canadian Association (*Tunghsianghui*), Formosa Cultural Foundation, and Society of Taiwanese-Canadian History in British Columbia. They all work to build a good profile for Taiwanese, to raise visibility of Taiwanese: the Taiwanese Cultural Festival, attended by 70,000 people, was awarded "best cultural event" in Canada for the sixth time in 2006. The subsequent themes of Taiwan Cultural Festivals were "Ilha Formosa" (2007), "The World Is an Island" (2008), and "A New Journey" (2009), attracting even larger number of participants.

> We organized the Taiwan Cultural Festival to show that we are different from [Mainland] Chinese. We support election campaigns for Members of Parliament who support Taiwan's position in the Canadian Parliament at the Federal level. We also help to promote a better

relationship between Canada and Taiwan, such as extending an invitation of the Mayor for a visit of Taiwan, so that he could meet Lee Teng-hui (Taiwan's former President). The Chinese embassy protested, but could not do anything . . . there are now more and more [Mainland] Chinese in Vancouver, buying up expensive property. They have already become Yellow Peril. (#7_ Susan)

Being interviewed earlier for my study of volunteers, Kirsten (#13) devoted herself to the TCCS,[7] which she co-founded to help immigrants, particularly women. She and her husband compiled a special issue, to commemorate the 20th Anniversary Celebration in 2011. Through volunteering, they have demonstrated a sense of self and belonging and a will to be part of the Canadian society:

> When you are working in an organization to help other Taiwanese immigrants, you do not anticipate benefit in return of any kind, but receive valuable experiences and knowledge while you are giving. My greatest gain in doing voluntary work is to set a good example for my children.

A strong sense of home and belonging to Canada are well stated by the early Taiwanese-Canadians, such as Titan (#4), who came to Canada in 1964 and co-founded the TCCS with ideals of increasing the visibility of Taiwanese:

> We should not act as if we are guests in the Canadian community. We should give back to the society, and be a part of it to win their respect. . . . The more you give, the more respect you will earn from the mainstream society. . . . I have my roots in Taiwan, where I spent one-sixth of my life; but Taiwan is not my home. I have already bought a space in a graveyard in Vancouver for use when I die.

The definition of home varies among individuals:

> Canada is my reality home, since my achievements are here. My husband, children and friends are all here. (#21_Fiona)

> Having lived in Canada since 1969, I am Canadian but I am [always] concerned with Taiwan (*kuanhsin* Taiwan 関心台灣). (#7_Susan)

> Taiwan is our home in our hearts. . . . I probably have no home anymore . . . everywhere is home. (#8_Sean)

> Taiwan is always in my heart, and my heart has never left Taiwan. (#9_Henry)

> Our hearts are with Taiwan—*hsinhsi* Taiwan (心繫台灣)—but we are not going back. Taiwan is now more modern than Canada [in the way people dress]. (#17_ Julita)

> My home (*lao chia* 老家) is in Taiwan; but if there is a sports competition like baseball game between Taiwan and Canada, I would cheer for Canada. (#23_Joe)

In contrast, Sean (#8) and several others noticed the lack of commitment by some newcomers in the late 1980s:

> I am not sure if I appreciate what the "new" migrants are doing in Canada—those who come to enjoy the welfare of Canada, but are not willing/prepared to settle permanently. Their children go to the local school, while they sit in immigration jail "坐移民監" while waiting to fulfill the requirement of citizenship, and then return to Taiwan. They behave like opportunists . . . [we are different] (#8_Sean).

> The new immigrants are "astronauts," business migrants who brings a lot of money with them. They do not need to struggle for a living. They are handicapped in spoken English and cannot integrate into the mainstream. Many could not find work, and have returned. (#17_Julita)

> They are the ones who bring their "*bento*" (便當) with them, they are flexible and never worry about their finances. It is not easy for the children of the old and new immigrants to be married. (wife of #19_Jacob)

Jean (#20) confirms my definition of early immigrants not by the year of immigration, but by the intention to settle down in Canada:

> "Identifying with Canada" is the main difference between me and the new immigrants who came with a lot of money. Their mindset is different from ours. We came to settle down. (#20_Jean)

> Everyone should have their own choice. Since they have their roots/business in Taiwan they need a transition before permanently settled in Canada. Language should not be a problem, if they try harder to participate, be in contact with and integrate with other Canadians. (#19_Jacob)

CONCLUSION

Activities within the transnational field comprise a whole gamut of economic, political and social initiatives—ranging from informal import-export businesses, to the rise of a class of binational professionals, to the campaigns of home country politicians among their expatriates. (Portes, Guarnizo, and Landolt 1999)

This chapter is an attempt to interpret early Taiwanese immigrants' experiences within a broader historical context by drawing attention to the structural (political) causes of mobility from the immigrants' point of view. The purpose is to give voice to a small *albeit* significant group that has played key roles in Taiwan's democratization movement. This study opens up a political sector as a type of transnationalism that has not been addressed and is unique to the Taiwanese-Canadians among the sub-ethnic Chinese. A specific group of Taiwanese immigrants who are self-identified as Taiwanese-Canadians has been presented, with their political background as the key factor for them to decide to stay, not economic or socio-cultural. Although they have left their hearts in Taiwan (*hsinhsi* Taiwan), it is unlikely that they want to return to live. Their efforts to return to visit their elderly parents have been met with various forms of interrogations by the Taiwan Garrison Command, such as detentions at the airport, instilling fear and worries by their families. They can never forget their experiences, and some still do not dare speak up and are unwilling to speak up in public. Being postwar baby-boomers, they were the elites of Taiwan in the 1970s—well-educated, multi-lingual, and extremely diligent and persevering in overcoming their hardships while settling down in Canada. Being "reluctant exiles," they have succeeded in planting their roots in Canada. Being *Taijiao*, rather than *Huachiao*, there is no reason for them to be lumped together with other Chinese in Canada or other early Chinese-Canadians from Taiwan in research. Let's hope that their voices are heard and their stories are documented by studies of this kind.

It is often hard for the host country population, or even researchers, to be sensitive enough to recognize the internal differences among the sub-groups of Chinese immigrants from a common source of emigration. Through this qualitative research, differences among sub-groups among ethnic Chinese immigrants can be distinguished, focusing on the early immigrants, whose diversity has not often been presented in the government statistics other than gender, year of arrival, and origin. Fieldwork allows me to get an "insider view" of the different groups I have studied so far, among the Taiwanese immigrants in Canada, with regard to gender, age, and political values, which impact their mobility patterns, paths of integration, adaptation, and identity formation. Even among the same ethnic group that arrived at similar times, political values can play an important role in their adaptation to the destination and the outcome of their migration.

As noted from their experiences, the employment issue among this well-educated group, as early as the 1970s, is similar to the situation of new Mainland Chinese immigrants who landed in the 1990s. Wang and Lo (2008) show that, although their levels of economic performance increases with length of residence in Canada, it would take more than 20 years for Chinese immigrants to close the earning gaps with the general population. This consistent finding suggests that discrimination at the structural level needs to be further investigated with regard to both early and recent immigrants.

This study allows me to draw the following conclusions regarding the early Taiwanese immigrants. They were well-educated and young professionals at the time of immigration, and they had developed good language and social skills/local knowledge in Canada. Their children are well-educated and have established families in Canada, and some have married Caucasians. They have a strong sense of commitment to Canadian citizenship, and they have a lot of [native] Canadian friends. They are at the same time proud of being Taiwanese and are keen on getting their culture represented in multicultural Canada, for example, establishing the TCCS in 1991and the Society of Taiwanese Canadian History in British Columbia 20 years later. While preserving the Taiwanese culture, their commitment to Canadian citizenship is unambiguous and consistent. Though reluctant to stay abroad at the beginning, they have planted their roots in Canada and have made Canada their home. It is a pity that these early immigrants could not come back to Taiwan to join the rank of "global talents" in the 1980s.

It should be noted that the main difference between them and the "new immigrants" is that they immigrated with their whole families and have made every effort to stay together and settle down. Their self-made identity of being Taiwanese-Canadian is not based on geography alone, but the past political history of Taiwan, of which they have played an important role in the democratic process of Taiwan. Even though staying abroad, they are still part of the contemporary political history of Taiwan. Politics should be taken up as an important issue in the study of transnationalism in Taiwan in the last six decades.

ACKNOWLEDGMENTS

This chapter is based on a larger project on the history, lived experiences, and paths of integration, self-identity, and sense of belonging of early Taiwanese migrants in Canada. This research was supported by National Science Council in Taiwan (ROC) and the College of Science, National Taiwan University. I am grateful to the Society of Taiwanese Canadian History in British Columbia, Satake Ruey, Ben Tseng, Jim Chen, and Peggy Yen for their research assistance and input. Earlier versions of the chapter were presented at the Conference on Immigration in Multi-ethnic Contexts: An International Comparison, Taipei, December 8–9, 2010, and at the Conference on Migration to and from Taiwan, London, June 29–30, 2011.

NOTES

1. The term "Taiwanese immigrant" has been used in the author's previous works in a purely geographical sense to refer to anyone who emigrated from

Taiwan, regardless of their place of birth, length of time in Taiwan, or other factors. Specifically, this chapter is focused on those who are "native" Taiwanese and have identified themselves as Taiwanese-Canadians.
2. The population of Taiwan is represented by four main groups that differ in terms of time of arrival, size, and language of use. The Taiwan indigenous population, the "aborigines," constitutes about 2% of the population. The Hoklos and Hakka, who are often referred to as "native Taiwanese," are ethnic Han Chinese who were in Taiwan before 1945 and their descendants, and they form about 70% and 12%, respectively. The fourth group consists of the "Mainlanders" and their descendants, who came to Taiwan from 1946 to 1950 when the Mainland fell to the communists.
3. The Taiwan Canadian Association or *Tunghsianghui* (同鄉會) initiated an oral history project with the purpose of building a database for liasing early Taiwanese compatriots. On July 4, 2010, the Society of Taiwanese Canadian History BC (hence, the Society) was formed with a membership of 30.
4. Thanks to the National Science Council, the Chiang Ching-Kuo Foundation, and the College of Science of National Taiwan University for their travel support, I have been able to conduct fieldwork quite a number of times in Canada, including Vancouver, Calgary, and Toronto, to study "astronaut families"—the 1.5 generation immigrants and early immigrants.
5. Eleven of the 24 interviews were conducted with wives present.
6. Martial Law was imposed after a political incident when Taiwanese uprising occurred on February 28, 1947, against the rule of the Nationalist Party when the Japanese Colonial period ended. It lasted for 40 years until 1987 when Martial Law was lifted and the period of the "White Terror" formally ended.
7. In 1990, several Taiwanese immigrants initiated the idea of forming an organization with the objectives of encouraging Taiwanese to form a bridge between Canada and Taiwan, enhance cultural exchange between the two countries, participate in activities in Canada, and help new immigrants understand the Canadian society. Formed in 1991, it was initiated by 34 members, with donations from many Taiwanese families. Registered with the Canadian government as an organization in 1992, the first president was Professor Chung-Yi LIN (林宗義). Membership now consists of 3,000 families, with 800 events organized per year.

REFERENCES

Avenarius, C. 2007. "Cooperation, Conflict and Integration among Sub-ethnic Immigrant Groups from Taiwan." *Population, Space and Place* 13:95–112.

Baum, J., and A. Sherry. 1999. "Identity Crisis." *Far Eastern Economic Review* 162:21–3.

Chiang, L. H. N. 2004. "Dynamics of Self-Employment and Ethnic Business among Taiwanese in Australia." *International Migration* 42(2):153–73.

Chiang, L. H. N. 2006. "Immigrant Taiwanese Women in the Process of Adapting to Life in Australia: Case Studies from Transnational Households." In *Experiences of Transnational Chinese Migrants in the Asia-Pacific*, edited by D. Ip, R. Hibbins, and E. Chiu, 69–86. New York: Nova Publishers.

Chiang, L. H. N. 2008. "Back to Taiwan: Adaptation and Self-Identity of Young Taiwanese Return Migrants from Australia." *Journal of Population Studies*, 36: 99–135.

Chiang, L. H. N. 2008. "'Astronaut Families': Transnational Lives of Middle-class Taiwanese Married Women in Canada." *Social and Cultural Geography* 9(5):505–18.

Chiang, L. H. N. 2009. "Volunteering: A Path to Integration by Taiwanese Middle-class Female Immigrants in Canada." *Journal of Geographical Science* 57:71–96.

Chiang, L. H. N. and L. C. Huang. 2009. "Reluctant Exiles: History, Lived Experiences and Identity of Taiwanese-Canadians." *Bulletin of the Geographical Society of China* (Taipei), 42:25–42. (in Chinese)

Chiang, L. H. N. 2011a. "Staying or Leaving: Taiwanese-Chinese Making Their Homes in New Zealand." In *Transmigration and the New Chinese: Theories and Practices from the New Zealand Experience*, edited by Manying Ip, 102–37. Hong Kong: Hong Kong Institute for the Humanities and Social Sciences (incorporating the Centre of Asian Studies).The University of Hong Kong.

Chiang, L. H. N. 2011b. "Return Migration: The Case of the 1.5 Generation of Taiwanese in Canada and New Zealand." *China Review* 11(2):91–124.

Chiang, L. H. N., and J. C. Hsu. 2006. "Taiwanese in Australia: Two Decades of Settlement Experiences." *Geography Research Forum* 26:32–60.

Chiang, L. H. N., and C. H. Yang. 2008. "Learning to Be Australian: Adaptation and Identity Formation of Young Taiwanese-Chinese Immigrants in Melbourne, Australia." *Pacific Affairs* 81(2):241–58.

Chu, Y. H., and J. W. Lin. 2001. "Political Development in 20th-Century Taiwan." *The China Quarterly* 165:102–29.

Gilmartin, M. 2008. "Migration, Identity and Belonging." *Geography Compass* 2(6):1837–52.

Ghosh, S., and L. Wang. 2003. "Transnationalism and Identity: A Tale of Two Faces and Multiple Lives." *The Canadian Geographer* 47(3):269–82.

Gold, T. 1993. "Taiwan's Quest for Identity in the Shadow of China." In *The Shadow of China: Political Developments in Taiwan Since 1949*, edited by Steve Tsang, 169–92. Honolulu: University of Hawaii Press.

Graham, E. 1999. "Breaking Out: The Opportunities and Challenges of Multi-method Research in Population Geography." *Professional Geographer* 51(1):76–89.

Ho, E. S., and R. D. Bedford. 2008. "Asian Transnational Families in New Zealand: Changing Dynamics and Policy Challenges." *International Migration* 46(4):42–62.

Hsu, J. C. R., and L. Chi. 2005. *A Survey Research of Contemporary Taiwanese Immigrants in Canada*. Taiwan, ROC: Overseas Compatriots Affairs Commission. (in Chinese)

Kong, L. 1999. "Globalisation and Singaporean Transmigration: Re-imagining and Negotiating National Identity." *Political Geography* 18(5):563–89.

Liu, I. C., and S. Y. Ho. 1999. "The Taiwanese/Chinese Identity of the Taiwan People." *Issues & Studies* 35(3):1–34.

Portes, A., L. E. Guarnizo, and P. Landolt. 1999. "The Study of Transnationalism: Pitfalls and Promise of an Emergent Research Field. *Ethnic and Racial Studies* 22(2):217–37.

Rigger, S. 2010. "Taiwan." In *Politics in China: An Introduction*, edited by William Joseph, 367–381. Oxford, UK: Oxford University Press.

Skeldon, R., eds. 1994. *Reluctant Exiles? Migration from Hong Kong and the New Overseas Chinese*. Armonk, NY: M. E. Sharpe.

Vertovec, S. 2001. "Transnationalism and Identity. *Journal of Ethnic and Migration Studies* 27(4):573–82.

Wang, F. 2005. "From Chinese Original Domicile to Taiwanese Ethnicity: An Analysis of Census Category Transformation in Taiwan." *Taiwanese Sociology* 9: 59–117. (in Chinese)

Wang, S., and L. Lo. 2005. "Chinese Immigrants in Canada: Their Changing Composition and Economic Performance." *International Migration* 43(3):35–71.

Wang, T. Y., and G. A. Chang. 2005. "Ethnicity and Politics in Taiwan: An Analysis of Mainlanders' Identity and Policy Preference." *Issues & Studies* 41(4):35–66.

Wong L. L. 2003. "Chinese Business Migration to Australia, Canada and the United States: State, Policy and the Global Immigration Marketplace." *Asian and Pacific Migration Journal* 12(3):301–35.

Wong, L. L. 2004. "Taiwanese Immigrant Entrepreneurs in Canada and Transnational Social Space." *International Migration* 42(2):113–52.

World Journal. 2003. "Nearly 80 per cent of Recent Mainland Chinese Immigrants Are Thinking of Returning." January 10:A1.

Wu, Y. S. 2001. "Liang'an Guanxi Zhong De Zhongguo Yishi Yu Taiwan Yishi (The Chinese/Taiwanese Identity in Cross-Straits Relations)." *China Affairs Quarterly* 4:71–89. (in Chinese)

Yu, Z., and L. H. N. Chiang. 2009. "Assimilation and Rising Taiwanese Identity: Taiwan-born Immigrants in the United States, 1990–2000." *Journal of Population Studies* 38:115–60.

Conclusion

13 Conclusion

Eric Fong, Lan-hung Nora Chiang, and Nancy Denton

The foregoing chapters have demonstrated the complexity of studying immigration in a multi-ethnic setting. The analysis has focused on the ecology of racial and ethnic residential patterns, intergroup relations, and intragroup diversity. The book includes studies based on three locations: Canada, Taiwan, and the United States. These places all have experienced an increase in racial and ethnic diversity, which began in the 1970s. Reasons for the increase include changes in immigration policies, local labor demands, and the growing connectedness of the global labor market. In this chapter, we highlight some common issues drawn from the studies reported.

INTEGRATION: THE REFERENCE GROUP OF THE STUDY

In the study of immigration, the most common approach is to contrast the performance of immigrant groups with the members of the host society. However, in a multi-ethnic society, the choice of reference group is not as simple or obvious as it is in a minority-majority society. In a multi-ethnic setting, the reference group can be another immigrant group or another group with a high proportion of the native-born population. However, as Iceland observed in his review, the choice of reference group can affect the interpretation of the results. Fong, drawing from Canadian data, explicitly demonstrated that groups may share neighborhoods with other groups, but that most of the residents are immigrant members of those groups so that integration with the native-born population cannot simply be assumed.

The issue reveals a major limitation of theories in the study of immigrant adaptation in a multi-ethnic society. Most studies of immigrant adaptation, guided by existing theories, tend to focus on how immigrants, usually a minority group, integrate into the majority group. The majority group commonly is considered to be a larger group that arrived in the country earlier and has a small proportion of immigrants. As a society becomes more multi-ethnic, especially growing with the size of the multiracial group, this view needs to be revised. In a multi-ethnic setting, there are many minority groups and many majority groups. Compounding the difficulty, there are significant proportions of immigrants among many of these groups, whether minority or majority. The theoretical vacuum leaves the choice of reference group to the discretion of the researcher.

The preceding chapters offer a few hints for understanding the integration of groups in multi-ethnic cities. The first focus is on comparing immigrants and native-born, such as Lin's chapter on the Taiwan labor force. It concentrates on understanding the dynamics between two groups without reference to their racial or ethnic backgrounds. This approach is best when most immigrant ethnic groups are relatively small and have similar demographic and socioeconomic backgrounds. However, the approach may not fully capture the differences within groups if there are considerable demographic and socioeconomic variations. Second, the chapter by Liao and Özcan suggests that the comparison should be across generations of the same group. As many have observed, integration cannot be complete in one generation. This comparison allows us to understand the progress without reference to other groups. Instead of comparing the performance of different groups in a society, this approach compares generations of the same group. The limitation is that all generations should have enough cases for sensible comparison. Third, Fong compares the native-born and immigrants of different races and ethnicities without reference to a specific group. The differentiation of native-born and immigrants of a racial and ethnic group allows us to better understand the interaction of the effects of growing racial and ethnic diversity and immigration. Similarly, Denton contrasts different multiracial groups with single racial groups. However, such analysis requires that each group have a certain number of native-born and immigrant members to allow for reliable analysis. Finally, Wang explores the integration of Asians and their contribution to the larger society as an indicator of integration. He looks at the achievements of minority groups in society without reference to other groups. Instead of emphasizing how groups improve their situation over years or generations, he discusses how much they contribute to the larger society. His approach is similar to the idea of the "melting pot" suggested by Gordon.

All the approaches reported in this book have their advantages and disadvantages. The outcome of using different approaches can vary. At the same time, through these studies, we have identified a serious need for theoretical development that directly addresses multi-group relations in order to provide guidance in determining the reference group.

INTEGRATION: VARIATIONS IN INTERGROUP RELATIONS

Chapters included in this book provide consistent findings about social relationships among groups from different countries. A clear pattern in all three countries studied is that all groups do not equally share the same closeness with all other groups. At the ecological level, Iceland shows that in the United States, whites are less likely to share neighborhoods with blacks and Hispanics but more likely to share with Asians. Fong shows that western and northern Europeans are less likely to share neighborhoods with minority groups in Canadian cities. Denton also illustrated diverse segregation levels among different multi-ethnic groups. Ley shows that residential segregation varies among groups over decades and that the definition of segregation can differ over generations.

At the intergroup level, Lalonde and Uskul focus on intergroup dating in Canada, and they find that Chinese Canadians and South Asian Canadians are less accepting of intergroup dating. The findings imply that close intergroup relationships may be less likely found among minority groups. Chen and Yi also show that there are variations in the social distance between local Taiwanese and immigrants from different countries. They find that Taiwanese are friendlier to immigrants from Japan, Europe, and North America than they are to those from South Korea, Mainland China, or Southeast Asia.

The authors provide some suggestions to explain the patterns. Based on findings from census tract data, Fong and Iceland suggest possible discrimination in the housing market. Ley argues for the importance of public discourse. Lalonde and Uskul suggest that there may be cultural differences, and that the adoption of a cultural inclusion discourse in society may foster intergroup intimate relationships. Chen and Yi, drawing from Taiwan data, argue that cultural ideology shapes intergroup social distance. Though we cannot conclude which are more significant, these findings together suggest that factors operating at different levels can shape the variations in social relationships among groups. These studies highlight the direction that future studies should take to explore the relative importance of these factors in shaping group relations in a multi-ethnic setting.

INTEGRATION: THE EFFECT OF POLICIES

The effect of policies in shaping immigrant adaptation in multi-ethnic cities is voiced by several of the authors, even though they have drawn their information and conclusions from places with substantial socioeconomic and demographic differences. Ley's study of the meaning of Chinese residential segregation in Vancouver as discussed by the public over the years suggests that the discourse has changed over time. The change from a negative connotation to a positive interpretation largely reflects the social discourse and the political economy of the larger society. In particular, the discourse on multiculturalism policies in the neoliberal society has changed the meaning of Chinese residential segregation. Ho explicitly suggests in her study that multiculturalism policies in Canada have fostered an environment for groups to maintain their ethnic identity. Such an environment is critical for new immigrants to seek help from co-ethnic members when they first arrive and helps ease their adaptation. However, for some new immigrants, multiculturalism also facilitates segregation and social distance from other groups. Thus, the policy can be seen as a two-edged sword for the integration of immigrants in multi-ethnic cities. Although most studies focus on the effects of policies in the host country, Chiang's chapter reminds us that the policies back home also can affect the integration of groups. From her in-depth interviews of early immigrants from Taiwan to Canada, she finds that their political experiences back home increase their desire to integrate into the new country. Given that the findings from different countries point to the importance of policies, future studies should develop a more theoretical understanding of the elements of policies that can facilitate or hinder the integration of immigrants.

FINAL THOUGHTS

Immigrant adaptation in multi-ethnic cities has posed a number of challenges to researchers. In this edited volume, researchers have addressed the issues of ecological residential patterns, intergroup relations, and intragroup diversity in different countries. The findings provide a comparative perspective on immigrant adaptation. They show that immigrant integration varies by groups as they are influenced by institutional factors (such as policies), intergroup relations, and socioeconomic differences among immigrants. These studies also have pointed out the limitations of existing theoretical frameworks that emphasize a minority-majority relationship. Future studies should theorize the relationship of immigrants with different groups in the context of adaptation in multi-ethnic cities, with consideration of institutional factors, intergroup relations, and individual socioeconomic factors. Further theorization of immigrant integration in a multi-ethnic society is important and urgent because it is related to the daily lives of many immigrants and has significant policy implications.

Contributors

Yu-Hua Chen is Associate Professor in the Department of Bio-Industry Communication and Development at National Taiwan University, Taiwan.

Lan-hung Nora Chiang is Professor in the Department of Geography at National Taiwan University, Taiwan.

Nancy Denton is Professor in the Department of Sociology at State University of New York at Albany, United States.

Paul Du is a GIS Analyst in the Center for the Study of Commercial Activity at Ryerson University

Eric Fong is a Professor of Sociology at the University of Toronto.

Elaine Lynn-Ee Ho is Assistant Professor in the Department of Geography at National University of Singapore.

John Iceland is Professor in the Department of Sociology at The Pennsylvania State University, United States.

Richard N. Lalonde is Professor in the Department of Psychology at York University, Canada.

David Ley is Canada Research Chair in the Department of Geography at University of British Columbia, Canada.

Tim F. Liao is Professor in the Department of Sociology at University of Illinois, United States.

Ji-Ping Lin is Associate Research Fellow in the Research Center for Humanities and Social Sciences at Academia Sinica, Taiwan.

Berkay Özcan is Lecturer in the Department of Social Policy at The London School of Economics and Political Science, United Kingdom.

Ayse K. Uskul is Associate Professor in the Department of Psychology at University of Essex, United Kingdom.

Shuguang Wang is a professor in the Department of Geography at Ryerson University.

Chin-Chun Yi is Research Fellow in the Institute of Sociology at Academia Sinica, Taiwan.

Index

Note: Page numbers followed by an "f" indicate figures. Page numbers followed by a "t" refer to tables.

A

adaptation: in multi-ethnic cities, 9–10, 197, 199–222, 287–288
Alaskan Natives, 112, 115, 121, 129–130, 133
alternative-theory challenges, 25–28
American Indians, 112–115, 124–125, 129–133
ANOVA, 145, 147, 149–151
Asian Canadians: gender effects of, 153–154; identity formation of, 143–144; inter-ethnic dating of, 141–142; inter-ethnic relationships for, 138–155; intermarriage of, 139–141; interracial dating of, 141–142. *See also* Canada
Asian immigrants: accepting immigrants, 176–178, 177f, 178t–179t; by age group, 202, 203t; attitudes toward, 184–194, 188t, 192t; in Canada, 4–5, 54–63, 199–222; by country of birth, 201–202, 201t; distribution of, 207t, 208t, 209f, 212f; diversity of, 199–222; education qualifications of, 202–206, 205t; impact on cities, 206–216, 212f, 214f; settlement patterns of, 206–211, 209f; societal interactions of, 217f; temples of, 214f; in United States, 4–5, 112–115, 121, 124–133; in Vancouver, 54–63
assimilation: with groups, 24–25, 27; immigration and, 226–227; as individual, 24–25, 27; intergroup relations and, 227–228; segmented assimilation, 15–17, 21, 25–35, 224–228; spatial assimilation, 6, 16–28, 32–33, 48
"astronaut strategy," 257, 267

B

biculturalism, 58, 154–155
blacks: in Canada, 36–38, 50n7; in reference group, 21, 42; in United States, 17, 38–39, 50n7
Bogardus, Emory S., 171–172, 191

C

Canada: Asian immigrants in, 4–5, 54–63, 199–222; bicultural Canadians, 58, 154–155; blacks in, 36–38, 50n7; Chinese Canadians, 138–155; Chinese immigrants to, 159–167; citizenship in, 60, 159–160, 256–257, 276–278; European Canadians, 144–153, 146t; growth of immigrants in, 3, 216–217, 258t; immigrant population of, 199; intergroup relations in, 138–155; multicultural cities in, 199–222; multiculturalism in, 159–167; multi-ethnic cities in, 31–38, 49–50; multi-ethnicity in, 31–53; population growth of, 3, 216–217, 258t; returnees from, 164–167; socio-spatial segregation in, 54–63; South Asian Canadians, 138–155; Taiwanese migrants in, 255–281. *See also* specific cities
Canadian identity, 8, 138–153, 151t, 164, 167, 274

Chen, Jim, 279
Chen, Yu-Hua, 8, 170, 287, 289
Chiang, Ching Kuo, 266
Chiang, Lan-Hung Nora, 3, 10, 255, 271, 285, 288, 289
China: attitudes toward, 184–187, 191
Chinatown, 55–61
Chinese Americans, 140, 142, 154
Chinese Canadians: comparing, 144–153, 146t; gender effects of, 153–154; identity formation of, 143–147, 146t; inter-ethnic dating of, 141–142; inter-ethnic relationships for, 138–155; intermarriage of, 139–141; interracial dating of, 141–142, 145–148. *See also* Canada
Chinese General Social Survey (CGSS), 176
Chinese immigrants: accepting immigrants from, 176–178, 177f, 178t–179t; associations of, 214f; attitudes toward, 184–194, 186t, 192t; multicultural controversy and, 162–164; multicultural polices and, 161–162; perspectives of, 159–167; returnees from Canada, 164–167; social distance of, 159–167
Choy, Wayson, 55
citizenship concerns, 60, 159–160, 176, 256–257, 276–278
cultural diversity, 162–163
Current Population Survey (CPS), 228–229

D

Darwinian teleology, 55, 56
dating: inter-ethnic dating, 8, 141–142, 153; intergroup dating, 138, 143, 149–151, 287; interracial dating, 138, 141–154
Denton, Nancy, 3, 8, 109, 285, 286, 287, 289
departure models, 73–74, 88–92, 90t–91t, 93t–94t, 100–101
destination-choice models, 73–74, 92–95, 100–101
dissimilarity: patterns of, 19–21, 19t–20t; segregation and, 26t
dissimilarity scores, 18f, 23f, 24f
diversity: in cities, 3–4, 8–9; cultural diversity, 162–163; ethnic diversity, 3–8, 31, 143, 147–148, 285–286; group diversity, 5, 10, 185, 288; intragroup diversity, 7–10, 285, 288; racial diversity, 3–8, 31, 285–286; religious diversity, 139; socioeconomic diversity, 9; in United States, 109–133
Du, Paul, 9, 199, 289

E

endogamy: definition of, 139; levels of, 140–141; norm of, 139, 142–143, 152
ethnic diversity, 3–8, 31, 143, 147–148, 285–286
"ethnic ghettos," 15
ethnic relationships, 138–155
ethnic residential patterns, 3–7, 13, 285
ethnic stratification, 6, 15–17, 62
Europe: accepting immigrants from, 176–178, 177f, 178t–179t; attitudes toward, 184–194, 189t, 192t; comparing immigrants from, 144–153, 146t
European Canadians, 144–153, 146t. *See also* Canada
exogamy: definition of, 138; practice of, 140–143; precursors to, 138; prevalence of, 152

F

families, generations of, 223–254, 235f, 236f. *See also* immigrant families
first-generation immigrants, 223–254
flights from "port of entry," 64–102
Foner, Nancy, 56
Fong, Eric, 3, 6, 7, 31, 285, 286, 287, 289
foreign labor intensity (FLI) regions, 81–88, 82f, 85t, 87t, 102n4
foreign labor skills, 65–69, 69f, 81–88, 85t, 90t, 92–100, 93t–94t, 96t, 97f–99f
Furnivall, J. S., 56

G

gender, effects of, 153–154
Gender, Group by, 146, 150
Geographic Information Systems (GIS), 81
"globalization of international migration" era, 3–4
Globe and Mail, The, 160, 161, 167

Goh, Robbie, 59
Good, Cam, 210
Gordon, Milton, 253
Group by Gender, 146, 150
Group by Generation, 149
group relations, 4–10, 107, 286–287. *See also* intergroup relations
"Guanxin Taiwan," 256

H

Harvey, David, 55, 56
heritage identity, 143–147, 150–151, 151t
Hierarchical Age-Period Cohort (HAPC) model, 230–232, 237
Hispanic immigrants, 19–21, 28, 227, 232–237, 238t, 248–250
Ho, Elaine Lynn-Ee, 8, 153, 159, 287, 289
home, sense of, 260, 274–276
Hoskins, Councillor, 57
hypodescent, 112, 130

I

Iceland, John, 5, 6, 7, 15, 285, 286, 287, 289
identity formation: of Chinese Canadians, 143–147, 146t; role of, 152–153; self-identity, 260, 263, 274–276; sense of home and, 274–276; of South Asian Canadians, 143–144; of Taiwanese migrants, 255–281
identity hypothesis, 144, 147, 150
immigrant adaptation: analyzing, 5–10; in multi-ethnic cities, 9–10, 197, 199–222, 287–288; study of, 4–5, 10, 285
immigrant families: analysis of, 234–254, 235f, 236f, 238t–247t, 251f; composition of, 41–48, 44t–47t, 202, 227–228; data collection on, 228–232; extended-family living, 225–226; generations of, 223–254, 235f, 236f, 238t; results on, 232–234, 233t
immigrant incorporation: debates on, 17–28; dissimilarity scores, 18–21, 18f, 23–24; reference groups, 21–24, 27; study of, 27–28; temporal issues of, 17–21, 27; theories of, 15–17
immigrant integration: assessing, 17–18, 27; data on, 15; effects of policies on, 287–288; family forms of, 9; understanding, 223; variations in, 286–288; ways of, 271–272
immigrant labor, 64–66, 80. *See also* labor market
immigrant residential incorporation, 15–29
immigrant residential patterns, 3–7, 31, 59. *See also* residential patterns
immigrants: acceptance of, 177f, 182–193, 192t; attitudes toward, 178t–179t, 182–194; composition of, 41–48, 44t–47t, 202, 227–228; first-generation immigrants, 223–254; flights from "port of entry," 64–102; second-generation immigrants, 223–254. *See also* specific regions
immigration: assimilation and, 226–227; labor market and, 64–102; study of, 4–5, 10, 27–28, 285–286
immigration "port of entry," 7, 67, 101
immigration procedures, 267–268
information theory index, 22, 22f
in-migration flows, 65–66, 70–74, 84, 94–101, 96t, 98f
inter-ethnic dating, 8, 141–142, 153
inter-ethnic relationships, 138–155
intergroup dating, 138, 143, 149–151, 151t, 287
intergroup relations: assimilation and, 227–228; cultural identities of, 149–151, 151t; dating, 138, 143, 149–151, 151t, 287; interactions within, 227–228, 249; in multi-ethnic cities, 4–10, 286; variations in, 286–287
interracial dating: of Chinese Canadians, 145–148; intergroup dating, 138; research on, 141–154; role of, 147–152; views on, 153
interracial relationships: openness to, 138; research on, 141–149; views on, 146–147, 152
intragroup diversity, 7–10, 285, 288
Iranian immigrants, 201–202
Iraqi immigrants, 202

J

Jade Peony, 55
Japan: accepting immigrants from, 176–178, 177f, 178t–179t; attitudes toward, 182–194, 183t, 192t

Japanese General Social Survey (JGSS), 176

K
Ka-shing, Li, 60
Kennedy, Ruby Jo Reeves, 226
Korea: accepting immigrants from, 176–178, 177f, 178t–179t; attitudes toward, 184–194, 185t, 192t
Korean General Social Survey (KGSS), 176

L
labor market: foreign labor intensity (FLI) regions, 81–88, 82f, 85t, 87t; foreign labor skills, 65–69, 69f, 81–88, 85t, 90t, 92–100, 93t–94t, 96t, 97f–99f; immigration and, 64–102
Lalonde, Richard N., 8, 9, 138, 287, 289
Latin American immigrants, 224–225, 230, 232–234, 237, 249–250
Lee, Teng-hui, 267, 270, 275
Ley, David, 7, 54, 67, 101, 287, 289
Liao, Tim F., 9, 223, 256, 286, 289
Lin, Ji-Ping, 7, 64, 286, 289

M
Maclean's, 199
Manpower Utilization Surveys (MUSs), 74–78, 78t–79t, 89
"melting pot," 59, 164, 226, 286
Middle East immigrants, 201–202, 230
migrants: acceptance of, 177f, 182–193, 192t; attitudes toward, 178t–179t, 182–194. *See also* immigrants
migration and labor market, 64–102. *See also* immigration
Ming-min, Peng, 269
multicultural cities: Asian immigrants in, 199–222; in Canada, 199–222; impact on, 206–216
multiculturalism: attitudes toward, 164–167; in Canada, 159–167; contradictory nature of, 159–167; controversy on, 162–164; experience of, 159–162; perspectives on, 159–167; practices of, 159–162
multi-ethnic cities: adaptation in, 9–10, 197, 199–222, 287–288; group relations in, 7–9, 107, 286; impact on, 206–216; residential patterns in, 3–7, 13, 250
multi-ethnic society: adaptation in, 5–6, 285–286; social distance in, 170–194
multinomial logistic regression: analysis of, 181–182; data collection and, 171, 176, 178; results of, 183t, 184–192, 185t–186t, 188t–190t
multiracial people: population of, 8, 109–115, 121–129, 133–134; in U.S. society, 109–133

N
Native Americans, 112–115, 124–125, 129–133
Native Hawaiians, 112–115, 121, 124, 127, 130–133
neoliberal government, 7, 54, 59–62, 287
neo-Marxists, 55–56
net migration flows, 64–65, 72–74, 84, 85t, 87t, 96–101, 96t, 99f
North America: accepting immigrants from, 176–178, 177f, 178t–179t; attitudes toward, 184–194, 190t, 192t

O
OLS regression models, 41, 44t, 46t
Oral History Project, 261–262, 279n3
out-migration flows, 65–68, 70–74, 88, 92, 96t, 97f, 98–101
Özcan, Berkay, 9, 223, 286, 290

P
Pacific Islanders, 112–115, 121, 124, 130–133
Pakistan immigrants, 148, 201–202, 219n1
Park, Robert, 55
partial residential integration, 31–53
Philippine immigrants, 69, 201, 206
Phillips, Trevor, 59
place stratification, 33–35, 48, 56, 62
plural societies, 54, 56–57, 59
"port of entry," 7, 67, 101
Public Use Microdata Sample (PUMS), 67

R
racial: diversity, 3–8, 31, 285–286; residential patterns, 3–7, 13, 285; stratification, 15–16, 62
regression models, 41, 44t, 46t

"reluctant exiles," 259, 263, 268–271, 277
residential incorporation: debates on, 17–28; spatial assimilation, 16–28; in United States, 15–29
residential integration: in Canada, 35–38, 39t; of new immigrant groups, 40–41; sharing neighborhoods, 41–48; suburban patterns, 31–53
residential patterns: comparing, 21–24, 28; ethnic patterns, 3–7, 13, 285; in multi-ethnic cities, 3–7, 13, 250; racial residential patterns, 3–7, 13, 285; socioeconomic resources and, 33–35; suburban residential patterns, 31–48
residential segregation: Asians and, 41, 110, 227; blacks and, 41; Hispanics and, 21, 110, 227, 249; levels of, 15–17, 287; research on, 25, 27; Taiwanese and, 191
Ruey, Satake, 279

S
second-generation immigrants, 223–254
segregation: meaning of, 57, 61–62; measure of, 55, 61–62; residential segregation, 15–17, 21, 25, 27, 41, 110, 191, 227, 249, 287; socio-spatial segregation, 54–63
self-identity, 260, 263, 274–276
sense of home, 260, 274–276
Smith, Adam, 55
social distance: cultural concerns and, 174–176, 287; determinants of, 172–176, 191; economic concerns and, 174; in multi-ethnic society, 170–194; perception of, 170–172, 191–192; scale of, 171–172, 191
Social Justice and the City, 55
socio-spatial segregation, 54–63
South Asian Canadians: gender effects of, 153–154; inter-ethnic dating of, 141–142; inter-ethnic relationships for, 138–155; intermarriage of, 139–141; interracial dating of, 141–142. *See also* Canada
South Korea: accepting immigrants from, 176–178, 177f, 178t–179t; attitudes toward, 184–194, 185t, 192t

Southeast Asia: accepting immigrants from, 176–178, 177f, 178t–179t; attitudes toward, 184–194, 188t, 192t; immigrants from, 69, 115, 170, 201, 201–202, 206, 263
Sri Lakan immigrants, 148, 201–202, 206, 218, 219n1
suburban residential patterns, 31–48
suburbanization distribution, 38–42, 39t, 40t
Sun, Yat-sen, 59
superordinate identity hypothesis, 144, 147, 150

T
Taiwan: attitudes toward migrants, 182–194; "black list" in, 263, 269–270; citizenship concerns in, 176; cultural concerns in, 174–176; data collection on, 73–88, 78t–79t, 102n5, 102n7, 176–182, 180t, 260–263, 264t–266t; departure models for, 88–92, 90t–91t, 93t–94t, 100–101; destination-choice models in, 92–95, 100–101; economic concerns in, 174; "Guanxin Taiwan," 256; identity formation of migrants, 255–281; identity politics in, 258–260; immigrants from, 64–102, 255–281; immigration background of, 173–174; immigration impact analysis, 73–77, 96–100, 102n7; in-migration in, 65–66, 70–74, 84, 94–101, 96t, 98f; labor market in, 64–102, 69f, 85t, 87t, 90t–91t, 93t–94t; martial law in, 259, 266–267, 270, 279n6; metropolitan areas in, 64–69, 81–83, 82f, 84–85, 86f, 102n3, 102n4; micro-migration models in, 88–95; migration from, 64–102; multi-ethnic society of, 4–5, 7–8, 170–194; net migration flows in, 64–65, 72–74, 84, 85t, 87t, 96–101, 96t, 99f; out-migration in, 65–68, 70–74, 88, 92, 96t, 97f, 98–101; pattern findings in, 84–88; politics in, 258–267; population of, 4, 10n1, 81, 279n2; regions of, 76f;

"reluctant exiles" from, 259, 263, 268–271, 277; research findings on, 266–276; "Taiwanese immigrant," 255–277, 278n1; "White Terror" in, 256, 259, 267–268, 279n6
Taiwan Cultural Festival, 261, 274–275
Taiwan Manpower Utilization Surveys (MUSs), 74–78, 89
Taiwan Social Change Survey (TSCS), 176
"Taiwanese immigrant," 255–277, 278n1. See also Taiwan
Taiwanese-Canadian Oral History Project, 261–262, 279n3
"Taiwan's Silicon Valley," 84
Thatcher, Margaret, 60
Thiel's H, 22, 22f
Toronto: immigrant composition in, 41–48; immigrant population of, 37, 199–200; multi-ethnic Toronto, 35–38, 49–50; sharing neighborhoods in, 41–48; study of, 37–50; suburbanization among groups, 38–42, 39t, 40t. See also Canada
Trudeau, Prime Minister, 58
Tseng, Ben, 279

U
United States: Asian immigrants in, 4–5, 112–115, 121, 124–133; blacks in, 17, 38–39, 50n7; data collection on, 110–113; dissimilarity of people in, 112, 128t, 129–133, 131t–132t; diversity in, 109–133; growth of immigrants in, 3; immigrant residential incorporation in, 15–30; multi-ethnic cities in, 31, 34, 36–38; multiracial adolescents in, 112, 114–115, 121–124; multiracial children in, 112, 114–115, 121–124, 122t–123t; multiracial combinations in, 109–112, 115–116, 116t–120t, 121–124, 122t, 130–133; multiracial locations in, 124–128, 125f, 126t; multiracial people in, 109–124; multiracial population of, 113–120, 113t, 116t–120t, 121–134, 125f, 126t; population of, 109–110; single race populations in, 110–113, 129
Uskul, Ayse K., 8, 9, 138, 287, 290

V
Vancouver: Asian immigrants in, 54–63; colonial Vancouver, 54–57, 61–62; immigrant population of, 199–200; immigrants in, 54–63; multicultural Vancouver, 57–59, 61–62; neoliberal Vancouver, 59–61; socio-spatial segregation in, 54–63. See also Canada
Vietnamese immigrants, 69, 115, 170, 201–202, 206, 263

W
Wang, Shuguang, 9, 199, 286, 290
Worlds in Motion, 109

Y
Yen, Peggy, 279
Yi, Chin-Chun, 8, 170, 287, 290